D1606873

Imagined Hinduism

Imagined Hinduism

British Protestant Missionary Constructions of Hinduism, 1793–1900

Geoffrey A. Oddie

SAGE Publications
New Delhi / Thousand Oaks / London

First published in 2006 by

Sage Publications India Pvt Ltd
B-42, Panchsheel Enclave
New Delhi 110 017
www.indiasage.com

Sage Publications Inc
2455 Teller Road
Thousand Oaks, California 91320

Sage Publications Ltd
1 Oliver's Yard, 55 City Road
London EC1Y 1SP

Published by Tejeshwar Singh for Sage Publications India Pvt Ltd, phototypeset in 10.5/12.5 Minion by Excellent Laser Typesetters, New Delhi, and printed at Chaman Enterprises, New Delhi.

Library of Congress Cataloging-in-Publication Data

Oddie, Geoffrey A., 1932–
    Imagined Hinduism: British Protestant missionary constructions of Hinduism, 1793–1900/Geoffrey A. Oddie.
        p. cm.
    Includes bibliographical references and index.
        1. Missions, British—India—History—18th century. 2. Missions, British—India—History—19th century. 3. Protestants—India—History—18th century. 4. Protestants—India—History—19th century. 5. Protestant churches—Relations—Hinduism. 6. Hinduism—Relations—Protestant churches. I. Title.

BV2420.033   294.507'041—dc22   2006   2005036060

ISBN: 0–7619–3448–0 (HB)   81–7829–591–1 (India–HB)
         0–7619–3487–1 (PB)   81–7829–637–3 (India–PB)

Sage Production Team: Malathi Ramamoorthy, Rrishi Raote, Girish Sharma, Sanjeev Sharma, Rajib Chatterjee and Santosh Rawat

To Ken Ballhatchet,
friend and mentor,
whose deeply-felt interest in Hindu–Christian relations
has inspired my own work on the subject

Contents

List of Illustrations

Acknowledgements

This was a long-term project and many people have helped me in my research and in bringing the book into its final form. I wish to thank in particular archivists Rosemary Seton of SOAS, Christine Penny, in charge of the CMS and CEZMS collections in Birmingham, and Sue Mills, of Regents Park College, Oxford. Others who have been encouraging and generous in giving of their time and advice, or who have been helpful in other ways are Brian Stanley, Dermot Killingley, Avril Powell, Barry Smith, Stuart Piggin, Ian Maxwell, Andrea Major, Jennifer Morawiecki, David Seton, Eric Lott, Richard Fox Young, Will Sweetman and Barbara Kearns (descendant of J.F. Kearns). Special thanks are also due to Nikki Whipps; and also to Anamika Mukharji and Rrishi Raote of Sage for their suggestions and technical assistance in the final stages of the production of the book. I wish also to acknowledge the generosity of the Australian Research Council and the University of Sydney for its financial assistance in enabling me during the initial stages of research to travel and exploit the resources of archives in both the United Kingdom and India. Last but not least, very special thanks are due to my family, for their patience, understanding and encouragement. I owe most to my wife Nola who, as usual, has been a tower of strength and support. She has not only helped with the proofreading, but also given advice and been helpful in ways beyond measure and for which no words of acknowledgement can suffice.

List of Abbreviations

AR	*Annual Report*
BMS	Baptist Missionary Society
CCO	*Calcutta Christian Observer*
CEZMS	Church of England Zenana Missionary Society
CLS	Christian Literature Society
CMG	*Church Missionary Gleaner*
CMI	*Church Missionary Intelligencer*
CMR	*Church Missionary Record*
CMS	Church Missionary Society
CMSJI	*Church Missionary Society Juvenile Instructor*
CMSMP	*Church Missionary Society Missionary Papers*
CMSQP	*Church Missionary Society Quarterly Papers*
CP	*Candidates' Papers* of the Council for World Mission
CS	Church of Scotland
CWM	Council for World Mission
FCS	Free Church of Scotland
FCSQMP	*Free Church of Scotland Missionary Papers*
HF	*Harvest Field*
HFRFCS	*Home and Foreign Record of the Free Church of Scotland*
IA	*Indian Antiquary: A Journal of Oriental Research*
ICHR	*Indian Church History Review*
IER	*Indian Evangelical Review*
IFE	*Indian Female Evangelist*
IOAOR	India Office and Oriental Records
IW	*India's Women and China's Daughters*
JMM	*Juvenile Missionary Magazine*
JO	*Juvenile Offering*
LMS	London Missionary Society
MCCM	*Madras Christian College Magazine*
MF	*Mission Field*
MMC	*Missionary Magazine and Chronicle*
MP	*Missionary Papers*
MR	*Missionary Register*
MS	*Missionary Sketches*
NLS	National Library of Scotland

PA	*Periodical Accounts*
PRWM	*Papers Relating to Wesleyan Missions*
RPC	Regents Park College
SA	Serampore Archives
SOAS	School of Oriental and African Studies
SPCK	Society for the Promotion of Christian Knowledge
SPG	Society for the Propagation of the Gospel
UPCS	United Presbyterian Church of Scotland
UPMR	*United Presbyterian Missionary Record*
WCC	William Carey Collection, Regents Park College
WMMS	Wesleyan Methodist Missionary Society
WMSMN	*Wesleyan Missionary Society Missionary Notices*

Introduction

The focus of this book is on the imagined world of Indian religion. More specifically, it explores the emergence and refinement of the idea of Hinduism as it developed among British Protestant missionaries from 1789 to 1900. As we shall see, a feeling among some European observers that India's dominant religion was somehow different from that of other pagan nations gradually gained wider acceptance in the seventeenth and eighteenth centuries. This growing conviction that there was something distinctive in Hindu tradition encouraged the formulation of the idea of 'the Hindu religion', or Hinduism. As a way of attempting to explore and understand non-Christian religious 'systems' the term Hinduism was then used increasingly as a category and concept, and as a label which has come to dominate the way in which Indian as well as Western scholars think about Indian religions.

Religion and Religions

In his seminal work entitled *The Meaning and End of Religion*, first published in 1962, Wilfred Cantwell Smith developed the view that the idea of 'religion' itself was a European and Western construct. It was, he wrote, a concept derived from the Romans, and further developed and influenced by Christianity and ideas of the European Enlightenment. This theme has subsequently been taken up by Peter Harrison, Richard King and others who have discussed in even greater detail the history and circumstances which affected European views of 'religion' and 'religions' in the seventeenth and eighteenth centuries.[1]

In contrast to the Romans, who continued to think of religion as ceremony, custom or tradition, as something which one did or performed, early Christians stressed the importance of attitude and belief. However, the initial emphasis on the significance of inner conviction was eventually matched, and perhaps even overshadowed, by a long process of objectification. The notion of religion as something expressed objectively in written creeds, doctrine or stated belief (a view nurtured in medieval

[1] Harrison 1999; King 1999; Sweetman 2003.

Europe and reflected in accusations of heresy and in the debates of the Reformation) persisted in Christian thinking throughout the colonial period. Furthermore, attached to these views was the notion of a basic source, a foundational scripture, a written text, which only those with the correct attitude or training, such as priests, scholars or pastors, had the right to interpret. During the Enlightenment, religion came to be thought of even more strongly as an objective reality, rather like natural objects which could be explored through scientific enquiry. It was a 'system', with its theologians, philosophers and priests, its institutions and people. It was also something which had a shape and boundaries and which, like other objects, could be compared or even arranged in an hierarchy of value from true to false, or from the most to the least beneficial.

The usual assumption of commentators in the seventeenth and eighteenth centuries was that there were four religions, namely Judaism, Christianity, Islam and Paganism or Heathenism.[2] This assumption is reflected in the correspondence of Ziegenbalg, one of the founders of the Tranquebar Protestant mission who, writing to Tamil religious leaders in the early eighteenth century, asked them: 'Among the Four different Religions of the World, which is the most proper to render us happy in the next World?'[3] The same idea of a fourfold religious system is reflected in William Carey's well-known *Enquiry* published in 1792. 'Paganism' or 'heathenism' as words used in these and other writings were very broad and loosely-defined terms which were meant to include all non-Christian religions apart from Judaism and Islam. According to Carey, for example, it was the religion of vast numbers of people in Africa, the Americas and Asia, including Australasia and the Pacific islands.

But while these terms continued to be popular, for example, among men and women applying for service with Protestant missionary societies in the nineteenth century, they were already losing something of their usefulness as descriptive categories in the broader circles of European discourse. Even if it was not seen as offensive, the term pagan or heathen was perceived increasingly as inadequate and imprecise. This, as noted above, was largely because of the new insights and knowledge acquired by Europeans through exploration, travel, business activity and missionary enterprise, in 'pagan' countries in the Americas and in the East, in the seventeenth and eighteenth centuries. The question inevitably arose as to whether paganism was really the same everywhere. Was there no difference,

[2] J.Z. Smith 1998: 271–72.
[3] Philips (tr.) 1719: Letter IV.

for example, between the form it took in India or Africa, and in other countries? Should not commentators revise their ideas and, instead of thinking of four religions, think in terms of many more? Only in this way could European observers and scholars begin to understand and deal with the different peoples overseas.

The evolution of dominant British and European ideas of India's distinctive religious traditions, ideas which affected British Protestant missionary views and understanding of Hinduism, will be discussed in Part 1. It also includes more detailed comment on the emergence of the concept of Hinduism in the second half of the eighteenth century, a development that culminated in the use of the term 'Hinduism' in Protestant circles in the last quarter of the century. Following the development and formulation of this idea there were constant disagreements among missionaries and others as to what it meant.

One of the objectives of this book is to explore the way in which Protestant missionary constructions of Hinduism related to the broader debates about the nature of Hinduism taking place among Europeans and Indian subjects generally. We attempt to discover something of what was different or especially influential in missionary views and propaganda, and also examine the overall context and general factors affecting missionary interpretations. What kind of ideas about Hinduism did the missionaries inherit? And how far was their depiction of Indian religion an echo of what travellers, other missionaries and orientalist scholars were saying? These questions also relate to the central themes and specific focus of this book which is on missionary knowledge and information. What did the Protestant missionaries really know about Hinduism? What were their presuppositions and sources of knowledge and information? How did they envisage Hinduism and what did they think it was?

A consideration of these issues raises further questions which are also explored in subsequent chapters. What did the missionaries do with what they knew, and why? How did they represent Hinduism to themselves, to each other, and to their supporters and the public at large? What was their purpose and specific agenda in depicting Hinduism in the way they did? For example, were missionary comments made for their own benefit and elucidation, or was their depiction of Hinduism deliberately constructed so as to influence government or other authorities, or to sway particular groups of people, Hindu or Christian? And lastly, what were the results of the missionary assessment, for themselves and for others, in Britain and in India itself?

As is apparent from these comments, questions about missionary knowledge and understanding of Hinduism, and the way in which it was represented, are linked with issues of evaluation. Whatever aspects of Hinduism came to their notice the missionaries tended to compare and evaluate, placing different ideas and practice on a scale of values, ranging from beliefs or practices they might approve to those which were evil or totally 'other'. As to their assessment of Hinduism as a whole, this has already been briefly considered in studies such as those of Kenneth Ballhatchet, Eric J. Sharpe and Kenneth Cracknell.[4] Ballhatchet, who roots his discussion in a broad context of change, distinguishes two main attitudes towards Hinduism during the nineteenth and twentieth centuries—one of hostility and another of sympathy, 'The former being predominant during the greater part of the nineteenth century and the latter thereafter.'[5] However, while there has been some discussion of missionary evaluations of Hinduism this has not been researched in any great detail over a long period of time. The emphasis has been on developments during the second half of the nineteenth century without a sufficient attempt to explore the basic factors that helped condition missionary responses to Hinduism in the late eighteenth and early nineteenth centuries. Especially conspicuous has been the absence of any detailed analysis of Protestant missionary presuppositions and assumptions which they carried with them and which were of considerable importance in their initial responses to India's religious and social life. But before considering some of the more important of these presuppositions, something might be said about the context of empire and some of the more general ways in which the presence of a British administration in India impinged upon missionary depictions of Hinduism.

Emergence of Protestant
Missionary Societies in Britain

The story of the establishment of British Protestant missionary societies is already so well known that only the briefest account needs to be given here. With the exception of women's missionary organizations (discussed in chapter 8), most of these societies were founded during the period from 1699 to c.1843. The establishment of the Church of England Society for

[4] Ballhatchet 1961: 344; Cracknell 1995: Ch. 1; Sharpe 1965: Chs 1 and 2.
[5] Ibid.: 344.

the Promotion of Christian Knowledge (SPCK) in 1699 was followed, two years later, by the founding of the Society for the Propagation of the Gospel (SPG). The institution of these organizations therefore pre-dates the Methodist and evangelical revivals that swept through Britain later in the eighteenth century. It was these revivals, however, which gave a much greater impetus to the missionary movement and which reflect the ebullient missionary spirit which led to the formation of evangelical missionary societies dedicated to missionary work overseas. Among the most important of these organizations which operated in India were the Particular Baptist Missionary Society (BMS) founded in 1792, the London Missionary Society (LMS) established in 1795 and the Church Missionary Society (CMS) established in 1799. These developments at the end of the century were followed by the founding of the Wesleyan Methodist Missionary Society (WMMS) between 1814 and 1818, the Foreign Mission Committee of the Church of Scotland (CS) in 1824 and, after the disruption in the Church of Scotland in 1843, the establishment of the Foreign Mission Committee of the Free Church of Scotland (FCS).

Evangelical and Other Protestant Views

The great majority of British Protestant missionaries working in India from 1793 to 1900 were employed by evangelical societies and thought of themselves as evangelicals. This was in spite of the fact that the term 'evangelical', which was somewhat vague, lost even more of its cutting edge and meaning as the years progressed.

In 1835 Henry Venn (later Clerical Secretary of the CMS) declared that evangelical clergy differed from others 'not so much in their systematic statement of doctrines, as in the relative importance which they assign to the particular parts of the Christian System, and in the vital operation of Christian doctrines upon the heart and conduct'. According to Bebbington, who quotes Venn and comments on the evangelical movement in the eighteenth and nineteenth centuries, there were four qualities or characteristics which were 'the special marks of Evangelical religion': these were 'conversionism' or a belief that lives needed to be changed; 'biblicism' or 'devotion' to the Bible; 'crucicentricism', a stress on the atoning work of Christ as the agency of salvation; and 'activism,' including an emphasis on preaching the gospel.[6] As the author appears to concede, these particular

---

[6] Bebbington 1989: Ch. 1.

features of Christianity were not confined to evangelicals. Non-evangelical leaders in the Church of England, for example, also appealed for 'repentance and amendment of life'. They too made use of scripture as the basis of certain ideas and teachings, espoused the doctrine of the atonement (the doctrine that Christ's death atoned for human sin) and were also involved in certain varieties of activism, such as the establishment of missionary societies and preaching the gospel. However, as Henry Venn (and Bebbington) suggest, it was largely a matter of priorities—evangelicals, as compared with other Protestant Christians, stressing the importance of different features within what Venn described as 'the Christian System'.

Other points of difference between evangelicals and other Protestants became more clearly apparent as a result of the rise of the Oxford or Tractarian Movement among Anglicans in the 1830s. Some Anglican clergy fearing disestablishment and withdrawal of state endowments, wished to assert that the Church of England was not dependent on the state and that it gained its authority from Christian truth and apostolic succession (the doctrine that bishops can trace their authority and office in an unbroken line back to the Apostles). These claims set out in a series of tracts written by John Henry Newman, Edward Pusey and other clergy residing in Oxford were linked with doctrines similar to those of the Roman Catholic Church. The Church of England, with its priesthood and sacraments, was the primary authority and means of grace. Scripture which for evangelicals was the basis of faith, the embodiment of revealed truth and primary means of communication between God and the individual, remained for these High Churchmen an important source for understanding Christian tradition. However, it was seen more as a text that could be interpreted correctly only by the Church and its councils rather than by individuals relying on their own imperfect insights or interpretation.

For some evangelicals, therefore, the emergence of the Oxford or Tractarian Movement signalled a return to principles which appeared to undermine the very basis of the Reformation; and controversies engendered by the rise of the movement and intensified by legal disputes spilled over into the mission field. This was mainly because the SPG, in the process of continuing to dispatch missionaries to India, included some men 'imbued with high-church principles'. Tensions in India were reflected in the fact that SPG missionaries were not usually participants or members of the more important local Protestant missionary organizations, such as the Calcutta, Bombay or Madras Missionary Conferences. Nor, with a few exceptions, did they participate in the more general Protestant gatherings such as the decennial conferences which became a feature of Protestant missions towards the end of the nineteenth century. Indeed, in some parts of India, such as Bengal, there was open rivalry between evangelical and High Church missionaries with each party accusing the other of confusing their converts and disrupting their work.[7]

In theory one might expect the attitude of High Churchmen towards 'Hinduism' to be slightly different, perhaps more sympathetic, compared with the response of evangelicals. High Churchmen, it might be surmised, had a much greater understanding of the role of traditional factors in religion, they were not anti-clerical or summarily dismissive of 'priestcraft' in the same vein as many of the evangelicals. Moreover, with their accent on what was jokingly described as 'smells and bells' they were more likely to be able to appreciate various forms of Hindu ritual. But if there were differences of this kind arising from the basic theology and nature of the Oxford or High Church movement, they were minimal compared with the attitudes and ideas about 'Hinduism' which they appear to have shared in common with evangelical missionaries. Like all Protestant missionaries of whatever hue, they were, as we shall see, tied into much the same basic assumptions about the nature of religions and Hinduism as a unified objective system, and to presuppositions about the dominance and role of brahmans in the Hindu system. But more importantly, and like most evangelicals (at least in the first half of the nineteenth century), they were operating from within what might be described as a comparatively rigid and exclusivist position. While for evangelicals there was no salvation except through the blood of Christ as revealed in scripture, for the High Church missionaries there was no salvation outside the church. As Max Müller (the well-known scholar and editor of Sanskrit texts) perceived, both parties had their own ideas and agenda which, in the thinking of Broad Churchmen like himself, had little relevance or significance for Christians who were trying to come to terms with the latest scientific

---

[7] The situation in western India in the early 1880s was little better. In a confidential note to George Smith (General Secretary of the FCS mission), John Murray Mitchell, writing from Puna in July 1882, expressed his alarm at the spread of High Church activity. He stated that by far the most active missions in Bombay were the Cowley fathers and the SPG and that the bishop was 'the highest of high churchmen'. The High Church party was, he believed, determined to take Puna by storm. He complained that the city was 'dreadfully altered' since he knew it some twenty years before when there were evangelical chaplains and an evangelical bishop. He pointed to the cordial relations which continued between the missionaries of the different evangelical societies, but warned that there was 'a strong continuous effort now to sweep all the Episcopalians into the net of Ritualism and to crush all Protestant Missions to the Heathen' (NLS, MS.7826, folios 110–11, Murray Mitchell to George Smith, 22/7/1882).

discoveries and new insights and knowledge about non-Christian religions.[8]

Though participants in the evangelical and Oxford movements continued to share many assumptions, the party spirit and sense of difference engendered by the rise of the latter created some problems for the SPG. According to Daniel O'Connor, the Oxford Movement and its controversies complicated the SPG's role, forcing it 'to steer a wavering course between the sensitive consciences of two opposing sets of supporters, while its many identifications with the movement (eg. Keble, Manning, Newman and Liddon etc) only served to deepen the divide with the CMS'.[9] Ritualism was, in fact, repeatedly attacked at CMS annual meetings.[10]

While fear of the Tractarian movement persisted among some evangelicals, a further cause of anxiety was the rise of new forms of theology and the Broad Church movement, also within the Church of England.[11] One of the central characteristics of the movement was a greater acceptance of diversity of opinion and willingness to engage in discussion with other leaders of thought in contemporary society. This was a process that further encouraged innovative, independent thinking on questions of faith and other issues, such as the relationship between Christianity and non-Christian religions. While evangelicals prioritized scripture and High Churchmen the church as the basis of faith, Broad Churchmen placed more emphasis on the role of reason. But once again the difference, for example between the views of some missionaries who continued to call themselves 'evangelicals' in the second half of the nineteenth century and the views of Broad Churchmen, was not always a sharply-defined one but more a matter of degree.

The emergence of Broad Church trends within the Church of England became increasingly apparent as a result of controversies such as those which erupted over the issue of hell and eternal punishment sparked by the publication of F. D. Maurice's *Theological Essays* in 1853.[12] From about that period on, and especially in the 1860s, church leaders and educated

[8] According to Müller's vicar, with whom he shared a great deal towards the end of his life, his view was that 'to base religion upon the verbal inspiration of a book, upon miracles, or upon ecclesiastical authority, was like trusting for the support of a building to wooden props or scaffolding with the decay of which the whole building must fall' (Max Müller Papers. MS. Eng.C.2814).

[9] O'Connor et al. 2000: 61–2.

[10] Nemer 1981: 23–4.

[11] Ibid.: 20–5.

[12] For an overview of these and other controversies, see especially Chadwick 1970.

Christians more generally were involved in heated debates and discussion of new ideas and discoveries which for some seemed to threaten the very basis of the Christian faith. The publication of Darwin's *The Origin of Species* in 1859, coupled with new findings in geology, challenged literal interpretations of the Genesis story and suggested that the earth was much older than Old Testament accounts appeared to suggest. Doubts were also raised about the historicity of the great flood, the miracles said to be performed by Jesus, and other so-called 'factual' or historical events in the New Testament. Of special significance was the influence of the Broad Church movement in stimulating more liberal movements among dissenters. Thus, the views of Maurice, Müller and other Broad Churchmen on the relationship between Christianity and non-Christian religions raised questions and stimulated debate in circles outside the Church of England.

Missionaries in the Context of Empire

Critics of Edward Said's book *Orientalism: Western Conceptions of the Orient*, have already noted the author's failure to draw an adequate distinction between colonialism on the one hand and the missionary movement on the other.[13] The present writer has argued that the main difference between the two movements was clearly apparent in their aims and objectives, colonizers being intent on the acquisition and maintenance of empire and missionaries on the saving of souls and the establishment of Christian communities which would survive and outlast all forms of political domination. These and other arguments pointing to differences as well as similarities between missionaries and empire-builders, have recently been explored in Andrew Porter's monumental study which includes an analysis of 'religion versus empire' in India.[14]

The burgeoning Protestant missionary movement was, Porter argues, encouraged by what evangelicals interpreted as signs of the time, a providential theology in which world events were readily interpreted as auguries for the success of Britain's missionary enterprise. European expansion overseas, including exploration, the spread of commerce and the extension of European political control were all seen as developments providing opportunities for mission both within and outside the context of empire. The essential point for historians is, therefore, to recognize the essentially

[13] Oddie 1994; Cox 2000: 9–11.
[14] A. Porter 2004.

autonomous character and distinctive purpose of Protestant missions. According to Porter,

> Early nineteenth-century evangelical views of the relationship between missionary religion and imperial or indigenous authority were distinguished by their sense of self-sufficiency under divine superintendence, rather than by any conscious or actual dependence by them on secular agencies or dynamism. Recognition by evangelicals of limiting conditions, whether imposed by governments or material circumstances, must always be clearly distinguished from both reliance on or subservience to them.... For the missionary, faith placed empire in perspective. 'Empire' like 'civilization' was at best something to be turned to missionary advantage, a means to an end but equally something to be ignored or rejected out of hand if it failed to serve the missionary's main purpose.[15]

However, as Porter himself points out, even when these basic differences of agenda and purpose (reflected in instances of serious conflict between missionaries and colonial officials) are fully acknowledged, the fact remains that the missionary movement, including missionary work in India during the period under discussion, was clearly influenced by the ideas and ethos of British rule.[16] Though separate, imperial and missionary movements affected each other—the imperial context being, to a greater or less extent, one of the factors influencing the way in which missionaries thought about their work, lived and carried out their separate tasks. Indeed, one may well ask what difference the imperial context made to the way in which the missionaries viewed or represented Hinduism.

First, and as we shall see in chapter 2, British missionary constructions of Hinduism were greatly affected by the writings of officials and other individuals associated with early British rule. Depictions of Hinduism by Charles Grant, Claudius Buchanan and Bishop Heber were all derived from their time in India when they were working in some sort of official association with empire. Grant, a commercial agent and later Director of the East India Company, was one of the first to enunciate the way in which evangelicals might respond to Hinduism. Claudius Buchanan, a Company chaplain and later Vice-Provost of Wellesley's College of Fort William, Bishop Heber, who was one of the first bishops to be appointed to the Company's ecclesiastical establishment, and other Company employees had some influence on missionary thinking. Moreover, and as we shall

[15] Ibid.: 116.
[16] Ibid.: 316.

note in chapter 3, early British orientalist discoveries relating to Hinduism (some of them made in the course of attempting to introduce a more effective administration) also had a considerable influence on Protestant models and depictions of Hinduism. Added to this was the introduction of the census and other administrative material relating to religion. The section in the census on religion, together with the statistics and tables relating to the size and distribution of the different religious communities, was noted and often cited in missionary reports.[17]

Second, imperial policies determined, at least to some degree, what aspects of Hinduism would emerge and become topics of public debate. During the first half of the nineteenth century one of the missionary concerns was with the Company's supposed 'religious neutrality' and the example the Company set as a 'Christian' administration. The focus was on the Company's alliance with 'the Hindu system' and on its tardiness in suppressing practices such as female infanticide, sati and hook-swinging. These and other customs became therefore even more prominent and high-profile issues in missionary comment. Also of increasing concern was the Company's involvement in the management and upkeep of Hindu temples, and the part British officials played in the conduct of Hindu religious festivals. Hence, in their attempts to change the Company's policies by bringing pressure to bear on it via the British public, Parliament and Company officials, the missionaries and their supporters repeatedly drew attention to these aspects of Hindu religious life and activity.

Third, the missionaries' association with empire quite possibly reinforced some of the more negative characteristics of their overall evaluation of Hinduism. While both official and non-official European attitudes to Hindus and Hinduism varied, the presence of other Europeans and increasing opportunities for mixing with them, especially in towns and cities, must have consolidated the missionaries' sense of isolation from the indigenous population. The 'us and them' mentality so clearly depicted in Said's idea of orientalism was not always easy to overcome and was clearly reflected in the continuing conservative missionary views of Hinduism which portrayed it as irrational, immoral and inhumane.

Mixed with a sense of difference was a general sense of superiority which was, if anything, encouraged by the growth of empire and the missionaries' association with the ruling elite. Britain's acquisition of the greatest empire since Roman times and exhilaration in her industrial, scientific and technological achievements, all encouraged a feeling of superiority which

---

[17] See, for example, *CMI*, Vol. XI, 1875: 257–71.

was not infrequently linked with the blessings of British Protestant Christianity. The feeling that the Hindu was inferior and had nothing to offer religiously, was, if anything, reinforced by India's apparent lack of material and scientific progress.[18] Indeed, in the eyes of some missionary candidates, missionary effort was all the more necessary because of the *overall* inferior position of pagan peoples. When applying for service with the LMS, J. J. Dennis declared, for example, that it was the missionary's duty 'to preach the word...to refine the taste—raise the morals—and promote the industry and civilization of the natives'.[19] In his application in 1888, E. S. Oakley was equally concerned and, at the same time, condescending. Missionaries, he felt, should be motivated both by 'the love of souls which should inspire the Christian with enthusiasm for the spread of the Gospel, and the human sympathy which should prompt us to seek the moral and social welfare of less favoured races than our own'.[20]

Some Basic Missionary Presuppositions, 1739–1850

Even though Protestant missionaries, like Protestant theologians, were divided on a number of issues, they all tended to operate within much the same paradigm of thought and assumption. Indeed, many of them were probably not conscious of the way in which these common assumptions affected their understanding and evaluation of other religious movements.

One of these assumptions was about the very nature, centrality and evil character of idol worship.[21] The influences affecting missionary attitudes and responses to this issue go back to the time of Old Testament prophets, to at least as early as the prophet Jeremiah in the seventh century BCE. As one of the missionaries declared, 'the Bible everywhere condemns the practice, by precept and example, by prohibitions and threatenings' (W. R. James 1888).[22] Idols, wrote the prophet Jeremiah, 'are both stupid and foolish; the instruction of idols is but wood.... They are the work of the

---

[18] In 1864, John Stephenson, a missionary with the SPG, was 'a little vexed' by the attitude of his Hindu pundit towards England's undoubted achievements. 'Whenever I spoke of England's greatness, as exemplified in her railways, and ships, and commerce, and so on,' wrote Stephenson, 'he always produced some fabulous King of Madura who "knew all about it".' *Augustine's College, Occasional Papers*, No. 82, 4/10/1864: 11.

[19] SOAS. LMS CP, Dennis to Committee, 23/12/1853.

[20] SOAS, LMS CP, Oakley to Committee, 6/9/1888.

[21] See especially Stanley 1990: 63–5.

[22] W. R. James, 'Idolatry: What is it and Why is it Condemned?', *IER*, Vol. XV, 1888: 220–34.

craftsman and of the hands of the goldsmith.... But the Lord is the true God; he is the living God and the everlasting King.'[23] Similarly, in the New Testament Paul, when speaking to the Athenians, declared that 'we ought not to think that the Deity is like gold, or silver, or stone, a representation by the art and imagination of man'.[24] The main objections to idolatry as expressed in these and other passages of Scripture were that it was 'stupid' or irrational; it involved the neglect of the worship of 'the *one* true god', and was conducive to polytheism; and third, it involved worshipping the created thing instead of the Creator, a practice which led to every kind of corruption of religion and morals. One of the most notorious of these 'corruptions' associated with the worship of idols in ancient Egypt, Babylonia and Israel, and a practice condemned by the prophets, was the performance of fertility rites and the existence of temple prostitution associated with the deity.[25] Not only did missionaries become aware of the existence of what they saw as similar centres of temple prostitution in south India, but they were also inclined to suspect (at least initially) that all the chief seats of idol worship in India were 'cesspools of immorality'.[26] Increasing their sense of repugnance at what appeared to be idol worship was their reading of the book of Kings, referring to the sacrifice of sons and daughters to the god Molech[27]—a custom practised by Semitic peoples—which reinforced the view that idol worship encouraged the rise of cruel and barbaric practices.

Antipathy towards the worship of idols was not however the prerogative and preserve of Protestants alone. As Brian Stanley remarks, determination to extirpate 'pagan idolatry' was a dominant motif in the sixteenth-century Spanish conquest of Central and South America and was, if anything, 'even more sweeping than in later Protestant missionary thought'.[28] An examination of Jesuit material suggests a similar drive to defeat idolatry in India. Thus, according to Father de la Lane, the Indians were 'truly idolaters' as they worshipped strange gods,[29] and in the opinion of Father Bouchet, they were formerly Christians who had fallen back into the 'errors of Idolatry'.[30] Referring to the same subject de la Lane claimed that the brahmans of Trichinopoly were in the process of deifying a former

---

[23] Bible (RSV): Jeremiah 10:8–10.
[24] Ibid.: Acts 17:29.
[25] Richardson 1950.
[26] W. R. James 1888: 232.
[27] Bible: 2 Kings 23:10.
[28] Stanley 2001: 9–10.
[29] Lockman 1743, Vol. 2: 377.
[30] Ibid.: 277.

king.[31] He also claimed that the 'Idol-Priests' of Sri Rangam were involved in an annual ritual in which they procured a wife for their gods and afterwards abused her.[32] In fact, the well-known dispute between Roberto Nobili and critics of his policy of adaptation was based on agreed assumptions about the evils of idolatry. The debate was not about whether idolatry was acceptable—clearly it was not—but about whether certain practices, such as the wearing of a modified brahmanical thread, were associated with an idolatrous system.

But no matter how much Catholics opposed idolatry, Protestants still saw them as using images in worship.[33] Indeed it is quite possible that the Protestant aversion to the use of 'idols' in Hindu worship was intensified by the fact that this practice and other rituals reminded them of much of what they had so vigorously opposed and attempted to abolish during the Reformation. However, much in this dispute over objects was dependent on interpretation—on how one interpreted the use of images and objects in worship, whether in the Roman Catholic, High Anglican or Hindu tradition. As Nobili and others argued, what really mattered was what was going on in the mind of the devotee.[34] This very point was at the heart of J. Murray Mitchell's research and interviews with Hindus in western India in 1841. As a result of this and subsequent research, Mitchell, a missionary of the Church of Scotland, noted the complexity of the issue and the fact that many Hindu devotees had different views. He also realized that in commonplace Hindu worship, there was a special ceremony invoking the spirit into the image (or removing it) and hence an established distinction between the spirit and the image itself.[35]

A second factor affecting Protestant missionary views and evaluation of Hinduism, linked with the first, was Hindu attitudes towards human sexuality. Once again Protestant and Catholics had much in common in their response to Hindu attitudes and practice, inheriting views of sex and sexuality which went back to well before the Reformation.[36] In an important overview of eighteenth-century British attitudes and practice,

[31] Ibid.: 379.

[32] Ibid.: 383.

[33] See, for example, reference to idols and institutions and practices 'characteristic equally of Hinduism and Popery' in the Protestant missionary periodical CCO, Vol. VI, May 1837: 433.

[34] Zupanov 1999: 97–8.

[35] Mitchell 1899: 84–5, 273.

[36] As far as Catholic attitudes were concerned, the French *philosophe* Diderot (1713–84) may not have been alone in noting the Catholic Church's 'morbid obsession with chastity and its kill joy attitudes towards eroticism' (Porter 1990: 62).

Roy Porter suggests that 'the most marked feature' of Georgian sexuality was 'its public nature, its openness and visibility'.[37] These characteristics, together with tolerance, a confessed enjoyment of sexual pleasures and an 'exultation in sexual freedom', stood in marked contrast to dissenting attitudes and the views of evangelicals, which were becoming increasingly influential towards the end of the century. But even before the rise of the evangelical movement, some Anglicans, notably those influenced by the continental Pietist movement, were concerned about declining standards of sexual morality. For Thomas Bray and other founders of the SPCK (1699) and the SPG (1701), education and the maintenance of Christian standards also involved 'the reformation of manners'.[38] This included the encouragement and introduction of stricter codes of sexual conduct at court and among the upper and middle classes.

The evangelicals, therefore, were not alone in advocating a return to what they believed were the traditional and appropriate Christian views on sexuality. But while, according to Eric Trudgill, it was evangelicalism that did most to establish what he describes as 'the anti pleasure principle', 'the whole spectrum of Victorian religion, from the austere puritanism of Methodism and the Nonconformist sects, through the Establishment Church, to the moral earnestness of the Oxford Movement, showed a similar asceticism'.[39] As he also remarks, it was believed that the only safeguard against Satan and his insidious 'little by little' wiles was persistent vigilance and self-examination, especially in sexual matters. 'The slightest deviation from the strictest rectitude could be the beginning of disaster; to listen to even a mildly equivocal joke, to look at even a mildly suggestive picture was to flirt with spiritual suicide.'[40]

The Protestant missionaries operating in India, and long imbued with these values, were amongst those most strongly opposed to the public display of sex and sexuality. This included iconographic representation as well as displays of nakedness and evidence of sexual activity or prostitution in public places. However, the missionaries were probably less united in their views of sex within marriage,[41] and more varied in the emphasis

[37] R. Porter 1982.
[38] Thompson 1951: 12–15; Brunner 1988: 24.
[39] Trudgill 1976: 13.
[40] Ibid.: 15.
[41] Peter Gardella, who has studied the development of sexual attitudes in nineteenth-century America has noted, for example, a diversity of evangelical attitudes. These included the approach of those who brought sex-like ecstasy into conversion and the attitude of those who viewed sex as a positive act in Christian marriage (Gardella 1985).

they placed on sexual matters than is sometimes suggested. Further, linked with notions of sexual purity and abstinence was the idea of asceticism— a practice greatly, though not universally, admired by evangelicals. Indeed a certain admiration for the ascetic ideal was possibly one of the reasons why the biographies of the missionaries David Brainerd (1718–47) and Henry Martyn (1781–1812) were so widely read by missionary candidates who may well have admired their stoic and single-minded devotion and dedication to the missionary cause.

A third development affecting the missionary estimate of Hinduism was the growth of what is often referred to as the Enlightenment stress on rationality and science. The same influences which in the seventeenth and eighteenth centuries encouraged the idea that religions were 'systems' which could be explored like scientific objects, also strengthened the notion that rational religion was superior to those based on dogma or superstition. As Bebbington and Piggin have argued, the evangelicals placed considerable stress on the need for rational enquiry. This approach was encouraged in missionary training colleges such as the LMS college at Gosport, in Scottish theological colleges such as Andrews and elsewhere. The works of Francis Bacon, Locke and other exponents of the new experimental and inductive thinking were well known and highly regarded among leading evangelical teachers. In some cases scientific subjects such as anatomy, botany, chemistry, astronomy and geology were taught as part of the curriculum in the colleges where missionary training took place,[42] while missionaries, writing from India, not infrequently displayed an interest in scientific subjects and an awareness of the importance of scientific progress, experiment and investigation. As we shall see, this attitude towards the importance of rationality and rational enquiry affected missionary responses to Hinduism in at least three ways. It served to underline the idea that the worship of dumb idols was irrational, it served to highlight what the missionaries perceived as the absurdity of Hindu mythology respecting creation and natural phenomena and, third, it reinforced their antipathy towards lower-caste practices of 'devil worship' or shamanism which, once again, were seen as dangerously irrational.

As Piggin has shown, missionaries of various denominations tended to distance themselves from what was known as 'enthusiasm' which for them implied 'false inspiration' or 'fanaticism'. Among its symptoms were a belief in special personal revelation, a related conviction of being inspired or possessed by the deity, suspension of personal accountability

[42] Piggin 1984: 174, 176, 212, 220–21.

and responsibility in favour of total dependence on the provision of the deity, and a reliance on the spirit's guidance as expressed through impulses, visions and dreams.[43] All of these characteristics, in evidence in the Christian tradition, and regarded as suspect by most Protestant missionaries in India, were also apparent in different types of Hindu religiosity. This included the shamanistic-like practices (which the missionaries dubbed 'devil worship') of the lower classes in Tinnevelly district and in other parts of India. The critical attitudes that candidates for the mission field evinced towards 'enthusiasm' in certain circles in the Protestant tradition, therefore, subsequently reinforced their aversion to 'devil worship', which was also seen as the unleashing of irrational, chaotic and uncontrolled spiritual forces.[44]

According to George Pettitt, a CMS missionary resident in Tinnevelly, the lower classes, excluded from the worship of brahmanic gods,

> contented themselves with propitiating, by worship and sacrifices, a host of imaginary demons, both male and female, supposed by them to be of a ferocious and bloodthirsty nature, and to have the power of inflicting physical evils, and even death, upon mankind.[45]

Edward Sargent, a missionary working in the same district, used the familiar 'us' and 'them' dichotomy in describing the worship of 'the common Pey or devil'. Addressing his friends in England, he asked them to contrast in their imagination 'a wild, frantic worshipper of a Pei [Pey] with a sincere, devout worshipper of our blessed Saviour', and with grateful heart 'thank God that they have in any way contributed toward such a happy change in the character of even a single individual'.[46] Pettitt, who

---

[43] Piggin 1984: 65–72; Bebbington 1989: 52–3.

[44] Protestant missionary explanations of possession varied. While the German missionary Rhenius, who was working in the CMS Tinnevelly mission in the 1820s, seemed to think that 'devil worshippers' were possessed by the 'great Enemy of Man', his German assistant was not always so sure. Describing one such incident of supposed 'possession', he declared that the sepoy (Indian soldier) involved 'played' the devil and was running about 'pretending to be possessed of the Evil spirit' (*MR*,1823, 447–48). The attitude of later, mid-nineteenth century, British missionaries who witnessed 'devil worship' in the same district appears to have been mostly non-committal. According to Pettitt, neither Sargent nor the scholarly Robert Caldwell (subsequently consecrated Bishop of Tinnevelly) 'meant to declare these cases real possessions; while yet both they and myself feel unable positively to deny that such cases do occur among these deluded people' (Pettitt 1851: 492). See also the LMS missionary Samuel Mateer's description of 'possession' and his remarks on the same issue (Mateer 1871: 215–19).

[45] Pettitt 1851: 483–84.

[46] *CMI*, Vol. 1, No. 2, June 1849: 34.

based his remarks partly on his own experience, declared that when 'devil dancing' was required, the people 'are mad with this noisy and disgusting worship, the villages are illuminated with fires, the tom-tom beats all night, the blood of numerous victims flows upon altars, while the yells of maddened dancers and infatuated spectators rend the air'.[47]

Another widespread and deep-seated conviction among evangelicals, and one shared by continental Pietists, and by Protestants associated with the older non-evangelical societies, was that what mattered was the primacy of personal and inner religion. As Andrew Walls has pointed out, the distinction was between the 'real' or 'inward' expression of Christianity and the 'nominal' or 'formal' practice which had been characteristic of so much church-going in the eighteenth century.[48] As will become apparent, what is especially noticeable about the Protestant accounts of Hinduism in the first half of the nineteenth century is that they place a great deal of weight on its formalism, its rules and the externals of ritual and ceremony. While stressing the importance of inner religion for themselves they tended to objectify the religion of others, spending little time in attempting to discover the Hindus' inner life. Certainly there was the tendency to think in terms of different, competing religious systems and to measure them as one would measure outward objects. Yet in one sense this is not what the evangelicals were doing with their own religion, and what is especially mystifying is why Carey and others (who dwelt on the importance of their own inner religion) so readily dismissed Hinduism as being all about externals when there was so little attempt to explore the Hindus' inner life. This is perhaps a measure of the superficiality of initial contact.

A final underlying influence that might be mentioned which affected a small number of missionaries, was democratic and republican sentiment. Ideas of liberty and social equality reflected in the history of the Independent and Baptist movements in Britain in the seventeenth and eighteenth centuries, and in agitation for parliamentary reform, became increasingly popular as a result of the American and French revolutions. Expelled from the English Church–State establishment for non-conformity, early Baptist leaders were at the forefront of the struggle for religious toleration and the right of every individual to follow the dictates of conscience. Indeed, when the American War of Independence broke out in 1775 most Baptist leaders, as well as dissenters generally, sided with their co-religionists on the other side of the Atlantic,

---

[47] Pettitt 1851: 294.
[48] Walls 1996.

where fear of the establishment of a state-supported episcopacy had been a contributing factor to the revolt.[49] Like so many leaders of Enlightenment thinking, the Baptists generally had developed a strong dislike and suspicion of traditional religious and political institutions. Among these institutions were the oppressive hierarchies of 'despotism' and 'priestcraft', two of the features which the Baptist William Ward identified as central to Hinduism.

The influence of radical, egalitarian and democratic ideas on the early life of a number of Baptists who subsequently became missionaries in India in the late eighteenth or early nineteenth centuries is apparent from a variety of sources. Among those affected by democratic and other contemporary developments were Carey and Ward, both of them commentators on Hinduism and influential in the formation of British Protestant ideas and attitudes towards Indian religions in the nineteenth century. Like evangelicals generally, both were advocates of an end to the slave trade. Carey, as one of his biographers writes, was 'a whole-souled Emancipationist'; and his sisters never heard him pray without reference to this traffic 'so inhuman and accursed'. Ward, who at the age of 21 became editor of the Derby *Mercury,* also campaigned against the slave trade.[50]

Less 'safe' but still in keeping with the radical Baptist political and social tradition, was Carey and Ward's involvement in some other public issues of the day. Ward was a member of a branch of London's Society for Political Information—one of a number of organizations pushing for democratic reform. Acting in this capacity he drew up a document known as the Derby Address. In this he declared that 'all true Government is instituted for the general good; is legalised by the general will; and all its actions are, or ought to be, directed for the general happiness and prosperity of all honest citizens'. Long afterwards, in 1822, when he had been working as a missionary in Bengal for twenty-three years, something of his former radical perspective was still apparent in his comment that 'neither greatness nor goodness descends by blood'.

The struggle for representation and parliamentary reform, the plight of the American colonists and the outbreak of the French revolution also encouraged the young Carey in his radical thinking. He greeted the French revolution as 'God's answer to the recent concerted prayings of his people', and declared that it was 'a glorious door opened, and likely to be opened much wider, for the gospel, by the spread of civil and religious liberty, and

[49] Watts 1978, Vol. 1: 480. See also Brown 1986: 132.
[50] Potts 1993: 28.

by the diminution of papal power'. Carey was, according to his grandson
S. Pearce Carey, 'hotly republican' and was sternly reproved by his friend
and mentor Andrew Fuller (1754–1815) 'for not drinking the King's health'.[51]
Like Rousseau, Carey was convinced of 'the common and equal rights of
all men'. A few years before his departure for India, he joined the Philosophical Institute in Leicester. An open forum for the discussion of political and other contemporary issues, it was founded by Richard Phillips,
an outspoken Quaker and one who was both sympathetic to the Revolution and enthusiastic enough about Tom Paine's ideas to sell copies of his
Rights of Man.[52]

But while both Carey and Ward harboured what the British authorities
viewed as dangerous and subversive ideas, they realized that the open
expression of these sentiments would have to be given up for the larger
cause of mission. Once in India, Carey dropped his republican sentiments
'for things of greater consequence', and because he believed that 'the Bible
teaches me to act as a peaceful subject under that Govt. which is established', provided it 'does not interfere in religious matters, or attempt to
constrain my Conscience'.[53] According to Potts, in spite of Ward's obvious
qualifications in printing and for preaching the gospel, the leaders of the
BMS hesitated to adopt him as one of their missionaries, and 'not until
Andrew Fuller, John Ryland and others become convinced that he had
truly renounced politics did they agree to send him'.[54] But while both these
men had officially renounced their former views and become firm advocates of the Raj, their support was, as already argued, provisional and based
on the idea that British rule was best for missions. Furthermore, the deeper
values, no longer articulated in political comment, remained. These are
reflected in the missionaries' continued commitment to the freedom and
rights of the individual—values which were felt to be diametrically opposed to those of oppressive regimes, hierarchies and inherited power,
features which both men, and Ward in particular, felt were important
characteristics of 'the Hindu system'.

Thus, social, political and other so-called secular developments occurring in Britain prior to the missionaries' departure overseas were among
the factors affecting their responses to Hindu religious beliefs and practice.

---

[51] S. P. Carey 1926: 7. Fuller was author of *The Gospel Worthy of All Acceptance* (1785),
which was one of Carey's favourite texts and a classic statement of eighteenth-century
evangelical Calvinism (Bebbington 1989: 64–5).

[52] S. P. Carey 1926: 63–4.

[53] Potts 1967: 171.

[54] Potts 1993: 33.

Also influential were earlier British and European representations of Hindu religion, commentaries, illustrations and the like, which influenced the missionaries' ideas and expectations of the Hindu world. It included the whole world of imagination, which the missionaries inherited and brought with them as they stepped ashore and prepared for their first meeting with Hindus whose souls they had come to save. It is these inherited ideas of Indian religion, ideas common in Britain and embodied in the earlier literature and narrative accounts, which we discuss in the first three chapters.

Missionary Attitudes towards Knowledge and the Study of Indian Religion

A basic factor shaping missionary understanding and representations of Hinduism was the missionary's level of curiosity, drive or willingness to learn more about it. However, as missionaries started with the assumption that Christianity was superior to all other systems, there usually had to be special reasons for their taking up the study of Hinduism or non-Christian religions. Indeed, in some cases, there was a positive aversion to studying the details of Hindu religion—an attitude encouraged, for example, by comments in the widely-read CMS *Missionary Papers*. Referring to brahman accounts of the stories and symbolism associated with the worship of Shiva and Parvati, the writer maintained it would be 'a waste of time to read what they say'.[55]

The Rev. J. C. T. Winckler, writing from south India in a letter published in the *Church Missionary Record* in 1832, remarked that:

> I find it necessary for a Missionary to make himself well acquainted with the literature and mythology, and, as much as possible, with the mystical theology of the Hindoos. I confess, that, in the beginning of my residence and labours in India, I thought the time lost if spent in the acquisition of these things; I thought the simple exhibition of the Gospel truths sufficient to make impressions on the native mind; and hence, when anything like Hindoo Mythology or doctrines were brought before us in conversation

---

[55] *Missionary Papers* (*MP*) No. XXIII, 1821. See also the comments of M. A. Sherring, a missionary who had already completed twenty-five years of service with the LMS in north India. Writing in his biography of the Rev. William Smith, he referred to a class of missionaries who, though they may have had an excellent knowledge of the colloquial tongue, 'may have a positive dislike amounting [to] repugnance to the study of its classical literature' (Sherring 1879: 11).

with the Natives, through an indirected zeal I was pre-emptory in condemning the whole without discrimination. I have reason to think, that other newly-arrived Missionaries are but too prone to fall into the same error.[56]

However, as Winckler pointed out, missionaries got nowhere and would continue to fail in their efforts to attract a following if they ignored Hindu belief and practice. It seemed to be necessary therefore to learn more of what was often called 'the Hindu mind', to study the Hindus' world view, and the way in which Hindus might understand or interpret the Christian Gospel.

One view common in the early nineteenth century was that the missionary should study Hinduism and other non-Christian religions in order to know and understand the enemy's strength and weakness, and so as to undermine and destroy his defenses. Thus, according to Alexander Duff, the missionary should be like Sultan Babar who conquered India as a result of all his diligent enquiry. After years of spying in the enemy's camp, of getting to know the entire system, what, asked Duff, was the result?

> With the light of *facts* so numerous, minute and accurate, his measures of aggression were contrived and adopted with such skill and precision to the end in view, that the outcast exile from the confines of the Tartarian desert, speedily became the sovereign Conqueror seated on the throne of Delhi.[57]

Thus Christian missionaries would be able to conquer Hinduism only if they had an intimate knowledge of all details of the Hindu system.

Another version of this same view is reflected in the Rev. William Buyer's comments on missionary training. Writing in 1836 he argued that unless the missionary studied the Hindu system he would never be able to meet the arguments of his native opponents.[58] Nor would he be able to combat, in a variety of new forms, 'all the metaphysical difficulties that have been brought against Christianity by the infidel philosophers of Europe'. Unless the missionary, before entering the work, was 'well furnished with information', he would 'always labour under far greater disadvantages than an ill-instructed minister at home, who can apply to numerous sources of improvement entirely beyond the reach of the Missionary'.[59]

---

[56] *CMR*, September 1832: 397.

[57] Duff 1840: 38.

[58] For another version of the same point see *Proceedings of the South India Missionary Conference*, 1858: 230–31.

[59] *Chronicle*, No. VI, November 1836: 88.

Arguments about the importance of knowledge in subverting Hinduism were supplemented by other views based on the missionaries' experience of attempting to preach. According to the Serampore Baptists writing in 1806, to know about Hindu thought, religious teaching and practice 'is of the highest consequence, if we would gain their [the Hindus'] attention to our discourse, and would avoid being barbarians to them'.[60] According to Winckler, what the missionaries were finding was that if they were ignorant of Hindu literature and theology and condemned Hindu ideas out of hand, then people were not prepared to listen to them. Much the same point was made by T. E. Slater when applying for service with the LMS in 1861 when he argued that a general knowledge, as well as 'an acquaintance with the different modes of thought, in connection with the religious systems of the Heathen', would be necessary 'to show to the more learned of the natives, that the Christian Teachers were not merely religious enthusiasts'.[61]

A third argument, more closely related to what were perceived as Hindu needs, was the view expressed in a review of Monier-Williams' *Indian Wisdom* in the *Church Missionary Intelligencer* in 1875.[62] According to the writer it was of 'the utmost importance' that Christians who wished to convey the glad tidings of salvation to those who are still ignorant of them should have 'a reasonable familiarity with the mental and spiritual condition of the races whom they seek to influence'. This was so that the missionary could identify 'the peculiar phase of the disorder which is presented to them' and, depending on their peculiar evils or disorder, could apply the most appropriate form of healing.

Another reason given for studying Hinduism, and a view which shall become clearly apparent in chapter 10, was the argument based on the need for further effective communication. Even if the missionary gained the Hindu's attention and respect, and had some knowledge of the spiritual condition of local people, there was still the need to clearly link the Christian message with Hindu thought and feeling. If the missionary was to move from the known to the unknown, then he or she had to know how and where to begin. Thus, as we shall see, the need for acceptance and the pressures involved in attempting to preach and interact with Hindus inevitably encouraged a much more serious and very deliberate attempt to study different aspects of Hinduism.

[60] *PA*, Vol. 3, 1806: 200.
[61] SOAS, LMS. CP, Slater to Committee, 27/8/1861.
[62] June 1875: 193–94.

But even among missionaries there were those who wanted to carry their pursuit of knowledge much further than others. How, for example, can one compare the labours of a newly-arrived missionary who felt some sort of reluctant obligation to know something of Hinduism with the driven determination of others, passionate in their pursuit of knowledge and understanding? It was this kind of drive and determination which was exemplified in Murray Mitchell's detailed researches into popular practice and in Caldwell's decision to spend a year studying Tamil and gathering information on the beliefs and customs of the people of Tinnevelly district. Furthermore, in the case of these and other missionaries, such as John Robson and J. McKenzie Cobban, one is left with a clear impression that while knowledge was important for missionary purposes and for practical reasons, it was also well worth pursuing for its own sake. In that sense missionary scholars such as those mentioned above were, perhaps, little different from the freelance orientalists of the late eighteenth century whose hobby and passion it was to discover something more of the unknown world of India's religion and culture.

1

Winds of Influence: Hinduism in the British Imagination, 1600–1800

1

Hinduism in Travel and Missionary Accounts, 1600–1800

B ritish Protestant missionaries and their supporters of the late eighteenth and early nineteenth centuries were not only influenced by
ideas and assumptions as discussed in the previous chapter, but also
by early European imagery and constructions of Indian religion. Like
others of their generation they inherited a world of ideas and information
about people of other faiths, of paradigm and prejudice, which were
bound to affect their response and interpretation of what became known
as 'Hinduism'.

In attempting to promote their views they either knowingly or at a less
conscious level built on many of the earlier representations and ways of
thinking about India's religious life which had gradually emerged and
proved influential in the seventeenth and eighteenth centuries. Missionary
and other Protestant views as expressed in books, circulars, magazines and
at public meetings at a later date, were, indeed, all the more effective
because they were able to tap into the public's deep-seated residual memory.
This 'information', or more strictly speaking, mythology, was embedded
in oral tradition and in a vast and growing literature produced by British
and European writers, travellers, missionaries and oriental scholars over
previous generations.

Clearly Protestant missionary characterizations of Hinduism did not
develop in isolation, or as if other Europeans had not written or spoken
on the subject before. But what new discoveries did they think they were
making and how new were their views and interpretation? Were there
specific Protestant missionary insights or contributions to an ongoing
debate? How far, for example, did Protestant missionaries, from the time
of Carey to 1850, merely select and recycle ideas and information which
other European commentators had already discussed? And if there were
parallels, for example, between what the Jesuits were saying and later
Protestant accounts, was this similarity largely accidental? Was it because
Protestants were heavily influenced by Jesuit accounts, or was it because

they were confronted by similar phenomena and, perhaps, deep down and in spite of all their differences, continued to share in much the same Christian and European world view?

Travellers' Accounts

It cannot be assumed that all European travel accounts (prior to the late eighteenth century) referring to religion in India were either available in Britain or, if available, were in a language which could be deciphered by English readers. For this reason, and for the sake of brevity, the following discussion is restricted to a consideration of the principal commentaries available in translation, or in accounts written in English. The latter (the British versions) emerged as an additional source of 'knowledge' in the wake of early Portuguese, Italian and other European commentaries and, significantly, after the formation of the English East India Company in 1600.

One of the first of the European accounts to become well known in Britain was that of the Italian adventurer Ludovico di Varthema who, in 1503, visited Cambay (in present-day Gujarat) and Goa and sailed down the west coast, visiting several important cities further inland. His *Itinerario*, described by a subsequent commentator as 'one of the most accurate and valuable descriptions [of India] then available to Englishmen,' was translated from Latin into English in 1577.[1] The appearance of this commentary was followed, during the last years of Elizabeth's reign, by the translation and publication of another popular and influential travel account. Written by John Huyghen van Linschoten, a Dutch Protestant adventurer, and translated into English in 1598, it included an even more substantial section on 'Gentile' religion in India than was contained in Varthema's account. *The Travels of Pietro Della Valle in India* (1586–1652), another influential Italian travel account commenting on Indian religious belief and practice, was translated by G. Havers into English in 1664. Lastly, and in addition to these works which incorporated accounts of religion mostly in coastal areas, was the translation and publication of the more detailed descriptions of religion in the interior and in the Mughal empire, in the works of the well-known French travellers such as Francois Bernier and Jean-Baptiste Tavernier. According to a recent commentator, Bernier's *History*, which ran into eight editions in the French original over the period from 1670 to 1725 and three in English translation from 1671 to

[1] Sencourt 1923: 69–70.

1684, exerted 'a lasting influence' over later authors.[2] Tavernier's work was also popular with English readers. Five English editions of his travels in India were published between 1677 and 1688.[3]

In addition to these foreign accounts, which contributed to the development of British ideas and imagery associated with Indian religious teachings and practice, was an increasing number of English or British descriptions especially of the west coast of Hindustan (India north of the 'Nerbudda').[4] Among the best known of the sixteenth and seventeenth century English travellers who commented on religion were Ralph Fitch, a pioneering merchant adventurer who journeyed extensively in north India and Bengal between 1583 and 1591, Nicholas Withington, commercial agent with the newly-formed East India Company from 1612 to 1616, Edward Terry, chaplain to Sir Thomas Roe, the English ambassador to the Court of the Great Mughal, Henry Lord, Company chaplain at Surat from 1624 to 1629 and author of *A Displaye of Two Forraigne Sects in the East Indies*, John Fryer, a Company surgeon, in India from 1672 to 1681, and John Ovington, a Company chaplain resident at Surat (c. 1689–92).

Like their precursors, British travellers in India during the eighteenth century (as distinct from administrators and others who were becoming more settled in the country) continued to give their impressions of Indian religious ideas and practice. Among the best known of these was the Scottish sea captain Alexander Hamilton, who was in the Indies from 1688 to 1723. Others were Captain Cope, who wrote *A New History of the East Indies*, published in 1754, J. H. Grose, author of *A Voyage to the East Indies* (1757), and William Hodges, author of *Travels in India During the Years 1780, 1781, 1782 & 1783* (1793).

Unlike the British Protestant missionaries, the British and European travellers mentioned above pursued a variety of different occupations. Furthermore, their religious beliefs and views of the world were somewhat varied. One of them, Varthema, appears to have adopted Islam and visited Mecca and other Islamic holy sites before travelling in India.[5] All the rest were Christians, Pietro Della Valle and Bernier being Catholics.[6] Bernier belonged to the French intellectual circle known as the Sceptics, and had

---

[2] Teltscher 1995: 14. The popularity and long-term importance of Bernier's work is also attested by the fact that further editions of his work appeared in English in 1745, 1808 and 1811.

[3] Teltscher 1995: 4.

[4] For a discussion of the changes in meaning of the term 'Hindustan', see Barrow 2003.

[5] Varthema 1863: xxvi–xxviii.

[6] Della Valle 1892, Vol. 1: i–ix; Bernier 1916, Vol. 1: xix.

been secretary to the philosopher Pierre Gassendi, whose work (reconcil-
ing Christianity and the new science) he popularized.[7] Tavernier, who
travelled with Bernier for some weeks, was a French Protestant,[8] while
most of the remaining authors, as far as can be ascertained, were also
Protestants, but with varying views. As already indicated, three of the
travellers were Church of England Company chaplains. John Fryer was
also a member of the Church of England, but one who was strongly
opposed to Puritan 'Phanaticks'.[9] Last, there was the influential Dutch
Protestant, van Linschoten, a self-conscious advocate of Protestant faith,
who wrote about the need for converting the 'Gentiles' in much the same
vein as British Protestant missionaries two centuries later! Having given
an account of 'Gentile' religion in India, he gave thanks to God

> that it hath pleased him to illuminate us with the truth of his holy Gospel,
> and that we are not borne [or brought up] among those Heathens, and
> divelish Idolaters, and to desire God that it would please him of his gracious
> goodnesse to open their eyes and to give them the truth of his holy word
> among them...for they are in all things like us, made after Gods owne
> Image.[10]

What then did these travellers think of Indian religion? What were the
impressions they sought to convey? First, it is clearly apparent that they
thought of Indian religion as part of a broader and more universal phenomenon. Non-Muslims were classified as pagans, idolaters, heathens or
gentiles or, in other words, followers of some kind of broad international
religious system not restricted to India. Thus according to Varthema's
travels, the kings of the various countries in south India were 'pagans'. They
included the powerful king of Bisinegar (Vijayanagar) who was a pagan
'with all his kingdom, that is to say, idolaters'.[11] Other travellers relied to
a much greater extent on the terms 'gentile' or 'heathen'. According to Della
Valle the people of India were mostly 'Gentiles'[12] and the same term is used
frequently by Fitch, Terry, Ovington and others. The word 'gentoo', derived
from the Portuguese word for 'gentile', also became increasingly popular

---

[7] Teltscher 1995: 29.

[8] Tavernier 1977, Vol. 1: x.

[9] Fryer 1909: xxxii–xxxiii. Indeed, he appears to have surprised his travelling companions
by fasting on 30 January 'for the Execrable Death of the Martyr Charles the First'.

[10] Linschoten 1885: 299–300.

[11] Varthema 1863: 126.

[12] Della Valle 1892: 67.

and was used widely in travel literature in the eighteenth century. 'The Gentoos are comprehended and known to the Europeans under that common appellation,' wrote Grose in his *Voyage to the East Indies*. The word, he explained, was 'derived from the corrupt Portuguese Lingua Franca, generalized over the maritime coasts of India, signifying Gentiles or Heathens'.[13]

However, in spite of the linking of religion in India with religions elsewhere, the occasional use of the term 'Indian' or 'Hindu' as a qualifying adjective with reference to religion on the subcontinent helped pave the way for a later and increasingly popular idea that there was, after all, something unique about Indian beliefs and practice.

The question of whether India had a distinctive form of religion left open the further question as to whether it was a unified all-India system or some sort of combination of different units. Was the heathenism of India constructed in such a way as to suggest a pan-Indian unified system, or is the reader left with the overall impression that Indian religion was like the political map of the subcontinent for much of the seventeenth and eighteenth centuries—fragmented and under the control of competing groups?

On the question of a unified system within India, travellers appear to give very different or even contradictory accounts. They either disagree with each other (even during much the same period) or they present the reader with a text which is inconclusive or can be read either way. Some authors, like Terry, Lord, Tavernier, Linschoten and Hamilton were inclined to emphasize diversity, drawing attention to regional, doctrinal and other differences. In contrast to their arguments, Della Valle, Fryer and Bernier were all inclined to highlight commonalities, while Grose, a Writer in the East India Company, adopted a position somewhere in the middle. Referring to 'Gentoo Mythology' in his *Voyage to the East Indies*, published in 1757, he declared that 'the bottom of that religion is every where nearly the same'. 'Yet,' he wrote, 'in various parts of that extensive country called Indostan, there are such various modes of opinions and practice built upon it, as would require many volumes to specify the differences.'[14]

Whatever conviction there was among travellers that India's faith and worship was a unified pan-Indian system was probably reinforced by a feeling that (despite the presence of sannyasis, or holy men) it was brahmans who were ultimately in control.

[13] Grose 1772: 231.
[14] Ibid., Vol. 1: 182.

There had long been a tradition in Europe concerning the wisdom and learning of the brahmans—a tradition which appears to have come down from the time of Greek contact with north Indian states. What better measure, then, could one adopt than to consult the brahmans when attempting to understand 'heathen' faith and practice? The brahmans were, in the words of John Fryer, 'Doctors of Divinity',[15] while according to Tavernier they were the teachers and ministers of the law.[16] Pietro Della Valle stressed the importance of being able to consult with brahmans, and subsequently sought out and talked with an old brahman who showed him books written in the Devanagari script.[17] Edward Terry, the English chaplain at Surat, made it quite clear that he had had discussions with brahmans on a range of philosophical and religious issues[18] while, in his account, Bernier made frequent reference to his discussions with pundits—one of whom was his 'constant companion' for three years.[19] Grose also referred to the discourse he had with brahmans on the Indian treatment of cows, and stressed the point that 'They have a learned language peculiar to themselves called Hanscrit, in which the Vedham, Shaster, and other of their books of their law are written.'[20]

The brahmans' dominance and priestly control, which was apparent in many different parts of India was, according to many of the same accounts, enforced through the caste hierarchy and in other ways.

Varthema, Della Valle, Linschoten, Tavernier, Hamilton and Grose all refer to brahmans as being at the apex of the varna system. Linschoten, for example, stressed their political importance and influence over kings, underlining his conviction that 'the King doth nothing without their counsell and consent'.[21] Della Valle described them not only as priests, astrologers and physicians, but also as 'secretaries to Princes'.[22] According to Hamilton the 'Nambouries' [Nambudiris] of Calicut were 'the first' in both capacities of 'church and state'.[23]

There is therefore plenty of evidence to suggest that European commentators, to a varying degree, believed that the brahmans had exclusive

[15] Fryer 1909: 94.
[16] Tavernier 1977, Vol. 2: 142–43.
[17] Della Valle 1892, Vol. 1: 72, 75.
[18] Foster 1968: 321.
[19] Bernier 1916: 325, 329, 342–43.
[20] Grose 1772: 184, 202.
[21] Linschoten 1885, Vol. 1: 247.
[22] Della Valle 1892: 81.
[23] Hamilton 1727: 375.

control over sacred knowledge, that they also possessed considerable secular power and control over governments, and, third, that they not only invented, but also controlled the caste system. It is perhaps in these comments that we see the seeds of the popular European and later missionary view that the lower orders were little more than ignorant and abject slaves in the hands of a manipulative and self-interested priesthood. If there was an inclination to religious unity then it was enforced (according to this view) 'cunningly', and through the mechanisms of religious, political and social control.

Della Valle noted that brahmans were much respected by the 'ignoble' who tried their best not to defile them.[24] According to Linschoten the brahmans were 'very subtil in writing and casting accounts, whereby they make other simple Indians beleeve what they will'. The common people, he said, believed them to be prophets[25] while, according to Nicholas Withington, merchant in India from 1612 to 1616, they received the alms or tithes of their parishioners, 'beeinge esteemed marvaylous holye'.[26] Bernier declared that they were held 'in great veneration', and also added that they were 'enriched by the alms of the people'.[27] He argued further that the brahmans played 'wicked and detestable tricks and impostures' and, like Hamilton and Ovington, stressed the way in which they foisted ideas and superstitions on gullible and ignorant people.[28]

Some travel, narratives also underline the role brahmans played in some of the more sensational public rituals. Both Tavernier and Bernier drew attention to what they believed was the key role brahmans played in the performance of sati, as well as in the burial of widows alive.[29]

For many travellers, therefore, a focus on the role and activity of the brahmans confirmed the idea that Indian religion was a unified and priest-controlled system. As we shall see, these views of Indian religion as an integrated brahmanical invention (which were even more strongly developed in Jesuit and orientalist writings) became essential ingredients in the dominant Protestant paradigm of 'Hinduism' in the late eighteenth and early nineteenth centuries.

India's religion not only featured brahmans, but included other special communities or features which seemed to the traveller to cry out for

---

[24] Della Valle 1892: 81.
[25] Linschoten 1885: 248.
[26] Foster 1968: 221–22.
[27] Bernier 1916: 305.
[28] Hamilton 1727: 317; Ovington 1929: 195.
[29] Bernier 1916: 313; Tavernier 1977, Vol. 2: 163, 165–66.

comment. While brahmans were discussed in terms of political power, control and domination familiar to readers in Europe, it was the *differences* between European and Indian society which tended to fascinate. The position of the brahmans was important and instructive, but the really interesting (even weird) thing about Indian religion was the sannyasis or holy men and a range of shocking and extraordinary beliefs and customs. Travel accounts were meant to be entertaining as well as instructive, and one of the best ways of holding the reader's attention was by recounting tales of belief and practice that seemed extraordinary to people who simply assumed that the world was constructed in a certain predictable, God-given way. As we shall see, almost all of these 'peculiarities' of Indian religion were taken up and discussed in nineteenth-century missionary literature, by missionaries or their supporters who, in most cases, recycled the old and well-established arguments.

Just how the Hindu ascetic or yogi fitted into the overall picture (if it was thought there was one), or how he or she related to the brahman, was seldom discussed. Female yogis were occasionally mentioned, but it was the male who held centre stage; and what, for most travellers, was most striking about him was his extraordinary appearance, feats of endurance (supposed or otherwise), relationship with ordinary people, and sexual habits.

Pietro Della Valle, describing his first sighting of yogis on the banks of the river near Ahmedabad in the early seventeenth century, referred to their hideous appearance and devil-like attributes, perhaps subconsciously linking them with the gods in what Partha Mitter has described as 'the monster tradition'.[30]

The ascetics' extraordinary feats of self-torture was a subject of special fascination. Not all accounts refer to the same forms of discipline; but commonly mentioned is the practice of ascetics holding their arm or arms elevated in the air 'so that the joints become so stiff they are never able to lower them again,'[31] and also the practice of never sitting or lying down— a custom which, according to Fryer, a medical officer, resulted in practitioners having legs 'swoln as big as their Bodies'.[32] Other customs, such as going on pilgrimage in heavy chains, being entombed for days without drinking or eating, gazing at the sun, or enduring the five fires for forty days, are reported in various accounts. Implied in some comments, such as those of Fryer, was the idea that some practices were 'unnatural' or 'irrational' in that they led to the abuse of the body. Other travellers

---

[30] Della Valle 1892: 100–101; Mitter 1992.
[31] Tavernier 1977, Vol. 2: 157.
[32] Fryer 1909: 260.

claimed that ascetics who performed such extraordinary exercises were motivated by spiritual pride, arrogance and the desire to impress and exploit ordinary believers. Fearing the curses of holy men, people gave them alms and ministered to their everyday needs. Then there were the stories and rumours of the fakirs' more spectacular feats involving the exercise of magical power. While some writers who entertained readers with stories of these supposed supernatural events dismissed the ascetics involved as frauds or cheats, others such as Bernier and Grose confessed that they were unsure what to believe or how to interpret the stories they heard.[33]

Last, there was the yogis' sexuality including their relationship with women. While there was comment on their nakedness and some admiration for their apparent self-control in public (notwithstanding the attentions of Hindu women) there were also disapproving remarks about their relationship with women in public and in private. Indeed, the authors of these accounts were almost as concerned with the looseness of Hindu women as they were with the lust and hypocrisy of the Hindu mendicant.

Unlike the brahmans it was the yogis who highlighted for European readers much of what was different, mysterious, bizarre and irrational in 'Eastern' practice. For Protestants and even for Roman Catholics (who were more accustomed to the idea of ascetic practices), here, surely, in the naked or near-naked figure of the Hindu fakir, was a person who was almost totally 'other'. His appearance, physical 'feats' and sexual habits not only cried out for explanation, but gave free rein to the author's (and reader's) imagination. In drawing attention to ascetics in their early nineteenth century accounts, therefore, Protestant missionaries were building on a long tradition of European comment, and especially on the more negative constructions of the fakir phenomena.

What then of Indian gods and other manifestations of Indian religion? Partha Mitter has already drawn attention to the 'monster' tradition of Indian deities in European art and travel literature.[34] The notion of Indian gods as monsters or demons is, as he points out, clearly apparent in early travel literature. Though he argues that, by the mid-nineteenth century, the rise of scientific interest and information about Indian mythology tended to dissolve the age-old monster tradition, it will be argued in a subsequent chapter that the idea of the Indian gods being both ugly and

[33] Bernier 1916: 316–23 and Grose 1772: 196–99.
[34] Mitter 1977.

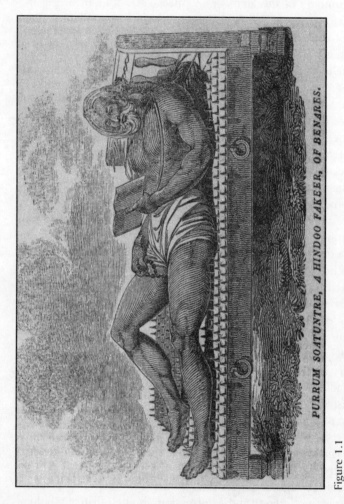

PURRUM SOATUNTRE, A HINDOO FAKEER, OF BENARES.

Figure 1.1
'Purrum Soatuntre, a Hindoo Fakeer, of Benares'

This sketch of a 'devotee' who was living on a small Government pension and whose ordinary position was 'reclining on a bed of iron spikes' was originally commissioned by Jonathan Duncan, orientalist scholar and Resident and Superintendent of Benares, 1788–94. It was first published in *Asiatic Researches* (the journal of the Bengal Asiatic Society) and subsequently reproduced in the *Missionary Register* and CMS *Missionary Papers* in 1819.

irrational (ideas closely linked with the tradition) lingered on even longer, especially in the more popular forms of missionary society literature.

The demonic and ugly appearance of gods was for some European travellers a symbolic reminder of the irrational and misguided devotion they could inspire. One powerful illustration of the gods' effect could be seen, for example, in the travellers' depiction of 'deluded' devotees throwing themselves beneath the wheels of a gigantic temple cart, a practice frequently referred to in travel literature. The best known and most famous example of this custom was what took place at the annual festival in honour of the god Jagannath (a form of Vishnu) at his temple in Puri, Orissa. It was not merely the size of the coach, however, but the strength of the 'devotion' or 'fanaticism' of devotees that attracted the attention of Europeans—Bernier's account accessible to English readers in translation in 1686[35] being supplemented by Hamilton's graphic description published in 1727.

While reference to temple carts crushing 'deluded votaries' was common enough, even more frequent were accounts of widow-burning or sati. Indeed, most stories of Indian religion must have seemed incomplete without the compulsory reference to the burning or burial of these women. The literature on the subject, which has been discussed by Kate Teltscher, Lati Mani and other historians in recent years, not only provides a context and background for the later debates on the subject, but also for the subsequent Protestant missionary depictions of Hinduism from the time of Carey until well after the practice was prohibited in 1829.[36]

One point that later became the subject of controversy was the issue of whether sati was enjoined in Hindu scripture. This, however, was not a matter of much concern for much of the seventeenth and eighteenth centuries. Quite sufficient for most commentators was their conviction that brahmans were the guardians of Indian religion and that they were active in encouraging the practice. Sati was therefore, for them, a religious as well as a social practice.

Another reaction among European travellers, and one which sometimes marked them off from Protestant missionaries of a later era, was their attitude to the woman involved. For some commentators, such as the English merchant traveller Nicholas Withington, the sati was an independent-minded heroic figure, loyal to the memory of her husband and determined to rejoin him in the afterlife. However, the woman

---

[35] Bernier 1916: 304.
[36] Mani 1998; Major 2004; Teltscher 1995.

Figure 1.2
Hook-swinging at the 'Hindoo Festival of "Churruck Poojah"' (Bengal)
A Sketch, 'however rude', from Bishop Heber's *Narrative* of 1828 (Vol. 1: 99).

involved appears to have been viewed increasingly in much the same way as missionaries saw her, as an innocent victim of a brutal and shocking system. Far from being hailed as a custom expressing the Hindu woman's courage and devotion, it was condemned as a practice involving compulsion, and one which was little more than the terrifying murder of innocents for the gratification of priests, family and others implicated in maintaining the practice.

Finally, among other more influential reminders of Indian 'barbarity', 'superstition' or irrationality and 'cruelty' was the practice of 'hook-swinging'—a custom which Hindu reformers, as well as missionaries, strongly condemned and campaigned against in the nineteenth century.[37] The ritual, which was usually performed by lower-class members of Hindu society (with some encouragement and support from traditional or even new elites), was the practice of being suspended or 'swung' from hooks. In many cases, it was enacted at annual festivals in honour of Shiva, Kali or local-level female deities. Portuguese observers appear to have been the first to record the practice which was described for English readers in travel narratives such as those of Hamilton[38] and Ovington.

Once again it was the 'difference' between this and anything else that Europeans had seen or experienced that made for interesting reading. Furthermore, it was also seen as confirmation of the 'cruelties' inherent in the religious system.

In summary we may say that some travellers' accounts may have encouraged the missionary argument that Indian heathenism was a unified coherent whole. Such tales also drew attention to the crucial role and importance of the brahmans in the religious system and provided English readers, including missionaries, with a background of image and story. This included what appeared to be the strangest, and sometimes most horrifying, details of certain types of custom and practice—externals of Indian religion which, at a later date, were given prominence in missionary propaganda.

At least up until about the 1850s, missionaries and their supporters were not especially original in the topics connected with Indian religion that they chose to discuss. Nor were they alone in condemning the Hindu system.[39] But while travellers sometimes found something they could admire, the missionaries tended to select and incorporate the negative

[37] Oddie 1995.
[38] Hamilton 1727: 360–61. For earlier references, see Della Valle 1892 (Vol. 2: 259) and Tavernier 1977 (Vol. 2: 198–99).
[39] Grose 1772: 203; Ives 1773: 26.

material in a less ambiguous general indictment of Indian religion and
society.

Catholic and Jesuit Constructions, 1550–1800

The most important and influential Catholic commentators on Hinduism
from about the mid-sixteenth to the mid-eighteenth century were the
Jesuits active mostly in south India during this period.

As is well known, the Society of Jesus adopted a policy, followed by later
Protestant missionary societies, of requiring missionaries to give an account of their activities in reports and letters home. Many òf these letters,
subsequently known as *Lettres Edifiantes et Curieuses*, were printed or
published for wider circulation—so that the missionaries themselves would
be better acquainted with what colleagues were doing in other parts of the
mission field, and also so that the public generally would be better informed and more inclined to support the mission.

While it is true that Jesuit letters from India had been contributing to
European knowledge of Indian religions since the sixteenth century, the
earliest information was somewhat superficial. As Donald Lach has shown,
the earliest of the Jesuit letters, even when dealing with religious questions,
were concerned 'primarily with outer trappings'. Like many of the early
European travellers, the Jesuits, having only recently arrived, tended to
focus on what was different, curious or even sensational in Hindu rituals
and practice. Thus, writing from Ormuz about 'the superstitions of the
Gentiles' [Hindus] living there, Fr. Barzaeus remarked on the worship of
cows, which were allowed to walk unmolested around the streets of the
city. He noted that the humble Hindus refused to take life or eat anything
that had been killed, but also claimed that, while living austerely on
vegetables and harming nobody, these people barbarically sacrificed themselves to their gods by slashing each other with razors, hurling themselves
under carts, and burning widows alive.[40] Elsewhere there are descriptions
of purificatory rituals, Hindu temples, the worship of images, festivals,
processions and other epiphenomena.

As Will Sweetman's work demonstrates, however, Jesuit knowledge and
understanding of Indian religions began to penetrate beneath the surface
and gradually expanded as the Jesuits came into closer contact with
brahmans and other high-caste Hindus. Sweetman points out that Jesuits
tended to remain in India and at their posts for a long period of time. In

[40] Lach 1968: 439–40.

addition, their policy of living inland, away from other Europeans, and of integrating as closely as possible with indigenous communities by adopting their lifestyle; their assiduity and outstanding skill in learning Sanskrit, Tamil and other languages; and their increasing opportunities to consult with brahmans and other high-caste Hindus both before and after their conversion, were all factors which encouraged a deeper understanding of Hindu ideas as well as practice. Moreover, as their knowledge of Hindu religious literature and teachings (as well as practice) in their own locality gradually improved, they had increasing opportunity to compare the local religious scenario with the situation in other parts of India. They not only read reports of Jesuit missions elsewhere, but were often moved from one part of India to another, for example from Tamil Nadu to Bengal, or vice versa.[41]

According to Sweetman, it was largely for these reasons that the Jesuits not only acquired a much greater knowledge and understanding of local beliefs and practice, but also developed 'the concept of a pan-Indian religion'.[42]

In the first place, he argues that Roberto Nobili (1557–1656), the well-known founder of the Jesuit Madurai mission, not only had no conception of 'Hinduism' as a unified entity or pan-Indian religion, but 'explicitly asserts that the non-Muslim inhabitants of India have several different religions'.[43] According to Sweetman, Nobili's approach is clearly apparent in his *Narrative Fundamentorum*, where he (Nobili) claims that there were among these 'gentiles', several sects, which 'entirely disagree with one another in the question of religion'.[44] Indeed, Nobili makes it clear that these differences went beyond the type of religious difference between Catholics and other Christians, even to the extent that they refused to use symbols in common.

Sweetman's argument is that the later Jesuits continued to recognize diversity in their accounts of Hindu belief and practice, referring, for example, to the six systems of Hindu philosophy, differences concerning the soul and conflicts between Shaivites and Vaishnavites. But the implication of the author's thesis is that these differences were seen increasingly as differences *within* an overall system. Indeed he establishes, with reference to detailed evidence, that at least some of the French Jesuits of the seventeenth and eighteenth centuries treated 'the system of religion

---

[41] Sweetman 2003: 130–34.
[42] Ibid.: 128.
[43] Ibid.: 59.
[44] Ibid.: 61.

recognised among the Indians' as a coherent religious entity. While, according to Sweetman, the Jesuits had 'no single term equivalent to Hinduism', they expressed 'the same idea' in various ways.[45] Notable among the Jesuit writers were Pierre de la Lane (in India from 1704) and Le Caron, who both offered summaries of 'the religion of the Indians', Jean Venant Bouchet, who noted that one of the points of 'the Indian doctrine' is that the gods may be changed into men, and the men into gods, and Jean Calmette (in India from 1725 or 1726) who referred to the original books of 'the religion of the Indes'. As further evidence of the same development, Sweetman also refers to the use of the term 'Gentilism' in contrast to 'Christianisme'.

While on the one hand Sweetman establishes a very good case for the Jesuits having the idea of a pan-Indian religion even before the use of the term 'Hinduism', Ines G. Zupanov in her *Disputed Mission* (1999) has focused on the Jesuit development of a brahmanical model. By this she implies at least five interrelated characteristics. First, there was their practice of selecting brahmans as 'the key group' for understanding Indian religion and society, and, related to this, 'a top down' view of Indian religion and culture; second, their privileging of the written text (in this case brahmanical Sanskrit texts) and the conviction that 'textual knowledge' was 'true knowledge'; third, the reference to Sanskritic and brahmanical religious words and terminology as the standard usage when describing Indian religious phenomena; fourth, the devaluing of popular religion which, in some cases, was considered as 'no religion at all'; and, finally, the assumption that the brahmanical model provided 'a template for the behaviour of the common people'.[46] These views and assumptions, she argues, were reflected not only in Nobilis' writings, but became widely accepted throughout the Madurai mission. Furthermore, and as a result of the influence of Jesuit writings,

> The primacy of Brahmanism as a general social model of Indian civilization, privileged by the missionaries in Madurai, became axiomatic in the centuries to follow. Jesuit 'descriptive' documents from the 17th and 18th centuries provided the blueprint for the Brahman-centred perspective.[47]

Though Zupanov does mention Protestants, there is in fact no evidence that the creation of the British Protestant missionary model of Brahmanism was a direct result of Catholic or Jesuit influence. As we shall argue,

[45] Ibid.: 129.
[46] Zupanov 1999: 36.
[47] Ibid.: 27.

the first fully developed British Protestant missionary exposition of both the pan-Indian and brahmanical model of Hinduism appears in William Ward's *Writings, Religion, and Manners of the Hindoos*, which was first published in 1811. There is no evidence, at least to date, that Ward was directly influenced by a reading of Jesuit accounts. Moreover, an examination of candidates' papers of LMS and CMS recruits in training during the early nineteenth century suggests that they were, by and large, confined in their reading to a world of Protestant thinking and adventure, if not anti-Catholic sentiment. There was some interest in Catholic missions, reflected, for example, in Bogue's lectures to candidates at the LMS seminary at Gosport where he referred to the zeal and labours of Roman Catholic missionaries.[48] However, this does not necessarily mean that students were familiarized with Jesuit views of Indian religion. Indeed, it does not appear that Bogue was especially interested in non-Christian religions. Second, the Jesuit accounts (modified by missionary administrators) were originally written in French. Nor do the two volumes of letters translated by John Lockman as *Travels of the Jesuits, into Various Parts of the World*, and published in 1743, include a great deal of material on Indian religion. There are some comments on brahmans and brahman belief, but little in the way of a systematic account.

While it seems unlikely that the dominant Protestant model of Hinduism, as it appears in Ward's account of 1811, was directly influenced by Jesuit writing, Abbé Dubois' depictions of Indian religion, *confirming* established Protestant accounts, were reported and discussed in Protestant circles at a later date. The Abbé's remarks on Indian ascetics were reproduced in the *Missionary Register* of 1819,[49] while his description of Hinduism as 'Brahmanism', confirming and reinforcing the dominant British Protestant view, was quoted at length in James Hough's influential *History of Christianity in India*, published in 1839.

In his account of the Madurai mission, Hough (who had been an East India Company chaplain stationed at Madras) drew attention to the brahmans' influence and control over the minds of the Hindu people. Referring to the way in which they maintained 'the preeminence they have usurped over all other castes of Hindoos' he added that 'for this purpose it is one of the most complete schemes ever devised to enslave mankind'. Consolidating his argument with a description taken from Dubois' *Letters on the State of Christianity in India*, published in 1823, he remarked that

[48] Piggin 1984: 176.
[49] *MR* July 1819: 324–26.

'the Hindoos are described as divided into two classes, "the imposters and the dupes. The latter include the bulk of the Indian population; and the former is composed of the whole tribe of brahmins". In underlining an argument which had already appeared in Ward's *History*, Hough then proceeded to quote with approval a passage from the Abbé's work which, because of its importance, is well worth quoting in full.

> No one among the contrivers and leaders of false religions was ever able to devise so well-framed a system of imposture as the brahmins have done, in order to preserve unimpaired their religious control over the other castes, and to keep the latter in that state of stupidity and ignorance in which they are immersed. It is a sin, it is a crime, in every Hindoo not born a brahmin, to endeavour to emerge from that state of ignorance, and to aspire to the lowest degree of knowledge: and it is considered a sacrilege for him to presume to calculate on what day fall [sic] the new and full moon. Every one of inferior caste is obliged to learn this and similar matters, and to be guided in the most common occurrences of life by his religious teachers. He is forbidden by his institutions to lay any claim whatever to either sacred or profane science, or to intermeddle in any way with the one or the other. His religious leaders have engrossed, as their absolute and exclusive inheritance, all that is included in the term *science*, fearing lest, if an access, even to profane science, were given to the other tribes, this, by causing them to exert their own reason and judgement, should lead them to discover the heap of religious absurdities and extravagances imposed upon their credulity by an interested priesthood.[50]

These and other remarks about the brahmans' 'system of imposture' which first appeared in Dubois' *Letters on the State of Christianity in India* in 1823[51] cannot be taken as an example of Catholic influence on the formation or origins of the dominant Protestant view. Rather they were comments which reinforced pre-existing Protestant views and a model of Hinduism which was derived more from travellers' accounts and from close contact with oriental scholars in Bengal than from Jesuit sources of information.

Ziegenbalg and Early Protestant Missionary Accounts

A third source of ideas about what became known as Hinduism, and one more important to members of the Church of England than to other

[50] Hough 1839, Vol. 2: 226–27.
[51] Dubois 1977: 48–9.

Protestants, was the Tranquebar mission and the Society for the Promotion of Christian Knowledge (SPCK). Bartholomaeus Ziegenbalg (1682–1719) and Heinrich Plutschau (1677–1747), the first Protestant missionaries to arrive in India, settled in the Danish enclave of Tranquebar in 1706. Educated in Germany, in Berlin and at the University of Halle under the celebrated A. H. Francke (a man well known for the depth of his devotion, scholarship and administrative ability), they were representatives of the new Protestant spiritual and revivalist movement known as Pietism which was sweeping across northern Europe in the late seventeenth and early eighteenth centuries.

One of the missionaries' first and most immediate priorities was to learn the languages. Of the two, Ziegenbalg was the more linguistically gifted and the one who, according to Brijraj Singh,[52] wrote all the reports and other literature on the religion and customs of the local people. Ziegenbalg not only made a close study of the Jesuit mission in Madurai, but was determined to discover what the Tamils (or 'Malabarians')[53] thought about their own customs and religion, as well as about Christianity. Hence the origin of the remarkable 'conferences' and correspondence which the Tranquebar missionaries initiated and conducted with 'learned natives', enquiring into their ideas, theology and way of life. Indeed, from the earliest stages in his construction of what he described as Malabar 'Heathenism', Ziegenbalg was involved in building a picture of a local religion heavily reliant on high-caste non-brahman as well as brahman sources of information.

His developing views are reflected in a range of sources. These include his correspondence with Halle, and separate reports on his dialogue and conferences with 'the heathen'. While some of this material was translated into English soon after it appeared in German, the greater part of his work on local religion was either not translated into English until the second half of the nineteenth century, or was lost until rediscovered in the 1920s. Thus Ziegenbalg's *Genealogy of the Malabar Gods*, written in 1713, did not appear in English until W. Germann published his translation of it in 1867; and a second major work, his *Malabarisches Heidenthum*, remained largely unknown until rediscovered in the archives at Halle and published for the first time in Holland, only in 1926.

---

[52] Singh 1999: 12.
[53] The word Malabar or 'pepper coast', applied originally to Kerala, was extended by the Portuguese to include Tamil Nadu. In Ziegenbalg's usage the Malabarians were the people speaking Tamil (Crooke 1968).

The Ziegenbalg material on Indian 'heathenism' available in Britain in the early eighteenth century was, therefore, only a part of what he wrote. Nevertheless, in spite of its incompleteness and the probability that most of it was read in translation, it was significant for providing an additional new and interesting source of information. Furthermore, it included not the first Protestant comment on Indian religion, but the first Protestant *missionary* comment and assessment of it.

Initially, information about the Tranquebar mission was confined largely to British royalty and court circles. The British royalty's connections with the Danish royal family were, in fact, crucial in the early process of disseminating information about developments in Tranquebar. Heinrich W. Ludolf (1655–1712), soon to be the husband of Queen Anne, was an exponent of a pan-confessional inward form of Christianity and also an enthusiastic ambassador for Francke's work and ideas at Halle. Ludolf, together with Anthony William Boehm (1673–1722) who studied theology at Halle and was appointed the Consort's chaplain in London, strongly supported the idea of British funding and involvement in the mission.[54] While Ludolf and other Lutherans continued to exert their influence in favour of obtaining British support for the mission, it was Boehm who, through his translation and editorial projects, became the earliest, best-known and most effective publicist in Britain for the Tranquebar mission's work in south India.

In 1709 Boehm published a translation of missionaries' letters in which they described their work and the difficulties associated with the early days of the mission. Though some of the topics, such as the narrative of their voyage and a description of their settlement at Tranquebar, have little to do with 'Hinduism', other letters, such as Ziegenbalg's depiction of 'the Divinity and Philosophy of the Malabarians', are relevant and gave readers some idea of the missionary's first impressions. Entitled *Propagation of the Gospel in the East*, the collection was initially dedicated to the SPG in the hope that the society would assist in encouraging and funding the Tranquebar project. However, as the SPG felt itself bound by its charter not to go beyond the English plantations and colonies, the SPCK was approached instead. Members of this society were interested. Ziegenbalg and Plutschau were admitted as corresponding members in September 1710.[55] Ludolf was also admitted as a corresponding member, and other Lutherans, including Boehm, joined the society. A subscription for the Tranquebar

[54] For these and other details, see Brunner 1988.
[55] Ibid.: 104.

mission was opened and the Malabar or East India Mission Committee of the SPCK came into operation in November of the same year.

Though the initial intention of the society was to support the Tranquebar mission financially through a public appeal, the committee was soon busy organizing other forms of assistance. This included other forms of material help, such as a printing press that could print Tamil characters, books, food and clothing, in addition to assistance in finding Englishmen suitable to work as missionaries in India. When the Committee failed to procure appropriate candidates for the task, it devoted greater attention to the supervision, as well as the material support, of the German Lutheran missionaries already in the field. It was not only the SPCK but also the official body of the Church of England (represented in the person of the Archbishop of Canterbury) which endorsed the experiment—Archbishop Wake describing the lot of the Tranquebar missionaries as 'higher than that of prelates, patriarchs, and popes', and their recompense 'more magnificent'.[56]

According to Brunner, 'it was Boehm alone' who, during the period from 1709 to 1721, kept the East India mission before the benefactors and English public.[57] His *Propagation of the Gospel in the East*, which by 1718 had been published in three editions, was updated to include thirty-seven new 'letters' detailing correspondence between the Tranquebar missionaries and the Malabar 'heathens'.[58] Another additional source of information was translations 'from the high Dutch' (German) by John Thomas Philipps, a Welsh philanthropist who like Boehm was an active member of the SPCK. The tract, entitled *An Account of the Religion, Manners, and Learning of the People of Malabar in the East Indies in Several Letters Written by Some of the Most Learned Men of that Country to the Danish Missionaries*, was published in 1717. This was followed by Philipps' translation and publication of a second and much more substantial collection of reports and letters from Tranquebar two years later. Dedicated to King George I, they were entitled *Thirty Four Conferences between the Danish Missionaries and the Malabarian Brahmans (or Heathen Priests) in the East Indies, Concerning the Truth of the Christian Religion: Together with Some Letters Written by the Heathens to the Said Missionaries*.[59]

These letters and reports, translated and published by Boehm and Philipps, were gradually supplemented and eventually replaced by

[56] Ibid.: 54.
[57] Ibid.: 112.
[58] Ibid.: 103.
[59] For comment on this source, see Grafe 1972.

publications put out by the SPCK itself. In 1734 the society, having been
for many years engaged in philanthropic and religious activities, finding
that 'their Designs are not so generally known as they could wish', resolved
to annex to the sermons preached at its anniversary meetings annual
accounts of the society's proceedings.[60] These included reports of its East
India Mission. From that time onwards, and throughout the rest of the
eighteenth century, SPCK benefactors, subscribers and others interested
in the society's progress, received fairly regular reports of the missionaries
and missions supported by the society in different parts of south India
such as Madras, Cuddalore and eventually Trichinopoly. This material also
included some information and comment on Hindu religious belief and
practice.

What, then, was the kind of picture of south Indian religion, conveyed
through translation and in the pamphlets, booklets and annual reports as
discussed above? What kind of impressions were the British readers likely
to gain? How far, if at all, did this information differ from other sources,
for example travellers' accounts of India during much the same period?

All the reports and other material make it clear that the missionaries
and Malabarians confined their discussion to the nature of 'Malabar' or
the Tamil region. But, while the focus was on a regional phenomenon,
there was still a feeling on the part of the Tranquebar missionaries that
'Malabar religion' was a part of something very much greater. Indeed, their
European views, categories and assumptions about 'religion' underline
and shape much of their discussion with the Malabarian religious elites
and people. Like Europeans elsewhere the missionaries assumed that there
were four religions in the world—and yet the reader is sometimes left with
the impression that there were more, and that the Malabar religion was
different from other forms of heathenism. In the subtitle of his *Propagation of the Gospel*, Boehm refers to 'the religion' of the Malabarians (1714),
and in an account of a conversion of a pandaram (non-brahman ascetic
or priest) in 1765, the latter is reported as saying that he had weighed
'the Malabar religion' against Christianity.[61] While these comments give
the impression that the Malabar religion was distinctive, they also give the
impression that it was a unified or coherent system. Yet, on this latter point
there is also apparent contradiction. The impression of unity is undermined, or at least modified, in other translations and comments, where

[60] *An Account of the Origins and Designs of the Society for Promoting Christian Knowledge*
(1734).
[61] SPCK, *AR* 1765: 88–93.

the Malabarians are reported as saying that they had many different opinions[62] and were divided into many different 'sects'. In one particular case, however, these divisions were compared with the different sects among Christians and therefore implied that the Malabarians had an overall system within which were many different 'sects'.[63]

While readers wondering whether Malabarians had one or more religions were presented with evidence which could be interpreted either way, there was a clearer and more consistent depiction of the nature of religious leadership. In this case, the Tranquebar missionaries viewed Malabarian religion more from a higher-caste than from a strictly brahmanical perspective. The top-down view of Indian religion and society, clearly apparent in Jesuit discourse, was tempered by a greater recognition of the role and importance of the lower castes. The implication of the pamphlets and annual reports and other literature was that the religious leadership of the people was shared by high-caste non-brahmans and brahmans.

Philipps refers to 'brahmanical learning', which he reminds his readers was 'famous among the Ancients'. He also quotes a Malabarian explanation that the rules Malabarians adopt 'in order to obtain Salvation' all depend

> on the Instruction of the Bramans, taken out of the four Books of the Law, and the six Systems, which shew us what Sins and Vices we ought to avoid, and what Virtues we should diligently practice.[64]

But also clear in this and other material is the role and religious status of high-caste non-brahmans. A reading of the thirty-four Conferences makes it clearly apparent that Ziegenbalg and his colleagues consulted with non-brahmans (poets, philosophers, physicians and others[65]) as well as with brahmans because they recognized the importance and extensive influence of non-brahmans in the Tamil religious system. In his *Account*, Philipps quotes a letter from a Malabarian correspondent explaining that if the missionaries want to know more about Malabarian doctrines and practice they should consult brahmans 'and sudras' as the proper persons to satisfy their enquiries.[66] The role and importance of the (non-brahman) pandarams also becomes clear in the SPCK annual reports. Considerable space was given to the conversion of a pandaram at Cuddalore in 1764.

---

[62] Philipps 1719: 342.
[63] Ibid.: 212.
[64] Philipps 1717: 11.
[65] Philipps 1719. Conferences 12, 13 and 15. See also Hudson 2000: 12–16.
[66] Hudson 2000: 16.

This included an account of his life, together with a translation of a letter from his former superior (the head of the non-brahman mutt at Dharmapuram in Tanjavur district) protesting against his conversion, and details of the convert's reply.[67]

The picture of 'heathenism' which emerges from these accounts of Malabar religion is somewhat different from the one represented especially in the travel literature as discussed above. The Tranquebar material gives the impression that the Tamil or Malabar religion was more effectively under the control and guidance of high-caste non-brahmans (sharing in the leadership with brahmans) than was 'heathenism' as depicted more generally in the travel accounts already mentioned. Indeed, this portrayal of Indian religion does not fit easily with what became the dominant model of Hinduism among Protestant missionary commentators in the early nineteenth century, where Indian religion is represented as being a brahman-constructed system under their continuing and total control. However, while the Tranquebar material suggests a brahman/high-caste non-brahman sharing of leadership, it was the brahmans who were, almost invariably, blamed for the worst aspects of the Malabar system. In that sense the Tranquebar reports and letters available in Britain served to reinforce anti-Brahmanism in much the same way as travel and Jesuit literature.

In almost all their reports published in Britain the missionaries are unashamedly anti-brahman, portraying themselves as champions of the poor and oppressed. Anti-brahman feeling among missionaries as well as among ordinary people appears as a powerful element in Philipps' *Account*, in his *Thirty Four Conferences* and in the SPCK annual reports. For example, in a conference between 'several brahmans and others', the missionaries described the brahmans as 'crafty, sensual and covetous Priests' who were responsible for public calamities, and who had 'most effaced from the Minds of Men' the difference between good and evil.

One of the causes of great offence appears to have been the brahmans' control and monopoly of knowledge. While on his travels one of the missionaries met several brahmans and asked them, 'How long will you go on Sirs, to delude the ignorant People?' A Malabarian physician was reported as saying that the brahmans seldom suffered laymen to read

[67] SPCK, *AR* 1765: 88–93. See also a reference to the activities of 'Pandarams and other Priests' in *AR* 1776.

their sacred books. According to Philipps' *Account*, another commentator remarked that

> When we come to our Bramans, and ask them: Good Sirs, what must we do to save our Souls? They will give us no other Answer, but 'That we should make them large Offerings, and give them part of our Possessions; and then for certain we should be saved'.[68]

Complaints of brahmanical oppression also appeared in a variety of different accounts. One of the most dramatic of these is a report of ill feeling and conflict between brahmans on the one hand and non-brahmans and pariahs on the other.[69] Having heard a missionary denouncing the evil deeds of wicked men, 'the People' cried out:

> Sir, 'tis all true what you say; and we have learnt more of you, than we have of the *Bramans* all the time of our Lives; for they never come near us, unless to eat and drink at Weddings and Buryings, to receive their Dole of boil'd Rice and Clothes, that at such times are distributed among them; and the poorer sort of Families dare not so much as appear in their Neighbourhood, because they call themselves *Holy Men*; and other poor Families they call Common and Unclean.

Then, according to the same account, some of the brahmans 'reproved the people' and the missionary, interjecting, pointed out that, unlike brahmans, the poorer people [the pariahs in particular] were very laborious and 'not ashamed' to do 'the meanest Drudgies', which, 'though mean and slavish, yet must be done by some or other'. Turning to the brahmans he remarked that 'it would be strange if those men had any respect for you'.

> You guess very well, said a Braman: There is an eternal Hatred between us and the Bareyers [pariahs]: For we are descended from the God *Biruma*, and designed for the Joys of Heaven; but they are the Off-spring of some Earthly-minded Men, and are ordained for the Torments of Hell and eternal Misery; and 'tis therefore in pursuance to this Odium, they affront us openly, and very often have the Impudence to throw Stones at us, when we are passing by their Habitations.

Many years later, in 1776, the SPCK published another account of the brahmans' 'incredible oppression' in the vicinity of Cuddalore. When

---

[68] Philipps 1717: 41. .
[69] Philipps 1719: Conference 21.

describing their role in the administration and the 'arbitrary' imposition of taxes on ordinary people the Rev. Gericke, the SPCK representative at Cuddalore, claimed that the people were 'weary of the Burden' and that the brahmans were 'hated and detested' all over the country.[70]

The influence of the SPCK/Tranquebar publications in Britain prior to 1793 (the date on which Carey set foot in India) is difficult to estimate. Most of the reports and pamphlets, including depictions of and comment on Hinduism, probably came to the notice of a comparatively small but highly placed readership. In 1712 there were 450 members of the society, eighty of whom were 'residing members', namely, those living in or near London who might be expected to attend committee meetings.[71] In 1763 there were still only 'six hundred'–odd subscribing and corresponding members of the society 'in Great Britain and Foreign Parts'.[72] However, these numbers more than doubled during the next thirty years—the annual report for 1793 computing the total number of subscribing members as 1,345 men and 240 'ladies'.[73] But despite the comparatively small number of its official supporters, the society (thanks in part to its royal connections) had the ear of the official establishment throughout the eighteenth century. Benefactors and subscribers included lords, bishops and gentry, as well as a large number of well-placed clergy.[74] Composed of some 'High' as well as of 'non-party' churchmen and -women[75] it had strong connections with the SPG. The SPG, which was more clearly the official missionary arm of the Church of England was, according to its first historian H. P. Thompson, 'brought into being' partly through the work of the SPCK, 'whose members largely formed its foundation list'.[76] Indeed, throughout the eighteenth century (and after) bishops and leading churchmen belonged to both societies.[77] The significance of this overlapping membership, mutual sympathy and interpenetration is that when the time came to appoint SPG missionaries for India in the nineteenth century, the society, and possibly also candidates, were more likely to have a better knowledge of India and of 'Hinduism' than, for example, missionaries

[70] SPCK, *AR* 1776: 83.
[71] Brunner 1988: 27.
[72] SPCK, *AR* 1763.
[73] SPCK, *AR* 1773.
[74] See, for example, the benefactors listed in SPCK annual reports for 1733, 1739 and 1742, and also Brunner's account of the status and prominence of the founders of the SPCK (pp. 23–5).
[75] Brunner 1988: 27.
[76] Thompson 1951: 16–17.
[77] Clarke 1959: 75.

of the Baptist or other evangelical societies who did not have the same long-term association with Protestant activity in India.

Lastly, the Tranquebar/SPCK depictions of Malabar religion were important not only because they supplemented travel and other accounts of Indian religion in the eighteenth century, providing those interested in the mission with further knowledge and information. They were also important because they were *Protestant* accounts, which model the different ways in which Protestants might react and come to terms with Indian heathenism. What was of fundamental importance to readers was not just accounts of Malabarian religious thought and practice, but missionary reaction, comment and judgement—or, in other words, the point or moral of the story. The missionaries from Ziegenbalg onwards spelt out in no uncertain terms what they thought was either admirable or wrong with Malabar 'heathenism,' and, in the latter case, their fierce anti-Brahmanism foreshadowed the anti-Brahmanism of William Ward and Alexander Duff. Indeed, the missionaries' remarks, even more than the commentaries of Protestant travellers (many of whom were not especially interested in theology) contributed to the further building of Protestant views and evaluations of Hinduism in the nineteenth century.

We have argued in this chapter that British Protestant missionary constructions and evaluations of Hinduism cannot be adequately understood without reference to the assumptions and overall context of ideas and imagery of Indian heathenism circulating in Britain in the seventeenth and eighteenth centuries. As we shall note, there was little in the missionaries' chief arguments and forms of representation in the early nineteenth century that was new or original. The notion that India had a unified religious system was there in travel, Jesuit and Tranquebar accounts. Furthermore, the idea that this system was invented by brahmans who continued to control and manipulate religious belief and practice even among the common people was a view frequently expressed in travel literature as well as by Jesuits. This view of exclusive brahman control was not, however, so strongly endorsed by informants connected with the Tranquebar mission who drew attention to the significant role which high-caste non-brahmans as well as brahmans played in Malabar religion. All of these commentators were, however, influenced by a top-down view of India's religion, a notion which, like so many of their other ideas, was shaped by Christian models and ideas of leadership. Finally, there was, in almost all of this literature, a fascination with certain kinds of custom and practice, with aspects of Indian heathenism sometimes praised, but more often condemned. These external manifestations of Hindu

religious life were also picked up and highlighted in subsequent missionary propaganda.

Many of the attitudes and forms of representation which developed
during the period roughly from 1500 to 1770 appear in the subsequent
accounts of prominent individuals who, while not missionaries, spoke and
wrote against Hinduism and on behalf of Protestant missions in India.
Among the most influential or significant of these authors, active during
what might be described as the gestation period of British Protestant
missions to India in the late eighteenth and early nineteenth centuries,
were highly-placed public figures who also happened to be members of
the Church of England. These men were Charles Grant, Claudius Buchanan
and Bishop Heber. It is to their accounts of Hinduism that we must now
turn.

2

Hinduism as Represented by Protestant Friends of Mission in the Late Eighteenth and Early Nineteenth Centuries

Of the three prominent individuals considered as commentators on Hinduism in this chapter, Charles Grant (1746–1823), Claudius Buchanan (1766–1815) and Bishop Reginald Heber (1783–1826), it was Heber alone who, as Bishop of Calcutta, liked to think of himself as a missionary. However, like Heber, 'chief of missionaries', Grant and Buchanan were also in their own way actively involved in supporting Protestant missions in India. While all three men were, to a greater or lesser extent, influential in what they wrote about Hinduism as well as about Christian mission, the circumstances of their writing and their intentions in making comments on Indian religion were markedly different. In writing his *Observations on the State of Society among the Asiatic Subjects of Great Britain*, Grant, a director of the East India Company, wrote with the specific aim of influencing Henry Dundas, a friend, member of Cabinet, and President of the Board of Control.[1] Buchanan's writings, including *Christian Researches in Asia*, in which he described the horrors of Jagannath, were intended for a general readership and were part of a broad propaganda campaign designed to alert as many people as possible to what he claimed was the true nature of Indian religion.[2] By way of contrast with these works, Heber's journal was not written in order to influence either public or missionary policy. It was a purely private exercise incorporating his own personal reflections and undertaken largely for the benefit of his wife Amelia who, pregnant with their first child, was unable to accompany her husband on his tour of northern India.[3] It was only at a later date,

---

[1] Embree 1962: 141–42; Morris 1904: 324–25; Grant to David Scott, 11/12/1793 in Philips 1951: 11. For the earliest text of *Observations* see IOAOR. MSS. EUR. E. 93. For the copy reproduced in *Parliamentary Papers* 1813 see *PP* 1812–13, Vol. X, Paper No. 282.

[2] On Buchanan's activities in connection with India see, especially, Davidson 1990.

[3] The bishop was compelled to leave his wife in Calcutta when he embarked on his journey for the Upper Provinces in June 1824 (see Heber 1828, Vol. 1: 107). As his widow

and after the Bishop's tragic death in Trichinopoly in 1826 that his wife decided to release what was essentially a private journal for publication.

Charles Grant and the Naming of Hinduism

Born in Scotland in 1746, Charles Grant was the eldest son in a family of five children. After elementary schooling and the death of his father at an early age, he was engaged as an apprentice to William Forsyth, 'a pious and God-fearing man' and merchant and ship-owner of Cromarty. Five years later, in 1763, Charles obtained employment as a clerk in his cousin's mercantile house in the city of London. After gaining promotion to senior clerk he resigned his position and sailed for India in 1765. While in Bengal, he acquired an intimate and detailed knowledge of the Company's operations throughout the province where he lived and worked for a period of more than thirty years. His first appointment was as an assistant to Richard Becker (one of the most prominent of the East India Company's servants) in private business affairs from 1768 to 1771 and this was followed by longer-term employment as a Company servant from 1774 until his return to England in 1790.

As is clearly apparent from his *Observations*, Grant was shocked by the corruption, miseries and exploitation which characterized the early years of British administration. Incidents which came under his personal observation included the famine of 1767, and the continuing injustice and suffering which he noted especially during his period as Commercial Resident at Malda (a district in the far north of Bengal) from 1780 to 1787. His sense of outrage and social concern, apparent even *before* his spiritual crisis and conversion to evangelical Christianity in 1776,[4] was subsequently combined with a growing belief in the importance of personal accountability and the need for a strict code of personal moral conduct as key factors in any attempt at socio-economic reform.

While reflecting on what might be described as the Bengal–British problem, Grant wrote to friends in England explaining what he had come to believe was the inescapable nexus between the moral conduct of Indian

---

explained in the preface to her husband's *Narrative*, although it was written in the shape of a diary, 'the greater part of the work' formed his correspondence with her (ibid., Vol. 1, Preface: v).

[4] For a discussion of the context and nature of Grant's conversion experience see, especially, Morris 1904: 57–65; and Embree 1962: 49–54.

Company servants and the quality of the Company's administration—
spelling out in detail the argument which was subsequently the basis of his
thesis in his *Observations*. In a letter to Thomas Raikes written in October
1784 (shortly after Pitt's India Bill was passed into law), he remarked that

> although inquiries into the evils that afflict the people and the means of
> redressing them are now deservedly become a business of Government, yet
> I shall fear all remedies will prove ineffectual which have no respect to the
> moral and intellectual state of the inhabitants.[5]

What he was thinking of was the extent of their 'corruption' and 'depravity'
and their need for instruction in 'integrity, truth and faithfulness', a reform
which he linked with the importance of their being 'acquainted with the
truth and excellence of Revelation', and 'with the improvements and rights
of man'. These arguments were again repeated in a letter to William
Wilberforce in 1787 when he stressed that there was no possibility of an
improved system of administration in Bengal without 'reformation of the
morals of the People'.[6]

For Grant, therefore, the fundamental issue was a moral one, and his
basic task, when he began writing his *Observations*, was to persuade
Dundas (and through him other influential persons) of the centrality of
the moral issue and of the need to introduce Christianity and Western
education as the only and most effective panacea for India's ills. This was
a project which he believed would not only facilitate conversion, but would
lead to a radical moral and social revolution which ultimately would
improve the Company's administration, help protect its interests and
promote the well-being and contentment of the entire population.[7] Having
examined the writings of earlier commentators and the evidence derived
from his own life and experience in Bengal there was, he argued, every
reason to reject the superficial view that Hindus were a people 'in whom
the mild and gentle qualities predominate'.[8] And once having recognized

---

[5] Morris 1904: 96–7.

[6] Ibid.: 111–12.

[7] Grant's essay was written 'chiefly' in 1792 at a time when the English were increasingly
concerned with the dangers of the French Revolution. While therefore the *Observations* were
radical in that they aimed not merely at conversion, but at an even broader moral and social
revolution, they were necessarily politically conservative. Indeed, Grant took considerable
pains to show that the introduction of Christianity would not only not threaten British
commercial and political interests, but, on the contrary, would, by improving morals,
improve the administration and also strengthen bonds between ruler and ruled.

[8] Grant 1792: 31.

what he emphasized was the Hindus' 'universal depravity' the next step in
his argument was to explain the root cause of their condition. Could it be
said that this depravity was the result of climatic conditions? Was it an
outcome of the decline of the political system, or was it the result of the
Hindu religious order? Incomparably more important than any other
cause, he argued, was 'false religion'—change that, and one changes the
basic tone and character of the entire society.

As Stokes has argued, Grant's *Observations*, including his diagnosis and
proposed remedies for the evils of Indian society, 'gives a fair exhibition
of the Evangelical mentality'.[9] However, while his views of Hinduism in
particular foreshadow many of the ideas and arguments expressed by
evangelical missionaries in India during the first half of the nineteenth
century, the immediate impact of his *Observations* appears to have been
limited, and confined very largely to certain chosen members of the
Clapham sect. Written hastily for Henry Dundas, Grant's 'essay' was
subsequently shown to a few of his most trusted evangelical friends, such
as Wilberforce, Henry Thornton and Hanna Moore. He also showed it to
Claudius Buchanan, who was one of his appointees as chaplain with the
East India Company, on the eve of the latter's departure for India in
1796.[10] Copies were printed and circulated for the information and use
of fellow directors when Grant became a member of the Board of
Directors in the following year; but the pamphlet was still not released
for public scrutiny, and remained inaccessible to missionaries, as well as
the reading public, at least up until 1813. It was only then, twenty-one
years after its completion in 1792 that, on Wilberforce's recommendation,
it was printed as a parliamentary paper on the eve of the East India
Company Charter debates of 1813. It was also printed as a parliamentary
paper in 1833.

But though these *Observations* were little known at least up until 1813,
and were not available in the same way as Buchanan's *Asiatic Researches*,
they are nevertheless important, as they indicate two major developments.
First, and as others have implied, they highlight many of the features which
evangelicals, including missionaries, thought they saw in Hinduism—at
least during the first half of the nineteenth century. And second, and in
a way that has not hitherto been recognized, they provide important
evidence about use of the term 'Hindooism' during the last quarter of the
eighteenth century.

[9] Stokes 1992: 29.
[10] Davidson 1990: 146; Pearson 1819, Vol. 2.

The 'essay' confirms the fact that Grant was one of the first Europeans (if not the first) to use the term 'Hindooism' in both his private and semi-official correspondence. He used the term in correspondence with Thomas Raikes in September 1787 when he claimed that some opposed his original proposal for a Protestant mission in Bengal and Bihar on the plea that 'Hindooism is a very good system, that is, that the few moral precepts which glimmer amongst its infinity of absurdities and enormities, are a sufficient Code for future happiness.'[11] He used the same term in a letter to John Thomas (who was appointed to run the mission) when, in about the same year, he explained that 'in case of converting any of the Natives, as soon as they renounce Hindooism, they must suffer dreadful excommunications in civil life, unless they are under the immediate protection of the English'.[12] Grant also uses the word in his *Observations* written a few years later. He referred to the twenty-eight rivers mentioned in the *Ain-i Akbari*, beginning with the Ganges and traversing the whole continent to that of the Indus, 'so that all the professors of Hindooism are within reach as antidote against the consequences of guilt'.[13] He mentioned 'the great extent of the continent over which Hindooism has anciently spread',[14] and he also remarked that the history of 'Romish' missions proved that 'it is practicable to induce multitudes of professors of Hindooism to embrace a new faith'.[15]

Richard King, as recently as 1999, reiterates the views of Cantwell Smith, Stietencron and others when he suggests that 'the term Hinduism seems first to have made an appearance in the early nineteenth century, and gradually gained provenance in the decades thereafter'.[16] However, as we have shown, the term was in use among Europeans in Bengal at least as early as 1780s. It was then that it began or was beginning to replace the more clumsy and lengthy expressions such as 'the Hindoo religion' or 'the Hindoo creed' etc. Also significant is the fact that Grant seems to have assumed that an England-based recipient of his letter would already understand the meaning of the word when he used it in his letter to Raikes in England in September 1787.[17] But whatever the case, Grant was one of the first to popularize the term in evangelical, missionary and official

[11] Morris 1904: 110.
[12] Ibid.: 105.
[13] Grant 1792: 60.
[14] Ibid.: 74.
[15] Ibid.: 87.
[16] King 1999: 100.
[17] Morris 1904: 110.

circles. This is highly significant, as its increasing usage implies the consolidation of a particular kind of idea or model; it also helped to empower
the missionary movement in its attempt to demolish what it saw as the
opposing system. The Hindu religion, having acquired its own special
name, was now seen even more clearly as the obverse of Christianity, as
a distinctive and unified religious 'system', with clear boundaries marking
it off from Christianity and other religions. The emergence of the term,
as indicated in earlier chapters, was the product of an expanding European
knowledge and increased experience, combined with a recognition that
existing limited European categories of 'religion' were no longer adequate
as a description of the unusual or less common features of Indian religion.
Moreover, its increasing acceptance and usage as seen, for example, in an
entry in Ward's Diary in 1800,[18] stimulated further questions of meaning.
Once having accepted the existence of Hinduism, Europeans and Indians
alike were bound to ask more questions about its primary features, its
development and how it might relate to other religions. Lastly, the word
was increasingly there to utilize as a tool and label, as a short and ready
reference, and as something which friends and foes alike might use in
religious discussion or debate.

Major Features of Grant's Imagined Hindu System

Apart from bringing the term Hinduism into public prominence, Grant's
'essay' also highlights many of the leading ideas prominent in the mainline
missionary model of Hinduism, especially in the earlier phases of the
British Protestant movement.

In Grant's view, as in the estimation of many other British and European commentators of this period, Hinduism was Brahmanism and Brahmanism was Hinduism. 'Nothing is more plain,' he wrote when referring
to the caste system, 'than that this whole fabric is the work of a crafty and
imperious priesthood.'[19] Referring to popular rites and ceremonies, he
added that:

> In all these rites, and in whatever regards the civil and personal, as well as
> the religious concerns of the Hindoos, the Brahmins have made themselves
> indispensably necessary. They formed the religion, they are the sole exclusive
> depositories of its ordinances, they are the expounders of them, they are,

---

[18] Serampore College Archives, Diary, 29/12/1800.
[19] Grant 1792: 45.

under a Hindoo sovereign, authorized to assist in the government of public affairs, in effect to control it; they are the administrators of the law. . . they are the sole ministers, either officiating or directing, in all the vast train of ceremonies, observances, ablutions, defilements, purifications, penances, and the works of supererogation, of which their religion exists: the endless questions arising about caste are determined by them.[20]

The production of the *Observations* coincided with debates in Parliament and increasing agitation for the abolition of the slave trade. It is not surprising therefore that in this context and in view of Grant's own understanding of the crucial role of brahmans in Hinduism, that he should compare it with a form of slavery. Continuing his detailed account of the brahman's comprehensive control, he explained that:

A Hindoo, from the hour of his birth, through the different stages of his existence, in infancy, in youth, in manhood, in old age, and in death, in all the relations, and in all the casualties of life, is subject to an accumulation of burdensome rites, with which the preservation of his caste, his credit, and place in society, are strictly connected: nay for his conduct in former states of being, preceding his birth, these absolute lords of his faith, conscience, and conduct [the brahmans] bring him to account, nor do they resign their dominion over him when he is dead. The return he has for this unbounded subjection, is an indulgence in perpetual deviations, even from those few principles of morality which his religion acknowledges. It is thus that abject slavery, and unparalleled depravity, have become distinguishing characteristics of the Hindoos.[21]

The clear implication of these and other sentiments in Grant's account was that the people were essentially victims 'held down' by what he described as 'this vast system of imposition'. They were not viewed by the author as having a mind or agency of their own, or of following their own independently-constructed religious traditions. Controlled through the instruments of fear and ignorance they were, according to this view, bound, like slaves, waiting only for coming of liberators and the exultant moment of liberation.

Linked with this exposition of what Grant argued was a system of overall brahmanical control were at least three criticisms which recur in subsequent missionary literature.

(*a*) Hindu ideas and worship were based on ignorance and irrationality. Thus in Grant's opinion Hinduism was a 'superstition' based on ignorance

---

[20] Ibid.: 74.
[21] Ibid.

of the deity's true nature and the type of worship and service that God requires. No service, he averred, was offered to God in popular Hinduism worthy of 'a rational mind'.[22] The legends and histories of the innumerable activities of Hindu deities were 'in the highest degree extravagant, absurd, ridiculous and incredible' and the people, stupefied by their own system, were deliberately kept in the deepest ignorance.[23] Underlying these remarks was not only Grant's literal view of Hindu scripture (a view which paralleled the literalism in his interpretation of Christian scripture) but also allegiance to the idea of 'rationality'. This was, as we have noted, a commonly accepted presupposition associated with the European enlightenment and one which included the notion that religion, whatever it was, should in some degree be subject to the rules of enlightened rational enquiry. Also in evidence in Grant's remarks cited above was his typically Protestant Christian insistence that the basic texts and teachings of scripture should be made freely available to all and not kept merely as the preserve of an exclusive and exploitative clerical elite.

(b) Hinduism was bound up with practices that were cruel and inhuman. Grant foreshadowed many a missionary argument when he held that the gods were responsible for 'the most detestable cruelties and injustice',[24] and described in some detail cruelties associated with the worship and propitiation of Hindu deities. These included the earlier practice of human sacrifice, and 'the practice still common of swinging from hooks fixed in the muscles of the back, and attached to ropes, with a lever to raise the body to a considerable height'.[25] And apart from these cruelties associated with Hindu worship there was also, in Grant's view, their maltreatment of women.[26]

(c) Deeply embedded in Hindu religious teaching and practice was gross sexual immorality. Here, as in the case of many later missionary critics, Grant appears to have been disturbed by anything which associated sexual activity with the Godhead, or which sanctioned what many English people regarded as 'deviant' forms of sexuality. 'The most enormous and strange impurities... [and] the most filthy and abominable conceits' were to be found in the history and mythology of Hindu deities.[27] Troops of

[22] Ibid.: 65.
[23] Ibid.
[24] Ibid.: 64.
[25] Ibid.: 66.
[26] 'Women', he wrote, 'were the most inoffensive and suffering of the Hindoo race' (ibid.: 30).
[27] Ibid.: 64.

prostitutes attached to the temples were brought up as servants of the 'idol', danced in its processions, and were recognized as part of the temple establishment.[28] In addition, those who, like the author had the opportunity of living among the natives in the interior of the country, had reason to fear that 'the purity of the female character' was not always 'so well preserved in reality, as in appearance'.[29]

Running as a scarcely visible sub-theme through this long and sometimes vitriolic account, was a final but important concession. This was Grant's conviction that in spite of the current enormities of their religious and social system, Hindus still retained the residue of reason and conscience—the barely visible traces of the original revelation. For him as for missionaries who followed in subsequent generations, the Hindus, as depraved and selfish as they might appear, were not totally 'other'. They were the descendants of Noah and, as such, were one of the branches of the once unified human race, created and blessed by God in the Garden of Eden. According to Grant, conscience 'though smothered' was 'not extinct',[30] while for their part it was still possible that brahmans retained in ancient texts evidence of a more rational belief in the one supreme being. Indeed according to his account there were still 'rays of original truth scattered through the system'.[31] Like the Bengal-based secular orientalist scholars of his day Grant appears to have accepted the idea that Hindus lived in a better age in the past. But if, for them, it was a golden age, for him it appeared to have been something more like silver. But whatever the case, there were long years of steep decline and eventually, the modern period, when 'the feeble stirrings of natural conscience were over borne by example and practice' and when original truths were 'overwhelmed in the mass of polytheism and idolatry'.[32]

Claudius Buchanan and Jagannath

It was Claudius Buchanan, military chaplain and subsequently professor and Vice-Provost of Wellesley's College in Calcutta (1800–1806), who

[28] Ibid.: 66.
[29] Ibid.: 30. While Grant attacked the 'Jogi' for abandoning his wife, children and connections and for being 'useless' (ibid.: 73), unlike Hamilton and many later missionary commentators he refrained from describing or even suggesting what might have been his sexual habits.
[30] Ibid.: 62.
[31] Ibid.: 65, 72.
[32] Ibid.: 28, 65.

appears to have had a more immediate and greater influence on Protestant missionary perceptions of Hinduism than did Charles Grant. Buchanan's relationship with Grant was, in fact, very close. As a director of the East India Company, Grant used his authority and power of patronage to fill vacancies in the Company's chaplaincy service with evangelical missionaries, and it was he who, with the assistance of Charles Simeon of Cambridge, chose Buchanan as his first appointee.[33]

As noted above, Buchanan had read a copy of the *Observations* and it is apparent that he and Grant shared views in common on many aspects of Indian religion. Both claimed, for example, that their investigation of Hindu religion provided ample evidence of the Hindu's moral depravity and spiritual darkness and that these conditions were sufficient, if not the only reason, for their wanting to promote Christian teaching. Furthermore, Buchanan's claims with respect to Hindu character, and some of his arguments criticizing aspects of popular religious practice, are strikingly similar to comments in Grant's essay. His references to Hindu religious activity in the *Memoir of the Expediency of an Ecclesiastical Establishment for British India* (1805) and in subsequent publications were, however, less comprehensive and systematic than Grant's comments in the latter's closely argued *Observations*. Moreover, while Grant operated in a fairly discreet and private manner in attempting to influence the affairs of state, Buchanan's approach was flamboyant. As Davidson has shown, he was primarily a propagandist intent on influencing public opinion and on bringing pressure to bear on the East India Company through broad-based public feeling. It was Buchanan and not Grant who, building on the imagery of Jagannath, captured the public's imagination, and dwelt on an issue which seemed to encapsulate all of the horrors and evils of the Hindu system.

Buchanan's basic purpose in writing the *Memoir of the Expediency of an Ecclesiastical Establishment for British India* was to bring pressure to bear on the authorities for a more regular and properly organized ecclesiastical establishment. This he argued, should be designed not only to meet the obvious religious needs of Europeans, but should also include a more active government policy encouraging the development of 'civilization' among the natives. This could be done, he believed, through the suppression of certain types of Hindu practice and also through the extension of Christian missionary activity. High on his list of problems to tackle were 'sanguinary superstitions' which, he contended, were 'still

[33] Davidson 1990: 56.

subsisting' and which inflicted immediate death or tended to lead to death.[34] These customs included the offering of children to the goddess Ganga, various forms of voluntary death, infanticide, the exposing of the sick in rivers, the burning or burial alive of widows, hook-swinging and different types of self-torture such as those practised at the *charak puja* in Bengal.[35] Citing as his source the views of the Fort William pundits, he argued that many of these activities had no sanction in Hindu scripture and were performed merely in consequence of vows or in compliance with custom; and these practices, he urged, should be suppressed.

Jagannath in Buchanan's Propaganda

Buchanan's focus on Hindu popular practice, specifically on those customs which he believed should be suppressed, was continued in his *Christian Researches in Asia*, an even more popular book which described his travels and discoveries while on tour in various parts of India outside Bengal during the period 1806–07. Among the objectives of the tour was a determination 'to investigate the state of Superstition at the most celebrated Temples of the Hindoos'.[36] This included his much-publicized visit to Jagannath at Puri. Indeed, it was his account of this episode, more than any other, which appears to have affected his readers' imagination and chimed in with many earlier travellers' tales of their visits to the same spot. As noted in an earlier chapter, Bernier's account available in English translations from 1686 was supplemented by Hamilton's description in his travels published in 1727. While, therefore, some of his readers were almost certainly familiar with stories of devotees lying down or falling beneath the ponderous wheels of Jagannath's chariot at Puri, Buchanan's graphic first-hand account, together with comments taken from the leaves of his journal, symbolized afresh all that seemed to be inhuman, cruel and lascivious in Hindu popular practice.

There were four major criticisms of the pilgrimage and devotions at Puri that Buchanan stressed in his account, and which were subsequently given prominence in public debate.

The first of his claims was that pilgrims died in large numbers from disease and starvation either en route to Puri or on the return journey. His

---

[34] See the Appendix to his *Memoir of the Expediency of an Ecclesiastical Establishment for British India*, reprinted in Davidson 1990 (p. 91).
[35] Davidson 1990, Appendix: 91–100.
[36] Buchanan 1811: 7.

PROCESSION OF JUGGERNAUT, AT THE GRAND HINDOO FESTIVAL OF THE RUTT JATTRA.

Figure 2.1
Procession of Jagannath's Car

This etching, which shows a body being crushed beneath the car's front wheels, appeared in the *Missionary Register* and the CMS *Missionary Papers* in 1817. Such was the fascination with this aspect of Hindu practice (the term 'juggernaut' passing into the English language) that the same drawing was reproduced in the *Free Church of Scotland's Quarterly Papers* (No. XLIV, December 1870) more than fifty years later.

first mention of the condition and death of pilgrims while on the journey was made in his journal while he was travelling to the Jagannath temple in Puri on 30 May 1806:

> We know we are approaching Juggernaut (and yet we are more than fifty miles from it) by the human bones we have seen for some days strewed by the way. At this place [Buddruck, in Orissa] we have been joined by several large bodies of pilgrims, perhaps 2000 in number, who have come from various parts of Northern India. Some of them, with whom I have conversed, say, that they have been two months on their march, travelling slowly in the hottest season of the year, with their wives and children. Some old persons are among them who wish to die at Juggernaut. Numbers of pilgrims die on the road; and their bodies generally remain unburied. On a plain by the river, near the Pilgrim's Caravansera at this place, there are more than a hundred skulls. The dogs, jackals, and vultures, seem to live here on human prey. The vultures exhibit a shocking *tameness*. The obscene animals will not leave the body sometimes till we come close to them. This Buddruck is a horrid place. Wherever I turn my eyes, I meet death in some shape or other. Surely Juggernaut cannot be worse than Buddruck.[37]

Second, quite apart from the circumstances which led to even younger pilgrims dying from exhaustion, starvation, or disease, was the high proportion of accidents. The most notable of these was the incident of people being crushed to death in the stampede to get through the temple gates, or in the crush and melee of enormous numbers of devotees desperately attempting to view the deity. On 12 June, according to Buchanan's own account, when he was near the outer gate of the temple he became separated from the rest of the party and was nearly crushed in the crowd. After being rescued by Mr Hunter (the European Superintendent and one of his former students) he was told that such accidents occurred and that many had been 'crushed to death' by 'the pressure of the mob'.[38]

Third, there were the well-known incidents when during the great *Ratha Yatra*, or car festival, devotees sacrificed themselves beneath the slow-moving wheels of the vehicle.

[37] Ibid.: 17–18. These comments were supplemented a fortnight later, after his viewing of the temple, when he remarked he had visited the sand plains by the sea, 'in some places whitened with the bones of the pilgrims; and another place a little way out of town, called by the English, the Golgotha, where the dead bodies are usually cast forth; and where dogs and vultures are ever seen' (pp. 21–2).

[38] Ibid.: 19–20.

During the first day of the feast Buchanan also witnessed the movement of the car. Amidst acclamation and the excited shouting of the vast
multitude of worshippers, it was pulled by 'thousands of men, women and
children' by means of six cables, each 'the size and length of a ship's cable'.

After the tower had proceeded some way [he wrote], a pilgrim announced
that he was ready to offer himself a sacrifice to the idol. He laid himself down
in the road before the tower, as it was moving along, lying on his face, with
his arms stretched forwards. The multitude passed round him, leaving the
space clear, and he was crushed to death by the wheels of the tower. A shout
of joy was raised to the God. He is said to *smile* when the libation of the blood
is made. The People threw cowries, or small money, on the body of the
victim, in approbation of the deed. He was left to view a considerable time,
and was then carried by the *Hurries* [lowest caste of Hindus] to the Golgotha,
where I have just been viewing his remains.[39]

Finally, in Bernier's account of the Jagannath festival more than 120 years
earlier, he claimed that the brahmans of the place exploited the situation
by attracting and impregnating young damsels. And for Buchanan, who
may or may not have read this account, the sexual aspects of the occasion
were even more damaging. For him Jagannath was not only associated with
the dark forces of death and blood, but was also closely linked with the evils
of abandoned promiscuity and vice. Being a European, he was not permitted inside the temple, but noted from an extract of its official published
accounts that the temple's annual expenses included 'wages for the *cour-
tesans*'.[40] He remarked that the outside of the temple was adorned with
representations 'numerous and various' of that vice which, he declared,
constituted the essence of Jagannath's worship. Not only were the walls and
gates covered with 'indecent emblems, in massive and durable sculpture',[41]
but he also thought he saw evidence of further immorality in the proceedings he witnessed in the temple precincts. These included the singing of
'licentious songs recounting the amours of their gods'. A high priest
mounted the car in front of the idol, and pronounced 'his obscene stanzas'
in the ears of the people 'who responded at intervals in the same strain'.
Furthermore, a boy, about twelve years old, was encouraged to do something 'yet more lascivious' through expression and gesture in urging the god
along.[42] When challenged on these points, and asked how he knew what was

[39] Ibid.: 27.
[40] Ibid.: 31.
[41] Ibid.: 21.
[42] Ibid.: 36.

being said when he was ignorant of the language, Buchanan replied that
he had two translations of the language, one from 'the indecent gestures of
the priest', whose attitude too plainly interpreted his words, and another
from his servants around him 'who could translate every word he uttered'.[43]

Thus, while for some Hindus, Jagannath was another version of Krishna,
a benevolent and playful god, for Buchanan he was the symbol of 'obscenity and blood'.[44] To make this absolutely clear to his European readers he
compared his worship with the worship of the god Moloch in the Old
Testament, and with the ancient feasts of Bacchus which, he claimed,
included 'the same obscenities, the same bloody rites, and the same emblem
of the generative power'.[45]

Though Buchanan used the term 'Hinduism' once in his *Memoirs*, for
most of the time previous to his visit to Puri, he appears to have been
unconvinced that there was any structural unity or commonality of belief
or practice in Hindu religion. Unlike Grant and most of the Protestant
missionaries of the first half of the nineteenth century, he was explicit in
rejecting the unitary model. For example, referring to the diversity of belief
among Hindus in his *Memoirs*, he declared that there was no such thing as
an hierarchy of brahmanical faith in Hindustan, fixed by certain tenets, and
guided by an infallible head.[46] 'They have no ecclesiastical polity, church
government, synods, or assemblies,' he wrote. The Hindu schools of learning were all different. 'Benares has acquired a higher celebrity for learning
than the other schools. But a Brahmin at Benares, or of Calcutta, acknowledges no jurisdiction of a Brahmin at Benares, or of any other Brahmin in
Hindoostan.' The brahmanical system, from Cape Comorin to Tibet, was,
he averred, 'purely republican, or rather anarchical'—the brahmans of one
province often differing in their creed and customs from those of another.[47]

In view of these earlier comments it is somewhat surprising therefore
that, after his visit to Puri, Buchanan began to insist that what he found
there was symbolic and a significant pointer to more general attitudes and
practice throughout 'Hindoostan'. As 'the horrid solemnities' continued,
he recalled in his diary, 'This, thought I, is the worship of the Brahmins
of Hindoostan! And their worship in the sublimest degree!... What then,'

[43] Letter 1, replying to statements by Charles Buller M.P. in Buchanan 1814 (p. 20).
[44] Buchanan 1811: 27.
[45] Buchanan 1814: 35.
[46] Davidson 1990, Appendix: 25–6.
[47] Note also Buchanan's comments in a letter to friends in 1806 when he declared that
'in Hindostan alone there is a great variety of religions; and there are some tribes which
have no cast or certain religion at all' (Pearson 1819, Vol. 1: 394).

he asked, 'shall we think of their private manners, and their moral principles? For it is equally true of India as of Europe; if you would know the state of the people, look at the state of the Temple'.[48] Presumably carried away by his visit and determined to strike a blow against 'blood and obscenity' he overstated his case, and in doing so became one of the architects of the idea that Indian religiosity had some sort of unity and essence. The basic message and point of his account was that the festival of Jagannath did not merely stand by itself, but that it was a clear indication of what was going on in brahmanical religion more generally. And for this reason the impact of his description was all the more effective. Jagannath became increasingly a symbol for the worst and most horrific aspects of the India-wide Hindu system. Moreover, it was also represented as a clear example of a misguided policy—a policy in which the East India Company encouraged still further the evils inherent in Hindu pilgrimage and worship. Hence those who wished to attack the government's 'connexion with Idolatry' saw Buchanan's description as a useful illustration of the more general malaise.

According to Buchanan's biographer, the circulation of the *Researches* was immense. The first edition of 1,700 copies was soon exhausted, and before the end of the year three others had been printed.[49] One year later, in 1812, the book was in its eleventh edition. Moreover, extracts from the work describing Buchanan's visit to the temple were reprinted in missionary periodicals. The editor of the CMS-produced *Missionary Register* remarked that 'Dr. Buchanan's affecting representations, in his Christian Researches, of the abominations attending the worship of this Idol [Jagannath] have made a general and deep impression.'[50] The *Baptist Magazine* in 1811 and the CMS *Missionary Papers* in 1814, 1816 and 1817 also included extracts from Buchanan's account. In most cases these were accompanied by illustrations of the temple cart and were presented in such a way as to imply that what was happening at Puri was *symptomatic* of what was happening elsewhere.[51] The influence of Buchanan's work is also

---

[48] See also his *Apology*, where he argued that phallic worship was widespread in Hindu worship. 'Phallic worship,' he wrote, citing a passage in Sonnerat, 'includes the Hindoo Triad, Brahma, Vishnoo, and Sheva. The pedestal is the type of Brahma, the Yoni that of Vishnoo, and the Lingam or Phallus that of Sheva' (Buchanan 1814: 37).

[49] Pearson 1819, Vol. 2: 247.

[50] *MR* July 1817: 74.

[51] See for example *MP*, No. 7, Michaelmas 1817, in which Buchanan is quoted as writing, 'And this, thought I, is the worship of the Brahmins of Hindoostan!' and where he also refers to his 'Ruminating long on the wide and extended empire of Moloch in the Heathen World'.

reflected in the letters and application papers of young men applying for positions in the mission field. A glance at applications for service with the CMS and London Missionary Society (LMS) during the period from about 1820 to 1840 shows that biographies of Buchanan and his *Researches in Asia* were among the books most widely read by applicants at the time.[52] Buchanan's influence in shaping the mainline idea of Hinduism is also reflected in more general missionary commentary. For example, writing in his influential volume *India and India Missions*, published in 1839, Alexander Duff made the most of Buchanan's commentary. Recalling his first sight of the temple at Puri across the horizon as his ship approached Calcutta, and reflecting on Buchanan's work and other commentaries, Duff remarked that if the traveller thought that he had not only 'seen the worst but seen it all', then he was sadly mistaken: for what was important to recognize was that the worship of Jagannath, the very emblem of 'cruelty and vice', was not confined to Puri, but took place at shrines all over Bengal, 'so that there are not merely hundreds of thousands, but literally millions, simultaneously engaged in the celebration of orgies, so stained with licentiousness and blood, that, in comparison, we might almost pronounce the Bacchanalia of Greece and Rome innocent and pure!'[53]

Bishop Heber and Hinduism

A third advocate of Protestant missions and significant commentator on Hinduism was Reginald Heber, Bishop of Calcutta from 1822 to 1826. His importance as a writer and commentator on Indian religion is, however, not so much because his views on the subject were especially influential, but for a somewhat different reason. His work reminds us that not all those who advocated the extension of Protestant missions in India and who wrote about Hinduism, were strictly evangelical. In other words, his comments on Hinduism provide us with insights and a better understanding of the limits and parameters of the Protestant (including non-evangelical) imagination. How far do Heber's publications present the reader with a

[52] CMS Archives. CMS Committee Minutes, G/C1, Vol. 2, Seager, 1/1/1830; W. Hawkins, 1/3/1831; R. Morewood, 8/6/1830; G/Ac3, Answers to Printed Questions, B. La Roche, 11/10/1820; J. Marsh,18/5/1825. CWM Archives, LMS Candidates Papers, Answers to Printed Questions, Box 26. S. Martin, 22/4/1836, Fol. 2: 424; R. Thompson 30/11/1836, Fol. 2. 272; H. Dickson, 3/3/1837, Fol. 3, 410; G. M. Jackson, 21/7/1840, Fol. 6, 452; R. Logan, 2/9/1840, Fol. 6, 430.
[53] Duff 1840: 221–24.

different type of commentary from another Protestant perspective? As is clearly apparent from his early correspondence Heber was critical of 'that hateful spirit of party'[54] which he detected especially among evangelicals and which sometimes led to their adopting a narrow-minded judgemental attitude towards other Christians who disagreed with their views.[55] As one who from an early age was concerned with mission, Heber felt especially strongly the need to overcome party prejudice and to encourage both evangelical as well as non-evangelical missionary societies. He spoke at meetings of the Society for the Propagation of the Gospel (SPG), CMS and Bible Society and, when appointed Bishop of Calcutta, wrote enthusiastically to Horton Wilmot, one of his closest friends, about his role as bishop and 'the first among missionaries' in promoting a broader spirit of collaboration.[56] In his own view, therefore, he stood for something which was more inclusive than the *evangelical* Protestant tradition, and his representations of Hinduism should be seen in that light, and as reflecting the responses of a person who was more comfortable with what subsequently became known as the 'Broad Church' approach.

Consecrated as the second Bishop of Calcutta in 1823, Heber had ultimate responsibility for the oversight of the Anglican ecclesiastical establishment throughout a newly-organized diocese which included India and extended as far south as the British settlements in New South Wales. In addition to the management and oversight of clergy and chaplains responsible for the religious welfare of European congregations, the bishop was also 'the conductor' of Anglican missions in the three Presidencies of India,[57] and as such was responsible for making decisions affecting the conduct, policy and morale of missionaries and officials connected with the Society for the Promotion of Christian Knowledge (SPCK), SPG and CMS—organizations which, as already noted, spanned the entire range of the Anglican theological spectrum. During the short period before his untimely death in 1826, Heber, who was, therefore, in a powerful and influential position, was consulted on a wide variety of issues relating to Hinduism and Christianity. Not the least of these and one of the most perplexing was the question of caste as well as the issue of how far it was permissible to continue to accommodate other Hindu customs in Christian activity and worship.

---

[54] A. Heber 1830, Vol. 1: 492.
[55] Ibid.: 359, 526.
[56] Ibid., Vol. 2: 116. See also his letter to Wynn, Vol. 2: 106.
[57] R. Heber 1828, Vol. 3: 391.

But Heber's understanding and assessment of Hinduism was important not only because of his position as a pioneer bishop who was expected to draw up guidelines on issues relating to Hinduism for the benefit of missionaries and clergy, but also because he made frequent reference to the subject in his widely-read *Narrative of a Journey through the Upper Provinces of India from Calcutta to Bombay, 1824–1825*, a narrative which was supplemented with a shorter account of his travels in Ceylon and south India in 1825–26. As Laird has pointed out in his introduction to selections from the journal (published in 1971) the journal was 'very well received' by contemporaries.[58] Three editions were published in 1828 alone, a fourth followed in 1829 and a fifth in 1844. The *Edinburgh Review* called it 'the most instructive and important publication that has ever been given to the world, on the actual state and condition of our Indian empire' and the *Quarterly Review* declared it 'one of the most delightful books in the language'. Sir John Shore, a former Governor-General and Member of the Board of Control, praised Heber's 'accuracy of observations, extent of information, and above all, penetration beyond the surface' of Indian affairs.

The journal was the outcome of what was for Heber not merely a journey of discovery and orientation, but an episcopal visitation in which he attempted to visit and minister to nascent Anglican communities scattered in different parts of the country. For this reason he attempted, as far as possible, to be present and to preach at Anglican services somewhere where there was a congregation on a Sunday. In addition to his duties such as preaching, consecrating churches and burial grounds and administering baptism and confirmation, he frequently inspected Christian schools and offered advice and counsel to individuals.

As noted earlier in the chapter, the greater part of his journal was written for the benefit of Amelia, the bishop's wife, who at the last moment, and for reasons of health, was unable to accompany her husband on his travels. It was therefore very different from Buchanan's *Researches* or Grant's *Observations* in the sense that it was more private than public and was not intended as a work of propaganda to persuade readers of the importance and necessity of promoting Christianity in India. Unlike some of the passages in his correspondence with influential leaders in England, Heber's comments on Hindus and Hinduism in his *Narrative* were more the tentative reflections of a man grappling to understand than the comments of an advocate, passionate and apparently certain of where he stood.

[58] Laird 1971: 35.

His remarks are primarily the comments of a writer attempting to inter-pret and represent Hinduism to himself, for his own and for his wife's satisfaction, rather than for the benefit or instruction of readers generally.

In his attempts to extend his knowledge and deepen his understanding of India and its people, including Hinduism, the bishop did not have the advantage of long-term residence, a sophisticated knowledge of a regional language or even familiarity with a range of Hindu texts. Like most Europeans when they first arrived in India, he brought with himself his own ideas and preconceptions and remained largely dependent on inter-preters and on the comments and advice of those around. Among his informants were British officials such as governors, residents, collectors, magistrates and Dr Smith (his medical attendant), and also missionaries and clergy, such as his friend, Archdeacon Corrie, who had been a chaplain and missionary in Bengal and northern India for more than fifteen years.[59] But probably also persuasive were the bishop's Indian sources of inform-ation. While towards the end of his tour he was able to communicate a little more effectively in Hindustani, he remained largely dependent on members of his entourage for comment and advice, especially on Abdulla, his guide through much of the journey. One of the Archdeacon's converts from Islam, and a man whom the bishop believed was intelligent and 'extremely well informed', Abdulla frequently acted as interpreter and remained as Heber's most consistent and long-term source of knowledge and information on topics relating to the people's religious and social condition. Like Buchanan and most of the missionaries, Heber's know-ledge of Hinduism was therefore derived, at least in some measure (and apart from his own direct observation), from Indian as well as from European sources of information.[60]

Hinduism in Heber's Narrative

One of the most striking differences between Heber's Narrative and Grant's Observations is in their view of the character of the people. Laird notes that

[59] As the effective founder of Anglican missions in the Ganges delta, Corrie had baptized many converts and was well informed about political, social and religious developments in that region. In Heber's own words Corrie, 'from his pleasing manners, his candid method of conversing with them on religious topics, his perfect knowledge of Hindoostanee, and his acquaintance with the topics most discussed among their own learned men' was 'a great favourite among the pundits of Benares, and the syuds and other learned Mussulmans at Agra, who seem to like conversing with him even where they differ most in their opinion' (R. Heber 1828, Vol. 3: 339).

[60] For references to Abdulla's comments and advice, see R. Heber 1828, Vol. 1 (pp. 125, 161, 164, 174–75, 205, 230, 248, 305, 310, 421) and Vol. 2 (pp. 126, 208, 341).

in Heber's earlier account of his travels in Russia he displayed 'a generous readiness to think well of the people whom he encountered',[61] and the same warmth of feeling and generosity of spirit pervade the narrative of his journeys throughout north and south India. While Grant stressed the Hindus' 'moral depravity' and 'abandoned selfishness', Heber found much in their character and behaviour which he liked and admired. In fact, he believed that Indian people had often been misrepresented. In a letter to Horton in December 1823 he declared that 'I do not by any means assent to the pictures of depravity and general worthlessness which some have drawn of the Hindoos. They are decidedly, by nature, a mild, pleasing, and intelligent race; parsimonious; and where an object is held out to them, most industrious and persevering.'[62] He noted in his journal the goodwill and generosity of the sepoys among whom he travelled, the concern they felt for relatives and the generosity of the people at large who were ever ready to give alms in support of mendicants.[63] In a report to his old friend William Wynn, President of the Board of Control, he wrote, in March 1825, that

> of the people, so far as their natural character is concerned, I have led to form, on the whole, a very favourable opinion. They have unhappily, many of the vices arising from slavery, from an unsettled state of society, and immoral and erroneous systems of religion.[64]

Thus unlike Grant and some evangelical missionaries who were inclined to offer a mono-causal explanation for the shortcomings in the attitude and behaviour of the people, Heber saw the explanation as more complex and varied. Their failures, he insisted in this letter and elsewhere, were the result of a number of factors, only one of which was the Hindu religion—political, economic and other conditions also affecting attitudes and conduct.[65]

But though Heber thought well of the people, he was increasingly disturbed by their religion. Indeed, his appreciative response to Hindu character was not matched by his remarks on what he described as a truly 'horrible' religious system. Hindus, in other words, were an admirable people, not because of but despite their religious beliefs and practice.

[61] Laird 1971: 17.
[62] A. Heber 1830, Vol. 3: 254.
[63] R. Heber 1828, Vol. 1: 225; Vol. 2: 98, 115.
[64] Ibid., Vol. 3: 333.
[65] Ibid., Vol. 1: 294, 311.

In a very general sense, Heber's construction of Hinduism was not very different from that of his evangelical contemporaries. He had read Sir William Jones on the Hindu religion before his arrival in India in 1823 and, like the Bengal orientalists, Jesuits, and many of the early British Protestant missionaries, he adopted the view that Hinduism was a discrete system—a religion with its own boundaries and distinctive forms of belief and practice. He used the term 'Hindooism',[66] also referring to it as 'a creed', 'the Hindoo faith', a 'system' or even as 'the superstition of India', all of these references and concepts underlining the idea of some kind of Hindu religious unity. Hinduism, or as he sometimes preferred to call it, 'the religion of Brahma', was clearly distinct from the religion of tribals such as 'the Puharrees' he encountered near Burdwan,[67] or the Bheels of western India.[68] 'Buddhist' was distinct from 'brahminical' worship,[69] and the Jains were 'a body of sectaries' held in detestation by 'the Hindoos'—the latter being a term Heber used in a religious sense.[70] Furthermore, as with the orientalists and other Protestant observers, Hinduism was conflated with Brahmanism. Thus Hindus could be the 'zealous followers of Brahma',[71] 'the votaries of Brahma'[72] or people who professed 'the Brahminical faith'.[73] In Heber's case stress on the brahmanical nature of Hinduism appears to have sprung from his long-term conviction (which he confessed in conversation with Swami Narain) that 'Hindoos called the God and Father of all, not Krishna [or some other name] but Brihm'.[74] In other words, like Sir William Jones, he held that all Hindus were monotheists and that underlying all basic beliefs and practices (no matter how diverse) was a sense of the operation of the one universal spirit ('Brihm'). Consistent with this view was the bishop's conviction that popular worship was somehow also part and parcel of the one overall brahmanical system. When on his travels near 'Ramghur' he observed what he described as rudely-carved stones, 'with symbols of Brahminical idolatry'. For him,

[66] For his use of the term 'Hindooism' see R. Heber 1828, Vol. 1: 351, 410; Vol. 2: 327; and Vol. 3: 17, 36; for his references to Indian religion as 'a creed', Vol. 1: 379, 433–34; as 'a faith', Vol. 1: 380; as a 'system', Vol. 3: 36; and as 'the religion of Brahma', Vol. 2: 495.
[67] Ibid., Vol. 1: 279.
[68] Ibid., Vol. 2: 495.
[69] Ibid., Vol. 1, 284.
[70] Ibid.: 385.
[71] Ibid.: 379.
[72] Ibid., Vol. 2: 425.
[73] Ibid., Vol. 1: 279.
[74] Ibid., Vol. 3: 38–9.

these images so clearly associated with 'idol worship' were also a part of the one brahmanical system.[75]

While Heber was inclined to agree with many of his contemporaries, including an increasing number of Protestant missionaries, that Hinduism was an India-wide unified and brahmanical system, his assessment of its basic defects was somewhat different from the verdict of Buchanan and Grant. It is true that all of them thought of Hinduism or Brahmanism as being morally indefensible. But what did this really mean? Did the criticisms they offered reflect precisely the same value systems, or were they disunited in what they believed were fundamental evils of Hinduism?

One of Heber's most comprehensive indictments of Hinduism was in a letter to his long-term friend and confidant, Wilmot, in March 1824, six months after his arrival in India.

> Of all idolatries which I have ever read or heard of, the religion of the Hindoos, in which I have taken some pains to inform myself, really appears to me the worst, both in the degrading notions which it gives to the Deity; in the endless round of its burdensome ceremonies, which occupy the time and distract the thoughts, without either instructing or interesting its votaries; in the filthy acts of uncleanness and cruelty, not only permitted, but enjoined, and inseparably interwoven with those ceremonies; in the system of castes, a system which tends, more that anything else the Devil has yet invented, to destroy the feelings of general benevolence, and to make nine-tenths of mankind the hopeless slaves of the remainder; and in the total absence of any popular system of morals, or any single lesson which the people at large ever hear, to live virtuously and do good to each other. I do not say, indeed, that there are not some scattered lessons of this kind to be found in their ancient books; but those books are neither accessible to the people at large, nor are these last permitted to read them; and in general all the sins that a Sudra is taught to fear are, killing a cow, offending a Brahmin, or neglecting one of the many frivolous rites by which their deities are supposed to be conciliated.[76]

Quite apart from the question of caste, which in subsequent discussion he argued was a civil distinction and therefore not part of Hinduism, there is the issue of the underlying basis of the bishop's assault. Leaving aside the question of caste, on what grounds therefore did he condemn 'the Hindu system'? What was his criteria or system of values and, above all, what weight did he give to particular problems? Were for example, the 'degrading notions' of the deity, 'burdensome ceremonies', 'uncleanness' and 'cruelty' all features of Hinduism which were equally reprehensible or were some aspects more deeply distressing than others? Once again the reader is confronted with a mirror—in this case a list of Heber's criticisms which reflect his basic values and priorities honed and developed in the context of English Christianity and conditioning his responses to what he thought he knew of the Hindu religion.

It might be noted that in this catalogue of complaints there is no mention of the 'irrationality' or 'absurdity' of Hinduism, the concern with the intellectual viability of 'the Hindu system' which attracted the attention of some other Protestant critics. Furthermore, 'the filthy acts of uncleanness' which strike the reader in Heber's indictment were never a *major* theme in his *Narrative*. Indeed compared with Ward and Buchanan, especially when the latter was involved in debate with Government officials over the 'obscenities' of Jagannath, Heber's reference to sexual immorality in Hindu mythology and iconography was comparatively restrained. In subsequent accounts of his journeys he described the Hindu women he observed as 'modest',[77] and on one occasion remarked that the sepoys in his escort were seldom 'indecent'.[78] Though apprehensive at first, he found nothing offensive in nautch dancing.[79] Lastly, in spite of his reference to 'filthy uncleanness' in connection with Hindu deities, his *Narrative* is relatively free from the outbursts of indignation at the sight of Hindu iconography which affected some other Protestant accounts.

What appears to have disturbed Heber much more than the 'irrationality', or indecency in Hinduism, or even its capacity to lead souls into eternal damnation, was what he felt was its lack of compassion in the here and now. His delight in the entirety of God's creation, his sensitivity to nature and care for all living things was reflected in his love of animals. The story of the miserable pariah dog which attached itself to Heber's retinue, which was fed by the bishop and followed his camp for days, only to be stopped by the frightening precipitous nature of the country, is also a story of the bishop's feeling for lesser creatures. His favourite horse Cabul, the pariah dog and all other animals including even tigers, were included in his embrace. Indeed, one of the most disappointing things he believed he had discovered about the Hindus was their ill-treatment of animals. En route from Monghyr to Baxar he remarked that 'it seems to me that the tender mercies of the Hindoos towards animals are exhausted

[77] Ibid., Vol. 1: 225, 306.
[78] Ibid., Vol. 2: 487.
[79] Ibid.: 320.

on cows only; for oxen they have no pity,—they are treated with much severity, but I have not here seen them shew such marks of cruelty as those near Calcutta'.[80] In a letter to Horton in 1823 he expressed his surprise at finding that though Hindus considered it as a grievous crime to kill a cow or a bullock for the purpose of eating, 'yet they treat their draft oxen, no less than their horses, with a degree of barbarous severity which would turn an English hackney-coachman sick'.[81]

The treatment of some classes of people including the lower castes and also sufferers from leprosy also aroused Heber's indignation. Referring to one of a number of the latter he met near 'Muttra' he wrote,

> I have seen, I think, fewer of these objects in Hindostan than in Bengal, but those I have seen are in every respect most pitiable. In addition to the horrors of the disease itself, the accursed religion of the Hindoos holds them out as objects of Heaven's wrath, and, unless they expiate their sins by being buried alive, as doomed in a future life to Padalon! They are consequently deprived of caste, can possess no property, and share far less than most other mendicants in the alms which Hindoo bounty dispenses in general with a tolerably liberal hand.[82]

In common with Grant and others he also complained of the treatment of women in Hindu society—though here again it is important to note that he was not convinced that all forms of moral conduct sprang from 'the Hindu religion'. While in Lucknow and acting on the advice of the Resident, he followed the usual custom of distributing alms to beggars at the palace gates. Seeing 'one poor old woman' he gave her half a rupee 'on account of her great age and infirmities'. Observing that his Indian escorts seemed to think that 'it was strange to give more to a woman than to most of the men', he remarked that he had noticed on many occasions

> that all through India any thing is thought good enough for the weaker sex, and that the roughest words, the poorest garments, the scantiest alms, the most degrading labour, and the hardest blows, are generally their portion. The same chuprassee, [police officer] who, in clearing the way before a great man, speaks civilly enough to those of his own sex, cuffs and kicks any unfortunate female who crosses his path without warning or forbearance.[83]

[80] Ibid., Vol. 1: 311.
[81] Ibid., Vol. 3: 252. However, at a later date he commented more favourably on the treatment of animals in Hindu animal hospitals (ibid.: Vol. 3, 67).
[82] Ibid., Vol. 2: 330.
[83] Ibid.: 71.

A second indication of the bishop's feeling about the treatment of women appeared towards the end of his travels in south India when he referred to the everyday life of the *devadasi* or temple women. In spite of the widespread belief that their dancing was 'more indecent' than the performance of *nach* girls in north India, 'their general appearance and manner' seemed to Heber 'to be far from immodest', and their air 'even more respectable than the generality of the lower classes of India'. But, he continued,

> the money which they acquire in the practice of their profession is hallowed to their wicked gods, whose ministers are said to turn them out without remorse, or with a very scanty provision, when age or sickness renders them unfit for their occupation. Most of them, however, die young. Surely, the more one sees of this hideous idolatry, the more one must abhor it, and bless God for having taught us better.[84]

As will be apparent from these remarks, it was not so much the immorality of temple dancing (the usual complaint of evangelical missionaries) but the treatment of the women that Heber found especially offensive.

While there can be no doubt about Heber's increasingly hostile attitude towards what he thought of as Hinduism (like Carey the more he saw the more he seemed to dislike what he found), the stress he placed on particular evils within 'the system' was somewhat different from that of many of his contemporaries. There was as much or more concern with the inhumanity associated with 'the Hindu religion' and less with its weakness as an intellectual system, or as a movement deeply tainted by sexual immorality.

Laird has suggested that 'perhaps the most attractive feature of Heber's Journal is the strong sense of the fundamental one-ness of mankind which he conveys; he does not give the impression that in passing from England to India he encountered a completely different order of human beings'.[85] Like Christians generally the bishop espoused the idea of a general as well as a specific revelation. God was operating through his creation and in the laws of nature, and people in all cultures and countries could therefore perceive something of God and his purpose for humankind through what the bishop described as 'the light of natural reason and conscience'.[86] While Charles Grant adhered to the same doctrine, the difference between his and the bishop's view, lay in the way in which they perceived the people's

[84] Ibid., Vol. 3: 219–20.
[85] Laird 1971: 32.
[86] R. Heber 1829: 201.

response and subsequent history. According to Grant the better conceptions of God's nature, 'the rays of original truth scattered through their system' had been overwhelmed by polytheism and idolatry.[87] In Heber's view much of the moral goodness and sensitivity was still there and clearly apparent in the people's attitudes and behaviour. His journey to India was therefore, less than Grant's sojourn, a visit to 'another country' where all was completely different. And if Grant's sense of the 'otherness' of India's people and culture was modified by his belief in the basic commonality of the human race, this sense of commonality and a shared humanity comes through even more strongly in Heber's *Narrative*.

Heber's liberal-minded inclusive approach (strengthened by, or strengthening, his theology) is also apparent in his attitude to the fate of the heathen in the afterlife. He went further than many other Protestants, and certainly further than most evangelicals, in suggesting that 'the heathen' were not necessarily always destitute of the grace of God. According to the views he expressed in a sermon preached in England in 1820 and in his sixth Bampton lecture, if the heathen did have some understanding of God, and 'diligently' sought Him, then who was to say they might not please God and 'obtain a seat in one of those many mansions which our Father's house contains'?[88] The strength of the bishop's feeling on this issue is apparent in his charge to clergy of the Calcutta diocese where he condemned those missionaries who taught that non-Christians were 'under the sentence of reprobation from God'.[89] There was always the need for mission, and the great majority of people were not 'innocent and conscientious followers of the law of nature'; but in some places, even for example, in the 'aweful and besotted darkness' of Benaras, 'God may have much people in this city'.[90]

Lastly, in spite of his frequent attacks on 'the Hindu system', there is some indication that on at least two occasions, experience was beginning to moderate his views. His sweeping condemnation of Hinduism as seen in his letter to Wilmot, written soon after his arrival in Calcutta, and his later confession that the more he saw of Hinduism the more he disliked it, these reactions need to be balanced against some few rare moments when Heber felt he could sense a connection between his own insights and Hindu spirituality. For example, when visiting a shrine at Chunar fort, and

[87] Grant 1792: 65.
[88] Laird 1971: 33.
[89] Ibid.
[90] R. Heber 1828, Vol. 1: 375.

being told that Hindus believed that Vishnu was seated there at certain times of the day, he remarked,

> I own I felt some little emotion in standing on this mimic 'mount Calasay.' I was struck with the absence of idols, and with the feeling of propriety which made even a Hindoo reject external symbols in the supposed actual presence of the Deity, and I prayed that God would in his own good time instruct these poor people, in what manner, and how truly he is indeed present both here and every where.[91]

On another occasion he was reflecting on the custom, widespread in north India, of casting the clay image of the deity into the water at the conclusion of Durga Puja and other festivals. Having discussed the theory that this practice may have originated from the custom of throwing a living sacrifice into the water, he offered a more charitable interpretation, declaring that it seemed 'rather to typify the inferiority confessed by the Hindoos themselves, of all their symbols of the God of nature, than to recall the memory of an ancient piece of inhumanity'.[92]

There were, therefore, some links and points of contact between Heber's views and these rituals. His sense that, at least somewhere, one could find commonalities with aspects of the Hindu system, was a conviction in line with later Broad Church theology. It was also a feeling which would grow with the missionary movement and strengthen the notion that Indian Christianity could be constructed, at least in part, on the basis of Hindu teachings and practice.

[91] Ibid.: 409.
[92] Ibid., Vol. 2: 391–92.

3

Orientalist Models and Missionary Scholarship

Earlier travel and missionary accounts, together with the comments of individuals such as those mentioned in the previous chapter, were not the only sources of influence on British Protestant missionary constructions of Hinduism. Another source, and one of more immediate importance to them, was the work of British orientalists. The term 'orientalist', as used here, applies to Sir William Jones, Nathaniel Halhed, H. H. Wilson and other European scholars of Indian languages and literature who were active in the later eighteenth and the nineteenth centuries.

The emergence and rise to prominence of individuals, and eventually, a self-conscious group of scholars subsequently known as orientalists, first occurred in India in Bengal, after Plassey, and as a result of the establishment of British rule. Many of them, in the province as officials in a fledgling administration, were engaged in the work of studying and translating mostly Sanskrit texts in the last quarter of the eighteenth century. While earlier European accounts helped lay the foundation of what became the Protestant missionary model of Hinduism as an all-embracing brahmanical system, it was the Bengal-based orientalist constructions which were crucial in consolidating this type of interpretation. Though the missionaries were never completely united in the way in which they conceived of Hinduism, it was the brahmanical pan-Indian model of India's religion which held sway. It was this model which became the dominant missionary paradigm, especially during the first half of the nineteenth century; and it was this model which dovetailed with the predominant orientalist notion of what constituted India's 'real' religion.

Most previous writers, including Bearce and Marshall,[1] have contrasted the attitudes of orientalists with those of the evangelicals. But while there were differences there were also important ideas, including presuppositions and views of religion, which orientalists and missionaries, as well as some of the travellers and other Europeans, shared in common. Indeed, as scholars studying eastern languages and literature, Protestant missionaries

---

[1] Bearce 1961: 20–26, 78–88; Marshall 1970: 197.

such as William Carey, Robert Caldwell and others were equally, with administrators and secular European scholars, 'orientalists' in the sense above. What is especially relevant is sequence. The Bengal administrative and secular orientalists were working in India prior to the arrival of British Protestant missionaries and provided one of the influential environments in which missionary ideas and missionary orientalism developed.

The work and achievements of British secular orientalists in Bengal have been the subject of a number of important studies, such as those of Mukherjee, Cannon, Kopf, Schwab, Kejariwal, Rocher, Trautmann,[2] and most importantly for our purposes, P. J. Marshall in his *British Discovery of Hinduism in the Eighteenth Century* (1970). It is clear from these and other sources that the phenomenon of British orientalism during this period was partly a reaction to early British misrule and the need for financial and administrative reform which Warren Hastings in particular believed would only succeed if British territories were governed largely along traditional lines and in such a way as to help reconcile Indians with British administration. But curiosity and an admiration for India's civilization were also factors encouraging European involvement in oriental studies.[3]

Two of the earliest and most influential of the Bengal-based British writers on Hinduism, both of them in the Company's service prior to Hastings' administration, were John Zephaniah Holwell, well known for his account of the Black Hole of Calcutta incident and Governor of Bengal for a short period in 1767, and Alexander Dow, an ensign in the Company's Bengal Army who had risen to the rank of colonel by the time he died in India in 1779. Holwell's account of Indian religion appeared as a chapter entitled 'The Religious Tenets of the Gentoos' in his *Interesting Historical Events relative to the Provinces of Bengal and the Empire of Indostan* published in 1767 and Alexander Dow's 'dissertation' on the same subject appeared in the first volume of his *History of Hindustan*, published in 1768. Both men were, as Kopf aptly remarks, 'isolated individuals' who, while working in the Company's service, acquired 'an intellectual appreciation of Indian civilization'.[4]

The few British scholars engaged in independent study such as these were brought closer together and greatly encouraged as a result of Hastings'

---

[2] Cannon 1970; Kejariwal 1988; Kopf 1969; Mukherjee 1987; Rocher 1994; Schwab 1984; Trautmann 1997.

[3] For a detailed discussion of the diverse motivations of orientalists see, especially, Rocher 1994.

[4] Kopf 1969: 15.

appointment and policy of developing oriental studies, first as Governor (1772–74) and subsequently as Governor-General (1774–85). Hastings, who like many other employees of the English Company arrived in India at the impressionable age of 17, soon became an ardent admirer of India's cultural achievements. He learnt both Persian and the common dialects of Bengal, collected Indian paintings and manuscripts and quoted the *Gita* in letters to his wife.[5] His love of learning and enthusiasm for India's ancient culture, as well as pragmatic administrative considerations, were all factors which informed his policy and which suggested the idea that he should encourage oriental learning. Convinced of the need to reconcile Indians to British rule and seeing no reason why they should be governed by English laws, he introduced financial inducements for those able to translate Hindu and Muslim laws into English for the use of Company servants and also for the translation of Company regulations into the languages of the people.

Saddled with arrogant and incompetent civil servants, Hastings looked to the younger generation for the development of his policies. He soon gathered around himself men whom he inspired with a love of oriental literature. Among the earliest of these were Charles Wilkins who arrived in India in 1770, Nathaniel Halhed who arrived two years later and Sir William Jones, the most famous of them all, who reached Calcutta in 1783. Like Holwell and Dow before them, all of them contributed something further to British if not general European knowledge and understanding of Hinduism, helping to create in the process a broader arena of knowledge and to raise issues which Protestant missionaries, among others, felt compelled to address. Halhed who was a writer in the Company's service, was an excellent linguist proficient in Persian, Bengali and Sanskrit. Commissioned by Hastings to provide a clear and undisputed corpus of law which would replace the conflicting sources and rival interpretations, he and his pundits produced *The Code of Gentoo Laws* which was published in 1776. In a preface Halhed referred to a range of Hindu religious ideas and writings and, in subsequent years, translated several ancient Sanskrit texts like the *Bhagavata Purana*, the *Siva Purana*, the *Brahmavaivarta Purana* and perhaps most importantly, the *Mahabharata*, into English.[6] Wilkins, who was also a writer and friend of Halhed, applied himself to the study of Sanskrit, publishing an English translation of the *Gita*—a work which Marshall claims was 'the first translation into a European

[5] Mukherjee 1987: 73.
[6] Kejariwal 1988: 20.

language of any major Sanskrit work'.[7] Sir William Jones, the last of these scholars to arrive in India, made the greatest of all contributions to oriental studies. This was not only because of his own research, translations and writings but because he was the effective founder of the Asiatic Society, the first learned society of its kind in the East.

While an examination of their writings shows that orientalists differed at least to some degree in their views and interpretation of 'the Gentoo religion', it is also possible to detect shared assumptions and points of agreement in their comments and approach.

The most important unquestioned assumption appears to be that there was one unified Hindu religious system. This idea is explicit in language and general comment. Holwell, for example, refers to 'the Gentoo faith and worship' and 'the Gentoo Creed'[8] and, although he refers to two different scriptures, he goes on to argue that they were 'originally one'. Reinforcing this sense of a common unified 'Hindu religion' is an astonishing degree of generalization exemplified in Holwell's further comment on the Hindus' contempt for death, when he asserts that '*every* Gentoo' [my italics] meets that moment of dissolution, 'with a steady, noble, and philosophic resignation, flowing from the established principles of their faith'.[9] Halhed also bases his ideas on the notion of one unified system which he describes variously as 'the Hindoo religion', 'the Hindoo Dispensation' or 'the Gentoo religion',[10] while Dow refers to 'the Hindoo faith' and 'the Hindoo religion'.[11]

The notion of Hinduism being a discrete and unified brahmanical system, a view shared by Sir William Jones, was, even for British orientalists of the late eighteenth century, hardly a new idea. Apparent as an element in earlier European thinking, it was a theory which was further developed at a time when Western scholars were unaware of the diverse origins of Indian religions.

First, the idea of Indian religion as a unitary system was bolstered by what Trautmann has called 'the doctrine of the linguistic unity of India'.[12] This, he argues, emerged out of the conjuncture of British Sanskritists and their pundits under colonial conditions. Bengal orientalists such as Jones, H. T. Colebrooke, author of an important article on the relationship between Sanskrit and the vernacular dialects, and Alexander Hamilton, the

[7] Marshall 1970: 5.
[8] Ibid.: 59, 77.
[9] Ibid.: 96.
[10] Ibid.: 145, 181, 183.
[11] Ibid.: 111, 115, 139.
[12] Trautmann 1997: 136.

first Sanskrit professor in Britain, were convinced that all the modern languages of India were derived from Sanskrit.[13] This view was challenged by F. W. Ellis, a civil servant working in Madras, who demonstrated that the Dravidian languages of southern India (principally Tamil, Telugu, Kannada and Malayalam) are not descendants of Sanskrit, but comprise an independent family of languages. Although these findings are mentioned in Alexander Campbell's commentary on Telugu grammar in 1816, they do not, however, appear to have been fully accepted until the publication of Caldwell's *Comparative Grammar* in 1856. Hence, up until 1816, and even among some later commentators, the idea of India's basic linguistic unity remained an unquestioned belief.

Linked with the conviction that Sanskrit was the parent of all Indian languages including those of the south, was the assumption that Sanskrit *texts* contained all that was worth knowing of ancient Indian customs and religion. As Alexander Dow declared in 1768 the Sanskrit language was 'the grand repository of the religion, philosophy and history of the Hindoos'.[14] And it followed from this that if Europeans like Dow, Halhed, Jones, Wilkins and others had access to all the sacred Sanskrit texts, and if they could master the language then they would know and understand the entire range of Hindu religious teaching. Behind this idea were the assumptions that the essence of religion was reflected in the teaching of the clergy or religious elite, and that, as in Europe, the doctrines they taught were preserved in written texts. These views also clearly implied that the so-called 'religion' of 'the vulgar' or common people, including oral tradition and low-caste religious movements, was in some sense inferior, derivative, less interesting, or of little value, and certainly not 'the real thing'.

Belief in the basic linguistic unity of India, in the influence and power of priests to control the people, the tendency to privilege textual information, and presuppositions about what actually comprises religion: all of these predispositions were almost certainly confirmed and encouraged by the brahman pundits and 'consultants' whom the British employed in their attempts to introduce and construct a viable administration. The role of these pundits who worked for individual orientalist scholars, such as Sir William Jones, or who were employed as advisers and translators in Wellesley's College of Fort William (founded in 1800) has been explored in some of the literature already mentioned.[15]

---

[13] Ibid.: 141–48.
[14] Marshall 1970: 108.
[15] Kopf 1969: 108–26; Rocher 1994: 223–40.

Last but not least, as a factor facilitating the view that there was only the one unified Hindu system, was the eighteenth- and nineteenth-century scholars' ignorance of the Indus Valley civilization and cultures. Not only were the Bengal-based scholars ignorant of the fact that the southern languages were not derived from Sanskrit and that they therefore reflected a distinctive southern-type culture, but, like everyone during this period, they were also unaware of the existence of the ancient Indus Valley settlements, another important ingredient which has to be taken into account by anyone attempting to understand the nature and roots of so-called 'Hindu religion'. It was not until the period immediately prior to the First World War that European archaeologists and others began to suspect that ancient artefacts found in the vicinity of Mohenjodaro represented an ancient culture which predated that of the Aryan migrants who appeared to have entered the subcontinent at points further to the north-east. The consensus among leading scholars was (and may still be) that the discovery of ancient figurines, representations of various deities and other objects on these sites is an indication that some of the most important traditions within what has come to be called Hinduism (like Dravidian customs and practice reflected in Tamil tradition) were different in origin from those introduced by the Aryans and preserved and developed by brahmans in tightly-controlled oral tradition and in Sanskrit texts.

Unaware of what scholars now know and conditioned by other factors described above, the orientalists thought of Hinduism as an all-India unified phenomenon, based on Sanskrit and still controlled, policed and enforced by brahmans. If, in their view, Sanskrit was the key to the ideas and teaching of Hinduism the brahmans were the key to the overall functioning and continued viability of 'the Hindu system'. In other words, for the orientalists Hinduism was 'Brahmanism'—a view that remained common among British Protestant missionaries at least up until the mid-nineteenth century. Holwell, who was sympathetic to Hinduism, confessed that the people had been reduced to 'a slavish dependence on their Bramins',[16] while Halhed, who was equally sympathetic, referred to 'the sacred preeminence of the Braminical tribe'.[17] However, he argued that this was because the bulk of people had settled power upon them and that besides presenting them with endowments and benefactions in all parts of 'Hindostan' they paid them 'a degree of personal respect little short of idolatry'.[18] Referring to codes of Hindu law, Dow remarked that

[16] Marshall 1970: 65.
[17] Ibid.: 180.
[18] Ibid.: 142.

'the influence of the Brahmins is so great, and their characters as priests so sacred, that they escape in cases where no mercy would be shewn to the other tribes'.[19] Jones was likewise struck by what he felt was the power and pre-eminence of brahmans and, while acknowledging the beauties he discovered in the ordinances of Manu, described them as 'a system of despotism and priestcraft'.[20]

Linked with these ideas of the power and influence of brahmans was a conviction that if popular religion was different from the religion of the brahmans then this was because the brahmans themselves had introduced a mythology and practice which was meaningful and appropriate for the masses.[21] Referring to their ideas of early history, Dow claimed that 'the Brahmins of former ages wrote many volumes of romances upon the lives and actions of those pretended kings, inculcating, after their manner, morality by fable. This was the great fountain from which the religion of the vulgar in India was corrupted.'[22]

Apart from the orientalist perception of Indian religion as 'brahmanism' was a growing conviction, especially among the later secular scholars, that 'the Hindu system' had seen better days. This too was a view that proved to be influential among Protestant missionary writers such as Robson, Vaughan and others in the nineteenth century. Holwell, Halhed, Dow, Jones and later Colebrooke all stated that 'the Hindu religion' was once an uncorrupted monotheism. For example, writing in the first volume of his history Dow declared that 'the unity of God was always a fundamental tenet of the uncorrupted faith of the more learned Brahmins'.[23] Jones remarked in a lecture to the Asiatic Society that 'it must always be remembered, that the learned Indians, as they are instructed by their own books, in truth acknowledge only one Supreme Being'.[24] And Colebrooke, who was the first European to obtain the text of all four Vedas and to study them, argued that 'if the doctrines of the Veda, and even those of the Puranas, be closely examined, the Hindu theology will be found consistent with monotheism, though it contains the seeds of polytheism and idolatry'.[25] But if monotheism might be described as the essence of true Hinduism or at least the religion of 'the more learned brahmans', what were the beliefs of the

---

[19] Ibid.: 117.
[20] Quoted in Davidson 1990: 24.
[21] Marshall 1970: 58–9.
[22] Ibid.: 126.
[23] Marshall 1970: 127, 156.
[24] Ibid.: 214.
[25] Kejariwal 1988: 92, 99–101.

common people? And how far, if at all, had there been a decline from ancient standards?

Jones was one of the first to state his belief in the existence of a Hindu golden age. In his essay 'On the Hindus' he stated his conviction that no matter how 'degenerate and abased' the Hindus 'may now appear', 'in some early age they were splendid in arts and arms, happy in government; wise in legislation, and eminent in various knowledge'.[26] But while this statement appears to be more like a description of civil rather than religious society, the idea of a spiritual or religious golden age is at least implicit in comments elsewhere. For example, in his discourse on the gods of Greece, Italy and India he claimed that there had been a general union or affinity between the most distinguished inhabitants of the primitive world, 'at the time when they deviated, as they did too early deviate, from the rational adoration of the only true God'.[27] Furthermore, in his later work on the Hindus, Jones refers to the emergence of 'idolatry' in what he describes as 'the second, or silver, age of the Hindus'.[28]

The idea of a Hindu golden age, raised and discussed in the writings of Sir William Jones, was further developed by H. T. Colebrooke who not only learnt Sanskrit, but obtained a much greater knowledge of the contents of the Vedas than had been achieved by any other European scholar. He averred that many of the gods and 'corrupt' practices associated with Hinduism in the eighteenth and early nineteenth centuries were not mentioned in the Vedic texts. Writing in his influential essay 'On the Vedas or the Sacred Writings of the Hindus', published in 1805, he stressed that

> most of what is there taught [in the Vedas] is now obsolete; and in its stead new orders of religious devotees have been instituted; and new forms of religious ceremonies have been established. Rituals founded in the Puranas and observances borrowed from a *worst* source, the *Tantras,* have in great measure... [replaced] the Vedas.[29]

He found depicted in the Vedas a people who were more outgoing and apparently less mystical than those of a later period. It was a robust, beef-eating, comparatively egalitarian community free from many of the 'evils' which disturbed Europeans and especially missionaries in the nineteenth century. The social system appeared to be less rigid than it had subsequently become, 'almost every occupation' (though associated with a

---

[26] Marshall 1970: 251.
[27] Ibid.: 196.
[28] Ibid.: 256.
[29] Quoted in Kopf 1969: 41.

particular class) being open to most other classes in the community.[30] There were no temples; there was no evidence of idol worship and nothing to suggest the existence of laws compelling a widow to burn on her husband's funeral pyre.[31]

As we shall see, it was not especially difficult for Christians and evangelical missionaries to incorporate this new body of evidence about the Hindu past into their pre-existing biblically based ideas of history. One of the fundamental issues was how to explain the existence of similar beneficial ideas, such as monotheism, in the early stages of Hindu history. How could one explain the fact that there was much to admire in ancient Indian civilization?

While Holwell in particular argued that his dating of Hindu teachings called into question the usual Christian dating and biblical account of the world, Sir William Jones expressed a different opinion telling the Asiatic Society in his anniversary discourse in 1793 that ten years of study in India had only confirmed in his mind 'the Mosaick accounts of the primitive world'.[32] According to Marshall, his basic explanation for the similarities between religions was that the peoples of the earth had all originated as *Genesis* explained, in a single place, where they had all practised the 'rational adoration of the only true God' before their dispersal. The Indians preserved memories of this period of their history in the legends of the first and second Manus, who could be identified with Adam and Noah.[33] Hence, so long as Christians continued to take literally the biblical account of the creation and so long as the orthodox Christian system of early dating remained intact, it was comparatively easy for missionaries to argue that similarities between, for example, Hindu and Old Testament mythology, was the result of all peoples being the descendants of Noah, and of their having lived together prior to the great dispersion associated with the tower of Babel.

A second interpretation and one which had deep roots in both Catholic and Protestant tradition, was the argument which lay at the basis of the idea of natural religion—that no matter what religious *system* people constructed and followed, God was already active in the human conscience and reason, and apparent through 'the light of nature'. This view, discussed in greater detail in chapter 10, is clearly apparent among the Tranquebar missionaries. It also appears in the writings of the influential Anglican

---

[30] Quoted in Kejariwal 1988: 83.
[31] Kopf 1969: 40–41.
[32] Marshall 1970: 35.
[33] Ibid.: 37.

clergyman Thomas Maurice, author of *Indian Antiquities*, and is echoed in Baptist missionary comment and correspondence and in Protestant missionary discussion throughout the nineteenth century. God, as the *Acts of the Apostles* showed, had 'not left Himself without a witness', and it was therefore only to be expected that some knowledge of God (though perhaps not of his moral qualities) was 'observable in the history of various nations'.[34]

This view of Hinduism did not in the slightest way appear to threaten or undermine the case for Christian missions. Though some missionaries were interested in history and antiquity, they were essentially present-minded. If, in their view, there had been a golden age, this was followed by an obvious decline. It was in these latter circumstances (in the age of Kali or decline that Hindus themselves acknowledged) that missionaries discovered their vocation and were involved in the urgent task of rescuing the people from their present-day degraded condition.

Commonalities and Difference

Thus, basic orientalist ideas of Hinduism as discussed above re-emerged in missionary writings on Hinduism in the first half of the nineteenth century. They included the notion of Hinduism as Brahmanism—the one unified pan-Indian system created and controlled by brahmans, and also the idea of a golden age, of an original monotheism followed by a steady decline.

If, however, there were very basic and important points of agreement between the secular orientalists and British missionaries (a coincidence of views which is not recognized by current commentators), there were also differences in approach and in some of the ways they understood and depicted Hindu religion.

Whereas the missionaries believed that there was only one universal religion and panacea appropriate for the whole world, Halhed, like some other eighteenth-century thinkers, felt that 'nations' had developed religious systems which were not only different but which were especially suited to their people's needs. Urging toleration in religion, he argued that God had

> appointed to each tribe its own faith, and to every sect its own religion; and having introduced a numerous variety of casts, and a multiplicity of customs, He views in each particular place the mode of worship respectively appointed to it; sometimes He is employed with the attendants upon the

[34] Sutton 1833: 18.

mosque, in counting the sacred beads; sometimes He is in the temple, at the adoration of idols; the intimate of the Mussulman, and the friend of the Hindoo; the companion of the Christian, and the confidant of the Jew. Wherefore men of exalted notions, not being bent upon hatred and opposition, but considering the collected body of creatures as an object of the power of the Almighty, by investigating the contrarieties of sect, and the different customs of religion, have stamped themselves a lasting reputation upon the page of the world.[35]

Unlike the missionaries, many of the secular orientalist writers were dismayed at the extent of negative European comment on 'the Hindoo religion'. In his 'Religious Tenets of the Gentoos', Holwell attacked 'all the modern writers' for representing the Hindoos as 'a race of stupid and gross idolaters'.[36] Among those he ridiculed were people who 'from an intemperate zeal of religious vanity (now so much the fashion) presume to condemn, depreciate or invade the religious principles of others'.[37] His own contribution would, he hoped, 'extricate them in some degree' from 'the gross absurdities we have conceived of them'.[38] Dow who was not uncritical of Hinduism, complained that modern travellers had prejudiced Europe against the brahmans, 'and by a very unfair account, have thrown disgrace upon a system of religion and philosophy, which they did by no means investigate'.[39] Halhed hoped that his comments and translation of 'the Gentoo Code' would give readers a more precise idea of the customs and manners of the people who 'to their great injury', had long been 'misrepresented' in the Western world. He went out of his way to exonerate brahmans from the slur of 'self-interested partiality', referring, for example, to their 'moderation and self-denial' and explaining that the injunction on women burning themselves with their deceased husbands was 'plain, moderate and conditional'.[40] Sir William Jones adopted a somewhat similar sympathetic approach to Hindu tradition, expressing his admiration for many aspects of Hindu belief and practice. Though a devout Christian, he was attracted especially by the conception of the non-duality of God and the human soul as explained by Shankara in his commentary on the Vedanta, and by the transmigration of the soul.[41]

[35] Marshall 1970: 182–83. See also Holwell's comments in Marshall 1970 (p. 48).
[36] Ibid.: 48.
[37] Ibid.: 49.
[38] Ibid.: 50.
[39] Ibid.: 107–8.
[40] Ibid.: 170, 176, 179.
[41] Mukherjee 1987: 107.

While many orientalist writers, and especially Jones, were not entirely blind to defects in 'the Hindu religion', their overall sympathetic approach and attempt to rehabilitate Hinduism in the eyes of Europeans created a difficult problem for evangelicals who were trying to convince the public and the relevant British authorities that India was in desperate need of missionaries and the Christian Gospel. How the missionaries and their supporters responded to this situation, including the orientalists' sympathetic representation of Hinduism, is a part of our narrative.

A third major difference between secular orientalist and missionary views of Hinduism is at least partially bound up with differences in interest, focus and experience. Men like Jones, Halhed and other secular scholars were primarily interested in what is sometimes called 'the great tradition',[42] while the missionaries were much more interested in popular religion and in the ideas and practices of the middle and lower classes and castes in the population.

As noted above, orientalists concentrated on the work of collecting, translating and interpreting brahmanical texts. That was for many of them their delight and basic agenda. Most of them lived in Calcutta where they had considerable contact with pundits and brahmans. Sir William Jones, for one, also spent time in Krishnagar and travelled extensively throughout Bengal by boat in 1787.[43] He was, therefore, well aware of popular forms of Hinduism, but like so many other members of the Asiatic Society, was not especially interested in it. In fact, what is especially striking about his letters (included in Cannon's two-volume edition published in 1970) is how seldom Jones refers to popular practice. And when on one occasion, in a letter to Jonathan Duncan in 1790, he does mention popular forms of worship it is only to show his revulsion at what he saw. 'With all my admiration of the truly learned Brahmens,' he wrote, 'I abhor the sordid priestcraft of Durga's ministers, but such fraud no more affects the sound religion of the Hindus, than the lady of Loretto and the Romish impositions affect our own rational faith.'[44] Unlike the missionaries he was not attempting to evangelize the lower classes or at least those who participated in these practices, and so from Jones' point of view there was absolutely no reason why he should become interested in this type of phenomenon.

On the other hand, the missionaries had a different agenda. When they arrived in India in increasing numbers in the late eighteenth and early

[42] For an introduction to this idea, which seems to assume that there was only one great tradition, see especially Cohn 1971: 4–5.
[43] Cannon 1970, Vol. 2: 754.
[44] Ibid.: 856.

nineteenth centuries they settled in towns and villages throughout the countryside as well as in cities. They also attempted to make contact with a much broader range of people. These included untouchables and lower-caste Hindus who had their own particular attitudes and way of life. Given these circumstances the missionary depictions of Hinduism were bound to be more varied, broader in scope and more contemporaneous than depictions of 'the Hindu religion' drawn from descriptions and comments by orientalists interested primarily or even exclusively in ancient brahmanical texts. In some cases missionary accounts, unlike orientalist arguments, were based on a detailed knowledge of both Sanskrit texts *and* of the views and attitudes of common people. Missionaries such as William Carey, John Wilson, John Murray Mitchell, Robert Caldwell, Robert Noble,[45] Howard Campbell and others studied and knew Sanskrit, but they were also well known as students and speakers of at least one vernacular language and as commentators on popular religious movements. The missionaries therefore had a more all-encompassing and comprehensive approach to the study of Hinduism than was usually the case among secular orientalist scholars who, like Monier-Williams and John Muir, remained strongly committed to the study of the ancient textual material.

Government, Orientalism and Missionary Scholarship on Hinduism

The development of Bengal-based British orientalism in the late eighteenth and early nineteenth centuries was significant for the missionary movement and for missionary constructions of Hinduism, not only because what emerged as the dominant missionary paradigm was nurtured and encouraged in the orientalist environment, but also because of its practical and long-term consequences. As is well known, evangelicals and other Christians had the deepest regard for the work of Sir William Jones, for his scholarly achievements and above all for his defence of Old Testament chronology and history.[46] As Trautmann has pointed out, it was Jones who 'showed that Sanskrit literature is not an enemy but an ally of the Bible, supplying independent corroboration of the Bible's version of history after the flood'.[47] Not only was there a Christian recognition and

---

[45] Noble 1867: 166.
[46] See especially Morris 1904: 82–3; Wilkinson 1844: 43–4; Trautmann 1997: 74–80.
[47] Trautmann 1997: 74.

support for Jones' work, but an opportunity soon arose for more struc-
tured missionary involvement in official orientalist projects.

In 1800 Wellesley established his College at Fort William for the training
of civil servants for positions in the new, rapidly expanding imperial
administration. Writers, trained in Indian languages and in law, were to
follow a three-year course before going to Bengal, Bombay and Madras. In
order to staff the new college, the governing council turned for assistance
to the Asiatic Society and eventually to the Baptist missionaries at Serampore
College. H. T. Colebrooke was appointed as Professor in Sanskrit at Fort
William and the College Council also looked to fill other positions in
Arabic and Persian and in six modern Indian languages. Claudius Buchanan,
Vice-Provost and Professor, and one of the two Anglican clergy responsible
for College discipline and general administration, recommended William
Carey as one of the professors. In April 1801 Carey was appointed to the
college as 'Professor of the Bengalee and Shanscrit Languages'.[48] While
working as head of the Bengali department he also developed a close
relationship with Colebrooke in Sanskrit studies, the two men collaborat-
ing in the translation of *Hitopadesha* (a version of the famous *Panchatantra*
fables) in 1804. When, two years later, Colebrooke resigned his position it
was Carey who succeeded him as a full professor, at twice his former
salary.[49] Carey's initial appointment and rapid promotion in the college
made him better known to government circles[50] and eventually led to
extensive Serampore mission–government collaboration in the translation
of Sanskrit, Bengali and other texts. Not only was Carey, and through him
Serampore College, paid for this assistance, but the missionaries were also
able to utilize the services of the Fort William pundits. In the meantime
Carey, increasingly respected for his work as an oriental scholar, was
admitted to membership of the Asiatic Society (1806).

Missionary links with oriental studies through Wellesley's 'University
of the East' at Fort William lasted as long as Serampore College, which
was officially closed in 1807. In the meantime, however, similar training
colleges were established by the Directors of the East India Company in
Madras and Bombay.[51] The tripartite institutional basis of oriental studies
in Bengal (government, College and Asiatic Society) was reproduced in
Madras through the provincial government supervisory council, the newly-
established College of Fort St George and the Literary Society of Madras.

[48] RPC, Archives, WCC/7, Carey to father, 23/11/1801.
[49] Kopf 1969: 88–91.
[50] RPC, Archives, IN. 13, Carey to Morris, 25/2/1802.
[51] Trautmann 1997: 114.

And here, once again, was the possibility of missionary contact and collaboration in oriental studies.

While there has been very little study of the Madras developments, apart from Trautmann's pioneering work, there are some indications of missionary interest and interaction with the Madras orientalist scholars. One of the key officials in the Madras experiment was Francis Whyte Ellis who, after arriving in India, joined the civil service in 1796. He distinguished himself as a Sanskrit and Tamil scholar, becoming chairman of the Madras college council, a teacher in the college and a member of the Madras Literary Society.[52] The Methodist missionary Elijah Hoole, who arrived in Madras in 1814, four years after Ellis' premature and much lamented death, was a great admirer of his achievements, claiming that Ellis' unfinished work on the *Kural* was 'an invaluable manual to every Tamil scholar'.[53] In his book *Madras, Mysore and the South of India* he quoted lengthy passages from Ellis' translation of Tamil classics. These included extracts from the *Tiruvachagam* (the sacred utterances of the Tamil Shaiva saint Manikkavasagar) and the *Tiruvaimoli*, which Hoole described as 'the principal work in Tamil in which the tenets of the Vaishnavas are found'.[54] While in Madras he also secured the services of a number of the pundits employed in the government college. 'A friendly intercourse with some of the chief Moonshees of the College was highly valued by me,' he wrote. 'Among other advantages accruing from it, was the obtaining copies of rare and valuable books, which probably I should not otherwise have met with.'[55]

Some association with the government orientalist colleges, including Carey's important connection with the College of Fort William, gave to missionaries interested in oriental studies contact with pundits and other European scholars, and some access to facilities they may not otherwise have had. Their scholarly activities were also recognized and encouraged through their membership and activities in connection with learned societies such as the Bengal Asiatic Society and other scholarly associations in Bengal, Bombay and Madras.[56] Missionary studies of different aspects

[52] Buckland 1971: 149–50.

[53] Hoole 1844: 400.

[54] Hoole 1844: 380–85, 390–404. On the *Tiruvaimoli*, attributed to Tiruvaranga Perumal Araiyar, one of Ramanuja's gurus, see Jagadeesan 1977.

[55] Hoole 1844: 189.

[56] That the proceeding of these societies were followed with some interest is indicated by the fact that their proceedings were reported in some detail in missionary journals such as the *Calcutta Christian Observer*.

of Hinduism produced in this way, in the form of scholarly papers, essays and reviews, need to be taken into account in any discussions of missionary constructions of Hinduism during the period of William Carey to 1900 and after. In these circumstances the missionaries' primary focus was on the task of representing Hinduism to themselves and to each other as well as to non-missionary scholars and the world of learning. Consequently their publications in this particular regard cannot be classified with some other types of missionary literature, including material designed more as propaganda to arouse the public and encourage and justify missionary activity. The primary consideration in this case was the world of learning, rather than the world of mission; and in that sense the missionary contribution symbolized missionary involvement in the mainstream world of scholarly studies in religion.

The British Protestant missionaries contributed to many of the best-known and most highly esteemed India-based scholarly periodicals throughout the nineteenth century and in connection with leading learned societies. Contributions included notes and queries, articles and reviews on languages and literature, poetry, folklore, ethnology and anthropology, archaeology, history and religion. Many of these topics overlap, but amongst the most important papers on the study of Hinduism in particular were those reflecting the results of research, not only in Sanskrit literature, but on different aspects of popular religion in different parts of the subcontinent. Indeed, the missionaries' later-nineteenth century contribution to an understanding of a whole range of Indian religious traditions (involving middle and lower castes as well as brahmans), provided, as already noted, a more balanced overview of the subject than did the secular orientalist scholars still trapped within the Sanskritic brahmanical model.

Though the missionaries did much to popularize Sanskrit religious literature in a range of publications throughout the nineteenth century[57] specialist contributions to secular learned journals on the same subject were apparently few and far between. One of these rare contributions was the Rev. Maurice Phillips' article on the 'Cosmogony of the Vedas', which appeared in the *Madras Journal of Literature and Science* in 1887.[58]

---

[57] One of the most influential nineteenth-century Protestant missionary works on Sanskrit religious literature, which appeared in several editions, was W. J. Wilkins' book entitled *Hindu Mythology*, first published in 1882. The work, however, did not profess to supply new translations of Hindu scriptures, 'nor to give very much information that is not already scattered through many other books'.

[58] Third Series, 1886–87: 69–88.

More common than this type of article, which is representative of the kind of brahmanical topics usually studied by secular orientalist scholars, were British missionary contributions to the study of devotional and other forms of regional and local religion. Two of John Murray Mitchell's studies of popular movements in western India appeared in the *Indian Antiquary* in 1882. These comprised a study of the character and influence of the Marathi bhakti poet Tukaram (together with translations of his verse), and Mitchell's eyewitness account of the pilgrimage and annual festival at Pandharpur.[59] Also noteworthy are missionary studies of *Shaiva Siddhanta*. One of the first serious contributions was an article by the Rev. C. Egbert Kennet (1826–84) of the SPG, Madras, entitled 'Notes on the Saiva Siddhanta', published in the *Indian Antiquary* in 1873,[60] at a time when comparatively little was known by European scholars about the subject. The various editions of G. U. Pope's translations and commentaries on *Shaiva Siddhanta* are well known. The impact of his work was supplemented by G. McKenzie Cobban's remarks on the subject in the *Contemporary Review* in 1895.[61] Lastly, there was an influential article by Bishop Caldwell (SPG). This was a paper published in the *Journal of the Anthropological Society of Bombay* on 'Demonolatry in South India'—an account of low-caste religion and spirit possession which was referred to in the Madras Census.[62]

These and other studies of Hinduism appearing in learned journals were supplemented by a much greater volume and output of work which was published in the missionaries' own serial publications. The most important of these India-based journals, designed primarily for their own consumption, were the *Calcutta Christian Observer*, the *Indian Evangelical Review*,[63]

[59] *IA* March and June 1882. See also 'The story of Tukarama. From the Marathi-Prakrit. With an introduction by the Rev. J. Murray Mitchell', *The Journal of the Bombay Branch of the Royal Asiatic Society*, III (XII), January 1849.

[60] 'Notes on the Saiva Siddhanta', *IA*, Vol. 2, December 1873: 343–44.

[61] *The Contemporary Review*, Vol. LXVII, 1895: 853–63.

[62] This article was also published in the *IER*, Vol. XIV, 1887–88: 192–203.

[63] Commenting on the objectives of the *Indian Evangelical Review* (after the demise of the *Calcutta Christian Observer*), the editor of the *Review* remarked that 'The want of a general religious periodical, which should seek to represent the common faith of all Evangelical Christians in India, to be the exponent of their thoughts and convictions, to record the progress and results of Christian efforts, to offer facilities greater than our Indian newspapers can afford, for the free discussion of unsettled questions connected with such efforts, and to be a bond of union between all believers in the land, was quite generally felt' (*IER*, Vol. 1, 1873: 96).

the *Harvest Field*[64] and the *Madras Christian College Magazine*.[65] Unlike most of the missionary society journals appearing in Britain they were (within the Protestant world) ecumenical in spirit and orientation, and also journals in which the missionaries themselves maintained editorial control. To a greater or lesser degree they created space in which missionaries could discuss their own issues and represent Hinduism to themselves and each other. Unlike the professional 'secular' journals as discussed above they were less embedded in the context of the broader scholarly world and more in the environment of Christian theology and Christian mission. Nevertheless, they too included the more objective scholarly studies of a wide range of different aspects of Hinduism during the nineteenth century. Articles in these and other journals included discussion of a wide variety of local and contemporary movements. One of these commentaries was, for example, on the role and activity of the Shankara Acharya of the Sringeri mutt in Mysore[66] and other brief studies were by J. Hewlett (London Missionary Society, LMS) on Hindu monasteries and sects of Benares.[67] James Kennedy (LMS) gave an account of popular presentations of the *Gita* in northern India, W. Shoolbred (United Presbyterian Church of Scotland, UPCS) contributed an article on the 'Ram Sneh Religion' in Rajputana and J. Shillay, of the Irish Presbyterian Mission in Gujarat, an overview of the Tantric literature of India.[68] J. Knowles (LMS) wrote an eyewitness account of hook-swinging in Travancore in the *World Wide Magazine*.[69] In addition to these studies were articles on the kudumi or Hindu tuft (S. Mateer, LMS) and on Hindu domestic and women's rituals by J. E. Padfield (CMS).[70] Cobban discussed his translations of Tamil devotional poetry in the *Madras Christian College Magazine* (Vols 2, 3 and 8) while Slater contributed a paper on Keshab Chandra Sen (Vol. 1), an account which was later developed and published in book form in 1885. These studies of popular and contemporary

---

[64] *The Harvest Field*, the recognized organ of the Wesleyan Indian missions, and a journal which in the 1880s was described as 'keeping to strictly orthodox lines', included a wide range of diverse opinion from missionaries with liberal or modern to more conservative theological views (*IER*, Vol. X, 1884: 286).

[65] For further discussion of Protestant missionary journals published in India, see especially Oddie 1976: 41–3.

[66] *Free Church of Scotland Quarterly Missionary Paper*, No. XLI, December 1869. See the sketch of the head of the Sringeri monastery in 1869, Figure 10.1.

[67] *Chronicle*, September 1886: 361–66; *IER*, Vol. XVI: 288–99.

[68] *IER*, Vol. II: 336–43, 398–412; Vol. X, 1883: 508–11.

[69] *The World Wide Magazine*, Vol. 3, April–September 1899.

[70] *IER*, Vol. VIII, 1882: 95–106; *MCCM*, Vols 3, 4 and 12.

movements included some analysis of texts and literature, but for the most part they were more akin to present-day anthropological researches than to the study of ancient texts and commentaries that was the hallmark of secular oriental scholarship such as that which continued to develop in Bengal in the early nineteenth century. Again it was the missionaries who seem to have bridged both kinds of studies, who were involved in ethnography and who anticipated the work of anthropologists of later generations.[71]

[71] On the relationship between missionary and anthropological studies, see especially Woodberry 2004: 12–14.

2

The Construction of Missionary Models

4

Hinduism in Missionary Education and Training

The Colleges

During the first half of the nineteenth century, Protestant candidates selected for missionary work overseas were seldom provided with college courses designed to equip them for the specific tasks of the mission field.[1] They were usually trained in ordinary theological colleges or, if not, undertook similar studies in so-called 'missionary' institutions. In other words, the core of studies for the mission field was essentially the same as that for clergy and ministers preparing for work at home.

Most Church of Scotland candidates who went to India, like their colleagues preparing for their ministry in Scotland, studied arts (often including philosophy and science) and then divinity at one of the ancient universities and divinity halls attached to them. Baptist candidates were trained in their own general theological academies, such as those of Bristol, Horton and Stepney. Nor were candidates in the Church of England who became missionaries with the Society for the Propagation of the Gospel (SPG) offered any special training. Like some of the other societies, the SPG followed the financially convenient practice of not paying for the education of its candidates, accepting suitable applications among those already prepared for holy orders.[2]

The Church Missionary Society (CMS), which opened its own missionary training college at Islington in 1825, introduced a syllabus which contained little, if anything, which could be described as material preparing missionaries specifically for work overseas. The course of study was shaped by two considerations. One was the need to pass the examinations of the Bishop of London, a condition which necessitated a thorough grounding in the classical European languages of Greek and Latin. The other was the need to satisfy the CMS regulations that required the candidates to be able to read the scriptures in the original languages and

[1] Piggin 1984: Chs 6–9.
[2] Ibid.: 198–200.

'be acquainted with the entire outline of Ecclesiastical History, both general and English, with Church Polity and Rituals, with Evidences and Doctrines'. While, in the 1830s, subjects included chemistry and logic (studies not mentioned in the above requirements), there was nothing additional which would have been especially helpful for missionaries preparing for India. There were no classes studying oriental languages, Indian history or Indian philosophies or religions.[3]

By way of contrast with these policies there was some attempt on the part of the Wesleyan Methodist Missionary Society (WMMS) to do something specific for its candidates for India. After his return to England in 1828 Elijah Hoole, who had spent eight years in evangelistic work in the Madras Presidency, was involved in instructing Methodist candidates for work in south India.[4] While much of this time appears to have been spent in teaching the students Tamil, it almost certainly included some discussion of Hindu belief and practice. According to Piggin, the Methodist training institution subsequently established at Richmond in 1843 also 'bore more of a missionary aspect than theological institutions in other denominations'. However, it was still not exclusively designed for missionary training.[5] Funds were provided for the library to purchase missionary biographies and other suitable publications, such as works in Indian languages written by Wesleyan missionaries. But despite a certain awareness of the needs of missionary candidates and of Hoole's pioneering efforts, no provision was made in the syllabus for instruction in subjects with a specifically missionary orientation, such as indigenous languages and the customs and religious beliefs of native people.[6]

Nor was London Missionary Society (LMS) policy much more effective—at least in providing a long-lasting and relevant solution to the special needs of its missionary candidates. The directors of the society established a special academy for the purpose of training its missionaries at Gosport. The aim of the institution, which trained fifty missionaries for India from the time of its inception in 1789 until its closure in 1826, was to provide an education chiefly for those intended for 'India, or any other civilized country'.[7] Though the Principal and driving force behind the project, David Bogue, was committed to the organization and development of missions in India, even he does not appear to have been especially

[3] Oddie 1999: 14–16; Piggin 1984: 189–97.
[4] *WMS Missionary Notices*, Vol. VIII, 1835–38: 583.
[5] Piggin 1984: 208.
[6] Ibid.: 210.
[7] Ibid.: 157.

effective in developing in his students the relevant and necessary skills or qualifications. A surviving set of his lectures suggests that the information and advice he gave students intended for India was of a very general nature. He encouraged them to acquire 'an accurate knowledge' of the country and to study the language, but said nothing about the distinguishing features of 'heathen' religions or about what became known as Hinduism.[8] If, indeed, education at Gosport represented the best the LMS could do to provide missionary candidates with an appropriate training for the Indian mission field, then there is even less to be said in favour of the more ordinary training in some of the other Congregational academies in Britain. Though sometimes academically of a high standard, there was little that was special for those planning a future career in the mission field.

An examination of all of this evidence suggests then that an appropriate education, including the study of Hinduism, was largely absent in the preparation of candidates for India during the first half of the nineteenth century. But was the situation any better as the century progressed?

While, in some cases, missionary societies did little to make their courses more relevant for the mission field, in other instances there were improvements which included greater attention to the study of 'other' religions.

The CMS and WMMS are two examples of societies which appear to have done little in actual practice to improve training for India during the second half of the century. Indeed, it is quite possible that the preparation of Wesleyan missionaries for India was less relevant or effective during this period than it had been initially, and especially under Hoole's teaching and direction. On the other hand, the LMS, SPG and a few of the new women's missionary organizations proved to be more adaptable, introducing changes which included a greater opportunity for the study of Hinduism.

To one of the more influential and vocal supporters of the CMS, Sir Robert Montgomery (one of the 'Punjab School' of administrators) the situation at Islington was little short of outrageous. Comparing the CMS method of training its candidates for India unfavourably with the measures adopted for the preparation of men for the Indian Civil Service, he argued in a minute in 1868 that:

> So far as I know, the training of our Missionaries at Islington College is as follows. They just manage, during the two years they are there, to qualify themselves for ordination. They proceed to India without any special knowledge of the history of the country, ignorant of the language, ignorant of the

[8] Ibid.: 175–81.

systems of religion they have to refute, and ignorant of the habits and customs of the races they go to evangelise.

Our missionaries of the present day have to meet in argument Moham-medans, Moolvees, and Hindoo pundits, deeply read and versed in their own religions, and many of them well acquainted with the outlines of Christianity, and all the objections urged by European misbelievers. Our Missionaries ought to have a thorough knowledge of the systems of the religion they have to combat, and none should be allowed to preach in public till they have thoroughly mastered the languages, and have a deep and complete acquaintance with the Hindoo and Mohammedan systems, and considerable familiarity with native habits of thought.[9]

Though Montgomery's minute was supported by T. V. French (subse-quently Bishop of Lahore) and others, it appears to have had little effect— at least in encouraging serious attention to Hinduism. During what was described as a 'full & prolonged' discussion members of the executive of the CMS seemed to agree that it was desirable 'to enlarge the course of study' at Islington; and that, during the period of some months between their ordination as deacon and priest, prospective candidates for the mission field should take a course of study which would comprise a language component and 'such History, Mythology etc as may the better qualify them for their future labours'. A revised curriculum included, among other things, 'the study of evidences made prominent with a view to Mahammadan and heathen controversy' and 'a knowledge of Eastern manners and customs as may serve to illustrate the Scriptures'. In his report on the Church Missionary Institution for 1869 the principal reit-erated these changes as official policy.[10] However, in light of the fact that the numbers at Islington were in decline, that the focus of attention was shifting more to candidates drawn from the universities, and also in view of the fact that these reforms are nowhere mentioned in Stock's official history, it seems unlikely that they were especially effective, or made much difference to the CMS missionaries' knowledge of Hinduism.

Much of what Montgomery said about the inadequacy of the CMS system of training at Islington, could have been said of Wesleyan Meth-odist policy with regard to candidates also destined for India during the second half of the nineteenth century. As was the case at Islington, those

[9] CMS, G/CI, Committee Minutes, Vol. 37 (14/5/18–31/3/1868). Minute by Sir Robert Montgomery. K.C.B.: 718–21 (also printed and published C. M. House, 18/2/1868).
[10] CMS, G/CI, Committee Minutes, Vol. 38 (11/4/1868–1/3/1870). Report of the Insti-tution for 1869: 358.

selected for India were not taught or given any introductory lectures on Hinduism or any other religious system. The inadequacies of Methodist training, which were matters of deep concern to Methodist missionaries in India, were fully exposed at conferences and in papers published in the early 1890s. A gathering of Wesleyan missionaries held in Bombay in 1893 announced that Wesleyan missionaries coming to work in India were to be subject, not only to 'the ordinary ministerial probation of their church', but to 'a special missionary probation'—a statement which says a great deal about the absence of any specific training. The Rev. Henry Haig (WMMS) declared in a paper published in the *Harvest Field* the following year that specific missionary training was 'altogether wanting' and that men were selected 'as they are needed' and 'sent forth' with their only chance of beginning training being on the voyage out.[11] 'In my time when a man received his appointment his first business usually was to turn to his atlas to make out precisely in what corner of the world his lot was being cast.' In another paper the Rev. J. Hudson (WMMS) conceded that 'fitful attempts' had been made in the past to prepare men for the mission field, but then emphasized that 'no adequate scheme [had] been prepared and followed out'. Both he and Haig were especially concerned with the way in which this lack of training affected the missionary's capacity to understand and debate the basic issues and problems in what might be described as the Hindu–Christian encounter. Indeed, it was Hudson's opinion that a lack of appropriate training was the reason why Wesleyan missionaries failed to explore the issue of Hinduism at a greater depth.

> Hinduism has never made upon them the impression which so great a system ought to have made. They have not understood its attractions, they have not weighed its reasons, they have not thought it through and felt for themselves its fundamental unsatisfactoriness, they have not solemnly and conscientiously looked at all it has to say against Christianity and for its own superiority.[12]

Growing criticism and dissatisfaction with the inadequate preparation of missionaries by their societies did not, however, go completely unheeded during the second half of the nineteenth century.

Concern for a better and more effective policy was at the root of the LMS experiment in establishing their own special college at Highgate— a scheme which, unlike many other 'fitful attempts', lasted longer and

[11] *HF*, Vol. 5, March 1894: 321–26.
[12] *HF* September 1894: 328.

provided missionaries with an extra year's worth of training more useful
and certainly more relevant to their country of destination. The college
was opened at Highgate in 1863, moved to St John's Wood in 1870 and
finally closed in 1872. Its object was to provide for missionary students,
who had completed their ordinary college curriculum, some special training in 'the languages of the East', and in other subjects especially connected
with their future work.[13] The principal of the college, from 1863 until its
closure in 1872, was John Smith Wardlaw, MA, a retired missionary with
twenty years' service in south India. Most of the students were destined
for China or India. Eighteen of the graduates were sent to India, mostly
to south India over the ten year period during which the college was in
operation. A memo signed by Wardlaw, who appears to have done all the
teaching, shows that subjects of study for those going to India included
'Hindu philosophy' as well as Indian languages and history.[14] Among those
sent to India were two students who subsequently became well known for
their studies of Hinduism. William Joseph Wilkins, a printer and subsequently tin-plate worker at Wolverhampton,[15] and Thomas Ebenezer Slater,
who was initially trained as an architect,[16] were both products of the
college and became eminent as scholars of Hinduism. While Slater is
perhaps better known in historical and scholarly circles for his *Higher
Hinduism in Relation to Christianity*, Wilkins' work, much of it on the
Puranas and popular deities, was still on sale in street stalls in Bombay in
1998.[17]

Towards the end of the 1840s the SPG also began to display signs of
being more sensitive to the needs of candidates in training for India. In
1848 it asked the Rev. Peter Percival, a much admired Tamil scholar and
former Methodist missionary ordained as an Anglican, to lecture on
Hinduism at St Augustine's Missionary Institution, Canterbury. These
lectures subsequently formed the basis of Percival's book *The Land of the*

[13] CWM, Home Personal, Box 2, R. Wardlaw Thompson, 'Memoir of Dr. John Wardlaw',
p. 6; Piggin 1984: 159. The library appears to have included some of Monier-Williams's
works on India.

[14] CWM, Home Personal, Box 2, R. Wardlaw Thompson, 'Memoir of Dr. John Wardlaw',
memo dated 30/10/1869.

[15] CWM, *CP*. Wilkins to Directors, 21/10/1861.

[16] CWM, *CP*. Slater to Directors, 27/8/1861.

[17] His first work, *Hindu Mythology, Vedic and Puranic* (London, 1882), proved immediately successful and has remained popular ever since. The seventeenth impression of the
second edition (1882) was published by Rupa and Co. (Calcutta, Allahabad, Bombay and
Delhi) as a paperback in 1998.

Veda, published in London in 1854. The SPG, whose graduates, like those of the CMS, were drawn increasingly from the universities, also introduced a system of scholarships at Oxford and Cambridge which were offered on the condition that the applicant had some knowledge of Hinduism as well as other religions of India. In 1861, for example, an advertisement appeared in the *Mission Field*, the society's principal magazine, advertising 'missionary exhibitions' for Oxford and Cambridge—the award depending on the results of an examination which included the answering of questions on 'the Religious and Philosophical Systems of India'.[18]

Finally, there were also some important developments in theological training as a result of the rise of the women's missionary movement during the second half of the century. While the CMS appears to have done little to change the curriculum at Islington, the new and independent Church of England Zenana Missionary Society (CEZMS), founded in 1875, took the opportunity of doing something more relevant for its candidates about to depart for India. The women who undertook training at 'the Willows', the CEZMS training institution opened in 1880, were expected to attend classes on Hinduism as well as on Islam. It appears, not only from this evidence but also from their application papers submitted prior to their entering college, that they were better informed on the subject of Hinduism at the point of their departure for India than many of their male colleagues, such as the Methodist missionaries discussed above.

Indian Language Studies in Britain

While facilities for the study of Hinduism, especially in the first half of the nineteenth century were largely neglected, there was greater awareness of the need for language training. The need for missionaries destined for India to study the appropriate language (an obvious prerequisite for evangelization and understanding of local religion), was recognized by the governing bodies of most of the Protestant societies in Britain from the very beginning. The basic issue was not so much whether those preparing for the mission field should study a language, but how, when and where. As we shall see, some candidates (probably the minority) commenced language studies while still in Britain, others began on the long voyage out, and almost all either began, or continued their work with a munshi or teacher while in India.

[18] *MF*, Vol. VI, January 1861: 21.

One of the hurdles faced by missionary candidates studying Indian languages in Britain during the first half of the nineteenth century was the difficulty of obtaining qualified teachers. In this situation some candidates, and societies attempting to make arrangements for language preparation for them while they remained in Britain, relied on the services of ex-missionaries wherever they could be found. The CMS, LMS, WMMS and Baptist Missionary Society (BMS) all sent candidates to Henry Townley's short-lived institution for the study of 'Eastern languages', namely Bengali and Sanskrit, during the period 1824 to 1831.[19] John Reid, appointed to the LMS mission station at Bellary in 1830, spent over a month studying Kannada under the tutorship of the Rev. John Hands, a former missionary who had spent five years at the same station;[20] while, as noted above, some of the early Methodist candidates commenced their studies of south Indian languages while still in England, and under the guidance of Elijah Hoole.

Missionary candidates were also encouraged to take advantage of Sanskrit being taught in non-missionary institutions. J. S. Wardlaw and W. H. Drew (both of the LMS), studied Sanskrit under Francis Johnson, Professor of Sanskrit at Haileybury College.[21] Further opportunities for studying the language were opened up when H. H. Wilson was elected to the first chair of Sanskrit at Oxford in 1832. A. W. Wallis and W. K. Coles, both of them candidates with the SPG, and Robert Fox, destined for the CMS Telugu mission, studied Sanskrit under Wilson.[22] The establishment of Sanskrit studies at Oxford was followed by its introduction at Kings College London and in the universities of Glasgow and Edinburgh— Howard Campbell, of the LMS Telugu mission, being one of those who took advantage of Sanskrit at Edinburgh in the 1880s.[23]

The idea of introducing candidates to some Indian language while they were still in Britain was not entirely forgotten, and nor was it overlooked during the second half of the nineteenth century. Women candidates in training with the CEZMS, for example, were expected to commence their language studies while at home.[24] However, throughout the nineteenth century the primary focus of all Protestant missionary societies was on the

[19] Piggin 1984: 241.

[20] R. Wardlaw 1845: 92–4.

[21] Piggin 1984: 241–42; J. S. Wardlaw 1856: 29.

[22] Noble 1867: 120; Piggin 1984: 242.

[23] CWM, South India, Tamil, Correspondence, W. H. Campbell to Thompson, 18/4/1885 (Folder 4, Box 8).

[24] Morawiecki 1998: 191–202.

need for language training in India itself. This was where the best teachers were generally available and where the missionary could learn the language in the context of his or her special sphere of activity.

While a few missionaries had some acquaintance with one or more Indian languages prior to their embarkation for India, it was more common for them to begin their studies on the long voyage out. This they did with the help of dictionaries, grammars or any other aids, such as the occasional linguist they employed or met on board.[25]

Most of these forays into language study prior to arrival in India were, however, preliminary or introductory, and, for the great majority of men and women, the serious and sustained study of language was begun only after their arrival in the country and as a result of their securing or being given the services of a munshi or pundit.

Pundits and Language Study in India

As the ability to function in the vernacular language became increasingly valued and recognized as a sine qua non for the professional missionary, the need for formal qualifications and the place of munshis in the missionary system became likewise increasingly recognized as essential. The usual practice of making arrangements with a munshi or pundit were formalized increasingly by the missionary societies and their local committees as the century progressed. Hence, some societies like the LMS and SPG provided the missionary with a munshi allowance and also began to

---

[25] The party of Methodist missionaries who left for India and Ceylon in August 1837 took with them Israel, 'a native of India', by whose aid they expected to make 'considerable progress' in Tamil studies (including colloquial usage and correct pronunciation) in the weeks ahead (*MN*, Vol. VIII, 1835–38: 551). The young Robert Caldwell, who was subsequently author of *A Comparative Grammar of the Dravidian or South Indian Family of Languages* (1856) was fortunate in meeting C. P. Brown, the linguist and expert in Telugu, on board the same ship (Wyatt 1894: 12). Other missionaries such as Noble and Fox (CMS), Edmund Crisp, Arthur and John Horner (WMMS), John Abbs and James Kennedy (LMS) may not have had the same degree of help or encouragement during the long weeks at sea. Nevertheless, some of them were pleased with the progress they made (Abbs 1870: 26; CWM, South India, Canarese, 1836–40, incoming corr., Box 4, F. 2, Rice to Ellis, 29/4/1837; and Tamil 1817–24, incoming corr., Box 1, F. 3, Crisp to Burder, 3/4/1837). On the other hand, James Kennedy and William Drew were less satisfied with their work on the outward journey—Kennedy, who was destined for Benares, confessing that he could not make much of the Hindustani grammar (Kennedy 1884: 13; CWM, South India, Tamil, 1817–24, incoming corr., Box 5, F. 1, J. Drew to Sec.).

insist on the need to pass language examinations. For example, the Calcutta Diocesan Committee (the local organization representing the SPG) declared in its regulations of about 1880 that 'Every Missionary, ordained or lay, and every Catechist and School master of the Society is required to pass, within one year of the date of his arrival in the country, or of his entering the service of the Society, an examination as to his competency to read, write and converse in the vernacular of the Mission.'[26]

There was also a move on the part of missionary societies to detail the specific outcomes required in language examinations. Thus according to the CMS committee in Madras, missionaries belonging to the CEZMS and the CMS in the 1890s were expected to demonstrate that they had developed the following skills:

> To translate, within a given time, in English a page (8vo) from an approved Text Book. To translate, within a given time, with accuracy of grammar and fair accuracy of idiom, a page (8vo) of narrative English and ten English sentences. Etymology and syntax. To write, within a given time, a short exposition of one of the Parables. To read aloud with facility, and to translate from a book not previously studied and a selected portion of the Bible. To translate with readiness a paper of short conversational sentences to be read out by the Examiner. To read and translate an ordinary Vernacular letter. To converse with Natives, not employed in the Mission, on ordinary and religious subjects with such fluency and accuracy as to be easily intelligible.[27]

It was generally recognized that language studies would occupy a substantial part of the missionaries' time and attention—one or two years or even longer. Language requirements were increasingly formalized and underscored in statements of mission society by-laws and policy, and as Jeffrey Cox has noted, in a few cases, would-be missionaries unable to pass their examinations, were 'disconnected' or sent home. Indeed, a successful career in the mission field came to depend more and more on the results of language examinations and, by implication, on the assistance of pundits or teachers, most of whom were Hindu.

The term 'munshi' was Arabic in origin. In its strictest sense it applied especially to teachers of Arabic, Persian or Urdu. However, it was also used more loosely in mission circles to refer to a 'native' teacher of one or more of the languages spoken in different parts of the subcontinent. While

---

[26] SPG, *AR* 1880: xxii.
[27] *IW* April 1899: 71.

munshis in the stricter sense were usually Muslims, many of the munshis who taught British missionaries throughout the nineteenth century were, in fact, Hindus. The term therefore was used to include both the munshi in the strictest sense and the Sanskrit pundit or pandit (from pandita or learned man).[28] Indeed, the words 'munshi' or 'pundit' were sometimes used interchangeably in the same passage simply to signify a native teacher of an Indian language or languages.[29]

Reading the Person: The Pundit as an Example of 'The Learned Hindu'

The hiring of a munshi or pundit was a significant event which marked the beginning of what could become a long-term personal and developing relationship. Furthermore, it was an experience which in some cases could colour the missionary's understanding and ideas of Hinduism. Even if the relationship between missionary and pundit failed to develop, even if the missionary's regular meetings with the munshi never went beyond a business-like arrangement, contact with the munshi was often important in conveying first impressions and in providing some insight into the Hindu religion and way of life. Newly-arrived missionaries soon became familiar with their native servants; but the pundit was different. In many instances he was the first learned or educated Indian the missionary met, the first representative of 'real' Hinduism and a person with whom the missionary could have a considered and in-depth discussion about Hindu beliefs and customs. And more than a source of knowledge conveyed verbally, he was in his person, conduct and appearance an example and symbol of the Hindu religion and way of life. While part of the missionary's world of educated persons and mentor, he was, at the same time, a significant representation of the missionary's 'other'.

It is hardly surprising that some missionaries, eager to learn as quickly and as much as possible, not only focused on the language they were studying, but also on the munshi in the hope that he, in his behaviour and

[28] Hobson-Jobson (Crooke 1968); CWM, Incoming Correspondence, South India, Tamil, Box 3, F. 3. Report of the first general meeting of the Madras District C'tee, 2/9/1827 and 4/10/1827.

[29] See, for example, the LMS Madras District Committee's regulations in relation to missionary pay and conditions in 1827 (CWM, Incoming Correspondence, South India, Tamil, Box 2, F. 3, Jacket B, J. Crisp to Sec., 15/10/1827).

as a person, would somehow betray the essence of what it was to be a Hindu. Recalling his experience of studying Hindi in Benares in 1839, James Kennedy (LMS) remarked that 'I felt myself studying the native character as well.' In working with his pundit he believed he had obtained illustrations of 'the patience, the courtesy, and also flattering, cozening character of the people'.[30] Thomas Hodson (WMMS) and William Drew (LMS) also drew general conclusions from the experience of meeting their teacher. They interpreted their pundit's reluctance to be drawn on the respective merits of Christianity and Hinduism as indifference to 'the truth'—an indifference typical of Hindus generally.

Referring to the attitude of his pundit, Drew concluded that Hindus had reduced religion 'to an almost unmeaning thing.' According to the missionary, they saw their 'system' either as a path to the gratification of their worst passions, or superstition in the most trifling forms, or unintelligible mystery. It was, in every way, something to be laughed at.

> 'Tell me, Chiniah,' I said solemnly one day to my Moonshee, 'what are your hopes of salvation?—how do you expect to be saved?' An unmeaning laugh, with 'I don't know,' was his indifferent but affecting reply. And as they do not know so they do not care. They will turn aside the weightiest arguments with a smile or a stupid attempt at wit.[31]

The Pundits' Social Background and Religious Tradition: Implications for Missionary Views of Hinduism

Hindu pundits in missionary employment were drawn from different Hindu communities and represented a wide variety of different Hindu religious traditions. As noted in chapter 2 it was Claudius Buchanan who, working with them at Fort William College, soon discovered there were among the brahman pundits of northern India sharp differences of opinion and different views of what constituted 'the real' Hinduism. Even in Benares, he explained, brahman pundits used different books and were disunited—those of one school refusing to recognize or acknowledge those of another.

Much the same point about the different traditions among pundits was made some years later by James Kennedy, a LMS missionary of more

---

[30] Kennedy 1884: 31–2.

[31] J. S. Wardlaw 1856: 56. See also SOAS, WMMS Special Series (biographical), India Fiche, Box 21, Box No. 625 (2), Journal of T. Hodson, 1/8/1831.

than twenty years' experience of work in the Benares region. 'Pundits as a class,' he averred, 'keep themselves to one book, or books of the same order, and their knowledge of books outside their favourite circle is very limited.'[32] Thus while we know that some brahman pundits employed by missionaries, for example Mrtyunjay Vidyalankar who was one of Carey's most famous pundits, were exponents of *Advaita* Hinduism,[33] others such as Waidya Natha Iyer, Benjamin Bailey's pundit at Kottayam in Travancore, were almost certainly theists and followers of either Shiva or Vishnu.[34] Nor was there a guarantee that those who were said to expound the same system of philosophy, or way of salvation, adhered to the same interpretation.

Second, some missionary pundits were drawn from the higher ranks of the non-brahman class. Richard Young has already explored the philosophy of Arumuka Pillay (commonly known as Navalar) Peter Percival's Tamil-speaking pundit.[35] It was he who became one of the best known and most aggressive exponents of *Shaiva Siddhanta* during the second half of the nineteenth century. While in his view, salvation was through love of Shiva as the supreme being, Elijah Hoole's long-term friend and pundit, Govinda Moodley, belonged to 'the Vaishnava sect'. He argued for the supremacy of Vishnu, and, according to Hoole, 'would sometimes assure me that all the worship offered to any being, was, in effect, received by Vishnu, as supreme, and that worship of Christians was acceptable by him'.[36]

Apart from Arumuka Pillay and Govinda Moodley (both Tamil non-brahmans), Kennedy's teacher and also Carey's first and perhaps most influential pundit, were kayasthas or pundits belonging to the writer caste. Throughout the period 1793–1900 British missionaries were not therefore entirely dependent on brahman teachers as linguistic consultants. Clearly another important source of indigenous information was the non-brahman pundit: and, at least in the case of Ramram Basu (1759–1813), Carey's first teacher, he was strongly anti-brahman.[37] His views, fiercely critical of brahmans, were reflected especially in the publication of a pamphlet which, according to Kopf's account, attacked the brahmans, 'who were portrayed as conspiring, like the medieval Roman Catholic clergy, to

[32] Kennedy 1884: 163.
[33] Killingley 1993: 100.
[34] On the religious outlook of Iyers, see especially Thurston 1909: 269.
[35] Young and Jebanesan 1995.
[36] Hoole 1844: 383.
[37] For some biographical detail see Das 1978: 21, 74–5.

enshroud the world in ignorance and darkness'.[38] While there can be little doubt that most Hindu 'missionary pundits' were brahmans, the appointment and use of non-brahman pundits raises questions about their influence on missionary thinking. How far, for example, was missionary criticism of the 'brahmanical system' encouraged by non-brahman Hindus as well as by Christian pundits whom the missionaries employed from time to time?

Third, the fact that Hindu pundits employed by missionaries, like Hindu pundits in general, were drawn almost exclusively, if not wholly, from among the higher castes, has special significance for missionary views of Hinduism. It meant that, if anything, the pundits were likely to reinforce the convictions of those missionaries who viewed Hindu religion and society from the top down. While missionary preaching and the missionaries' contact with low and outcaste Hindus led them in a direction away from higher caste culture, an initial and important countervailing influence was that of the Hindu pundit who for many inexperienced missionaries seemed to symbolize 'the real Hinduism' or 'the' Hindu tradition. James Vaughan (CMS) a missionary of twenty-one years' experience of work in India among lower and higher-caste Hindus, was well aware of general differences in their theology and outlook. In his influential book *The Trident, the Crescent and the Cross*, he drew a distinction between polytheistic and pantheistic beliefs and stated that, 'without doubt, the Pundits, and learned class, gravitate more towards pantheism than do the common people'.[39] If this is in fact the case, then it would help explain why missionaries, influenced by pundits (and in common with many other European commentators) favoured pantheism as the essence or kernel of Hinduism. Imbued with elitist assumptions about religion and exposed to high-caste pundits from the very beginning, young missionaries were likely to adopt a higher-caste approach and view of the world.[40]

The learning of the vernacular in this context also had important implications for the missionaries' effectiveness in communicating with low- and outcaste Hindus, and in understanding their religious views. Describing his life and experience as a missionary in Mysore, William Arthur (WMMS) explained how he had become increasingly concerned

[38] Kopf 1969: 125. See also Richard Young's exposition of what is known of his views in Young 1987: 276–93.

[39] Vaughan 1876: 65.

[40] See chapter 9.

with his pundit's Kannada which he believed was not entirely appropriate for work among the lower classes.

> Feeling that an intimacy with a dialect of the ryots [cultivating classes] was essential to that familiar intercourse which is the surest way to confidence, I determined on acquiring it; and, among other means, requested my munshi to converse in it for an hour each day. To this he stoutly demurred, saying that it was an indignity to a learned Brahman, to be asked to speak the vulgar and broken Kanarese of the ryot; but, on being threatened with having a ryot munshi placed by his side, he first laughed heartedly at the idea of a ryot munshi, and then said he always thought the purpose of education was to gain polish, not vulgarity; but that if I were not content with a Brahman's education, without that of a ryot in addition, why then he could become a ryot, or anything else I pleased.[41]

What therefore is striking in all of this evidence is the extent to which indigenous knowledge and understanding, and even the way in which missionaries were taught the language, was tied to the pundit's social context and limited horizons. Indigenous knowledge, like European knowledge of Hinduism had its limitations. As Kennedy emphasized, the brahman pundits sometimes had little knowledge of other high-caste Hindu traditions. Nor could the brahman pundit be expected to know (and often did not want to know) about the nature of belief and practice prevalent among the common people. Indeed, the newly-arrived missionary asking his munshi questions about Hinduism and Hindu belief was likely to be given an answer reflecting all of these limitations.

Some Complicating Factors

No doubt further research will continue to underline the missionaries' dependence on Hindu comment and pundits' views. However, one important qualification which needs to be kept in mind is the obvious point that the British missionaries had their own presuppositions and agenda and that the questions they asked helped predetermine the kind of answers they received. The parameters of the debate were dictated largely by missionary needs, and by what they were interested in learning. Their notions of religion and what aspects of thought and practice they thought important to understand were not necessarily the subjects which Hindus

[41] Arthur 1902: 207–8.

themselves would have chosen to discuss, or viewed as important for an understanding of Hindu religious and social life.

Second, while there were cases where the missionary's knowledge and understanding of Hinduism was greatly enriched as a result of a close and trusting relationship, this should not blind us to situations which were radically different, where the missionary was treated less readily with an honest and straightforward opinion. The relationship between some missionaries and pundits was clearly complex and, in some cases, pundits may have felt pressure to deliberately misrepresent or withhold inform- ation, or to tell their 'pupils' whatever they seemed to want to hear.

One of these undoubtedly more complex situations arose over the issue of Christian conversion. Missionary records are full of accounts of the way in which missionaries attempted to confront and convert their teachers.[42] They also contain evidence of the way in which pundits attempted to hose down the issue, often in the politest and least confrontational manner. But even if they avoided a response on the first occasion, the issue was still there as an undertone, and as a continuing part of the context in which the dialogue between missionary and pundit was taking place. One strat- egy on the part of the pundit was noted by the Rev. Warth (CMS), who declared that whenever he conversed upon religious topics or, in other words, attempted to convince his pundit of 'the excellence' of the Gospel scheme, his teacher became sleepy, in a way in 'which I have observed in others'.[43] Another strategy was to say nothing, or to pretend to agree. Thus, according to the Rev. Richard Allnutt (CMS), Hindu munshis employed by the CMS, feeling threatened as a result of conversions to Christianity in the Tinnevelly district, bound themselves 'with an oath before their gods' not to be persuaded by missionary arguments to become Christians. 'Their determination,' wrote Allnutt, 'is to assent to everything and believe nothing.'[44] Another strategy was to laugh (and then be accused of not taking religion seriously), to point to obstacles, or even to say that while Christianity is not for me, later generations of my family might be more interested in conversion.[45] Another perhaps more obvious reaction de- signed to resist pressure was not only to oppose Christianity, but to try to focus the missionary's attention on what he or she might think were the

---

[42] *MR* October 1837: 464; *HF*, Vol. VI, No. 4, October 1885: 105–6; Allnutt 1911: 52; Kennedy 1884: 32; J. S. Wardlaw 1856: 56.

[43] *MR* October 1837: 464.

[44] Allnutt 1911: 52.

[45] *HF*, Vol. VI, No. 4, October 1885: 105–6.

more commendable aspects of Hindu faith and practice; or even concoct an interpretation of Hindu custom which would make it appear more like some acceptable aspect of Christianity.[46] In some circumstances, therefore, there was probably pressure to misrepresent. Indeed, a frank and open confession of what one really believed or how one felt, in front of a missionary sahib (especially an employer) could be difficult. Thus, according to Murray Mitchell, Krishna Sastri, an able pundit 'much employed' by the mission, gave a series of lectures on the relative claims of Hinduism and Christianity; but later when the missionaries arrived, he abstained from attacking Christianity.[47]

But not all reactions were devious or completely negative. Over time some pundits became increasingly attracted to Christianity, thought about conversion, and in some comparatively rare cases were baptized.[48] This process of gradual rapprochement with Christianity inevitably raised in-depth questions not only about Christianity, but also about the nature of Hindu beliefs and practice.[49] In conversing with pundits who were questioning their own faith, or contemplating conversion, the missionaries themselves were almost invariably increasing their knowledge and understanding of the pundits' religious background. They eventually learnt a great deal through the life histories and struggles of these few men who joined the Christian church.

---

[46] This may be one of the considerations which helps to explain why Robert Noble's pundit attempted to 'Christianize' his depiction of Hindu practice. He claimed that during the great 'annual ablutions' taking place by the sea, the people washed their sins away, not by bathing, but by entering the temple and offering prayers for 'pardon of their sins' and, second, that they used certain prescribed forms of prayer *understood by them and many of the people*. However, Noble, who had already studied Telugu, made his own independent enquiries, and as a result, was given a very different explanation. The brahmans and 'other respectable natives' he consulted declared, 'without a single exception', that the people performed their ablutions not to cleanse themselves before going to the temple, but to wash away their sins. Furthermore, not even the brahmans could enlighten the missionary on the meaning of the prayers involved. While Noble suggests that this episode demonstrated the unreliability of English-speaking pundits, this conclusion is not inconsistent with the idea that the pundit was attempting to deflect criticism of Hindu practice by making it appear more like Protestant Christianity (Noble 1867: 138).

[47] Mitchell 1899: 113.

[48] A well-known example is Carey's first pundit, Ramram Basu, who, while attracted to Christianity, was never baptized. For the baptism of pundits see Ashcroft 1909: 31; Barnes 1897: 74; Cheriyan 1935: 179; *IW* May 1899: 108; *MN*, Vol. XI, 1845–47: 80.

[49] For a detailed account of the discussions that arose between the Rev. W. Smith and his munshi ('an eminent pundit') in Benares in the 1860s see *CMR* 1868: 369–70.

The Pundits' Influence on Missionary Knowledge of Hinduism

The effect that contact with pundits had on missionary views and models of Hinduism is obviously complex, and will be explored in greater detail when we examine the views and comments of individual missionaries in the chapters that follow. As we shall argue, the pundits' influence was reflected in their role in the translation of Hindu texts, in their comments and explanation of a whole range of Hindu customs, rituals and practices, and perhaps more importantly, in what they seemed to suggest was the essence or core of Hindu belief and practice. The argument here is not that all missionaries were affected by pundits' views, but that, *in some cases*, the pundits' comments were one element in a complex of factors affecting missionary constructions of Hinduism.

5

The Emergence of a Dominant Paradigm

Carey and Ward, two of the 'Serampore trio' (which also included the schoolteacher Joshua Marshman) had much to say about what came to be called Hinduism—Carey as the first of the Serampore commentators and Ward as author of several versions of the *History, Literature and Mythology of the Hindoos*. Both men have already been mentioned as having much in common. This included their Particular Baptist background, their enthusiasm for the rights and freedom of the individual, their sympathy for the anti-slavery and republican movements and, in keeping with many of these views, their deep-seated hatred of 'despotism and priest-craft' wherever it was found. But there were also differences. While, in his early years in India, Carey had little to guide his thoughts on the mysteries of Hindu religion and was heavily dependent on his experience and the comments of Hindu pundits, Ward was more fortunate (at least from his point of view) in the sense that he was able to build to a much greater extent on the perceptions of other Protestant commentators. Not only were the circumstances surrounding the arrival of the two men in India different, but their approach to the subject of Indian religion also varied. Carey, rooted in the empirical tradition, and without the comments of other Europeans, found it difficult to generalize. On the other hand, Ward (who also believed in the importance of direct observation) was less restrained in his comments and much more willing to generalize. Whether, alongside other factors, this was a result of his training and work as a journalist, it was he rather than Carey who was inclined to paint the general picture and write as a theoretician and systematizer in his depiction of Hindu religion.

(a) William Carey: A Pioneer's Journey of Exploration

William Carey was not the first British Protestant missionary in India,[1] but he was, perhaps, the greatest of the pioneers. A passionate advocate and

---

[1] Potts 1967: 5–6.

indefatigable worker in the cause of foreign missions, he was influential in Christian circles in England well before the establishment of the Serampore mission in 1800. Undoubtedly his greatest achievement before leaving for India was the publication in 1792 of his *Enquiry into the Obligations of Christians to Use Means for the Conversion of the Heathens.* This was the most significant apologia for Protestant missions to emerge at the beginning of the modern era, and was also one of the influences leading to the formation of the Baptist Missionary Society (BMS) some months later.[2] The foundation of the BMS was in itself significant as it was followed by the establishment of a number of other Protestant mostly denominational British associations with much the same purpose.

The *Enquiry* is also remarkable as an indicator of Carey's thinking only one year before his departure for India. As was common during this period, he divided the inhabitants of the world into Christian, Jewish, 'Mahometan', and pagan[3] and argued, on the basis of his own detailed tables giving populations and religion for all the continents and countries of the world, that nearly three-fifths of the world's inhabitants lived in 'pagan darkness'. After surveying the rise and growth of missions over the past 1,700 odd years, he remarked that

> It must undoubtedly strike every considerate mind, what a vast proportion of the sons of Adam there are, who yet remain in the most deplorable state of heathen darkness, without any means of knowing the true God, except what are afforded them by the works of nature; and utterly destitute of the knowledge of the gospel of Christ, or any means of obtaining it.[4]

Carey's reading of Cook's voyages was 'the first thing' to engage his mind to think of missions.[5] Initially, he had thought of going to Tahiti or West Africa, but not to India which appears to have been somewhat less in the forefront of his plans or imagination. His *Enquiry* refers to 'India *beyond the Ganges*', and 'Indostan', but these are places which he lists along with all other countries of the world, there being nothing in his treatise which suggests any special interest in India even then. Indeed, it was only late in 1792, after publication of the *Enquiry* and the formation of the BMS, when he met Dr John Thomas (recently returned from working as a Baptist missionary near Malda in the north of Bengal) that

---

[2] Smith 1885: 37–8.
[3] Carey 1792: 380.
[4] Ibid.: 62–3.
[5] Carey 1836: 18.

Carey appears to have become conscious of specific needs and opportunities for work in that part of the world. It was only at a meeting of the newly-established Baptist Missionary Society in October, where Thomas was present and made a plea for help, that Carey volunteered to go.[6] Like some of the least-prepared missionaries who followed in his footsteps, Carey had, therefore, very little time to make enquiries or to study or reflect on life and religion in Bengal before his departure from England five months later.

The period from the time of his arrival in India in 1793 until he was joined by Ward and Marshman and moved to Serampore near Calcutta seven years later was a crucial stage in developing his knowledge and understanding of Hinduism. After his appointment as Professor of Bengali and Sanskrit in the East India Company's College of Fort William in 1801 he became increasingly immersed in linguistic and literary pursuits which gave him additional insights into Hindu teachings and mythology. However, because of the pressure of teaching, the work of translation, the increasing need for pastoral care among an expanding Christian community, and other demands, he had less time for direct contact with ordinary Hindus and much less time, or even inclination, to write reports or comment on ordinary Hindu religious activities. Indeed, as he confessed in a note to his father, 'the Business of the Mission' gave him little time to write any letters at all.[7] While his knowledge, especially of Hindu scripture, continued to develop during the period from about 1800 until his death in 1834, it is his feelings, observations and comments on Hindu religious ideas and practice upon his arrival, while he was staying at Debhatta (in the Sundarbans south of Calcutta) and especially during his longer period of residence in Madnabati in northern Bengal (1794–1800), which give historians the best insight into his formative years and the variety of factors affecting his understanding and construction of Hinduism.

His letters and journals written during this period reveal, in some detail, his motivation, the way in which he acquired his knowledge and the way in which he was constantly attempting to interpret new ideas and experience. As part of this story, the unfolding of which is clearly apparent when we place these documents in chronological order, is the impact of newly-acquired information on his thinking and the surprising fragility of his tentative and changing interpretations.

---

[6] For an account of this meeting and the circumstances in which Carey volunteered for Bengal, see Carey 1926, Ch. 9; Smith 1885: 40–1.

[7] [RPC] WCC/7 Carey to Father, 23/11/1801.

What then did Carey know of 'Paganism' (as he called it) in India before his arrival there in 1793? How did he acquire his knowledge while in Bengal during the period 1793 to about 1800? What was the nature of his experience? Who were his informants and what were his sources of information? What overall impression of Hindu religion did he gain and attempt to convey to others?

Motivation and Love of Learning

Carey has often been acknowledged as a man of science, who even in childhood had been fascinated by plants and insects, and longed to know more about the natural world around.[8] His thirst for knowledge and delight in geology and zoology, as well as botany, extended to geography and different peoples, cultures and languages in other more remote parts of the world.[9] Like Captain Cook, whose journals he read with avidity and whose voyages inspired his interest in Tahiti, he too was an explorer—and one who, upon arrival in India, was determined to explore and discover more about the religions, customs and habits of the people he had come to serve.

Carey's motives in studying Hinduism, however, were not only the satisfaction of his own curiosity or the acquisition of knowledge for its own sake. Some of his supporters at home also wanted to know more about Hindu religion and expected their well-placed friend, ardent for the welfare of Hindu souls, to supply the answers. John Rippon, editor of the *Baptist Annual Register*, was, for example, one of those who wrote frequently, asking questions. 'Your letter is full of questions; to many of which I cannot reply,' quipped Carey. 'A life-time is too short, perhaps, to investigate the mythology of the Hindoos.'[10] Another reason for his searching enquiry into Indian religions was so that he and his colleagues would be more effective as evangelists in discussion and argument, and in persuading the Hindus to accept the Christian message. For example, referring to his reading of Hindu scriptures in 1796, he wrote that 'I find an acquaintance with them very useful, as I have never yet met with a Hindoo who

[8] Carey 1926, Ch. 31; Davidson 1990: 71–2; Smith 1885: 4.

[9] See especially Daniel and Hedlund 1993: 259–96. Thomas, Carey's brother, later recalled that 'I only recollect that he was from a boy, remarkably studious, deeply and fully bent on learning all he could, and always resolutely determined never to give up any point or particle of any thing in which his mind was set, till he had arrived at a clear knowledge and sense of the subject' (Carey 1836: 39).

[10] *Baptist Annual Register*, Vol. II, Carey to Rippon, 7/10/1795: 411; Vol. III, 10 /12/1796.

was proof against the absurdities of his own shasters.'[11] In addition, Carey was a practical reformer who in order to encourage the process of reform, and eliminate 'certain dreadful practices,' needed more of the relevant details, to make further inquiries and obtain more information both for propaganda purposes and as a basis for effective government intervention.

Nevertheless, alongside these stated and obvious reasons for wanting to study Hindu religious traditions, the reader can sense in his journal entries and correspondence an unbounded enthusiasm and thirst for knowledge generally, not only for information on religion or languages, but for a whole range of topics. His sense of delight in discovery, and wide-ranging interests in both science and the humanities are clearly apparent, as are his extraordinary powers of observation and attention to detail, his humility, including a sense of his own limitations in the task of discovery, his willingness to change his mind, and his determination to think things through. As becomes apparent to anyone who reads his diary, all of this, for Carey, was also a part of his inward spiritual journey, his effort to get to know God's created order, good and evil, to reflect upon his findings, and to do what little he could in working out his own eternal destiny. The outward and visible world, including Hinduism, had for Carey and prob-ably for many other missionaries of the period, its inward and very per-sonal meaning. It was part of an inner life which Carey nurtured through prayer, Bible readings and devotional works, such as those of Jonathan Edwards which he took with him during his long voyage out to India and which he continued to read after his arrival.

Early Impressions, Observation and New Learning

There is no evidence that Carey used the term 'Hinduism' before Ward had started using it in 1800. The 'pagans' he mentions in connection with India in his *Enquiry* are usually described as the 'heathen' in his subsequent letters and journals. What then did he know of Hindu pagans or heathens when he first sailed down the Hugli and stepped ashore in 1793?

According to Potts, 'an unsigned and undated (*c*.1789) essay on the Psalms in Carey's handwriting' shows his familiarity with the work of Sir William Jones before 1793.[12] There are, however, difficulties with this view, as, according to a more recent scholar, the only reference to Jones in the essay cites a work which was not published until 1799—six years after

[11] Carey to Fuller, 23/4/1796 in *Periodical Accounts* (*PA*), Vol. 1: 299. See also reports of his conversation with Hindus, Carey to P., 2/1/1797, *PA*, Vol. 1: 357.
[12] Potts 1967: 251.

Carey's departure for Bengal![13] If, therefore, the letter was originally written by Carey, the reference to Jones must have been an interpolation and, at least to date, there is no available evidence that Carey had read anything of Jones' work prior to the former's sailing for India.

What we do know for certain is that Carey had heard something (however unreliable) about India and its religion from his colleague, Dr John Thomas, the ex-surgeon who had worked for three years in Grant's mission at Gumalti (1787–89) in Malda, situated, as we have seen, in the extreme north-western part of Bengal. Thomas, who returned to England in 1792, was recruited by the BMS as one of its missionaries for the proposed Baptist mission in Bengal.[14] According to S. Pearce Carey, William Carey first heard Thomas give an account of Hindu customs and practice at a meeting of the BMS in January 1793, when, referring to India's spiritual and material needs, Thomas drew attention to 'its pilgrimages and penances, its swingings and sati' as well as to its Vedic hymns.[15] In a subsequent paper, published in both the *Baptist Annual Register* and *Periodical Accounts*, Thomas not only referred to his qualifications and experience as a missionary in Bengal, but also described in varying detail the religious life and condition of the Hindu population.[16]

He began with a straightforward though somewhat misleading description of Hindu scripture, including a reference to the four Vedas which he described as 'laws' and which he claimed were 'the fountain of *all* their books of theology' (his italics). He also referred to the eighteen Puranas which he thought were 'commentaries on the Vedas'. His fundamental purpose, however, appears to have been not only to awaken an interest in the Bengal mission, but to demonstrate its feasibility and the likelihood of its success. For this reason he chose to emphasize both similarities and differences between Hindu religious traditions on the one hand and Christianity on the other. One of the less attractive aspects of Hindu sacred literature was, he suggested, the books that held up for veneration characters which were 'very profligate' and which contained strange doctrines, 'evidently of an infernal origin which have a dreadful effect on their [the Hindus'] minds and manners'.[17] On the other hand, he gave a decided impression that there were points of contact between Hindus and

[13] Davidson 1990: 66.

[14] For the origin of the Baptist Missionary Society and its mission in Bengal, see Stanley 1993: 1–20.

[15] Carey 1926: 103.

[16] *PA*, Vol. 1: 13–32.

[17] *PA*, Vol. 1: 19.

Christians and ways in which missionaries could build on the Hindu doctrine and belief. 'That there is one great God, Omnipotent, Omnipresent, and Omniscient; that he is to be worshipped and served; that the soul is immortal; that all have sinned; and that some Atonement is necessary,' wrote Thomas, 'are truths commonly believed among them.' As an illustration of the felt necessity for 'atonement for sin' he referred to human sacrifice, which he described as 'rare', to voluntary tortures such as '*sitting in one position for years*', or walking on spikes, to performances at the *charak puja* and especially to hook-swinging which he described in detail and referred to as a ceremony which could be seen 'in almost every town once a year'.[18]

It is not clear how far these views influenced Carey, apart from the fact that, in his early correspondence, he made remarks similar to Thomas' about the mild and friendly character of the people and was interested in seeing for himself how far the people were seeking 'atonement for sin', an idea which he later explicitly rejected as a satisfactory explanation for hook-swinging. But whatever the case, and whatever ideas he carried with him, Carey's own dynamic and ongoing exploration of Hindu religious life began as soon as he arrived in Calcutta and so long as he continued to live and work in Bengal.

Apart from what he had heard before he arrived in India, Carey's earliest sources of information about what was to be known as Hinduism were derived from people like his servants, a few interpreters and from his own direct observation.

The progress of his knowledge and increasing insight into Hindu faith and practice can, at least to some extent, be mapped through his description of specific rituals and forms of worship, as well as in his comments on ideas and teachings. Indeed his journey of discovery was a presage of what happened to many Protestant missionaries in subsequent generations, who began with the outward activity, the sights and sounds, often at the grassroots level, and only gradually began to explore the inner life of Hindu thought and devotion as they mastered the language and became better acquainted either with the oral tradition or with Hindu religious writing.

Among the first, most 'striking' and 'singular' observances to attract Carey's attention were hook-swinging and sati, two of the more sensational rituals which appeared to be radically different from anything he had heard of in his own society. They were, moreover, public as opposed

[18] *PA*, Vol. 1: 27–9.

to private rituals and were therefore more within the purview of Europeans who were usually debarred, by the rules of pollution and purity, from entering high-caste Hindu homes.

A careful reading of Carey's successive accounts of hook-swinging in particular illustrates his powers of observation and the gradual increase in his knowledge and understanding of particular Hindu rituals.

A few weeks after his arrival, he remarked that 'the practice of swinging by the back is very common, I have seen the scars arising from it in the backs of many persons, and a person now lives in the same house with me who carries them in his flesh'.[19] Nearly four months later (while he was still at Debhatta in the Sundarbans) during the *charak puja* celebrations in April 1794 he wrote what was possibly his first eyewitness account of hook-swinging procedures.[20] 'Today,' he explained in his journal on 10 April, 'the cursed mode of Self-torturing was varied, a large pole was erected, and a Bamboo fixed across the top, and the swinging by Hooks fixed in the Back was attended to. I went out to see it.' After being suspended and swung around for what Carey estimated was half an hour, one of the swingers seemed especially keen to demonstrate some of the techniques involved. He showed Carey how the hooks were fastened, and asking another performer to participate, demonstrated how they were taken out of the shoulder and the wounds treated with a leaf.

When observing the practice at Madnabati in the following year Carey noted that the swinging there was practised only 'by the hurry, or lowest *cast* of the Hindoos'. And while at the same place a year later, he witnessed what he believed was the amazing strength of the human skin which prevented performers falling or being thrown to the ground. In a reply to a query from England, he explained that:

They use no precaution whatever except that in the swinging in the Southern parts they fasten a cloth round the waist; and the hooks have hold both of the cloth and the flesh: but even this is not done in this neighbourhood. I saw last year [1795] a heavy man swing. I saw the hooks put in. He swang [sic] off gently at first; but afterwards was whirled around very fast; and at last took a log of wood, near half a hundred weight, suspended by a cord in his mouth, with which he swung for near a quarter of an hour. The skin, by bearing all this weight, was drawn from its natural position at least six inches.... I have never heard of an instance in which any mischief followed.[21]

[19] Carey to church at Leicester, 25 /12/1793, *PA*, Vol. 1: 58–9. See also RPC, WCL, Vol. 10, Carey to Sisters, 4/12/1793.

[20] RPC, Carey's Journal, 10/4/1794.

[21] Answers to various Questions put to Mr Carey, *PA*, Vol. 1: 413.

While in these accounts, Carey was still not commenting on why he thought individuals swung (except that this was some sort of devotion) he was fascinated by the question of the origin of the practice, and consulted his pundit who said that the performance was nowhere commanded in the Shastras, but 'is entirely their own invention'. When giving an even more elaborate eyewitness account of swinging at Madnabati in 1798[22] he described, in greater detail, the preparations for the exhibition, the offerings laid carefully at the base of the pole, the precise way in which the hooks were inserted, the way in which the man was raised for swinging, and the treatment of his wounds after the event was over. On this latter occasion his account was not only much more elaborate, but his questions and comments more reflective and searching. In trying to discover 'the origin and intention' of the custom he was able to employ his increasing language skills, confer with brahmans and probably others, and come to the somewhat tentative conclusion that hook-swinging 'is not considered in the light of an atonement [as Thomas had argued]; but as a custom or show: it is however generally done in consequence of a vow made in distress'.

The importance of first-hand experience as a factor in Carey's increasing understanding of Hindu practice can also be seen in his comments on sati. In his earliest remarks he referred to what he had been told about the custom and about scriptural references to it. In a letter to his church in Leicester in 1793 he wrote that 'Burning women with their husbands, is a practice too frequent. We were at Nuddea (an eminent place for learning) last Lord's day, and were informed that about a month ago two women devoted themselves in this manner.'[23] In 1795 Colebrooke quoted Sanskrit works recommending sati in his article entitled 'On the Duties of a Faithful Hindu Widow' in Asiatic Researches.[24] Three years later, Carey, who had possibly seen Colebrooke's work, referred to the same subject of Sanskrit texts approving sati in a letter to John Sutcliff in England.[25] By that stage Carey had studied Sanskrit[26] and was able to read some of the Hindu scriptures for himself. 'Having just read a Shanscrit book, called Soordhee Sungraha, which is a collection of laws from the Shasters,' he wrote, 'I shall give you an extract from it.' In it, the author quoted passages from

[22] RPC, Carey to Sutcliff, 5/4/1798; and PA, Vol. 1: 495–97.

[23] Carey to Church in Leicester, 25/12/1793 in PA, Vol. 1: 56–8.

[24] Asiatic Researches, Vol. IV, 1795: 209–19.

[25] Carey to S (Olney) 10/10/1798 in PA, Vol. 1: 473–76.

[26] Carey to BMS, 28/12/1796 in PA, Vol. 1: 348.

144 IMAGINED HINDUISM

different Sanskrit sources which, for the most part, laid down the conditions in which sati could take place.

Even by this time, Carey had not witnessed a sati or felt what he later described as the 'horror' for himself. However, an opportunity to witness the event came by accident four years later when, accompanied by a friend (probably the Rev. Nathaniel Forsyth, the first LMS missionary in India) he was returning from Calcutta. In a passage which has become one of the best-known missionary descriptions of a Hindu practice, Carey described in graphic detail his first sighting, inner turmoil and feeling, and personal involvement in attempting to save the widow's life.[27] Like Bernier and Job Charnock, the reputed founder of Calcutta, he was therefore an active participant as well as observer attempting to influence the outcome of events as they unfolded before him.

Seeing that preparations were underway for the widow's burning, he enquired as to whether the act was voluntary or forced (an issue which raised in the mind of many Christians the question of whether it was suicide or murder). Having been told that it was 'perfectly voluntary' he indicated he did not believe it and told the people he was determined to stay 'to see the murder'. Then he appears to have changed his mind acting as if he really thought the woman's action was voluntary. He urged her not to throw away her life, and to fear nothing, for no evil would follow her refusing to burn.

Then followed his very graphic description of the woman's death—a description which reminds the reader of travellers' accounts depicting the sati as the tragic heroine. In spite of his feelings of disgust and horror Carey could not help noting the woman's composure, her dignity, attention to the details of the ritual and determination to see things through. However, in his view, there was still some hope that, as the flames began to torment her body, the sati would change her mind and leap or rush for safety. But to his absolute horror he saw that there were bamboo poles pinning her down 'like the levers of a press' and making any escape impossible. Protesting vehemently against the use of force and unable to bear watching any longer, the two missionaries left the scene—Carey, no doubt, never to forget, and even more determined to suppress the practice.

Carey's enquiries into the nature and limits of Hindu religion, were not, however, confined to the more dramatic or 'singular' rituals such as hook-swinging or those, like sati or the drowning of infants at Sagar, involving

[27] Carey to Ryland, 1/4/1799, *PA*, Vol. 2: 26–7. This account was subsequently quoted in Dodwell 1958: 134. See also Carey 1926: 176–77; Walker 1926: 45–6.

the death and apparent suffering of individuals. He was also very particular in his observation and note-taking on different forms of Hindu celebration and worship. His correspondence and journals record a wide range of festivals and other events which came under his personal observation. Apart from references to what he observed at the *charak puja*, they include descriptions of festivals in honour of Sarasvati, the goddess of learning, Krishna celebrations, a visit to a temple while on a preaching tour and a lengthy eyewitness account of sun-worship rituals.[28]

Carey was also involved in discussion with pundits and others about more abstract Hindu teachings and philosophical ideas. These included Hindu ideas of life after death, the role of imagery in the inner reflection and life of the worshipper and Hindu ideas of creation, the world and the natural order.

Soon after his arrival in Calcutta, and while learning Bengali, he spent some time with his munshi on a translation of the Old Testament into Bengali. On 27 January 1794, the very day in which he and his assistant had corrected the first chapter of Genesis, he received a visit from a pundit and another man from Nadia—a well-known centre of Sanskrit learning. Carey showed the visitors his translation and noted that the pundit seemed much pleased with the account of the creation, 'only they [the Hindus] have an imaginary place somewhere beneath the Earth, and he thought that should have been mentioned likewise'. Carey, ever the man of the enlightenment and modern science, explained that 'the Earth was a Planet, & that Heavens and Earth included all the Material Creation'. He then goes on in his diary to describe Hindu views—a view of cosmology and the cosmograph which coincides with teachings on the subject in the *Vishnu Purana*.[29] These included the notion that the world is composed of 'Seven Deeps or Lands'—a theory which Carey illustrated with a sketch. This shows land in the middle, surrounded by water, which in turn is surrounded by a 'deep' or circle of land, which is also surrounded by water and so on. Carey also emphasized that Hindu chronology, including the idea of the four 'jugas' or ages of the world, each of which is terminated by a Deluge or some other universal calamity, was 'equally ridiculous'. These accounts, he continued, 'are so connected with their religious opinions that the Mosaic account of the creation, and Biblical Chronology are very strange to them'.

---

[28] See *PA*, Vol. 1, Journal entries, 3/2/1794: 167; 16/3/1794: 170; 26 May 1794: 178; Carey to S., 5/4/1799: 404–6.

[29] For a summary of these ideas see Eliade 1987, Vol. 4: 109–10.

Carey's interest in much the same questions continued, and was something he pursued in the textual material. Writing to Dr Rippon from Madnabati in December 1796 he remarked that he had been several days extracting 'the Hindoo account of the beginning of the world', from the *Mahabharata*. This material he explained, gave 'an account of the Hindoo notions of the first creation of man and peopling of the earth'. But, he confessed, this was 'the more popular account' and he still had a lot more work to do.

> I have not yet seen the account, so often mentioned by writers, of the four casts of Hindoos being produced from the four parts of Burmmha's body; it may be probably found in some other Shasters; but it is a lifetimes' work to get them all and read them; not to mention that a very difficult language, viz the Shanserit, must first be learned.[30]

It was the textual aspect of Carey's research into Indian religion (as opposed to the more experiential approach) which gradually took over and became predominant—especially after his appointment as Professor of Sanskrit and Bengali at Fort William College in 1801. It was after that that Carey and his colleagues, making full use of the availability of Hindu pundits, began work on translating the *Ramayana* and other texts—the first volume of the *Ramayana* being published in 1806.[31]

In the meantime, however, Carey's increasing skills in conversation in the colloquial languages enabled him to explore, still further, some of the attitudes and ideas behind Hindu practice. One of his conversations was, for example, with a brahman during the Sarasvati festival in Malda in January 1795. Curious to know more about what Hindus thought about their idols, he engaged the man in conversation. The latter disputed the idea that the idol was some form of representation and told Carey quite bluntly that '*this image was God*'.[32] Later in the year, while at Madnabati, Carey thought he had discovered more clues as to why the common people worshipped subordinate deities. The people, he wrote,

> universally tell me that their deptas [subordinate gods], whose images they worship, have a power to afflict their persons, to spoil their crops, and to kill their children, and will infallibly do this if they neglect to make offerings to them; so that from what I can learn, bodily and carnal fear is the only spring of all their worship.[33]

[30] Carey to Rippon, 10/12/1796, *The Baptist Annual Register*, Vol. 111: 62–5.
[31] RPC IN13, Carey to Fuller, 18/11/1806.
[32] Carey to Fuller, 30/1/1795, *PA*, Vol. 1: 130–31.
[33] Carey to BMS, 30/12/1795, *PA*, Vol. 1: 227.

Then again on another occasion he wrote in his journal that he had 'frequent opportunities of discoursing with the natives' about the 'horrid self-tormenting modes of worship such as falling on spikes of iron, dancing with threads or bamboos thrust through their sides, etc.'[34]

Pundits as Consultants

Especially important in the growth of Carey's understanding of Hinduism were his pundits. They were not only his tutors in languages, and in the translation of texts, but were also one of his most important sources of information.

The effect of his pundit's comments in clarifying Hindu practice can, for example, be illustrated in his changing ideas about what was done with the image of the deity after worship. In a letter to a friend in Leicester in March 1795 referring to the Hindus generally he wrote that 'their idols are numerous' and that 'when the season of their idolatrous worship is over, the idol is always cast into some water'. However, when challenged on this issue by a correspondent from England nearly two years later, Carey consulted his pundit.[35] He confirmed the questioner's suggestion that some images were 'stationary' and explained that these images, of stone or other materials, were found especially in temples dedicated to Shiva and Kali. He continued:

> My pundit informs me that these are made by some King, or other great person, and are endowed with lands to maintain worship for the welfare of that family, and that during this time the officiating Brammhan makes every day small representative images of earth, which he worships at the river or waterside, and afterwards throws into the water with flowers and many other ceremonies.

It was one of Carey's pundits who explained how, during the *charak puja*, sannyasis who threw themselves from a great height onto spikes below, managed to avoid serious injury;[36] and it was also Carey's pundits who declared that neither hook-swinging nor sati were sanctioned in the Shastras.[37]

---

[34] Journal, 6–10/4/1795, *PA*, Vol. 1: 197.
[35] Carey to R.B. (Leicester), 12/3/1795, *PA*, Vol. 1: 138, 416.
[36] Answers to various questions put to Mr Carey, *PA*, Vol. 1: 410–11.
[37] Ibid.: 423.

Carey's first pundit, one who appears to have been important for his initial and developing understanding of Indian religions, was Ramram Basu. One of John Thomas' unbaptized 'converts', Basu was a kayastha by caste and hence someone who might be expected to be more critical of brahmans and brahmanical culture than the usual pundits, most of whom were brahmans.[38] Basu was 35 years old when he was employed by Carey as his Bengali teacher in 1793. Thomas described him as 'a person of more than ordinary capacity' and Carey had increasing admiration and respect for him as time progressed, until suddenly in 1796, he felt obliged to dismiss him 'for the credit of the gospel', because Basu had committed adultery and procured an abortion.[39]

During Carey's first three years in Bengal, however, the relationship between the two men appears to have become increasingly close. Writing to the BMS in October 1793 Carey declared that 'Ram Boshoo still keeps close to us; I have had much conversation with him, and find him a very sensible well-informed man.'[40] Four months later when building his house at Debhatta in the Sundarbans the missionary wrote that, 'Though deprived of a personal intercourse with my European friends, I have at least one religious friend, and that is *Ram Ram Boshoo*; he has indeed much timidity, but is a man of very good understanding, and well-informed.'[41] After Basu's dismissal in 1796 Carey again expressed his admiration for his 'natural abilities'[42] and five years later he decided to re-employ him as one of his pundits at Fort William College.[43] Apart from Basu's abilities as a teacher of Bengali and translator it appears from this and other evidence that he was much valued as someone who was 'well informed' and who could, therefore, answer some of Carey's questions about Bengali religion and society.[44] After Basu's dismissal Carey immediately employed another pundit whom he consulted on a number of religious issues.[45] Also significant for Carey's increasing insight into Indian religion and especially Hindu scripture was his selection and employment of pundits after his appointment as lecturer in Bengali at the College of Fort William in 1801. The most famous of these was Mrtyunjay Vidyalankar, one of India's finest

---

[38] Thomas to BMS, *PA*, Vol. 1: 19–20.

[39] Carey to Fuller, 17/6/1796, *PA*, Vol. 1: 303; Potts 1967: 82.

[40] Carey to BMS, 25/11/1793, *PA*, Vol. 1: 65.

[41] Carey to BMS, 15/2/1794, *PA*, Vol. 1: 74–5.

[42] Carey to Fuller, 17/6/1796, *PA*, Vol. 1: 303.

[43] Carey 1926: 206.

[44] Carey's Journal, 30/1/1794, *PA*, Vol. 1: 166–67.

[45] Carey to Fuller, 17/6/1796, *PA*, Vol. 1: 303.

Sanskrit scholars of the time, who was able to shed a great deal of further light on the question of how far sati was either enjoined or discouraged by Sanskrit texts.[46]

Interpretations and Changing Evaluation

If, then, these were Carey's observations and primary sources of information, what did he come to believe about Hindu religion or religions, and how was this phenomenon represented in his letters and journals?

Before commenting on this issue, it is important to note that, unlike his colleague William Ward, Carey wrote no major *systematic* treatise on Hindu religion. Though he had drawn attention to 'the grand picture' and organized the whole of the religious world in his *Enquiry*, his journals and correspondence, at least up until 1800, are very different. This is partly because his journal, in particular, is more like an inner dialogue in which he was having a private conversation with himself, than an exposition meant to be read as widely as possible. However, for whatever reason, his thinking, especially during this earlier period, appears to have been more exploratory and tentative and more like that of an astonished traveller than that of a commentator wanting to make clear-cut, bold or even dogmatic statements.

Nevertheless, though his comments were mostly scattered and anecdotal, it is possible to follow the way in which he was beginning, not only to accumulate knowledge, but to reflect on its implications and develop clearer outlines of an overall interpretation.

First, it appears from correspondence in July 1797 that, by then, he was beginning to draw a distinction between the religion of the Hindus and the religion of tribal peoples. Referring to the 'Hill People' of Bihar, he remarked that 'they are said to be a small people, and utterly distinct from Hindoos and Musselmans, in their language, manners and ways of thinking, having no cast: yet they are surrounded on every side with Hindoos'.[47]

Second, if in Carey's view there were differences between tribals, such as the hill people of Bihar, and Hindus, there were also differences in religious ideas and practice among the Hindus themselves, and in the different districts even within Bengal. Writing to Sutcliff he remarked that

---

[46] Bose 1960: 128–29; Kopf 1969: 205–6; Potts 1967: 148, 232. For his activities in the work of translation while in Carey's employment, see Hatcher 1996: 143–50.

[47] Carey to Ryland, 6/7/1797, *PA*, Vol. 1: 377.

It may be observed once for all that the Hindoo modes of worship, and their other customs differ considerably in different districts, which may best account for the apparently discordant and contradictory relations by several writers on the same subjects, whose descriptions have been taken from the practice in their respective neighbourhoods: while for the like reason mine may not exactly accord with any of them.[48]

On other occasions Carey pointed out that the minutiae of Hindu worship was so various that scarcely any of the Hindus themselves could give 'a tolerable account' of them.[49] For example, it seemed to him that the manner of sun worship was 'in some respects different in different places',[50] that the way in which hook-swinging was conducted was different in the southern and northern districts of Bengal, and that different Hindus believed different things about the possibility or nature of life after death.[51]

Third, reflecting on the nature of Hindu religion, he felt he could also draw a fundamental distinction between the religion of the ignorant and the learned. For example, in 1795 when he was able to converse more freely with the people, he declared that 'the common people, and the majority of Bramins account these idols to be so many deities: but the most learned acknowledge only one'.[52] The inference here and in some of Carey's other correspondence was that there was a difference between what was in sacred literature (known and understood by 'the most learned') and the belief and practice of the common people and brahmans also ignorant of what the scriptures contained. Implicit in this distinction is the idea familiar to Carey and others that there was a marked difference between the religion of the ignorant and unenlightened and religion as perceived by the enlightened few.

This view, which privileged literacy, erudition and the written text over devotion and the understanding among the illiterate, re-emerged in a convenient and slightly different form in Carey's proposals in the early nineteenth century. Disturbed by the incidence of sati and infanticide, he submitted a memorial to Wellesley's government in 1802 on murders committed under 'the pretence of religion'. As the East India Company was committed to a policy of non-interference in Hindu religious affairs, it

[48] Carey to Sutcliff, 5/4/1799, *PA*, Vol. 1: 493.
[49] Carey to BMS, 3–5/1/1794, *PA*, Vol. 1: 72.
[50] Carey to Sutcliff, 16/1/1798, *PA*, Vol. 1: 404.
[51] Carey to BMS, 18/3/1795, *PA*, Vol. 1: 146.
[52] Carey to R. B., 12/3/1795, *PA*, Vol. 1: 138.

greatly strengthened Carey's case (and the purpose of subsequent reformers including the Baptist missionary James Peggs and Rammohan Roy) if he and others argued that the so-called 'religious' customs of sati and of infanticide at Sagar were instances of 'pretended' as opposed to 'real' religion. This laid the basis for the next step in the argument that practices could be suppressed safely and without the Company having to abandon its existing policy of 'religious' neutrality. As we have seen, Carey was already becoming increasingly convinced that these 'murders' had no genuine sanction in the Shastras. In other words, like many other missionaries, he was simply placing an emphasis on the long-held Protestant tradition, that 'real religion' was scriptural and that usage or custom by itself, without a sanction or a basis in scripture, did not constitute the essence of 'real' religion.

Fourth, and in spite of the differences between elite and popular traditions, and variations in belief and practice among Hindus, Carey felt he could, after a number of years, detect some sort of cohesion or basic unity in what he eventually described as 'the Hindoo system'.[53] The brahmans, he believed, played a key role in maintaining the overall structure. Having described the brahman system of ranking in Hindu society (varna) he explained in a letter in July 1795 that 'no one of an inferior cast himself can make any offering to their god, but the common people bring their offerings to the Brammhan, who offers it to the Debta'.[54]

On another occasion he pointed to what he saw as the widespread veneration for brahmans and 'implicit obedience to all their dictates'.[55] This he argued was partly because of the traditional practice, still operating despite the introduction of British rule, whereby brahmans exercised the right of imposing fines 'on every other tribe' as a form of 'atonement' for even the most trivial offence. Furthermore, reverence for and fear of brahmans among the populace was reinforced by stories about the risks involved in offending brahmans and receiving a brahman's curse and the belief in their supernatural power.

In addition it appears to have been Carey's conviction that the unity of what he belatedly described as 'the Hindu system' was not merely structural. This view is reflected in a letter written in 1798, where he seems to suggest that fatalism, leading to indifference and moral apathy, was a common and unifying belief.

---

[53] Kopf 1969: 125.
[54] Carey to Ryland, 6/7/1797, PA, Vol. 1: 378.
[55] Carey to P., 23/11/1798, PA, Vol. 1: 483–85.

The Hindoos most generally believe themselves to be a sort of machines, which God acts upon in a physical manner, and that they are not accountable for their own actions. If a man be detected in thieving, or charged with murder, he will generally answer that his *Kopal*, or forehead, is bad. By this they mean that they were designed by God to commit such crimes: for it is a common opinion among Hindoos that the fate of every man is written in his forehead; and including in that opinion all moral actions, as well as their providential situations, they conclude that all their actions are chargeable on God, and not on themselves. This doctrine is almost constantly avowed when we attempt to press on them the sinfulness of sin, and the guilt of their conduct.[56]

Thus while recognizing religious differences among Hindus, there are some indications that Carey was, if anything, moving towards a unitary and brahmanical model more in line with Ward's exposition. What then was the relationship between Carey's increasing knowledge and understanding of Hinduism on the one hand and his evaluation of it on the other? What difference did his discoveries make to the way he judged it as a good or evil system?

J. N. Farquhar, a missionary commentator writing in the early part of the twentieth century, was too sweeping in his generalization when he declared that the more the early missionaries knew about Hinduism 'the more they disliked it.' But he was certainly correct in the case of William Carey. The more Carey knew of Hindu belief, and especially practice, the more he disliked it.

His first painful disappointment was with the character and moral behaviour of the great majority of people which, in his opinion, contrasted with the 'sublime Benevolence' of some passages in Hindu scripture.[57] Reflecting on the changes in his views, he explained to his friend Morris that, when first introduced amongst 'the natives', he formed 'a much better opinion of their morals, and customs, than I ought to have done; and, I believe, some others have formed a worse opinion than they ought'. They

[56] Ibid.: 482.

[57] His initial admiration for their 'simplicity of manners' and 'harmless behaviour' was soon overwhelmed by his impression of them as he settled down as planter and padre at Madnabati. Reflecting on the Hindus' character in his journal, he deplored especially their lack of sincerity, lying and avarice (RPC, Journal, 1–3/7/1794). In a letter to his old friend Robert Brewin, he even went so far as to declare that 'stories of the Hindus benevolence, humanity and meekness' were 'all false', and existed 'only in the doctrines of the shasters, which have been neither seen nor heard by the thousandth part of the people' (RPC, IN 13, Carey to Brewin, 12/3/1795; see also Carey to Arnold, 13/3/1795, in the same collection).

were 'certainly a very perfidious and deceitful people, bound in the chains of numerous superstitions, and very servile in their behaviour'. But he added, 'many of them are men of good learning'.[58]

Part of the problem (as Carey saw it at least at this time) was that 'the men of good learning' had so little influence on ignorant brahmans and the common people who continued to practice customs which he discovered were worse and more cruel than anything he had imagined. As early as April when commenting on the rituals of self torment associated with the *charak puja* he declared that:

Their horrid and idolatrous transactions have made such an impression on my mind as cannot, I think, be easily eradicated. Who would grudge to spend his life and his all, to deliver an otherwise amiable people from the misery and darkness of their present wretched state![59]

It was during the same year that he was confronted for the first time with visible evidence of infanticide. When riding near Malda he saw the remains of an infant who had died from deliberate exposure. This gruesome finding must surely have been an unforgettable incident which linked Carey's own personal experience with what became the wider debate among missionaries, officials and others about the practice of infanticide, including the custom whereby previously childless couples sacrificed their first-born infant to the goddess Ganga.[60] Adding to the impact of these encounters was Carey's experience of witnessing the burning of the widow in 1799. This was followed by his accidental presence, when he was on a preaching tour, at a similar event where a 14-year-old girl was burnt at the village of Chattera in August 1800.[61]

[58] Carey to Morris, 14/8/1795, *PA*, Vol. 1: 213.

[59] Journal, 11/4/1794, *PA*, Vol. 1: 174.

[60] Potts 1967: 140.

[61] Carey to Ryland, 15/8/1899, *PA*, Vol. 2: 78. As is well known, Carey was one of the chief advocates of suppression. In 1802, when submitting a memorial to Government on the evil of infanticide, he expressed the hope that 'other murders committed by the Hindoos, under the pretence of religion' would also be prohibited. George Udny, a long-time friend of the Baptists and member of the Governor-General's Council, asked Carey to supply the Council with full information on the practice, while Buchanan, Vice-Provost of Fort William College, also sought Carey's best advice 'respecting the way of putting a stop to women burning' so that he could put forward concrete suggestions to Wellesley, the Governor-General. Shortly afterwards, Carey, together with his colleagues, converts and pundits from Serampore and Fort William attempted to record, as accurately as possible, the number of satis which occurred each year within a thirty-mile radius of Calcutta (Ward 1817–20, Vol. IV: 144–45). He also used his position as a lecturer at Fort William College

Lastly, not only was Carey increasingly confronted, at an experiential and emotional level, with 'certain dreadful practices,' but also appears to have become increasingly disillusioned with what he found in Hindu scripture. Soon after arrival he bewailed the fact that so many millions of Hindus were ignorant of their own scriptures. In 1795 he argued, in a letter to Morris, that Hindu theology was much more refined than popular ideas and practice.[62] While out preaching a few months later, he remarked that there were 'many good observations and rules, such as ought to be regarded' in both the Hindu Shastras and in the Koran, but that they did not inform Hindus how God can forgive sin consistently with his justice, and save sinners in a way which justice and mercy can harmonize.[63] In this and in later remarks on Vishnu's avatars[64] he was critical of the fact that there was no resonance in these teachings and ideas of one of the central concerns of evangelical theology. In other words, the problem was not so much what Hindu scripture included, but what was left out.

However, as he became more familiar with Hindu popular literature in particular, the tone of his remarks became increasingly critical. For example, in a letter to Fuller in 1796, he remarked:

As may shew the depraved state of this people I shall now and then note some parts of their Mythology, as I find it represented in their shasters, which I have now begun to read, and which fill me with astonishment when I think that they are seriously believed by any rational creatures... The fears, quarrels, lusts etc of these *debtas* [subordinate gods] also, as recorded in their shasters, furnish arguments against them.[65]

A few years later, Carey's outrage at what he saw as the malign, deliberate and unfair criticism of 'the inspired writings' (the Bible) by some of the more strident 'infidel opposers of the Gospel' provoked in him a further blunt statement as to what he thought about Hindu scripture. Hindu feeling and opposition to missionary preaching was greatly intensified by the baptism of Krishna Pal, Gookul and their families at Serampore

---

to collect from pundits various texts referring to sati in the Shastras. These tended to confirm his earlier impression that the self-immolation of widows, though countenanced by Hindu law, was in no way commanded by it (Ingham 1956: 45).

[62] Carey to Morris, 14/8/1795, *PA*, Vol. 1: 213.
[63] Journal, 13–19/4/1795, *PA*, Vol. 1: 199.
[64] Carey to BMS, 11/1/1796, *PA*, Vol. 1: 229–30.
[65] Carey to Fuller, 23/4/1796, *PA*, Vol. 1: 299. See also his letter to Rippon, *Baptist Annual Register*, 10/12/1796, Vol. 111: 61–5.

in 1801. In a letter to Sutcliff in March 1802 Carey expressed surprise and exasperation at seeing how readily the more vociferous Hindu critics picked 'every flaw' they could in 'the inspired writings', and even distorted their meaning, so that they might make them appear inconsistent. And yet, he wrote,

> These very persons will labour to reconcile the grossest contradictions in the Writings which the Hindoos account sacred, and will stoop to the meanest artifices in order to apologize for the numerous glaring lies, and horrid violations of all decorum and decency, which abound in almost every page...but it seems, that anything will do with some people except the Word of God. These men ridicule the figurative language of Scripture, but will use allegory...to support the merit of the most worthless books that were ever published.

If then Carey was becoming increasingly disillusioned with the content, tone and character of Hindu religious literature, why did he spend increasing time in later years working on the translation of the *Ramayana* and other Hindu religious texts into English?

The story of how Carey and other members of the 'Serampore trio' became involved in the translation of Hindu classics has been told elsewhere and noted in a previous chapter. What is important for our purpose is Carey's motivation. Certainly, in proposing the translation of all the great Sanskrit classics, he believed he would be contributing to a more general knowledge and understanding of Indian tradition. This is evident from a much-celebrated speech he delivered in Sanskrit in September 1804. Like other scholars of his day he accepted the prevailing view of linguistic unity, including the notion that Sanskrit was the parent of the south Indian family of languages.[66] Speaking before the Governor-General, the principal civil and military officers of the Presidency, and 'many learned natives', he strongly defended the work of Wellesley's Fort William College, including the teaching of Sanskrit. This ancient language, he argued, was not only the parent of the modern vernaculars, but 'enriches the world with the history, learning and science of a distant age.[67]

But clearly Carey's purpose in spending so much time in translating Sanskrit texts was not only 'to enrich the world' with the knowledge and wisdom of the ancients, but also to encourage Christian mission. The most outstanding contribution that Hindus had made to the world through

[66] Trautmann 1997: 152.
[67] Smith 1885: 167.

Sanskrit literature was not, according to Carey, to be found in their religious texts, but in science and other non-religious subjects. Indeed, he appears to have believed that the more Christian readers knew about the character and values as represented in Hindu religious classics, such as the *Ramayana*, the more they would discern the superiority of their own tradition. Pointing out in a letter to Rippon in 1796 that the *Ramayana* was written in verse he went on to acknowledge its literary merits. 'The poetry,' he explained, 'is excellent, and appears to me, in its composition and subject, more like Homer's Iliad than any thing else.'[68] But in spite of its literary merits, a reading of the *Ramayana*, and indeed the rest of the *Mahabharata*, would, Carey believed, lead Rippon to 'bless God' for the Bible. 'Could I send accounts of the triumph of the Cross of our Lord Jesus Christ over these deep rooted idolatries, I am sure it would gladden your heart more than the longest detail of their religious books and vulgar opinions.'

Referring to Hindu religious books in his letter to Sutcliff in 1802, he remarked:

> I should think it time lost to translate any of them and only a sense of Duty excites me to read them—an idea however of the advantage that the friends of religion may obtain by having these mysterious sacred writings exposed to public view which have maintained their celebrity so long merely by being kept from the inspection of any but Brahmans.[69]

Linked with the idea of exposing Hindu scriptures to view were also financial and other considerations—at least in connection with Carey and Marshman's involvement in the official project of translating Hindu scriptures in the combined government, Asiatic Society and Serampore endeavour. This project was undoubtedly good for mission in a variety of ways. It helped raise the status and increase the good name of the mission in the highest circles. It allowed the missionaries increased access to the services of pundits and other facilities, and it also earned the mission an extra Rs 150 per month as payment for the missionaries' contribution to the project.[70] Both Carey and Marshman, the two missionaries involved, were well aware of the irony in the situation. Carey hoped the profits arising from this work, 'manufactured by Satan', would enable the mission

---

[68] Carey to Rippon, 10/12/1796, *The Baptist Annual Register*, Vol. 111: 65.

[69] Carey to Sutcliff, 17/3/1802, *PA*, Vol. 2: 233–34.

[70] Kejariwal 1988: 106.

to support two or three stations 'to destroy his empire'.[71] Marshman, writing in his journal, remarked that

> it makes us smile…when we consider that Satan will probably here be overshot in his own bow. He certainly did not intend when he dictated those vile and destructive fables, that the publishing of them to the enlightened world, should supply a fund for circulating the oracles of Truth.[72]

Carey's increasing dislike of Hindu teachings and practice brought him closer to the kind of position as outlined in William Ward's extraordinarily influential *Account of the Writings, Religion and Manners of the Hindoos*— a series of volumes the first edition of which was published in Serampore in 1811. In the long process of writing these volumes and seeing them through the press, Ward claimed that he had had the assistance of Carey 'in every proof-sheet', and that 'his opinion and mine is in almost every particular the same'.[73] While, as we shall see, there were certainly some differences between Carey's understanding and shifting evaluation of Hinduism (at least during the period 1793 to 1800) and Ward's subsequent *Account*, the two men were beginning to represent elements of Hinduism in similar ways and along lines which were later incorporated into the dominant Protestant paradigm echoed in the works especially of Bengal missionaries during the first half of the nineteenth century. And while, as Kopf has argued, Carey and Duff (see chapter 6) had very different ideas of education, they were not so far apart in their attitude towards Hindu moral behaviour, Hindu gods and religious teaching.

Carey was already beginning to think of Hindu religions as 'the Hindu religion' and to describe it as 'a system'. Like many other orientalist scholars he was also beginning to believe that the brahmans were extraordinarily powerful and a key to the whole 'system'.

Lastly, he was beginning to develop a critique of Hindu religion and 'idolatries' which would be still further developed and repeated, with slight variations, in much missionary literature throughout the nineteenth century. This critique was not based solely on the idea that Hindu teachings were false or inadequate in that they failed to acknowledge the seriousness of sin or Jesus Christ as the only hope for sinners. It was also based on other general enlightenment and/or evangelical principles. These ideas, some of which have been discussed in the introduction, included the ideas of rationality as defined by Western philosophers such as Bacon, Locke and

---

[71] Davidson 1990: 206.
[72] Quoted in Potts 1967: 91.
[73] Ward to Fuller, 12/1/1809, *PA*, Vol. 3: 558–59.

Hume. They also included ideas of humanity and justice (as reflected in, for example, the anti-slavery movement) and beliefs about sexuality and sexual purity as reflected in sections of British society even before the rise of the evangelical movement.

Many of Carey's objections were, as we have seen, to popular practice and the way in which a variety of Hindu deities were portrayed, or supposed to depict, the true nature of God. In this way he pointed to their moral defects, 'fears, quarrels and lusts etc' as failings that furnished arguments against them.[74] Second, his assumptions about the benefits and importance of the God-given gifts of rationality and reason were never far below the surface. According to one entry in Ward's diary during the *charak puja* celebrations of April 1802, for example, Carey asked one of the swingers when he came down at the end of his 'performance' why he was 'such a great fool'.[75] The more he read the more he was astonished at the 'absurdities' and irrationality as evidenced in Hindu mythology and scripture.

But the immoral behaviour of deities and irrationality as displayed in various aspects of Hindu religion were, for Carey, of much less moment than the cruelty and inhumanity it seemed to encourage. The evidence of infanticide, the burning of widows (even despite their wishes), the many cruel forms of self-inflicted punishment, such as those he witnessed on many occasions during the *charak puja*, the death of pilgrims through starvation and disease, and the callous exposure of the sick and dying on the banks of rivers, these were aspects of Hindu religion which disturbed him deeply. 'Idolatry destroys more than the sword', he wrote in a letter to a friend in 1812. 'The numbers who die in their long pilgrimages, either through want, or fatigue, or from dysenteries, and fevers, caught by lying out, and want of accommodation, is incredible.' In calculations which remind the reader of his *Inquiry* he argued that the mortality caused by Jagannath alone (at a conservative estimate) would be 120,000 in a year.

> Besides these, I calculate that 10,000 women annually burn with the bodies of their deceased husbands. The custom of half immersing persons supposed to be dying, undoubtedly occasions the premature death of many, and the multitudes destroyed in other methods would swell the catalogue to an extent almost exceeding credibility.... How much should every friend of the Redeemer, and of men, desire the universal spread of that gospel, which secures glory to God in the highest, and peace on earth.[76]

[74] Carey to Fuller, 23/4/1796, *PA*, Vol. 1: 299.
[75] RPC, Diary, April 1802: 78.
[76] Carey to Saffery, 20/1/1812, *PA*, Vol. IV: 447–48.

These basic arguments against what became increasingly known as Hinduism had been voiced by travellers, Jesuits and other Europeans before; but, reinforced by Carey's own first-hand experience and observation, they were even more compelling. His fresh first-hand accounts (which probably provided new information for some readers) helped consolidate the main-line arguments in evangelical and wider Christian propaganda. The throwing of infant children to the sharks at Sagar, the sati's suffering as she was held down and perished in the flames and 'cruel' forms of self-inflicted punishment were all events which were depicted increasingly in missionary literature and which were also incorporated into William Ward's monumental account.

(b) William Ward's *History*

Though Carey's descriptions and occasional comments set the tone and introduced some of the main themes in the missionary commentary on Indian religions, it was his colleague William Ward who, more than any of the other Serampore Baptists, influenced Protestant thinking and consolidated what became the predominant paradigm or overriding idea of Hinduism. Joshua Marshman had something to say about popular practice in *Periodical Publications*, but it was Ward who produced his most famous book which is still in some quarters regarded as an authority on Hinduism, at least as it was in the early nineteenth century.

William Ward was born in Derby in 1769.[77] He was therefore eight years younger than Carey, the man he admired and his colleague for twenty-four years. Ward did not follow his father's trade which was that of a skilled joiner and cabinet-maker, but instead was apprenticed to the owner of the *Derby Mercury*, becoming editor of the paper in 1789. He subsequently moved to London and then to Hull as editor of the *Advertiser and the Exchange Gazette*. While employed as a journalist and prior to his departure for India he became acquainted, at least to some degree, with Indian affairs. In January 1790 he refers to a translation by Sir William Jones and may well have read other works on Hindus such as Holwell's 'Religious Tenets of the Gentoos', Alexander Dow or even Halhed. In 1793 Ward met Carey and was persuaded to join the Baptist missionaries at Serampore.

The first edition of his book entitled *Account of the Writings, Religion, and Manners of the Hindoos*, begun soon after his arrival in India, was

---

[77] For these and other details about his early life, see especially Potts 1993: 27–34.

published in Serampore in 1811. Encouraged by the promise of subscriptions from 250 members of the civil service he published a new single volume version of his work in 1815.[78] Ward then decided that there was a market for his work in England—a hunch which not only proved correct, but which eventually led him to rival James Mill as one of the most widely-read European commentators on India during the first quarter of the nineteenth century. At least five two-volume editions of the work under slightly different titles were published in London between 1816 and 1818. These were followed by two four-volume editions. The first of these, also known somewhat mysteriously as the third edition, *A View of the History, Literature and the Religion of the Hindoos: Including a Minute Description of their Manners and Customs, and Translations from their Principal Works*, was published for the East India Company booksellers, Black, Parbury and Allen over the period 1817 to 1820. The second four-volume edition appeared in 1821 and a three-volume version, the last to appear before the author's death, was published in 1822.[79] Among the republications of Ward's work (in whole or in part) after his death in 1823 was a new and abridged edition published in Madras in 1863. Indeed, such is his enduring reputation that his third (1817–20) edition was reprinted in Delhi in 1990.

The sections on popular Hinduism were especially well received and were quoted in a wide range of missionary journals and magazines produced by missionary societies active in Britain. Furthermore, as we shall show, Ward's influence was not confined to the publication and circulation of these books.

Influences on Ward's Thinking

There are at least four major strands of influence which affected Ward's outlook. These factors are important to examine if one is to attempt to understand Ward's views; rather than adopting the approach of a more recent writer who does little more than condemn his work in an anachronistic 'post-colonial' critique.[80]

The first and most obvious influence was his religious conviction and views which he shared with so many others in the evangelical movement.

[78] Stennett 1825: 253.
[79] For further comment and information on the different editions of Ward's *Account* and the later *History of the Hindoos* published in Britain, see Mani 1998: 123–24, 215 (fn. 2).
[80] Sugirtharajah 2003, Ch. 3.

Though, like Carey, he was originally Anglican, his mother was attracted by the teachings of the Wesleyan Methodists. While working in Hull, Ward came into further contact with Dissenters and Methodists and was baptized into the Particular Baptist church on 28 August 1796. His views at about this time were relatively straightforward, as is indicated in an extract from one of his letters.

> If I were asked for my creed, I could soon give it: God is love. This is a faithful saying, and worthy of all acceptance, that Christ Jesus came into the world to save sinners. He that believeth, shall be saved. I will shew thee my faith by my works. If God so loved us, we ought also to love one another. He that believeth not, shall be damned.[81]

The notion that unbelievers (in Britain and elsewhere) needed to hear the Gospel before they could believe and be saved was, at least among evangelicals, axiomatic, as was the rider that those who did not believe were 'damned'.

But as Carey made clear in his *Inquiry*, an emphasis on the need to believe in the Christian revelation as a step in the process of salvation, was not the same thing as saying that the pagans or Hindus had no knowledge of God. Salvation through an acceptance of the merits of Christ's sacrifice on the cross was one thing, knowledge of God another. Indeed, the Baptist missionaries shared in Carey's views and, in voicing them, were no different from the medieval Catholic theologians, Tranquebar missionaries and Dutch Protestant commentators on paganism of earlier generations. Ward's view of what was regarded in the eighteenth century as the operation and influence of 'natural religion' in pagan or heathen societies is reflected, at least to some extent, in his work on the *Hindoos*[82] and also in an account of events on a voyage to India which he and other Baptist missionaries and friends made in 1820. While on board, they held a conference on 'the degree of knowledge of the natural and moral perfections existing in modern and heathen nations'.[83] According to one of their number, they came to the conclusion that 'a knowledge of the existing and natural perfections of God does not appear difficult to attain, and hence traces of it are observable in the history of various nations, as the African and American Indians, the Hindoos, Greeks, Romans, and ancient Britons

---

[81] Quoted in Potts 1993.

[82] See, for example, the appendix to Vol. 4 of Ward 1817–20, which draws attention to parallels between Old Testament and Hindu views of God.

[83] Sutton 1833: 3–19.

[handwritten margin note: not evolved to be a great religion in all aspects]

etc.' However, according to the same group, 'of God's moral perfections and the worship that is due to him little can be known, but from Divine revelation, either directly or indirectly'. Hence, some knowledge of God without a knowledge of Christ was of no avail and insufficient for salvation. Notwithstanding their insights, 'idolaters' could not inherit the kingdom, were 'unfit for heaven' and had 'no hope of obtaining salvation without Christ'.

A second major influence on Ward's thinking was ideas associated with the European Enlightenment. Like many of his contemporaries he was not only an evangelical and a missionary, but also a product of the Enlightenment. His enthusiasm for Enlightenment ideas becomes immediately apparent in the preface to his work published in Britain in 1820. After discussing some of the causes of change in European history, he remarked that

> The European mind, it must be recollected, has attained its present vigour and expansion by the operation of these causes and after the illumination of centuries; while we find the Hindoo still walking amidst the thick darkness of a long long night, uncheered by the twinkling of a single star, a single Bacon.[84]

Of Ward's commitment to ideas such as those of Francis Bacon and to the principles of universal happiness, rationality and science there can be no doubt. Great Britain, he argued, had no less a responsibility than the raising of India's population of sixty millions 'to a rational and happy existence, and through them the illumination and civilization of all Asia'.[85] In his view, the spread of knowledge, education and science were all linked together as crucial factors in the formation of a more rational and therefore more civilized country. Referring to the Hindus' sacred code, he argued that any system must be 'essentially vicious' which dooms the great mass of society to ignorance, and treats 'rational beings' as though they possessed no powers except those of 'an animal'.[86] He not only deplored the lack of educational opportunities in India, especially for women, but also bemoaned the neglect of scientific studies. If the Hindus had possessed 'all the advantages of European science', he declared, 'they would rank among the most polished nations'.[87] Finally, in a statement which

[84] Ward 1817–20, Vol. 1, Preface: xxvii.
[85] Ibid., Vol. 1, Preface: liv.
[86] Ibid., Vol. 1, Preface: xxxiv.
[87] Ibid., Vol. 1, Intro.: xxiii.

reflects his commitment to both missionary work and the Enlightenment, he declared that 'our present duties to this people seem to be comprised in imparting to them, first knowledge, and then sacred principles; and in this God-like work, Schools, as well as the extensive circulation of elementary works on the first principles of science, and of the Holy Scriptures'.[88]

A third major factor in Ward's thinking, and one linked with the Enlightenment, was the influence of the radical democratic/humanitarian movement—a late eighteenth century development which again affected his attitude to Hinduism. As noted in the introduction, local newspapers edited by Ward prior to his departure for India show a considerable interest in the suppression of the slave trade, a concern for the relief of various distressed people—widows, orphans, and others in the community—and a critical attitude towards inequality before the law.[89] Furthermore, it was Ward who drew up a document known as the Derby Address in which he espoused democratic principles declaring that 'all true Government is instituted for the general good; is legalised by the general will; and all its actions are, or ought to be, directed for the general happiness and prosperity of all honest citizens.'[90]

These Enlightenment and related ideas reinforced Ward's views of Hinduism derived from his reading of the Christian Gospels. Like Carey, he constantly criticized what he saw as 'irrational', 'absurd' or 'inhumane' in Hindu thought and behaviour. As a product of the Enlightenment, a radical in politics and Baptist, he was especially critical of traditional forms of authority, ideas and practice. Like many other evangelicals who were influenced by the same trends in Enlightenment thinking he condemned 'superstition and priest-craft', including institutional 'despotism', the irrationality and 'folly' of idol worship, and the manifold 'cruelties' involved in Hindu practice.

While these factors derived from Ward's English background greatly coloured his perception and representation of Hinduism, his contact with the members of the Asiatic Society of Bengal constituted a fourth important source of influence affecting his work. Even if he had felt so inclined, Ward was in no position to ignore the findings of a range of orientalist scholars who were publishing research and translations of important Hindu texts in the Asiatic Society's journal. As already noted, the Serampore missionaries' association with the Society became increasingly close in 1805 when Carey and his colleagues drew up plans for a cooperative

---

[88] Ibid., Vol. 1, Intro.: xii–xiii.
[89] Potts 1993: 28–30.
[90] Ibid.: 28–9.

translations venture involving the Asiatic Society, the College at Fort William and Serampore.[91] While Carey and Marshman worked with the Fort William pundits on a translation of the *Ramayana*, Ward made use of the college facilities, including the pundits' services, for his own work on the *Hindoos*.[92] It is not clear from his journal how often he came into direct contact with 'secular' orientalist scholars, but he was in charge of the printing department at Serampore which printed many of the Asiatic Society's publications including its highly esteemed *Asiatic Researches*.[93] Furthermore, he read and borrowed heavily from the works of Jones, Colebrooke, Wilkins and others when in the process of writing his account of the *Hindoos*. Indeed, large sections of his work, especially on Hindu philosophy, include extensive quotations taken directly from the work of oriental scholars.

These then were some of the influences on Ward's work. What was his purpose or agenda in writing the book? What did he actually know of Hinduism and what did he do with what he knew? How original was his account and what was its lasting effect?

Ward's Purposes in Writing His Account of Hindu Religion

In January 1809, in a letter to Andrew Fuller, General Secretary of the Baptist Missionary Society, Ward remarked that:

> I have been for the last five or six years employed in a work on the religion and manners of the Hindoos. It has been my desire to render it the most authentic and complete account that has been given of the subject. I have had the assistance of brother Carey in every proof-sheet; and his opinion and mine is in almost every particular the same. He and brother Marshman think the work would be read in England. It has been enquired for by numbers here ... you are aware that very pernicious impressions have been made on the public mind by the manner in which many writers on the Hindoo system have treated it. My desire is to counteract these impressions, and to represent things as they are.[94]

The mildness of these comments and the seemingly limited objectives of this first edition mask what was the beginning of a long-term and

---

[91] SA. Journal, 14/7/1805. Kopf 1969: 70; Kejariwal: 105–7; Daniel and Hedlund 1993: 248.

[92] Mani 1998: 124.

[93] Journal, 22/5/1801.

[94] Ward to Fuller, January 1809, quoted in Stennett 1825: 146.

passionate public crusade. In Ward's opinion, the romantic attitudes and naivety of European commentators who expressed favourable attitudes towards 'the Hindu system', prevented readers from seeing it for what it was and glossed over an enormity of evils. It was these evils which he felt in a better position to highlight, especially in the later editions.

When writing their journals, Carey, Marshman and Ward were coming to terms with everyday experience. They were primarily concerned with representing and thinking about aspects of Hinduism for their own benefit and sometimes also for the benefit of their own circle of supporters and friends. In this sense the journals were somewhat different from works of propaganda. Ward's *Hindoos* (as distinct from his own and especially Carey's journals) was, for example, designed primarily for wider public consumption. In the form it took, especially in the later editions, it was much more a work of passionate propaganda designed to argue and influence what Ward called 'the public mind'. The objective, in this case, was not so much to ask questions but to supply the answers; to remove ignorance and bias and present a compelling case against Hinduism and in favour of Protestant missions and Christian civilization in the subcontinent. In his *Hindoos* Ward was, therefore, following more in the footsteps of men like Buchanan and Grant than, for example, Heber. Unlike Carey, the shoe-maker and teacher, and unlike Heber, the parish priest, counsellor and traveller, Ward had been a journalist engaged in public debate. He was used to espousing causes and knew something about how to achieve his objectives.

Whatever details his volumes may contain, therefore, they are most patently geared to presenting one side in a series of public debates. These included the continuing controversy about whether there were compelling reasons for or against promoting Christianity in India and, underlying this debate, further questions about the attitude of the East India Company towards Christianity and Hinduism and its policies of 'religious toleration'. Lastly, in the later editions, there were explicit comments on the responsibilities of the British Government, and the urgent need for the authorities in India to become more active in social reform, especially on behalf of Indian women.

Ward hoped that his work would be of use in exposing what he described as 'the greatest piece of priest-craft and the most formidable system of idolatry that has ever existed in the world'.[95] His determination to counteract the effect of what he claimed were uncritical accounts of a

[95] Ward 1817–20, Vol. 1: xiv.

'detestable system' (an objective which he shared in common with both Grant and Buchanan) is reflected in many parts of the book where he attacks eighteenth-century writers on the subject. Among these were Voltaire, Gibbon and Hume, whom he argued had too much liking for 'Grecian and Roman idolatries'.[96] But reserved for special and lengthy condemnation were the views of Thomas Maurice, the Church of England clergyman whose work he had read on board ship and who, in Ward's opinion, painted a much too flattering picture of Hinduism.

> Mr. Maurice, a clergyman, has attempted to describe the Hindoo ceremonies, which he never saw, in the most captivating terms, and has painted these 'abominable idolatries' in the most florid colours. It might have been expected, (idolatry being in itself an act so degrading to man, so dishonourable to God,) that a christian divine would have been shocked while writing in this manner. If Mr. Maurice think [sic] there is something in Hindooism to excite the most sublime ideas, let him come and join in the dance before the idol,—or assist the bramhuns in crying *Huree bul! Huree bul!* while the fire is seizing the limbs of the young and unfortunate Hindoo widow,—or, let him attend at the sacrificing of animals before the images of Kalee or Doorga,—or, let him come and join in the dance, stark naked, in the public street, in open day, before the image of Doorga, in the presence of thousands of spectators, young and old, male and female. He will find, that the sight will never make these holy bramhuns, these mild and innocent Hindoos, blush for a moment'.[97]

In addition to his attempt to change public perceptions of Hinduism as a mild and congenial religion there was also Ward's crusade to obtain government legislation to suppress certain Hindu socio-religious practices, another objective which is clearly apparent in the later editions of his book.

The first edition was published in 1811 when the missionaries and their supporters were engaged in a campaign to gain easier access to East India Company territory in India. Moreover, as Lati Mani has emphasized, it was written and first published at a time when the Serampore missionaries were trying to prove that they were no threat to stability, but, on the contrary, friends and supporters of the British Government. While therefore, in 1811, the sensible approach was to maintain a low profile and to try to avoid saying anything which might offend the English authorities, the situation

[96] Ward 1811, Vol. 1: 301–11.
[97] Ibid., Vol. 1: 306.

was markedly different in 1820 when Ward's new four-volume edition became freely available. Memories of the Vellore mutiny (an uprising which intensified fears of the inflammatory effects of missionary meddling) had faded still further. And the missionaries who were also heartened by the growth of public support in Britain and the easing of restrictions on missionary activity in India in 1813, were clearly in a better position to state their case for changes in the administration's policy.[98] The new edition of Ward's book was, therefore, quite explicit about the role British authorities could and should play in reforming the Hindu system.

On the basis of surveys done in and around Serampore, Ward claimed in his book, in large print, that as a result of being burnt alive many thousands of widows were 'murdered' throughout Hindustan every year,[99] and argued not only for the suppression of sati, but for an even broader governmental reform agenda.

> The removal of the dying to the banks of the Ganges, the voluntary immolations at places the resort of pilgrims, and the burning of widows alive, entail so much misery on the Hindoo race, that every humane heart is rent in pieces whenever these horrible practices are brought into public notice. The great success which has attended the benevolent exertions of Government in certain cases, encourages us to hope, that the hand of mercy will, sooner or later, heal the wounds of a country bleeding at every pore from the fangs of superstition.[100]

Sources of Knowledge and Information

When Carey arrived in India he was comparatively isolated from other Europeans who may have been able to give him information on Hindu ideas and practice. Nor was he able to profit from the information and insights derived from a range of converts who could discuss their life and experience prior to their joining the Christian mission. For these reasons Carey relied heavily, not only on his own observations, but on the comments and advice of his pundits. Ward, on the other hand, was in a more fortunate position. He was based at Serampore where, unlike Carey for most of the period 1793 to 1799, he was not only in contact with other Europeans with a greater or lesser knowledge of Hinduism, but was able to discuss Hindu religious and social life with an increasing number of

---

[98] For these and other details see especially Potts 1967, Ch. 8.

[99] Ward 1817–20, Vol. 4: 114.

[100] Ibid., Vol. 1: 284.

converts. According to missionary calculations, the number of converts at Serampore, including Indians, rose from two in 1800 to seventy in 1821.[101]

Ward had three main sources of information. First, there were other European writings, and Europeans he could consult nearby. Of considerable importance for his book were the translations and commentaries of the eighteenth and early nineteenth century orientalists. As already noted, he was familiar with the work of Sir William Jones while still in England and, when in Bengal, met leading orientalist scholars of his day. In his book, he refers to the publications of the Bengal Asiatic Society and drew quite heavily on the researches of Jones, Wilford, Bentley, Wilkins and especially Colebrooke—though the latter was somewhat embarrassed by Ward's mistakes.[102]

Another European source of knowledge, and one which (apart from what he could learn from Thomas) was largely unavailable to Carey in his early years, was missionary literature and information. Ward not only profited from information supplied by Carey and other colleagues at Serampore but, as Acting Secretary of the mission for several years, received reports from Europeans working in more distant parts of Bengal and northern India.[103] He also had contact with evangelicals of other denominations, refers frequently in his diary to Claudius Buchanan, and had read Grant's *Observations*, extracts of which he included in his book.

Second, there was the knowledge Ward gained through his own observation and direct enquiry. Like so many other Europeans of Ward's generation interested in empirical and 'scientific' methodology, including Carey, he 'cultivated the habit of constant observation'.[104] In fact it was his own personal account of what he experienced, saw and heard (accounts that were both fresh and immediate) which greatly appealed to the imagination of his readers. His diary, in particular, is filled with references to a large range of Hindu festivals and different types of worship, such as ceremonies connected with Jagannath, Rama, Kali and Durga. As well as this, there are detailed eyewitness accounts of sati, hook-swinging and various forms of self-torture during the *charak puja*, temple cart processions, Hindu weddings, encounters with holy men, pilgrims and so forth. Many of these eyewitness accounts, entered first in his journal, were later incorporated into the book. From there they were copied as extracts,

---

[101] Potts 1967: 36.
[102] Schwab 1984: 339.
[103] Diary, 14/1/1810.
[104] Ward 1864, Biog. intro.: 3.

commented upon and reproduced in numerous missionary journals and magazines read by the British public.

Third, there were indigenous sources of information. One important source of this nature, especially relevant when considering Ward's translation of the *Puranas*, was the advice, comment and information supplied by Hindu pundits—an obvious and rich repository of knowledge and information which, as previously mentioned, had already been utilized by Carey and also by Buchanan in his *Memoir*. As Marshman's son pointed out, Ward was 'but imperfectly acquainted with Sanskrit',[105] and in his journal Ward readily admits that for the most abstract and philosophical parts of his work (which were undoubtedly the least interesting sections) he relied heavily on the pundits' translation and interpretation. Brahman pundits were employed in translation work at Serampore. There were thirty brahmans there in 1819[106] and these, together with the pundits at Fort William, were available not only for advice on the intricacies of translation, but also for comment on Hinduism more generally. References in Ward's diary make it perfectly clear that he made good use of the pundits in his employment, consulting them, not only on matters relating to translation, but also about contemporary Hindu practice.[107] For example, he drew heavily on the historical writings of Mrtyunjay, head pundit at Fort William, and also refers to the latter's exposition of Hindu ideas of God.[108] Ramnath Vidyavachaspati discussed with him the extent of Krishna worship throughout Bengal and also provided him with, what he claimed, was evidence of the practice of human sacrifice.[109] Other pundits provided Ward with further material which he used for his campaign against Hinduism. This included details relating to sati, thagi, self-mutilation, infanticide and the immoral nature of the songs and dances performed at religious festivals.[110]

Another indigenous source of knowledge was the information supplied by enquirers and converts. The converts and European missionaries living in close proximity at Serampore often met socially, for prayer and worship, or were involved in common evangelistic activity such as preaching in the countryside. The missionaries gradually gained greater knowledge of the converts' background and circumstances through events connected with

---

[105] Marshman 1859, Vol. 2: 443.
[106] Diary, 30/3/1800; *AR*, BMS, 1819: 33.
[107] Diary, 9/2/1806 and 9/3/1806.
[108] Ward 1817–20, Vol. 1: 30; Vol. 3: lxxxvii.
[109] Ward 1817–20, Vol. 1: 288; Vol. 4: 50.
[110] Ibid., Vol. 3: xxvii, xlix, lv; Vol. 4: 50, 101–2.

their conversion, from their testimony at baptism, as well as from information which emerged as a result of what were called 'experience meetings'.[111] Converts such as Ram Bose, Krishna Pal, Gookul, Kangali and others provided Ward and his colleagues with information on a wide variety of subjects such as sati, Jagannath celebrations and processions, child sacrifice at Sagar, brahmans and the moral state of the Hindus, Hindu 'sects' and gurus, and even the phenomenon of men worshipping their wives.[112]

Uses and Management of Knowledge and Information

Given that Ward's basic purpose was to counteract European impressions favourable to Hinduism, and also push for reform, it is only to be expected that he would use his material selectively to highlight those aspects of Hindu thought and practice which would contrast with the truth, moral superiority and benefits of the Christian Gospel. But the attempt to counteract favourable attitudes towards Hinduism was not the only factor affecting his overall approach. Equally, if not more powerful, were his basic assumptions especially about the brahmanical, unified and closely integrated nature of 'the Hindu religion.' This was a view, which tended to override alternative interpretations such as Buchanan's suggestion that there was no central authority and that, even among brahmans, there was only 'anarchy' and difference.

In stressing the idea of Hindu religion being 'the one unified pan-Indian system' Ward was hardly original. For Ward, as for his arch-enemy Maurice and many of the Bengal-based orientalists, the Hindu religion was 'a system'; and that was precisely why he, following in the footsteps of Charles Grant, introduced and used the word 'Hinduism'. In fact, Ward was one of the first Protestant missionaries, if not the first, to use the term 'Hindooism' in his writing when it appeared in his diary in December 1800. Describing a conversation between Carey and the Danish Governor on the subject of Hindu opposition to Christian conversion, he remarked that the Governor assured Carey he would take no notice of Hindu complaints so long as the Baptists brought no undue means 'to bring the people from Hindooism'.[113] It is, of course, unclear whether the Danish

---

[111] Diary, 22/12/1799; 3/1/1802.

[112] Diary, 4/1/1800; 24/6/1800; 19/3/1801; 22/9/1801; 24/2/1802; 3, 5, 6, 12, and 15/1/1802; 5/3/1803.

[113] Diary, 29/12/1800.

Governor actually used the word 'Hindooism', whether it was used by Carey in his report of what transpired, or whether (as seems most likely in view of Carey's habit of using alternative terms such as 'heathen' in his writing) this was Ward's own usage and summation of the conversation.

The transition in Ward's thinking prior to the use of the term, is illustrated in two earlier entries in the same diary. In June 1800, before he introduced the term 'Hindooism', he noted that one of the Serampore converts was writing a substantial piece against 'the whole Hindoo System', but, in the following February (having already introduced the term in his diary) he referred to the pamphlet being against 'Hindooism'. Here and in later parts of his diary the word was being used as a substitute for 'the Hindoo system' or even for 'the Hindoo superstition'.[114] Hence, for Ward, this religious phenomenon (in spite of its apparent diversity) was really a gigantic package, an integrated and basically coherent entity which could be compared to other 'systems' such as Christianity and those of Egypt, Greece and Rome.

Admittedly Ward states that, in his view, 'the opinions embraced by the more philosophical part of the Hindoo nation', were 'quite distinct from the popular superstition' and in volume 3 of his book he refers to deities worshipped 'by the lower orders only.' But these divisions 'within' were apparently of little moment when compared with the overall unified structure of the whole.

For Ward, as for some of his predecessors such as Grant (as well as for some European travellers, Jesuits and others) the key to the system and its binding force were the brahmans. It was the brahmans who were seen as providing the clue and entree into a proper understanding of Indian religion and society. Writing in his first edition of his work, Ward declared that 'I think it will be abundantly evident that the whole fabric of superstition is the work of brahmans.'[115] Hindus, he wrote on another occasion, 'were those under the transforming influence of the philosophy and superstition which may be denominated Hindooism; and … their conceptions on these transcendently important subjects are all regulated by systems invented by the Indian bramhun'.[116] But the entire system including 'the practice of the popular ceremonies', as well as its ideas and theology, was not only 'invented', but also 'administered' by brahmans.[117]

[114] Diary, 29/6/1800; 28/2/1801; 28/2, 14/3, 19/9 and 19/12/1802; 13/11/1804; 28/9/1805.
[115] Ward 1817–20, Vol. 1: 69.
[116] Ibid.: xix–xx.
[117] Ibid.: xxvi–xxx.

As one who had opposed despotism and the enslavement of the individual in Europe he, like Charles Grant, came to the conclusion that this power was a form of tyranny which led to the enslavement of the great bulk of the population. So great was the brahmans' power, he wrote, that they condemned 'nine tenths of the male population to mental, civil and bodily slavery'.[118] All their books were filled with accounts to establish brahmanism, and to raise the brahmans in the seat of God, so that many 'multitudes' believed they were inferior Gods.[119] Such was 'the power of enchantments possessed by brahmans' that they could persuade a man to inflict upon himself dreadful tortures, the widow to burn on her husband's funeral pyre and others to commit the most unspeakable crimes.[120] In fact, so exaggerated was Ward's view of the influence and the extent of brahman control that he seems to have believed that they had successfully stifled all opposition. Referring to Ram Bose's pamphlet against them, he suggested that this was the first piece in which brahmans had been opposed 'for these 4000 years perhaps'.[121]

According to Ward, not only was the entire system created *and administered* by brahmans, but it contained common brahmanical ideas and teachings which helped bind it together. Commenting on what might be described as the 'essence' of Hinduism in the first edition of his book published in 1811, he declared that 'the whole of the Hindoo religion may be comprised in abstraction of mind, and the performance of certain prescribed ceremonies'. At the basis of this argument were three points. First, 'The Hindoo philosophers in general, and particularly those of the Vedantu sect, consider the human as a portion of the Universal Soul: and that the mind is debased, ensnared, and kept separate from the Great Parent, by its connection with the body.' Second, Hindus have adopted a variety of techniques, such as subjugation of the body, so that the person may have his whole mind 'fixed on Brahma' as the only way of returning to the 'Great Parent', and third, *absorption* rather than some kind of continuing separate relationship with God, was the ultimate goal. 'The want of this abstraction of mind, and this subjugation of the passions, leads the Hindoo in general to despair of obtaining absorption in God, or perfect happiness, unless in some future birth.'[122]

---

[118] Ward 1811, Vol. 1: vii.
[119] Diary, 31/8/1801.
[120] Ward 1817–20, Vol. 1: xlii; Vol. 4: 113.
[121] Diary, 31/8/1800.
[122] Ward 1811, Vol. 1: xxiv.

Reiterating these views in his preface to the 1820 edition of his work he declared that he had given

a rapid view of the Hindoo sacred code, as a grand system, regular in all its parts, and proposing a defined and magnificent object, nothing less than the yogee absorption into the divine nature, and, to the common people, a gradual advance towards the same state.[123]

Ward was therefore the first British Protestant missionary to identify and describe what he claimed was the core of the Hindu system. Based to a large extent on Shankara's interpretation of Vedanta in the *Vedanta Sara* (a text which he quoted and had translated as an example of Hindu literature), it was an interpretation of Hinduism which he argued was validated in both ancient texts and in contemporary Hinduism. The doctrine, he claimed, was taught in many parts of Hindu writings, 'especially in the Durshunus',[124] and was referred to 'even in the conversations of the natives at the present time'.[125]

Ward's adoption of this pantheistic model of Hinduism was almost certainly influenced by his pundits. 'Respecting the Divine Being,' he wrote, 'the doctrine of the vedantu seems chiefly to prevail among the best informed of the Hindoo pundits.'[126] Two of his own 'best informed' pundits were Mrtyunjay Vidyalankar, head Sanskrit pundit at the College at Fort William, and Ramnath Vidyavachaspati, the second Sanskrit pundit in the same institution.[127] Both were brahmans,[128] and while the latter's philosophical views are unknown, Mrtyunjay was an *Advaita Vedantin*.[129]

But quite apart from the views and influence of his pundits, Ward was given to prioritizing textual and brahmanical literature at the expense of non-brahmanical writings and oral tradition. In other words, for him, as for so many other missionaries, the sacred Brahmanical texts were 'the real' Hinduism. Baptists including Ward, though in some ways socially radical, remained elitists in their views of the qualifications and expertise required in religious leadership. In their view the best preacher was not only one who had God in his heart, but one who knew the Bible—who, like the

[123] Ward 1817–20, Vol. 1: xxxiv; Vol. 3: lxx.
[124] Ward 1817–20, Vol. 3: ii.
[125] Ward 1811, Vol. 1: xxiv.
[126] Ward 1817–20, Vol. 2: 119.
[127] Ward 1817–20, Vol. 1: 30; Vol. 3: lxxxvii; Vol. 1: 288; Vol. 4: 50. Bose 1960: 195–96.
[128] Das 1978: 20.
[129] Killingley 1993: 100.

brahmans, knew the text and was able to expound its meaning to both the educated and illiterate people. And like so many European travellers, Jesuits, orientalist scholars and others, if one wanted to know about the essence of any religion then one consulted the priests and pundits and read what was supposed to be the authorized version.

In espousing *Advaita* Vedanta as the essence of Hinduism, Ward was being selective in his interpretation of brahmanical, let alone general Indian religious literature. In considering philosophical works he was either ignorant of some other alternative brahmanical or non-brahmanical texts and traditions opposed to Vedanta, or deliberately minimized their importance. In the philosophical part of his work he made a passing reference to the followers of Ramanuja. Describing them as 'a sect' he noted that they rejected the idea of absorption, 'pleading that it is far more pleasant to drink the sweet and cooling draught, than to be lost in the ocean'; and that 'the highest happiness of which we are capable is to be near the deity, partaking of his overflowing blessedness'.[130] But while the followers of Ramanuja warranted a mention, albeit as a 'sect', the author omits all reference to some of the other important movements in the same region. These included the followers of *Shaiva Siddhanta* in south India who insisted on the separateness of the soul and God; and also the followers of Madhva who taught the doctrine of dualism (dvaita).

Moreover, this top-down view of religion, including a privileging of what was understood as 'the correct text', meant that even Baptist missionaries tended to misunderstand and underrate the importance of popular movements. The greater the stress that Ward placed on the extent and effectiveness of brahman power and control, the more clearly he implied the powerlessness of the common people. Indeed, in this view they were 'victims' who were manipulated, deluded and forced into obedience to a higher authority. Intimidated and forced to conform, they seemed to have few ideas and very little sense of their own autonomy.

But where the lower classes were conspicuous or obvious in showing initiative and where their resolution and anti-brahman sentiments were clearly apparent Ward had also to take them into account. In that case he was faced with the problem of how to fit these movements into his Vedantic/pantheistic brahmanical model. Not surprisingly he turned to the Christian tradition and adopted the techniques and categories familiar in Christian history. The solution to the problem, he realized, was to relegate popular movements, as well as some brahmanical philosophies

---

[130] Ward 1817–20, Vol. 2: 292–93.

(such as that of Ramanuja) to a subordinate category within what he continued to call 'Hindooism'. Thus, he introduces the terms 'regular' and 'irregular', 'orthodox' and 'heterodox', 'sects' and 'seceders'. During the later medieval period the term 'sect' had sometimes been used to denote a distinct religion such as Islam,[131] but Ward uses the term in the more modern sense of a breakaway movement within an overarching religious system. 'Irregular' Hindoos, heterodox or sectarian movements, according to Ward, included Buddhists, Sikhs, Ramanuja's followers and several popular bhakti movements in Bengal such as the diverse and rapidly growing communities who revered Chaitanya as an incarnation or embodiment of God. Indeed, in Ward's own estimation, 'one fifth of the whole population of Bengal are supposed to be followers of Choitunyu, and of the Gosaees, his successors'.[132] These were people who, far from being Vedantists, insisted on the basic difference between God and the devotee.

Treatment of the Kartabhaja Movement

One of the more important religious developments associated with Chaitanya was the Kartabhaja movement which arose in Bengal in the eighteenth century. The Kartabhajas (karta = guru, bhaja = devotee) were, as the name suggests, worshippers of gurus, or rather the particular guru they believed was the true successor to Chaitanya and therefore the embodiment of God.[133] Generally speaking, they rejected almost all aspects of what might be described as 'Brahmanism', or Hinduism as described in so much detail in Ward's account. At the time Ward was writing, they had no written scriptures of their own and thus defied the common assumption that for something to be a 'religion' it had to have a written text. The Kartabhajas (like Ward himself) opposed idol worship and were strongly anti-brahman. They were not only not slaves to brahmans, or to any brahman-created system but, on the contrary, treasured their independence. Furthermore, they rejected the idea of inequality as expressed in the caste system. In fact, their most important regular ritual was the secret meeting where they worshipped God the Creator and, in defiance of caste rules, broke bread or ate rice and drank together.

---

[131] Biller 1985: 351–69.

[132] Ward 1817–20, Vol. 3: 222.

[133] For some of the more recent work on this sect, see especially Chakrabarty 1985, Ch. XX, and Oddie 1997.

Baptist converts such as Krishna and Gookul, drawn from the Kartabhaja movement, supplied the missionaries with 'many interesting particulars' concerning their earlier life in the Kartabhaja community;[134] and Ward's journal is replete with references to the Kartabhajas and other egalitarian anti-brahman movements very similar in character. For example, in April 1802 he noted that one of the disciples of Dulol, leader of the Kartabhajas at Ghospara who claimed 100,000 followers, had visited the mission several times[135] and, in the following month, he noted that four people, three of them Muslims, had come to enquire about 'the way'. But though they were born Muslims, he believed that they were to be 'classed among a pretty numerous body of people', Hindus and Muslims, who 'neither worship the debtahs [idols] nor mind Mahomet'. They were, in Ward's opinion, in a state of doubt,

> believing in one God, supposing it wrong to gratify the grosser vices; but mixing with all they believe many prejudices both of the Hindoos & Mussulmans. They seem to be expecting that God will make a Revelation of his will by somebody.[136]
>
> At Jessore, near where I was when I went out with Mr Short, an old man lives, who is in very great reputation, & who teaches all who come to him not to mind the Bengalee debthas or poojas, to worship in their minds on God, & to act with truth to all.—His disciples are said to amount to several lacks of people.[137]

Ward also records meeting enquirers at a place called Khorda 'connected with a large sect of men, who like the Ghosparrowites, reject the Hindu and Muslim systems'.[138] Somewhat later, he noted that many people he met at another village were 'inveterate foes of the Brahmans' and were led by a guru who abominated 'the vileness of the whole system'.[139]

---

[134] Reflecting on the history of the mission in an article written in 1836, J. C. Marshman, son of Joshua, noted that 'We have at Serampore Native Christians of long established character who were connected with the *Kurta Bhojas* before they embraced Christianity, nearly thirty years ago; and there are others, younger men, whose parents belonged to the sect.... It is a certain fact, that a considerable number of those who first received the Gospel in Jessore, were in a measure prepared to do so by an acquaintance with the religionists of Ghospara' (*Friend of India*, 14/1/1836).

[135] Diary, 12/4/1802.

[136] Diary, 27/5/1802.

[137] Diary, 14/7/1802.

[138] Diary, 10/8/1802.

[139] Diary, 18/10/1803.

What is especially striking about these accounts is the discrepancy between the amount of space taken up with references to the Kartabhajas and other popular movements in Bengal in Ward's diary (where the movements loom large), and the attention given to these same movements in his volumes on Hinduism. In spite of their increasing power and popularity, references to the Kartabhajas in the 1822 edition of his book are, for example, restricted to just one in over 1,400 pages of text. Indeed, reflection on the reasons for this discrepancy suggests a great deal about the objectives of Ward's book.

Clearly the Kartabhajas and other low-caste religious movements did not fit easily into Ward's model of what Hinduism was supposed to be. Too much attention to this group would throw doubt on the idea that it was a unified theological and religious system controlled by brahmans who kept 'nine-tenths of the population' in a condition of slavery. The Kartabhaja and other egalitarian religious movements (quite common in Bengal in the early nineteenth century) tended to contradict the long-held European assumption that the brahmans were the key to what was increasingly seen as the one overriding pan-Indian religion. But the other fact about the Kartabhajas, which was for Ward best left unsaid, was the deep commitment of so many of their followers to a moral and egalitarian lifestyle. As we have noted, Ward's basic purpose was to *contrast* Hinduism with Christianity, not to point to parallels and similarities. If he did too much of this, what was the purpose of mission? As he was so intent on demonizing 'the other', he could hardly afford to dwell for too long on Kartabhaja virtues, on their monotheism, rejection of caste and love of one another! Indeed writing in the *Friend of India* many years later J. C. Marshman, son of Joshua, remarked that the Kartabhajas recognized the two main principles of true religion 'the spirituality of divine worship and the obligation of mutual good will and love'.[140] Furthermore, as the present writer has argued elsewhere,[141] the similarities as well as differences between the Kartabhaja movement and evangelical Christianity was one of the reasons why so many Kartabhajas were converted to Christianity in the late 1830s and early 1840s.

Evaluation of Hinduism

Quite apart from questions about the nature and shape of religion were questions of evaluation. Ward's conscious purpose in his book, from the

[140] *Friend of India*, 11/4/1839.
[141] Oddie 1997.

very beginning, was to counteract the effect of more favourable or romantic views of Hinduism and to demonize not so much Hindus as the religious system which condemned them to hell. In the words he penned in his diary in 1801, 'Brahmans & the Devil' were both employed in the one work, 'destroying the souls of men'.[142] He did not, therefore, see it as his task to dwell on any merits that Hinduism, even in its wider sense, might possess, but rather to concentrate on its evils which, by way of contrast with the Christian Gospel, led inevitably to the enslavement, suffering and eternal damnation of India's Hindu population. An emphasis on the darker side of Hinduism was indeed necessary for the sake of the perishing heathen.

As with so many propagandists, his technique was to select, leaving out of account or playing down the better features while dwelling on the very worst teachings and practices he could possibly find. One illustration of this was his account of Hindu deities. 'Many' Hindu idols, he argued, 'were monstrous personifications of vice'.[143] This statement implies that even according to Ward's own criteria some idols were associated with 'virtue'. But instead of reading something about the virtue associated with idols and much about vice, all the reader is given are the details of vice. Another technique was to imply there was evidence where there was none—and to presume to know all about the evil and sensuous disposition of the Hindu heart; in other words, to question and disparage motives. Thus according to Ward the whole fabric of Hinduism was created by brahmans in order 'to aggrandise themselves'.[144] Furthermore it was not devotion which led Hindus to the temple, but 'a licentious appetite'.[145] In case his readers failed to get the message about the real nature of Hindu deities and the effects of idol worship, his work was loaded with colourful phraseology and a remarkable range of epithets. Amongst other things, Hindu worship was 'shocking' and 'affecting', the image of Kali 'a truly horrid figure'.[146] Shiva was associated with 'ludicrous stories', while the display of the lingam was 'a shocking violation of everything decent'.[147] Many idols were 'monstrous', 'indelicate' or 'indecent', while festivals in honour of the gods had 'the most pernicious effects' on the minds of the people and so on.[148]

[142] Diary, 7/2/1801.

[143] Ward 1817–20, Vol. 3, Intro.: xlvii.

[144] Ward 1811, Vol. 1: 69.

[145] Ward 1817–20, Vol. 3, Intro.: xxvi.

[146] Ibid., Vol. 1, Intro.: xxviix.

[147] Ibid., Vol. 1, Intro.: xxix.

[148] For a further elaboration of Ward's disparaging comments on Hinduism see Sugirtharajah 2003, Ch. 3.

As we shall see, it was not only Ward's insularity and model of Hinduism as an all-India monolith that disturbed his missionary and other critics, but also the basic unfairness of his picture of the Hindus. One of those critics was also an evangelical, the Rev. James Long of the CMS, who having lived for some years in Bengal declared that:

> Many of Mr. Ward's remarks respecting the cruelties and immoralities among the Hindus are no more applicable to the body of the people than a description of Billingsgate and the Old Bailey, in London, would be to the inhabitants of the east end of the town.[149]

Long also quoted F. D. Maurice as saying that 'Mr Ward can see only the hateful and the devilish; of what good it may be…what divine truth may be concealed in it he has not courage to enquire.'[150]

Legacy and Influence

While Ward's work contained a lot of new and detailed information about religion in Bengal, its basic assumption about the existence of the one unified Sanskritic system and the arguments about the evils of brahmanism were hardly new. What was important was that Ward picked up and promoted the idea of Hinduism. Indian 'paganism', 'the Hindu religion' or 'Hindu superstition' was now, quite simply, 'Hindooism'. Furthermore, for Ward especially, 'Hindooism' was a word for 'the Hindu other', for everything that was evil and different from Christianity. Indeed, in helping to popularize the term he helped develop a very valuable and effective weapon in the arsenal of Christian propaganda. As a result of its increasing usage, English-speaking commentators were tempted more strongly into stereotyping, oversimplification and misunderstanding. Certainly, for ordinary Christians in Britain, some of them directly influenced by Ward's depictions, the complex world of Hindu religions suddenly became clear and simple. Hinduism was a system 'out there' which could be compared with other systems like Christianity. The basic difference was that one system, Christianity, was good and the Hindu system, or Hinduism, was evil. And the message, at least in Ward's book, was that Christians should 'pity' and do everything in their power to help the unfortunate Hindu.

[149] Long 1848: 92–4.
[150] For the views and influence of F. D. Maurice (not to be confused with Thomas Maurice) see chapter. 8.

One of the reasons for the effectiveness and widespread impact of Ward's work was the fact that the influence of his views and writing were not confined to those who actually read the book. Extracts from his work appeared, for example, in numerous missionary periodicals published in Britain[151]—not only in the more sophisticated missionary journals such as the *Baptist Magazine, CMS Register* and *LMS Chronicle*, but also in the more popular missionary papers such as the CMS *Quarterly or Missionary Papers, Papers Relative to Wesleyan Missions* and probably also the LMS *Missionary Sketches*. As will become apparent in another chapter, the latter class of journals were more copiously illustrated, and designed specifically for the poorer, less well-educated subscribers, including working-class readers. Their distribution was far wider than that of the thicker and more elaborately produced publications that devoted less space to the issues and problems in the mission field and more to administration and maintenance.

By far the most frequently reproduced parts of Ward's book proved to be his accounts of popular religion. These included his accounts of Hindu deities and their festivals, devotees and popular practice—and especially those sections which highlighted the self-deception and irrationality of Hindu believers, the immorality of their 'supposed' deities and the inhumanity and cruelty of their religious customs. According to Ward, Hindus were not only 'deluded', for example in their understanding of how to deal with sin, but followed ways of worship that compounded the problem. Much in Hindu worship, in the lifestyle of ascetics and especially in the cult of Krishna, was shocking and 'indecent'. But especially prominent in the extracts (and perhaps even nauseating for some of the more sensitive readers), were Ward's accounts of cruel and inhuman customs. These included descriptions of the burial of widows alive (an account reproduced in at least four journals), his account of the horrors of sati, his detailed notice of the different forms of self-torture at the *charak puja*, his reference to the methods of leaving or disposing of the sick and dying on the banks of holy rivers, his discussion of human sacrifice and so on. These and other graphic descriptions tended to confirm much of what Carey had already been saying. They either created, or helped consolidate in the minds of thousands of British readers, an aversion to Hinduism, a pity for

---

[151] *Baptist Magazine*, 1813, Vol. V: 244–47, 332–33; *MR*, 1813: 215–18; 1817: 406–7; 1818: 253–55; 1819: 96, 326–27; 1822: 170, 173–75; 1823: 456; 1824: 564. *MMC*, No. 2, July 1836: 29–30; *MP*, Nos. 2, 1816: 8; 1817: 11; 1818: 16; 1819: 23; 1821: 26; 1822: 27; 1822: 31; 1823: 32; 1823: 33; 1824: 38; 1825: 39; 1825: 56; 1829; *PRWM*, No. LXIII, March 1836; No. LXV, September 1836.

its victims, and a longing for the day when the whole 'system' would be replaced by the Protestant Christian faith and way of life.

Ward and James Mill's *History of British India*

Ward's interpretation of Indian religion and his assault on it was reinforced by the publication of James Mill's *History of British India* in 1813 which contained a substantial chapter on 'Religion of the Hindus', other comments on religion and related issues scattered in different parts of the work.[152] Though their agendas were different in that Ward was an evangelical concerned with the propagation of Christianity in India while Mill was a writer who was using his history as a method of suggesting his own Utilitarian and modernizing policies for India, the two men were agreed on many points in their understanding and construction of Hindu religion.

The authors, who together had a profound effect on British perceptions of Hinduism, were working quite independently of each other—the one in Serampore and the other in London—apparently unaware of each other's research and writing until about 1818 when Mill read and favourably reviewed Ward's first (Serampore) and third (London) edition in the *Edinburgh Review*.[153]

Mill who in his history relied heavily on the work of the Bengal-based orientalists, followed the trend in thinking of Indian religion as a system. It was in his view one of 'the systems of superstition' which perhaps more than any other on earth was the product of an unscrupulous priestly class.[154] 'The Hindu religion' was, therefore, according to his history, a discrete brahmanical system of tyrannical oppression in which ceremonies were either invented or encouraged by the brahmans so that the rest of the population would be kept in abject submission in attempts to follow the right prescriptions for fear of offending God or suffering in the life to come. As with Ward, popular and philosophical Hinduism were all part of the one sinister plan to keep other castes in the population in religious as well as civil subjection.

We have already seen, in reviewing the Hindu form of government, that despotism, in one of its simplest and least artificial shapes, was established

---

[152] For recent comment on James Mill see especially Majeed 1992, and Trautmann1997 (pp. 117–24).

[153] *Edinburgh Review*, Vol. 29, No. LVIII, February 1818: 377–403.

[154] Mill 1826, Vol. 1, esp. Ch. VI.

in Hindustan, and confirmed by laws of Divine authority. We have seen likewise, that by a division of the people into castes, and the prejudices which the detestable views of the Brahmens raised to separate them, a degrading and pernicious system of subordination was established among the Hindus, and that the vices of such a system were there carried to a more destructive height than among any other people. And as we have seen that by a system of priestcraft, built upon the most enormous and tormenting superstition that ever harassed and degraded any portion of mankind, their minds were enchained more intolerably than their bodies; in short that, despotism and priestcraft taken together, the Hindus, in mind and body, were the most enslaved portion of the human race.[155]

The idea of Hinduism being a carefully contrived system, as reflected in Sanskritic texts and popular practice, the tyranny and control of brahmans (comparable to or even worse than the Catholic priests of the Dark Ages), the stress on 'the meanness, the absurdity, the folly of endless ceremonies in which the practical part of the Hindu religion consists'[156] the degree to which 'fantastic' ceremonies were exalted above moral duties, the perversion and uselessness of self-inflicted torment, the cruelty of 'barbarous' customs such as human sacrifice and sati, the sexual immorality associated with Hindu worship and more, these were points on which Mill and Ward were agreed. Small wonder then that Mill declared that the first volume of Ward's English publication contained 'an admirable view of the whole subject', or that he quoted Ward so frequently in the footnotes in his third edition of his *History*.

As Stokes has pointed out, certain broad similarities have often been detected in the thinking of Utilitarians and evangelicals.

Both had turned against the tolerance and respect for Indian civilization characteristic of the ages of Clive and Warren Hastings. Both agreed in many general aims. Evangelicalism and utilitarianism were movements of individualism, both seeking to liberate the individual from the slavery of custom and from the tyranny of noble and priest. Their end was to make the individual in every society a free, autonomous agent, leading a life of conscious deliberation and choice.[157]

The significance of Mill's *History* in so far as it dealt with the issue of 'the Hindu religion', is that it tended to reinforce what, we have argued,

[155] Mill 1826, Vol. 2: 166–67.
[156] Ibid., Vol. 1: 341–42.
[157] Stokes 1992: 54.

was becoming the dominant paradigm in the evangelical constructions of Hinduism in the early nineteenth century—the idea that Hinduism (in spite of some of its apparent confusions) was basically one brahmanical system and something which represented the very opposite of what Protestant Christianity and much of the thinking in the Enlightenment represented.

Mill's influence on British thinking and contribution to the paradigm was certainly important; but in some ways he was not as influential as Ward became at least at the grassroots level. Once published, Mill's *History* appears to have held the field unchallenged for twenty-five years, being reprinted in 1820, 1826 and 1840.[158] Indeed, the number of editions of the *History* was somewhat comparable with the number of editions of Ward's work—both men being regarded as standard authorities on the subject of Indian history or of Hindu religion, manners and customs respectively. Furthermore, Mill's work was used as a textbook at Haileybury College, for the training of the East India Company's civil servants, from 1809 to 1855, its influence on the mind of young men being such that Hayman Wilson, oral examiner at the College, was concerned lest the 'harsh and illiberal spirit' create a feeling of 'aversion' and destroy 'all sympathy between ruler and ruled'.[159] Yet in spite of its popularity, the influence of Mill's book was probably more restricted to middle and upper class readers than Ward's work, which was not only influential among the same sections of the population, but which was also used as source material for a substantial amount of literature designed for less exalted readers. It was Ward's construction of Hinduism rather than Mill's account which penetrated down to the popular and grassroots level.

[158] Philips 1961: 221.
[159] Ibid.: 225–26.

6

The Guardians—Consolidating the Paradigm: Duff, Mundy and Others

The dominance of a paradigm based on the idea of Hinduism as an all-embracing brahmanical 'system', an idea formulated primarily by Jesuits, and Bengal-based administrators, scholars and missionaries, was consolidated by George Mundy, Alexander Duff and a whole succession of missionary commentators who wrote on Hinduism during the second quarter of the nineteenth century. The belief that Sanskrit was the root of all vernacular languages (with the exception of tribal tongues) and hence that it was the key to an understanding of all Hindu religious texts, remained largely unchallenged, as was the idea that *written texts* express the essence of what the religion was all about. Furthermore, the assumption that Hinduism in Bengal was much the same as religion elsewhere in India (an idea implicit in Ward's book) remained for many an unquestioned presupposition and a part of the dominant view.

It was Alexander Duff who, in *India and India Missions* (written in 1839), did more than most other Protestant missionaries to consolidate these very general views about the nature and shape of Hinduism. It was also Duff who attempted to clarify notions about the essence, or central ideas, of Hinduism (which he identified as pantheism) and it was he who developed, still further, an intellectualist critique of the entire system. But before exploring the part he played in the Protestant missionary constructions of Hinduism, it is important to focus on the relevant aspects of his background and education, and to ask questions about what he actually knew of the religion in order to understand and to attempt to explain his views.

Alexander Duff was born on a property in north-east Perthshire in 1806. His father, James, was an agricultural labourer who subsequently obtained regular employment as a gardener. Both Duff's parents, who had come under the influence of the evangelical revival, were people of passionate religious faith—James Duff being especially active in keeping and superintending Sunday schools.[1] Alexander was sent to school at Kirkmichael at

[1] Maxwell 1995: 9–15.

the age of 8. After making rapid progress there, he attended the Grammar School at Perth where he concentrated on the study of Greek and Latin, becoming dux of the school at the age of fifteen.[2] He attended the University of St Andrews as an Arts student from 1821 to 1825 and as a student in divinity at St Mary's College from 1825 to 1829. Having accepted the Church of Scotland's invitation to become their first missionary, he was ordained and sailed for Calcutta in September 1829.

Duff spent some time after his arrival in India in assessing for himself the effectiveness of the more traditional Baptist and other missionary programmes. He noted what he felt was the failure of the missionaries to attract high-caste converts, and at the same time became increasingly aware of the growing importance and popularity of the English language among young men in Calcutta and its vicinity. He therefore decided to establish an Anglo-vernacular institution which would provide students with a modern Western-type education in English and which would also, as an almost certain consequence, attract more of Bengal's young men into missionary education. As is well known, Duff's system proved a highly successful experiment. The school opened in July 1830, attracted numbers beyond expectation and led to the conversion of several brahmans and other high-caste Hindus. Indeed, it was during these early years in Calcutta that Duff claimed that his educational efforts had done more to convert Hindus than decades of ineffective preaching.

India and India Missions

Why, then, in these circumstances and after four and a half years of service in India, and another five on leave in his homeland, did Duff decide to publish *India and India Missions*, a book in which he presented his overview of Hinduism?

The basic purpose of the book was to publicize and consolidate what he regarded as his distinctive achievement in educational missions. Linked with this was his attempt to arouse greater missionary zeal in the Church of Scotland so that congregations would participate more wholeheartedly and effectively in the missionary movement. He believed he had to challenge the assumptions of conservative evangelical Calvinists, who believed that preaching was the only effective and acceptable apostolic pattern of evangelism, with the idea that *educational* missions could play a vital part in extending Christianity among the educated classes. As Ian Maxwell has

[2] Smith 1879, Vol. 1: 16–17.

pointed out, the continuance of Duff's own mission was never in doubt.[3] However, it was subject to financial restraints, and Duff was well aware that its continued health, and the expansion of his work, would be assured only with the enthusiastic backing of Scottish Presbyterian congregations convinced of the need and effectiveness of his educational experiment.[4] For these reasons Duff campaigned extensively in Scotland during the years 1835–40 and decided to publish an account of his work and of the need for educational missions in *India and India Missions*. The book, written while Duff was recuperating from ill health, was a record and the substance of what he had 'so often endeavoured to enforce on the attention of his countrymen'.[5] It was divided into six chapters. The first was a discussion of civil society and the importance of India as a field of missions; the second was on the theory of Hinduism; the third on 'practical sketches of some of the leading superstitions and idolatries of eastern India'; the fourth was on the Gospel as 'the only effective instrument in regenerating India'; the fifth dealt with miscellaneous objections to the missionary enterprise; and the final chapter, which included an appendix, was an account of the rise and early progress of the Church of Scotland's mission. The sections on Hinduism were therefore part of a broader argument designed to explain the rationale and convince readers of the relevance and importance of educational missions, including the need to develop rational argument.

Duff's Knowledge of Hinduism

Duff's commentaries on Hinduism in his book and elsewhere raise questions about what he knew and how he acquired his information. In this case the historian has available more data on Duff's reading, and other sources of information, than is usually the case for similar studies of missionary preparation and writing. As with missionaries in general, there is the question of what Duff knew prior to embarking for India, and his subsequent acquisition of information, including knowledge and understanding of Hinduism gained through the direct experience of people and conditions in 'the mission field'.

Duff appears to have been better informed and had acquired much more detailed knowledge of Indian religions, while still in Britain, than his

---

[3] Maxwell 1995: 175.
[4] Ibid.: 171–72.
[5] Duff 1840: vi.

forebears such as Carey and Ward. He had the advantage of a more extended education, association with a student missionary organization and a much greater access to books and articles on Indian religion than most young candidates for the mission field appear to have had in an earlier period. Publications of the Bengal Asiatic Society, including translations of Sanskrit texts, such as those of Colebrooke, continued to arrive and to be available for readers in Britain. James Mill, among others, had produced his *History*, and Duff was also fortunate in being able to read more accounts from the mission field, including Ward's monumental work—a book which he singled out for special commendation in the introduction to his own volume.

However, it would be a mistake to assume that all of Duff's early ideas of Hinduism were acquired through reading. Reflecting on his childhood experience towards the end of his life, he recalled being shown pictures of Jagannath and other gods of India.

> Into a general knowledge of the objects and progress of modern missions I was initiated from my earliest youth by my revered father, whose catholic spirit rejoiced in tracing the triumph of the gospel in different lands, and in connection with the different branches of the Christian Church. Pictures of Jugganath and other heathen idols he was wont to exhibit, accompanying the exhibition with copious explanations, well fitted to create a feeling of horror towards idolatry and of compassion towards the poor blinded idolaters, and intermixing the whole with statements of the love of Jesus.[6]

It was therefore with deep feelings, coloured by his memories of childhood exposure to pictures of Jagannath, and reinforced by his reading of Buchanan's description, that Duff caught his first glimpse of the famous temple on the shoreline at Puri, as the ship on which he was sailing approached the mouth of the Ganges. In this case, childhood and later memories enhanced the significance of what was for Duff his first sighting of the temple towers.

Information on what Duff read as an undergraduate in the Faculty of Arts at St Andrews is available in the record of his borrowings from the University Library over the four-year period 1821–25.[7] This suggests that, at least initially, he was more interested in Africa than in India, but that some slight interest in Indian religion was beginning to emerge towards the end of his studies for his Arts degree. This may have been because of

[6] Smith 1879: Vol. 1: 10.
[7] Maxwell 1995: 226–28; St Andrews University Library Receipt Book, 1816–25, 1825 ff.

Chalmer's lectures on moral philosophy which raised questions about natural theology including the issue of how different religions (such as Indian religion) related to each other.[8] The same interest in India and Hinduism may also have been stimulated through Duff's participation in the activities of the St Andrews University Missionary Society, an association which he and other students founded in 1824.[9] The society, which encouraged discussion of missions in general, included in its library (of which Duff was the librarian) Buchanan's *Researches* and other books touching on India.[10]

One of the books which Duff borrowed in 1826, when he was a theological student at St Mary's, was the first volume of a work by Robert Adam entitled *The Religious World Displayed; or a View of the Four Grand Systems of Religion, Judaism, Paganism, Christianity and Mohammedanism* (1818). The work which, as the title suggests, divided the religious world into the usual four basic categories, described 'Hindus' as one of the 'chief sects of Paganism'.[11] It gave what was, for the most part, an unflattering account of Hindu thought and practice. Beginning with some innocuous comments on the Hindus' belief in the transmigration of souls, the sacredness of the cow and sanctity of rivers such as the Ganges and Indus, and their concerns with pollution, purity and so on, the author then moved into a heavy-handed attack on the whole 'system'. Quoting from a sermon delivered by Dr Joseph White in his Bampton lectures, published in 1784, he noted the Hindus' recognition of one God, but then remarked that this belief persisted alongside the worship of innumerable subordinate deities believed to have many vices and follies. 'With a blindness which has ever been found inseparable from Polytheism, they adore, as the attributes of their gods, the weakness and passions which deform and disgrace human nature.'[12] The article went on to describe in detail the many 'senseless ceremonies, and unreasonable mortifications', as well as the cruel and inhuman custom of sati, and the sacrifice of children to 'the goddess Gonza'.

Another book which Duff borrowed from the library in the following year was Thomas Maurice's *The History of Hindostan* (1820). The author was a liberal-minded Anglican cleric, scholar and poet who, as author of *Indian Antiquities*, had already incurred the wrath of William Ward, who

---

[8] Maxwell 1995: 57–8.
[9] Ibid.: 68–9. See also Piggin and Roxborogh 1985, Ch. 6.
[10] Ibid.: 68.
[11] Adam 1818: 160.
[12] Ibid.: 164.

disliked his sympathetic views of Hindu religion. Though *The History of Hindostan* was described as a history, it was, for the most part, a detailed account of Hindu cosmology, periodization and mythology, including a detailed illustrated account of the ten incarnations of 'Veeshnu'.

These items, and a separate collection of Joseph White's sermons published in 1785, and borrowed by Duff from the library in 1827, are significant not only because of what they claim about Hindu belief and practice, but also because of their assumptions about the nature of religion and what became known as Hinduism. There was the deeply-held conviction that the Hindu religion was a 'system'. This, as noted elsewhere, was the view of many orientalist scholars, one which paralleled Locke's idea of the whole of the universe being like a mechanical system, or a clock, wound up and set in motion by the Great Clockmaker Himself. For Duff, influenced by these ideas, and writing in *India and India Missions*, religion was also a system and hence something very different from later concepts of it as 'process'. Second, and also significant in view of Duff's subsequent argument, was the presupposition in Adam's account, and the view deeply embedded in Maurice's narrative, that 'Hindoo' religion was 'brahmanism'—a brahmanical construct in which all the leading ideas were formulated by the brahmans themselves.[13] Lastly, there was the conviction that the essential components of the 'real religion' could be found, not so much in what people did, or in popular practice, but in texts.

According to Duff, who was reminiscing more than thirty years after the event, it was when he was a student at college, perusing the article on India in Sir David Brewster's *Edinburgh Encyclopaedia*, that his soul was 'first drawn out as by a spell-like fascination towards India'.[14] This is a significant remark, not only because of what it tells us about Duff's view, on the eve of his departure from India in 1863, about his first feelings of attraction for the country, but also because the article almost certainly contained a considerable amount of information on Hindu religion.[15]

Hence, by the time he came to write his book in 1839, Duff had at his disposal a considerable array of secondary sources and information. His

---

[13] Maurice 1820: 49, 54, 56, 78, 87, 137, 158, 396–97.

[14] Smith 1879, Vol. 1: 43–4.

[15] While we have been unable to locate the earliest versions of the entry, the article, appearing in Volume 12 of the third (1830) edition of Brewster's *Edinburgh Encyclopaedia*, contains detailed references to Hindu religious teachings and practice. Like Duff in his subsequent writings it stresses the importance of the role of brahmans, emphasizes the essential unity of the Hindu religion and highlights issues such as the Jagannath festival and sati.

reading not only included the works as mentioned above, but a further list of references, some of which he identifies in his introduction.[16] Particular writings which he highlighted as being important for the chapters on Hinduism were works 'translated, in whole or in part, from the Sanskrit language: such as the Institutes of Manu, the Bhagavad Gita, the Ramayan, etc.', transactions of various Asiatic Societies and the writings of 'Sir W. Jones, Wilkins, Colebrooke, Vans Kennedy, and others; who have expatiated at large over the wide domains of Orientalism', and also works written by Protestant clergy and missionaries, such as Buchanan, Heber, Peggs and Ward. Works by Maurice and Mill are also mentioned, but only as authorities for the introductory chapter on the history of Western contacts with India and India's importance as a perfect field for the propagation of the gospel.

Duff's Experience of Calcutta

While Duff's use of written sources of information (including texts in translation) was quite extensive by the standards of his own day, his contact with the contemporary and living faith of the Hindus drawn from different backgrounds was more limited than that of older missionaries, such as Carey and Ward, who spoke the local language fluently, who discussed religion with people of different caste backgrounds and who travelled extensively on preaching tours throughout the countryside. Indeed, the relationship between Duff's reading and theories about Hinduism on the one hand, and his experience and contact with the reality of belief and practice in India is somewhat problematic. This is so much so that his overall response raises the question that if he had decided to follow Mill's example and never visited the country, would it have made much difference to the two chapters in *India and India Missions*?

Such evidence as there is suggests that Duff's experience in Calcutta was important, but only because it was unusually restricted and seemed to confirm much of what he had already read. Like Carey, Ward, and other men of the Enlightenment, he believed that first-hand observation was necessary; but what he saw, and the views of the limited range of people he met and consulted appear, if anything, to have consolidated his imagined world of the Hindu religion.

Most of what he had read about Hinduism was about Hinduism *in Bengal*. When he arrived in Bengal he was therefore not struck by the

[16] Duff 1840: vi–ix.

regional differences he may have noted if he had been operating in some other part of the subcontinent. So much of his reading having been about the situation in Bengal, his experience of Hindu festivals and of seeing different types of ritual and worship was not very different from what he expected. Believing in the importance of 'ocular' verification, he was assiduous in observing the events of the *charak puja*, in seeing for himself the processions of the sannyasis, men performing hook-swinging before his eyes, the bloody slaughter of goats at the temple of Kali ghat and so on. All these things, which are described in his book, largely confirmed his imagined picture of 'popular superstition'.

Nor was there anything new in what Duff saw, or in the people he seems to have met, to challenge his underlying assumptions, such as the idea that Hinduism was Brahmanism, or, in other words, a system ordered and controlled by brahmans. This, as already argued, was for many of Duff's British and European contemporaries the normative way of understanding the Hindu religion. In fact, Duff's convictions about the importance of brahmans were, if anything, reinforced by orientalist scholars in Bengal, by his meetings with Rammohan Roy, who insisted that 'real Hindooism' could be found only in brahmanical texts, and by the amount of time Duff spent with high-caste Hindus, especially brahmans, in the course of his work in educational missions. It is well known that Duff's work prior to his writing *India and India Missions* was almost entirely confined to establishing his Anglo-vernacular school system and giving public lectures—both activities aimed at attracting the interest of higher-caste Hindus alone.

Of course he made an effort to see what other missionaries were doing, to visit preaching stations (special places where missionaries preached to the common people) and to see what was happening in the Bengali language elementary schools. But he had some difficulty in learning Bengali. He was clearly delighted when the Rev. Townley (LMS) presented him with several Bengali works on the eve of his departure for India and hoped that these gifts might eventually prove 'of considerable service in his acquiring a thorough knowledge of the language'. But though he started learning Bengali with the help of a brahman pundit, once he arrived in Calcutta there is some doubt as to how far he progressed.[17] According to Laird, Duff did not think it worthwhile to acquire a mastery of Bengali during his early years in India, departing from 'the usual missionary custom of making a

[17] National Library of Scotland (NLS), Duff Collection: MS7530, F. 10, Duff to Inglis, 14/11/1829; Smith 1879, Vol. 1: 149.

study of the language his primary concern after arrival'.[18] But whatever the case, he did not see his future activities as being bound up in what the missionaries described as 'vernacular work'. On the contrary, he seems to have felt uncomfortable and was discouraged by the difficulties he encountered in attempting to preach in the vernacular. In one of the few descriptions of his visits to preaching stations during his early years in Bengal he reported in a letter to Dr Inglis, at the Edinburgh office, in July 1833 that:

> During the last twelve months Mr McKay & myself have been in the habit of occasionally accompanying, as opportunity offered, our respected Brethren to their native preaching places...those who attend are, for the most part, stragglers of the lowest orders of Natives—miserably ignorant, superstitious, & captious. They come most frequently, not to hear, inquire, or to be informed, but solely for the purpose of scoffing & blaspheming. You may easily imagine how difficult it is to make much impression on such persons.[19]

Nor did Duff's original evaluation of Hinduism seem to change with the years, or with his contact with it in Bengal. His basically negative attitude towards it was apparent not only in Scotland, but from the very first time he sailed up the Ganges and was forced to wade ashore. His hostility to the 'Hindu system', nurtured from childhood and reinforced by much of his reading, remained undisturbed or, if anything, was consolidated by the narrowness of the circles in which he moved. His arrival in India evoked remarks that are symbolic of his attitude throughout both chapters of the book he wrote ten years later. On board ship, progressing slowly up the river towards Calcutta, he had an occasional glimpse of a heathen temple, or of numbers of 'deluded idolaters' performing their ablutions in the Ganges— 'at this time the foulest & most impure of all streams', and when, after a severe storm, the ship keeled over on the bank and the passengers were forced to take to small boats and make for the shore, his encounter with the villagers was far from happy. In a note to Inglis he explained that:

> Here we had an experimental proof of the dark dissocializing genius of idolatry. Shattered, exhausted, and helpless as we were, the Hindoos shewed no tender meltings of compassion: they stood, coldly gazing at us—& then, suddenly disappearing out of view, the doors of their miserable huts were shut to escape the pollution—& the weary passengers, left exposed to the pitiless pelting of the storm.[20]

[18] Laird 1972: 208.
[19] NLS, Duff Collection, MS7530, F. 164, Duff to Inglis, 30/7/1833.
[20] Ibid., F. 24–6, Duff to Inglis, 28/5/1830.

His subsequent observation of the externals of popular practice, his mixing with other missionaries who were hardly sympathetic to Hinduism, his contact with Rammohan Roy and his friends and, above all, his in-depth discussion with *alienated* youth seemed to confirm the worst 'evils' in the system. The plain fact is that most of Duff's Bengali informants, and the students he attempted to convert, were already disenchanted with their own religion, and must have agreed with much of what he had to say about the irrationality of traditional Hindu forms of belief.[21] Many of the students who attended his lectures, or who became enquirers, came from the Hindoo College. Influenced by the new norms of Western critical thinking they were vague and unsure about many of the things they had formerly taken for granted, except that they no longer believed in their family's religious tradition. Under the influence of David Hare, Derozio and others they had imbibed some of the most radical ideas and teachings associated with the European Enlightenment. Among these was a dislike of inherited tradition and a belief in the self-serving propensity and irrationality of all religion.

In the light of these circumstances and other evidence it appears then that Duff's experience of India (during the four and a half years he was there from May 1830 to November 1834) had little effect on his understanding and responses to Hinduism. What it did do, however, was to confirm his ideas about the way it might be attacked and destroyed. It made him even more acutely aware of the outlook, thinking and arguments of deracinated youth, who, like himself, were profoundly influenced by the European intellectual movements of the time. The basis of his teaching, speaking and writing was therefore an appeal to reason, as well as to conscience, and to build his arguments on the foundation of the knowledge and ideas familiar to him in Scotland, and increasingly familiar to the young men who sat at his feet.

His Representation of Hinduism

In what way then did Duff depict or represent Hinduism in *India and India Missions*? First, the book consolidates the dominant view of Hinduism as brahmanism. Indeed, in order to describe 'the theory of Hinduism', Duff launched into an account of 'theoretic Brahmanism'.[22] Hinduism was Brahmanism and, in order to describe it, Duff deliberately excluded from

[21] See especially Bose 1960: 37–54.
[22] Duff 1840: vii–viii.

his mind everything except what an orthodox brahman would have said. In a revealing passage on his methodology he refers to his reading of a range of writings by orientalist scholars and continued:

> At the same time, in his choice and rejection of materials—in his exposition of the views and opinions which may be said to constitute Brahmanical orthodoxy—he [the author] has been guided solely by his own vivid recollection of oral discussions and mutual interrogatories, carried on for several years, in his familiar and habitual intercourse with the sons of Brahma on the banks of the Ganges. In fact, he had constantly before his mind's eye the image of a learned brahman of the orthodox school; and his endeavour has been to present such a statement of every division and subdivision of the complex theme, as experience has taught him to believe would be rendered by a skilful advocate and expounder of the Brahmanical creed, if required to act the part of Commentator and Interpreter.[23]

Duff's assumptions about the nature of 'real' religion, and his view that the essence of Hinduism was brahmanism, emerge even more clearly in subsequent chapters. Like many of his contemporaries, he believed that Sanskrit texts (assumed to be composed by brahmans) were the only original writings of the Hindus.[24] Hence if European scholars could gain access to them and translate their contents, they would be in possession of the entire corpus of ancient Hindu religious writing and documents which, like the Bible, would explain what the Hindu religion was all about. And, as was the case in Europe, it was these basic texts which, from Duff's point of view, seemed to offer a clue to understanding, and also gave a certain degree of unity and coherence to the entire system. As in Europe, wrote Duff, 'the great mass of people would be found appealing to a common written standard,—an authoritative record, believed by them to contain a divine revelation'.[25]

Moreover, what Duff described as 'the one stupendous system' was, he believed, held together vertically by the caste system, oppression and fear. The common people, in the thraldom of brahmans, and hankering after some kind of salvation in the life hereafter, were the slaves to an endless series of taboos and ceremonial regulations. Furthermore, the Hindu system was 'a national system', in operation throughout the subcontinent. Apart from the Muslims and the numerous 'aboriginal tribes' which, according to the author, constituted 'no more than an atom of the dense

[23] Ibid.
[24] Ibid.: 68–9.
[25] Ibid.: 65.

mass of the population of Hindustan', there existed, he suggested, the great majority of the people who were the followers of the 'Brahmanical system of superstition'. 'Speaking... in a *generic* sense,' he averred, 'the Brahmanical faith is the *national faith* of India, in the same way as Christianity is the national faith of Europe.'[26] Indeed, Duff's conviction of the intellectual as well as social/structural coherence of the one 'brahmanical' system, was so great that he believed that if one attacked and undermined one part of it, the entire structure would collapse. For example, once students began to realize that Hindu science was false then they would begin to doubt and would eventually reject the entire system. Each part of the apparatus, like that of a clock, depended for its viability on all the rest.

Pantheism as 'the Essence' of Hinduism

While Duff tended to echo the Jesuit and contemporary view that the Hindu religion was an integrated 'system' best viewed from the top down, some of his other views were less widely expressed. As he himself confessed, there was nothing original in his description of Hinduism. However, his idea that the essence of Hinduism was pantheism (as well as idolatry) and his focus on its weaknesses as an intellectual system were both aspects of Hinduism less frequently discussed, at least by Protestant authors.

As we noted in the preceding chapter, Ward suggested that Hinduism was 'a grand system' regular in all its parts, 'and proposing a defined and magnificent object, nothing less than the yogee absorption into the divine nature, and, to the common people, a gradual advance towards the same state'.[27] While this idea does not appear to have been developed or discussed at greater length (for example, under the heading of 'pantheism') it is, nevertheless, clear from Ward's account that he was referring to Hindu teaching about the ultimate absorption of the individual soul in Brahman. In doing so, he could have been echoing Wilkins' comments on the *Gita* (published in 1785) where the latter remarked that the Hindus believe that they are bound to transmigration until 'all their sins are done away' and aspire to 'Mooktee', eternal salvation, 'by which is understood a release from future transmigration, and an absorption in the nature of the Godhead, who is called Brahm'.[28]

[26] Ibid.: 67.
[27] Ward 1817–20, Vol. 1: xxxiv; also Ward 1811, Vol. 1: xxiv.
[28] Quoted in King 1999: 121.

What had been a remark in Ward's work became a major theme in Duff's commentary. By that time (1840) a great deal more was known about the Vedanta, the *Upanishads* and the Hindu doctrine of monism. A major event was Rammohan Roy's translation of an *Abridgement of the Vedant or Resolution of all the Veds* in English in 1816, and his translation of Shankara's *Mundaka Upanishad* three years later.[29] These works, together with T. E. Colebrooke's essays on the Vedanta, published in the *Transactions of the Royal Asiatic Society* in 1827,[30] highlighted what was known as 'pantheism'—a term coined by an English writer, John Toland (1670–1722)[31] to express the idea that all is in God. Discussion of issues relating to pantheism, or rather Vedantism, were prominent in the *Calcutta Christian Observer* (organ of the Calcutta Missionary Conference) edited by Duff and others in 1833. Not only was this the year of Rammohan Roy's death, but it was also a period of further reflection on the doctrines and teaching of the Brahma Sabha which was subsequently renamed the Brahmo Samaj. Entries in the *Observer* included a detailed description of Brahmo worship, discussion of the connection between the Vedas and the Vedant and 'Observations on the Veda and the Vedantic System' by 'Aliquis', who claimed to have consulted the pundits.[32] One of the issues that Duff addressed in a series of public lectures to young men in Calcutta in 1831 was the brahman doctrine of *maya* or illusion, which he rebutted as a variant of the Idealism of the Berkeleyan school.[33] In August 1833 he was reported as having spoken on the 'insuperable objections' to the Hindu notion of the soul being a part of God.[34] It is also noteworthy that Duff's disciple, Krishna Mohan Banerjea (1813–85) not only saw Rammohan's Vedantic message as a rival to his own, but considered it pernicious in its denial of the absolute reality of the world, and its identification of the self with God.[35] These views of Vedanta and pantheism expressed in the *Calcutta Christian Observer*, and in direct response to the activities of Rammohan and the Brahmo Samaj, re-emerge as the basis of Duff's remarks in *India and India Missions* published some years later.

While acknowledging variations in its philosophy, Duff argued that Hinduism was 'essentially a stupendous system of pantheism.[36] Developing

[29] For a discussion of this work see especially Killingley 1993.
[30] Cowell 1873, Vol. 1: 350–401.
[31] Eliade 1987, Vol. 2.
[32] *CCO*, Vol. 2, 1833.
[33] Maxwell 1995: 162.
[34] *CCO*, Vol. 2, 1833: 372.
[35] Killingley 1993: 103.
[36] Duff 1840: 61.

his own terminology, he described the different schools, 'all of them pantheistic,' as 'Spiritual Pantheism', 'Psycho-ideal Pantheism', 'Psycho-material Pantheism' and 'Psycho-material–mythologic Pantheism'. In complex prose, in which his sentences are sometimes half a page long, he engaged in sweeping generalizations, and in an overview of what he argued was the one overall Hindu system in which he attempted to show that the 'facts and doctrines of Christianity beautifully contrast with those of Hinduism'.[37] According to Duff, 'Brahm', 'the Supreme God of India', 'the Supreme God for more than a hundred millions of people!' was understood as being 'totally inoperative',[38] and a spirit without moral attributes. Furthermore, despite their differences, all the schools supposed that this spirit was the one ultimate and only reality.[39] Indeed, Hinduism was a system in which 'the hosts of heaven', 'the great elements', 'the herbs of the field and trees of the forest' and all creatures 'may be addressed as parts of the universal and sole-existing Brahm'.[40] For Duff, all Hindu accounts of creation were unsatisfactory in the sense that the visible universe did not appear to differ sufficiently from the one universal spirit. Breaking off from his account of the psycho-material view, he declared that 'here we cannot help pausing to notice how thoroughly, in every scheme of Hinduism, the creature is confounded with the Creator. The distinction between these is not merely lost:—it is utterly annihilated.'[41] Thus, despite Duff's apparent acknowledgement of diversity within Hinduism, he effectively reduced it to pantheism, a monistic philosophy in which the dualism of Madhava, the teachings of *Shaiva Siddhanta*, and the outpourings of the *bhakti* saints (agonizingly conscious of their separation from God) had little or no place. Couched in the flow of an astonishing rhetoric, these arguments gave impetus to the increasingly common view that pantheism was the kernel and essence of Hinduism.

Duff, Mundy and an Intellectual Critique

Duff's account of Hinduism in *India and India Missions* was also important for another reason. It developed further the view, already established among some Protestants, that revelation and reason went hand in hand

[37] Ibid.: 62.
[38] Ibid.: 55–7, 75.
[39] Ibid.: 85.
[40] Ibid.: 151.
[41] Ibid.: 106–7.

and that Hinduism was basically an irrational system. Though Duff was not the first among British Protestant missionaries to emphasize the irrationality of Hinduism, his arguments can be seen as helping to consolidate views already expounded in publications by John Wilson (1804–75), George Mundy (1796–1856) and others active in India earlier in the nineteenth century. What Duff was doing in his book was the same as what he did in lectures and in the classroom in Calcutta, where he brought into play all his training in logic and philosophy in a sustained attempt to demonstrate the weaknesses and lack of viability in Hindu belief.

One of the first and most important of the earlier Protestant works concentrating on what were thought to be intellectual weaknesses in Hindu texts and teachings was George Mundy's *Christianity and Hinduism Contrasted; or a Comparative View of the Evidence by which the Respective Claims to Divine Authority of the Bible and the Hindoo Shastrus are Supported* (1834). As the first edition, published in Bengali in 1827, was soon sold out, friends suggested the author should publish an English version. Encouraged by the reception of the first edition and well aware of the spread and increasing importance of English among higher-caste Bengalis, Mundy decided to publish a second and larger English edition, which appeared in 1834. It was, as he explained, 'very different from the first edition', incorporating, for example, new material from John Wilson's tract entitled *Exposure of Hindooism* (1832, 1834).

Mundy, who completed his training at the LMS institution at Gosport in 1819, was appointed as a catechist and schoolmaster to Chinsura.[42] This was a former Dutch trading settlement some miles north of Calcutta, where the LMS, funded by grants from the Bengal Government, had developed an extensive system of elementary schools. In 1818 there were thirty-six schools with 2,695 boys in regular attendance.[43] Mundy's main tasks were teaching and superintendence and, after a period of seven years at Chinsura spent mainly in contact with Hindu youth (some of whom became enquirers), he wrote the first edition of his book, published

[42] Mundy was an apprentice to a linen draper, and a Sunday schoolteacher, when he was accepted by the LMS as a candidate for the mission field. Like Carey and Ward he had little formal education, which, in his case, extended only to reading, writing and arithmetic. What he did have, however, over and above the meagre benefits many others enjoyed, was an opportunity for further instruction and training in a missionary college. This was the LMS institution at Gosport, which appears to have achieved a reasonably high standard of excellence and which included both the humanities and science in its curriculum (CWM, CP, Mundy to Directors, 25/2/1818; Sibree 1923).

[43] Laird 1972: 72–3.

in Bengali in 1827. It was, as might be expected in these circumstances, designed as a work which would convince thinking young men (stimulated by an increasing exposure to European ideas) of the superiority of Christianity over Hinduism. As a missionary reviewer stated, the book was 'the first effort to provide for the Hindu youth a concise and striking outline of the evidences of our faith'.[44]

Like Ward, Jesuit writers and others before him, Mundy believed that the Hindu religion was 'not framed by God, but by the Brahmans'.[45] He went on to claim that 'the intellect of the people' had been 'crippled' as a result of an overriding brahmanical control which kept them in a state of spiritual bondage.[46] Basing his comments on the assumption that Hinduism was supposed to be the one connected and unified system, he complained at several points in his analysis that it was full of contradictions. 'Mohemadans, Christians and Jews each have their book which they respectively believe to be of divine authority;' he wrote, 'but with the Hindoos it is otherwise; they have a variety of sacred books which they call shastrus, and of which the contents are almost as much opposed to each other as the Koran and the Bible.'[47] The account which the *Shastras* give of the Divine Being, he claimed in another passage, 'are so contradictory, and so much at variance with each other, that it is utterly impossible for any man who takes them for his guide to obtain any definite idea on this subject, or to satisfy his own mind as to what is true or what is false respecting it'.[48] Nothing, he believed, 'could be expected from sources so varied and a system so incongruous' as that of Hinduism, 'but confusion, contradiction and inconsistency'.[49]

Like Grant and the Serampore missionaries, the author was horrified by what he perceived as a lack of moral standards, sexual impropriety and a lack of benevolence in Hinduism.[50] But while these moral and general

---

[44] *CCO* 1836, Vol. 5: 424.

[45] Mundy 1834: 125.

[46] Ibid.: 126.

[47] Ibid.: 8.

[48] Ibid.: 41.

[49] Ibid.: 244.

[50] For example, he argued that the lives of principal and inferior deities were 'all marked by similar crimes'; they were all, more or less, adulterers, thieves, liars and murderers according to their own historic records. They quarrelled with each other, fought, and cursed, and kicked each other, and committed such crimes 'as would bring them to condign punishment' were they to make their appearance again in this world (Mundy 1834: 198). Mundy also quoted at length an Indian writer on the prevalence of Hindu sexual vices and obscenities all too apparent at Hindu festivals and on the banks of the Ganges; and, lastly,

humanistic considerations were given their place, there is in Mundy's book a greater appeal to critical acumen and intellectual criteria than is apparent in earlier Protestant missionary writings on Hinduism. Indeed, the sub-title of the work sets the tone of his approach. It was: 'a Comparative View of the *Evidence* by which the respective claims to Divine Authority of the Bible and Hindu Shastras are supported'. Amongst other things, readers are asked to consider the possibility that any revelation has to be consistent with what is known of God in the natural order. The work was written in the developing context of what one writer called 'Infidelity and Ratio-nalism',[51] and the arguments were therefore set out in a way which, it was hoped, would appeal to Hindus increasingly exposed to inductive and scientific reasoning. References to 'absurdities' in Hindu accounts of the origin and history of the world were claimed to be 'as much at variance with reason and the principles of sound philosophy', as their statements on a whole range of other subjects. Significant also was the author's condemnation of idolatry which he argued had 'a degrading influence' on 'the faculties of its adherents'. While, according to Mundy, some people argued that idolatry was the fruit of ignorance, the real situation was the other way round. Hindus who were taught to look upon a stone as God were encouraged to ignore the dictates of 'natural understanding' and were eventually reduced to a state of 'stupefaction'.[52]

The English edition of Mundy's book was published from Serampore in 1834, the same year that Duff left for Scotland where he remained for a period of six years until his return to Calcutta in 1840. Even if he did not have an opportunity of reading Mundy's work in India, there was still plenty of time for him to obtain a copy and read it while he was in Scotland and before he gave his lectures and published his own views of Hinduism in *India and India Missions*. Indeed, a review of Mundy's book appeared in the *Calcutta Christian Observer* in August 1836.[53] Apart from criticizing Mundy's literary style as too complex for those who were still in 'their infant acquaintance' with English, it commended the work as 'the first effort made to provide for the Hindu youth a concise and striking outline

---

he compared 'the supreme benevolence of Christianity' with the 'system of the Hindus', citing as examples of Hindu indifference to human welfare the usual examples of sati (which even though abolished, would still continue if Hindus had the power to do so), the drowning of parents and so on, and even the lifestyle of ascetics who renounced their social respon-sibilities, were selfish and did nothing for others.

[51] *CCO* 1836, Vol. 5: 424.
[52] Mundy 1834: 113–15.
[53] *CCO* 1836, Vol. 5: 422–23.

of the evidences of our faith'. It also commended the author for adopting the mode 'of contrast' which, the reviewer argued, was the best way of arresting attention and convincing the people 'among whom we labor'. The author of the review, penned under a Greek pseudonym, is not known. However, Duff himself had been active as one of the founders of the *Observer* a few years earlier (in 1832) and, even if he was not author of the article, it is highly likely he read it or knew of Mundy's work. In any case, the idea of exploring Hinduism as a rational construct and of pointing out its weaknesses alongside the superior rationality of the Christian Gospel (the basic approach to Hinduism in Duff's *India and India Missions*) was again not new. The inspiration and idea was there in Mundy's critique.

However, notwithstanding its lack of originality, it was Duff's depiction of Hinduism that grabbed the attention of Europeans (as well as some Indian readers). This was partly for the obvious reason that Duff's account was specifically written for the European Christian audience. But it was also because of his standing as a revered and successful Christian missionary, because of his dramatic success in winning over high caste enquirers to Christianity, and also because of his powers of persuasion and ability as a propagandist in capturing the attention of audiences, not only in Scotland but throughout Britain.

While Duff's book carries with it certain assumptions about the nature and shape of Hinduism, and while it directs attention to the usual criticism of Hindu religion as being immoral and inhumane, it also reflects his Baconian principles—a part of his thinking which is clearly seen in his assault on Hinduism as a rational system. Linked with this approach was his long exposure to ideas of natural religion—above all, to the idea that all human beings were rational creatures capable of being convinced through argument, inductive reasoning and logic. Among India's proud philosophers, he remarked, there were many who had been endowed 'with intellects as subtle and acute as any ever bestowed upon the children of men'.[54]

The tone of the second chapter on 'the grand theory of Hinduism' is set by Duff's constant reference to 'delusion', 'absurdities' and 'irrationality'. 'Our present purpose not being to expose, but simply to exhibit the system of Hinduism,' he wrote (somewhat unconvincingly), 'it has all along been taken for granted, that in the eye of the intelligent Christian, its best confutation must be the extravagance and absurdity of its tenets.'[55] It was a faith which, from the earliest infancy, 'demands the unconditional

---

[54] Duff 1840: 63.
[55] Ibid.: 199.

surrender of reason, and can brook no mental state, save that of unthinking acquiescence'.[56] 'What could be more affecting,' he declared, 'than to behold thousands intensely occupied in the investigation of the noblest truths, and only accumulating heaps of the vilest error.'[57] Among these errors was the idea of *maya*, which was so contrary to 'the dictates of reason' that even 'the great majority of the learned in the orthodox schools' required a system 'more level of ordinary comprehension', and offering 'less violence to the evidence of sense and consciousness'.[58] In Hinduism these 'errors', which extended to claims that it was possible to answer all the most complex questions, contrasted with the moderation of Christian belief in not claiming to know all and demonstrated that Christians 'were more truly the disciples of sound philosophy and an enlightened reason, than those who make the proudest pretension to both'.[59] Though 'the incoherencies, inconsistencies, and extravagancies of Hindu sacred writings' on the origin of the cosmos were 'interminable', on no subject perhaps was 'the multiplicity of varying accounts and discrepancies more astounding' than on the more recent past.[60] He attacked Hindu accounts of the origin of the physical universe and of geography and argued that 'the revelations of Hindu astronomy' were not, like those of the Bible, 'chiefly figurative and emblematic' but were to be understood in 'strictest literality'.[61] Furthermore, Hindu ideas of geology and history were but specimens of 'the interminable puerilities and extravagances' with which 'the annals of myriads of ages' were 'densely crowded', and which were 'constantly rehearsed and intensely admired by the millions of India'.[62] Indeed, according to Duff, 'the extravagances of Hinduism' were 'worse than worthless' when viewed as 'the pretended substitute for true history, or true science or true religion'.[63] As already mentioned, it was Duff's conviction that these ideas were extremely influential among the millions of Hindus he referred to as 'deluded votaries'.[64] 'The more anything transcends the bounds of nature and of truth,' wrote Duff, 'the greater is the gravity with which it is asserted, and the more unquestioning the credulity with which it is received.'[65]

[56] Ibid.: 141–42.
[57] Ibid.: 88.
[58] Ibid.: 98.
[59] Ibid.: 130.
[60] Ibid.: 119.
[61] Ibid.: 118.
[62] Ibid.: 139–40.
[63] Ibid.: 143–44.
[64] Ibid.: 87, 181.
[65] Ibid.: 141.

7

Hinduism in Missionary
Society Periodical Literature

In earlier chapters our focus has been on the Protestant missionary
experience, 'knowledge' and constructions of Hinduism as reflected in
missionary depictions and reports of their work in India. In this
chapter attention switches to the role of the Protestant missionary society
media in creating and cultivating ideas and images of Hinduism in Britain.
Hitherto little attention has been paid by historians to what missionary
societies in Britain did with written and illustrated material, or to the way
in which it was edited, repackaged and presented for the consumption of
the reading public. The key factor in this propaganda campaign was
missionary society periodical literature. Issuing from the missionary
society press in ever-increasing volume throughout the nineteenth
century, it was this material, especially in its more popular form, which
greatly increased the public's consciousness of Hindus and Hinduism. It
consolidated some of the earlier British impressions of Indian religion,
extended the range of imagery and issues discussed, and also helped create
a more coherent (though perhaps no less prejudiced) picture of what
Hinduism was supposed to be. Indeed, it was this literature, including a
great deal of graphic illustration, which further developed the general
impressions, ideas and feeling which continued to influence Christian
assumptions and thinking about Hinduism well into the twentieth
century. And it was this material which candidates for missionary work
usually read, sometimes to the exclusion of all other sources available,
about overseas mission.

The Growth of a Reading Public

The rise and development of the Protestant missionary movement in
Britain coincided with a rapid increase in education and literacy. There
was not only an increase in the different types of schools providing an

education, but an upsurge in the number of people able to read in the population. M. J. Quinlan has estimated that between 1780 and 1830, while the population of England doubled from about 7 to some 14 million, the number of readers quintupled from 1.5 to between 7 and 8 million.[1] These figures include an upsurge in the number of working-class readers. R. K. Webb has stated that by 1830, taking an average from many widely divergent areas, between two-thirds and three-quarters of the working classes in England could read.[2] The rapid growth of literacy, noted in surveys and contemporary comment, can be illustrated by the remarks of one observer, who told an SPCK committee in 1832 that 'the population of this country [was] for the first time becoming a *reading* population, actuated by tastes and habits unknown to preceding generations, and particularly susceptible to such an influence as that of the press.'[3] One of the signs of the time was a rapid increase in the number of newspapers. For example, between 1801 and 1831, when heavy taxation on newspapers curbed production, the output of officially stamped copies alone more than trebled, from 16,085,000 to 54,769,000 a year.[4] At the same time there was a rapidly growing demand for periodical literature. 'Every little sect among us,' wrote Thomas Carlyle in *Signs of the Times* in 1829, 'Unitarians, Utilitarians, Anabaptists, Phrenologists, each has its monthly or quarterly magazine.... [A]t no former era has literature, the printed communication of thought, been of such importance as it is now.'[5]

The organizers of Protestant missionary societies, like those connected with the SPCK, were well aware of the increasing role which the print media could play in influencing the ideas and attitudes of a growing number of people. Hence, the production of periodical literature soon became one of the main tasks of missionary societies organized in the first half of the nineteenth century; and it was also one of the tasks taken for granted by later societies, such as those organized by women and referred to in chapter 11 of this book. Their publications, including magazines and leaflets for children as well as for adults, incorporated an increasing amount of illustrated material and rapidly became one of the most potent forces affecting the British public's perception of India and Hinduism.

[1] Quinlan 1941: 160–61.
[2] Webb 1955: 22.
[3] Quoted in James 1976: 18.
[4] Ibid.: 17.
[5] Quoted in ibid.: 33.

The Missionary Register and Journals Representing Specific Societies

The first English missionary periodical, and one which included substantial comment on Indian religion, was the *Missionary Register*, a monthly magazine which began publication in January 1813. Edited by the Rev. Josiah Pratt, a founder member and Secretary of the CMS, its avowed object was 'to awaken the Public to the state of the Heathen World, by giving information derived from all quarters, and by regular reports of the proceedings of all Protestant Societies aiming at its conversion'.[6] Its broad scope and generosity of spirit is reflected in the fact that it carried news and reports of the work of the SPG, as well as that of evangelical societies overseas. Reports on India included missionary accounts of various aspects of Indian religion in different parts of the subcontinent, ranging from reports of conversations with brahmans to descriptions of the great mela at Allahabad, temple processions and 'devil worship' in south India. In 1817 the attractiveness of the journal was enhanced by the inclusion of woodcuts based on sketches usually of 'heathen' peoples, their environment and social and religious customs in different parts of the mission field. Copies of the journal, which were sent free to those who collected one shilling per week or more for the CMS, and also to members of other societies were, according to Charles Hole (an early historian of the society), 'in continual demand wherever the smallest association or penny-society was formed'.[7] The monthly circulation of the paper, distributed in Ireland as well as in Great Britain, rose from about 5,000 copies in 1814 to 7,500 in 1824.[8] Furthermore, as was commonly the practice during this period, each copy of the magazine was passed around among a number of people and, in some cases, read aloud in churches or elsewhere, for the benefit of those unable to read.[9]

[6] CMS Minutes, 20/4/1824.

[7] Hole 1896: 409.

[8] Ibid.; CMS Minutes, 20/4/1824.

[9] Thus, referring to the influence of the *Missionary Register* in their annual report of 1817, the CMS Committee remarked that 'not a few Clergymen, who enter with due zeal into the cause of Missions, have adopted, with very great advantage to their ministry, and to the edification of their parishoners, the practical reading to parties of them, monthly or at other times, the most interesting parts of the Missionary Register, and of conversing familiarly with them on the extension of Christ's kingdom, accompanied by prayer for the success of the Gospel. The Cottager and Labourer thus become, in the best sense, Citizens of the World' (CMS, *AR* 1817: 355).

In addition to the *Missionary Register*, which reported on the progress of all the different Protestant missions[10] there were numerous other missionary journals more strictly denominational in character. All the principal Protestant societies operating in India had their own information and propaganda outlets that gave more or less extensive coverage on Hindus and Indian religion. The extent of coverage depended partly on the newness of the mission, on the number and proportion of the society's missionaries working in India and perhaps also on other factors, such as the depth of public disquiet over specific issues such as the East India Company's conduct of socio-religious affairs.

While it is difficult to categorize this material, there appear to have been three overlapping levels of communication which were gradually developed as missionary societies broadened their base and reached down and outside the level of upper- and middle-class readers.

At one level there were the more intellectually demanding periodicals, which were written primarily for 'the use of educated men and women'—the readership being drawn primarily (though not exclusively) from the middle- or upper-class divisions of British society.[11] These magazines included articles which were critical or analytical (rather than merely descriptive) as well as illustrations and comment, subscription lists, and detailed information about the society's business and activities in the United Kingdom. Among them were the *Church Missionary Intelligencer*,[12] the Society for the Propagation of the Gospel (SPG) *Monthly Record*, which became the *Mission Field*,[13] various publications of the London Missionary Society (LMS) including the *Quarterly Chronicle* and its successor the *Missionary Magazine and Chronicle*, the *Wesleyan Missionary Notices*, the Baptist Missionary Society (BMS) *Missionary Herald*, and also periodicals which included home church as well as missionary information such as the *Home and Foreign Missionary Record of the Church of Scotland* and its equivalent for the Free Church of Scotland, which separated from the Church of Scotland in 1843.

---

[10] It ceased publication in 1855.

[11] Barnes 1906: 168–69; Stock 1902: 593.

[12] Edited by Joseph Ridgeway, the first number appeared in 1859—the committee's intention being to produce 'a superior monthly publication, in which articles on the geography, ethnology, religions, etc of the various Mission-fields could appear; and in which important missionary letters could be published at once, instead of waiting perhaps for some months' (Stock 1902: 593).

[13] Thompson 1951: 230.

Circulation figures are difficult to obtain. It appears that the extent of distribution depended on price and the committee's policy (for example in giving away free copies) as well as on the intrinsic appeal of the publication involved. In 1842 the circulation of the *Home and Foreign Missionary Record of the Church of Scotland* averaged 10,000 monthly, while the circulation of its equivalent published by the Free Church of Scotland was 18,260 monthly in 1856 and 20,560 in 1857.[14] The circulation of the SPG's *Mission Field* rose from 4,000 monthly in 1862 to 5,000 in 1869.[15] In 1875 when the *Church Missionary Record* and the *Church Missionary Intelligencer* began to be published in the one issue, the average printing was 4,600 a month.[16]

In addition to this more intellectually demanding 'highbrow' literature were smaller tracts, often known as 'quarterly papers', which were generally well illustrated and especially designed for circulation among less educated middle and working class readers.

One of the most successful of these popular level publications was the CMS quarterly usually published under the title of *Missionary Papers*.[17] Commencing publication in April 1816, it was designed as material for the use of 'Collectors' (persons collecting money on behalf of the Society), which they would carry with them and distribute to all regular contributors, even to those who gave the smallest amount. According to the Church Missionary Society (CMS) Committee, 'These Quarterly Papers consist of a few pages of striking Facts and Anecdotes, with Addresses and Exhortations, adapted to the level of the Labouring Classes and the Young; and are illustrated by engravings on Wood.'[18] The papers, which usually had a page-sized illustration (at a time when illustrations were not as common as in the late nineteenth century) and three pages of printed text, were an immediate success. They not only included pictures calculated to excite or astonish, but were couched in simple and direct language—much of the commentary coming direct from the pens of missionaries or converts in different parts of the mission field. Furthermore, they were uncluttered with the dreary details of missionary management and finance and generally required little effort to read and comprehend.

[14] Weir 1900: 48; *The Home and Foreign Record of the Free Church of Scotland*, Vol. 1 (new series): 3.

[15] SPG, *AR* 1862, 1867, 1869.

[16] Nemer 1981: 66.

[17] Its title was subsequently changed to *Church Missionary Paper*, presumably in order to distinguish it from similar periodicals published by other societies.

[18] CMS, *AR* 1817–18: xv.

Their appeal to the poorer and lower-class contributors as well as to the better-off sections of the community is apparent in remarks in the *Papers* themselves. Contributors, and hence those who received the quarterly, included children, scholars, servants, labouring people, widows and others.[19] Hence some knowledge and information about India and Hinduism (whatever the bias) was reaching right down to the level of the English cottager[20] or even illiterate workers. The success and influence of the CMS *Missionary Papers* (also known as *Quarterly Papers*) is also reflected in printing and circulation figures which show that it was the most widely circulating missionary paper in Britain in the nineteenth century and hence a powerful factor in the formation of deep-seated ideas and assumptions about the shape and character of Hinduism. In 1819 the circulation figure was 268,000 or 67,000 copies per quarter and by 1824 this figure had risen to 400,000 or 100,000 copies per quarter. In 1839–40 the society was printing 165,000 copies per quarter,[21] and in about 1905 a total of 700,000 papers or 175,000 copies each quarter.[22] These circulation figures are not comparable with figures for some of the publications put out by political radicals or even by the domestically orientated religious press during the equivalent period (for example 1815 to 1850).[23] However, it is important to recall that the CMS *Quarterly Paper* was only one of the CMS publications depicting Hindus and Hinduism and that the CMS itself was only one of the several Protestant societies also producing material on the same subject.

The success of the CMS *Quarterly Papers* apparently inspired other Protestant societies with the same idea. In 1818, two years after the popular CMS quarterly was launched, the London Missionary Society followed suit by launching its *Missionary Sketches*, for the use of the weekly and monthly subscribers to the London Missionary Society. Judging from the only copies which are available (those from 1841 onwards) the *Sketches* followed the CMS model of four pages, the first one being an illustration of missionary work or some object or custom overseas. The Wesleyan Missionary Society, also thinking in terms of a popular periodical, adopted

---

[19] *MP*, No. XXII, 1821.

[20] The cottagers who were referred to in the *Quarterly Papers* were traditionally those who resided at a reduced or nominal rental on the master's estate.

[21] CMS Committee Minutes, 23/7/1839 and 28/7/1840.

[22] Barnes 1906: 166.

[23] For figures on the printing or circulation of secular and domestically orientated papers and magazines in Britain during the nineteenth century see especially James 1976 and *The Newspaper Press Directory*.

the idea of a similar series, commencing publication of its *Papers Relative to the Wesleyan Missions, and to the State of Heathen Countries*, in 1820. Like the CMS and LMS tracts, it was a small four-page booklet usually including a woodcut on the front page.

Describing the nature of the Wesleyan *Quarterly Paper* in 1872 the authors of *The Missionary World* declared that:

> This little tractable of four pages, intended for gratuitous distribution among the subscribers, generally contains a well executed wood cut of some scene or object of Missionary interest, with a descriptive article, well calculated to awaken and sustain the zeal of all who take a part in the glorious enterprise.[24]

The SPG launched its *Quarterly Papers* in French and Welsh, as well as in English. Produced for 'gratuitous circulation', the papers were 'illustrated with wood-cuts', and gave 'general missionary information'.[25] In 1856 the society distributed 488,050 copies, or 122,000 per quarter, a circulation figure not far below that of the CMS.[26] Among other societies which published a quarterly, including material on Hinduism and India during the nineteenth century, was the Free Church of Scotland, which joined in the rush with its *Quarterly Missionary Paper*, the first number of which was produced in 1852. Copies of the paper, which appeared in a new format in 1857, were sent to missionary associations, of which there were 560, in connection with congregations of the Free Church of Scotland in 1858.[27]

Apart from these quarterly papers which were pitched at a popular readership, there were also periodicals which targeted specific groups, namely children and also women, the latter becoming increasingly involved in the women's missionary organizations during the second half of the century. Known affectionately as 'the little Green Book', one of the first illustrated magazines designed specifically for children was the *Church Missionary Juvenile Instructor* which appeared in 1842[28]—a periodical which soon attained a circulation of 80,000 copies per month.[29] *The Gospel Missionary*, a similar monthly magazine for children with a circulation of

---

[24] Boyce 1872: 415.
[25] SPG, *AR* 1853: XXXV; Boyce 1872: 415.
[26] SPG, *AR* 1857.
[27] *Free Church of Scotland Quarterly Papers*, No. IV, December 1858.
[28] Stock 1902: 592–93. It was edited successively by the Rev. Charles Hodgson, the Rev. R.C. Billing (subsequently Bishop of Bedford) and Miss E. S. Elliott.
[29] Stock 1902: 592.

23,500 per month in 1862, was published by the SPG.[30] Among other societies, the LMS produced the monthly *Juvenile Missionary Magazine* in 1844,[31] the Wesleyan Methodists the *Juvenile Offering*, and the BMS the *Juvenile Missionary Herald*.[32] The latter was intended chiefly for circulation among children and young people connected with the Sabbath-schools of the Baptist denomination. This material, which included references to Hinduism and Hindu practice was usually well illustrated and simply and clearly written. Much of it was in the form of anecdotes and stories about missionary adventure, the trials and bravery of converts and the way in which 'heathen' religion and customs impinged upon or oppressed people in their daily life. Added to this were exhortations, poems and other passages with a Christian devotional or moral message. The popularity of these periodicals, the most successful of which seem to have included something for everyone,[33] is reflected in circulation figures. In 1846 the editor of the LMS *Juvenile Missionary Magazine* claimed to have published more than 4 million copies during the previous two years (each copy being a monthly edition),[34] while, according to Findlay and Holdsworth, authors of the history of the Wesleyan Missionary Society, the *Juvenile Offering* was also a highly successful enterprise.

While it is comparatively easy to distinguish the 'highbrow' from popular and juvenile missionary literature, there was also an intermediate category of material which represented something of a compromise between the two extremes. The most obvious and successful example of this was the *Church Missionary Gleaner*, a paper which the CMS Committee hoped would 'occupy a place between the Church Missionary Record and the Quarterly Paper'.[35] After some initial difficulties, it greatly increased its circulation, which soared to 80,000 copies per month by the end of the century.[36] Writing in 1906, Irene Barnes, who was involved in CMS administration, remarked that in addition to popularly-written articles, terse and

---

[30] SPG, *AR* 1859, 1863.

[31] Soliciting the co-operation of friends of the LMS, and especially ministers and superintendents of schools, the Directors, writing in 1844, declared that the new monthly was an 'effort to interest the *Young* in cause of Missions'. The magazine they explained, would have a frontispiece 'in an embellished wrapper' and would be sold at one half penny per number or three shillings and sixpence per hundred (*Chronicle*, No. XCVII, June 1844: 96).

[32] Boyce 1872: 414.

[33] *Juvenile Missionary Magazine*, Vol. 1, June–December 1844, Preface.

[34] Ibid., Vol. 3, 1846, Preface.

[35] Committee Minutes, 14/1/1841.

[36] Stock 1902: 592; 'The Story of the "Gleaner"', *Gleaner*, 1 January 1918: 5–6.

pungent editorials, and the close contact between editor and readers, the magazine largely owed its attractiveness to its pictures.[37]

Aims, Organization and Personnel with Special Reference to Literature on Hinduism

The primary object of Protestant missionary society publications throughout the nineteenth century was to increase enthusiasm for 'the cause of mission', enlarge funding for the different missionary projects and help increase the number of people volunteering to become missionaries overseas.[38] Related to this task was the initial and important work of explaining to readers why foreign missions were at least as important as those at home and why the spiritual condition of particular peoples in different parts of the world cried out for immediate attention. The latter challenge necessitated an early educational programme in which readers were given more information on the context, religious background and special needs of the target populations.

In addition to these concerns, there were also subsidiary objectives— at least one of which was specific to India and aimed at changing government policies towards Hindu religious institutions and practice. The various missionary societies with missionaries in India, dissatisfied with what they perceived as the East India Company's lack of genuine 'religious neutrality' and its continued 'connexion with Idolatry' used their own periodicals in attempts to influence public opinion and force changes in Company policy. The issue of Hinduism as well as Christianity in India was therefore an important public question which took up additional space in missionary periodical literature during the first half of the nineteenth century.

Missionary society publications attacked what they saw as blatant discrimination against Indian Christians, for example, in rules disqualifying Christians from employment in the public service and in inheriting ancestral property.[39] But it was the British administration's continued refusal to suppress sati and other practices, and its official policy on the funding,

---

[37] Barnes 1906: 165.

[38] While some of the evangelicals such as Josiah Pratt (the founder of the *Missionary Register*) and early members of the LMS were generously ecumenical there were other advocates of mission, like some mission candidates, who were more concerned with the propagation of the views of their own denomination.

[39] *MR* September 1832.

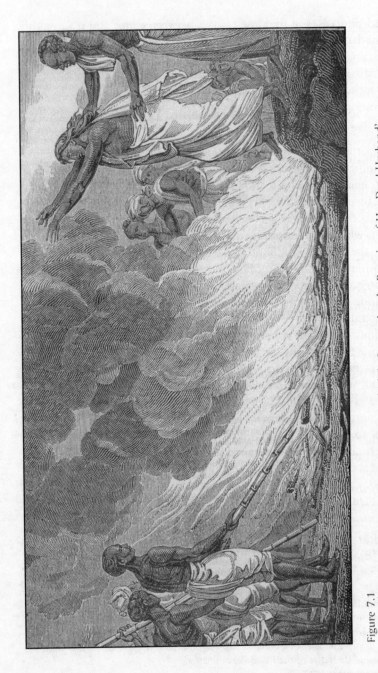

Figure 7.1

'A Hindoo Widow Casting Herself into the Fire, which is Consuming the Remains of Her Dead Husband'

This illustration, which appeared in *Missionary Papers* (No. XXXIV, 1824), was one of several British missionary society reproductions of Solvyns' painting—a work that the artist claimed was based on a ceremony which he himself attended.

care and management of temples and other Hindu institutions which attracted the greatest amount of attention and provoked the most frequent and sustained criticism in the missionary press.

The *Missionary Register*, as well as periodicals connected with the CMS, LMS, Baptist and other associations, all attacked the East India Company's prevarication and delay in outlawing the practice of sati. For example, articles in both the *Register* and CMS *Quarterly Papers* cited William Ward's plea for an end to the practice[40] and included engravings of widows preparing themselves, or being prepared, for death. One of the most disturbing of these illustrations was an engraving supposedly done by 'a native artist' which showed a woman about to cast herself into the billowing smoke and flames.[41] The engraving, which was in fact done by the Flemish artist Baltazard Solvyns (who arrived in Calcutta in 1791), was based on his attendance at the event in which the widow, 'full of courage and resolution' jumped into the flames.[42] However, as Hardgrave has pointed out, this etching is open to further interpretation and probably, for that reason, appeared in a number of missionary publications. Behind the woman appears to be a brahman priest who may be waiting to give her a push should she suddenly become frightened and change her mind. Standing on the same side and near the widow are others (perhaps her relatives?) encouraging her to jump, while in the foreground, on the opposite side of the picture, are two sturdy young men waiting with bamboo poles in their hands ready to hold the woman down once she is in the pit should she struggle and attempt escape. In this graphic material, readers (and those who had difficulty reading) were confronted with what was widely believed to be one of the most ghastly and inhuman customs of 'the Hindu system'.

As noted above, the *Missionary Register* and CMS and LMS periodicals were also outspoken in their attacks on the Company's patronage and management of Hindu temples.[43] Referring to the Government of India's apparent failure to implement the Directors' measures for the withdrawal of support for Hindu institutions, the *Missionary Register* cited with approval James Peggs' remarks on the Company's continued financial interest in the prevailing system.[44]

[40] *MR* June 1822 and CMS *MP* No. XXVI, 1822.

[41] CMS, *MP*, No. XXXIV, 1824.

[42] For a commentary on this etching and on some of Solvyns' other work see Hardgrave 1998.

[43] *Chronicle*, No. 9, February 1837: 140.

[44] *MR* November 1836: 511.

The *Missionary Register* and the LMS *Magazine and Chronicle* noted the progress of agitation against the Indian administration's continued association with 'Hindu idolatry'—the *Register* reporting the Rev. Edmund Crisp's detailed account of the ways in which the authorities were implicated in the day-to-day maintenance of temple establishments in south India.[45] In his speech at an anniversary meeting of the LMS, Crisp referred to the British officials' involvement in the repair of temples, the maintenance of temple services, the appointment and removal of staff (such as the rice boilers, musicians and even dancing girls), the recruitment of labour for the drawing of temple carts, and the huge profits which accrued to the public treasury. While Crisp was quoted as saying that the Company's involvement in the administration of temples of south India encouraged 'idolatry' and made it even more difficult for missionaries to counter arguments in favour of idol worship, the *Register* also drew attention to what was happening in the north. In a passage headed 'The Tottering of Juggernaut', it referred to a report from the Rev. Charles Lacey of the General Baptist Mission in Orissa, welcoming orders from the Supreme Government to the effect that the Pilgrim Tax was to be 'immediately and entirely abolished'.[46] In the next year, in July 1840, the *Register* reported that the Government had withdrawn all connection with 'idol shrines' in Allahabad, 'Gyah' and Puri.[47]

It was in the course of campaigns against these and other policies that the British public became, almost incidentally, better informed and more keenly aware of the variety and nature of practices supposedly associated with Hinduism. Indeed, the intensity and frequency of debates on issues relating to Indian religion not only created a receptive audience, for example at missionary anniversary meetings, but also led to the establishment of parliamentary committees of enquiry which provided the public, including supporters of Christian missions, with more data (however interpreted) on Hindu belief and practice.

Those ultimately responsible for the way in which 'Hinduism' was portrayed in Britain included missionaries and converts, editors who organized or commented on the material, artists who produced drawings and sketches for woodcuts—and finally, at a later date, photographers or photographic experts who supplied the increasingly popular photographic material.

[45] *MR* August 1837: 349–51.
[46] Ibid., July 1839: 352.
[47] Ibid., July 1840.

Much of the comment on Hinduism in periodical literature produced in Britain was by missionaries—often by those who were sufficiently motivated and interested enough to ask questions and explore the issues at length. Among the most renowned of these (all of them already referred to in earlier discussion) were William Ward (BMS), Alexander Duff (Free Church of Scotland, FCS), Elijah Hoole (Wesleyan Methodist Missionary Society, WMMS), Peter Percival (SPG), William Arthur (WMMS) and James Vaughan (CMS). In addition to these commentators were others who may not have written books specifically on the subject, but who were sufficiently interested to write and explore the topic for the benefit of readers. Notable among them were the older experienced missionaries, many of them fluent in the vernacular, who had spent many years in the field. Among them were George Gogerly, A. F. Lacroix and Charles Mead, all of them of the LMS, G. U. Pope (SPG), Samuel Hasell (CMS) and others.

The part played by editors in selecting material, writing the introduction to different passages, choosing contributors and making their own comments was also an important factor influencing the way in which Hinduism was depicted in Britain. It was the editor, sub-editor or editorial committee that decided, for example, which missionary letters, or extracts from letters and journals and other correspondence would appear in the society's journals. It was also their task, if necessary, to correct details and also, if it was felt desirable, to include editorial comment and to interpret the material for readers. Indeed it was sometimes this interpretative comment or gloss on the original report which created much of the journal's bias or particular slant on Hindu belief and practice.

These editorial tasks appear, for the most part, to have been in the hands of the mission secretaries or their offsiders. For example, in a lengthy minute detailing the work involved, the Rev. Josiah Pratt and his assistants in the CMS pointed out that there were three principal officers employed by the Society, Pratt (the Chief Secretary), the Rev. Edward Bickersteth (Assistant Secretary) and Danderson Coates, a lay assistant. While Pratt spent much of his time as editor of the *Missionary Register*, he and his assistants were also responsible for producing the Society's own publications, including the *Quarterly* or *Mission Papers*, which involved 'much greater labour than might appear from their size'.[48] Editorial work was also part of the many duties undertaken by Secretaries of the SPG throughout the nineteenth century,[49] and much the same practice appears to have been

[48] CMS Minutes, 20/4/1824.
[49] Thompson 1951: 230.

followed by the Baptist, Wesleyan and London missionary societies during the same period.

This work was occasionally supplemented by the enthusiastic labour of individuals apparently outside the committee structure. For example, the first series of the Free Church of Scotland's *Quarterly Mission Papers* (1852–57) was edited by Mr Justice Hawkins, formerly of the Bengal Appellate Court (Sudder Dewani Adulat);[50] and the *Church Missionary Gleaner*, which was eventually adopted as an official missionary publication, began its life on the private initiative of the Rev. Charles Hodgson, a clergyman who, for many years, was the Honorary Association Secretary for the CMS in Yorkshire.[51] In the case of the CMS, which probably produced more periodical literature than any other missionary society in Britain, the burden of work was greatly relieved by the establishment, for the first time in 1850, of a position entitled 'editorial secretary'—a position which was continued throughout the nineteenth century. The Rev. Joseph Ridgeway (Rector of High Roding, Essex), the first appointee, held the position for 21 years,[52] and was succeeded by Eugene Stock, who acted as the Society's editorial secretary from 1871 until after the turn of the century. The London Missionary Society also had an editorial secretary at the time of its centenary in 1895.[53]

Some mission secretaries, most notably Elijah Hoole, sole secretary for the WMMS (1834–51), and William Arthur, joint secretary for the same society (1851–68), had both been missionaries in India and were well known as commentators on Hinduism. But they were the exceptions rather than the rule. The great majority of missionary secretaries who dealt with India appear to have been ordinary clergy who had never lived there, or tried to learn its languages or interacted with its people for any length of time. It is certainly true that they had a passion for mission and often read a considerable amount of missionary correspondence from different parts of the subcontinent. However, their central task was to take the larger view and to consider the well-being and progress of missions as a whole, not only in India but in other parts of the world, wherever their society was operating or was planning to operate in the future. In other words, editors of missionary magazines, far from being specialists or having a

[50] *Foreign Missions of the Free Church of Scotland*, No. 1, 'India. A Field for Missionary Effort', Edinburgh (n.d.).

[51] *Gleaner*, 1/1/1918: 5–6.

[52] Stock 1899, Vol. 2: 51. During the whole of this period he edited the *Intelligencer* while the *CM Record* and other smaller papers were prepared under his supervision.

[53] Lovett 1899, Vol. 2: 720.

single minded focus on India, needed to be familiar with fields that might include the West Indies, China, Africa, the Middle East, the Pacific and other regions as well as India.

Second, the day-to-day task of editors, as distinct from missionaries, was publicity and propaganda in relation to the public 'at home'. Their primary and sometimes all-consuming task was to encourage subscriptions and a desire among readers to volunteer for service overseas. While workers in the field were occasionally concerned with what supporters would think, or with the attitude of the general public in Britain, concern with these issues was no more than one consideration in a range of issues that most missionaries were dealing with in their daily activity. Indeed, the different agendas and understandings of their respective role as missionary or editor appears occasionally to have led to differences of opinion. One example of this type of conflict is apparent in the correspondence between Pratt who, as noted above, was CMS Secretary and editor of the *Missionary Register*, and William Greenwood, the CMS' first English missionary to India. Though Pratt was clearly more liberal-minded, and adopted a more scholarly attitude to Hinduism than, for example, the editor of *Papers Relative to the Wesleyan Missions*, he nevertheless felt constrained to admonish Greenwood for failing to send home vivid accounts of pagan abominations.[54] Greenwood was, above all, concerned with evangelism among Hindus, Pratt with propaganda, including the encouragement of new recruits. Furthermore, while mission editors like Pratt focussed on the task of how to create an interest and arouse enthusiasm for mission, some missionaries, especially those with scholarly interests (like John Wilson, Murray Mitchell or John Robson) were, at certain points, less concerned with this single issue than with, for example, a scholarly understanding of Hindu tradition. In this sense they were very different from the editors of the LMS *Missionary Sketches* or the CMS *Quarterly Papers*, who were much more focussed on how to garner the public's money and support for missions in general.

Apart from the task of receiving, commissioning and editing written material, editors were also involved in procuring visual material. Illustrations were employed increasingly in missionary periodical literature and as a method of consolidating arguments about Hindu belief and practice. In fact, it was quite possibly the visual statement (such as the depictions of sati already mentioned), that left the most powerful impression, especially in an age when illustrated material was not as common as it became

[54] CMS, CI 1/EZ/18, J. Pratt to W. Greenwood, 28/7/1818 (quoted in Piggin 1984: 140).

later in the nineteenth century. Commenting on this issue, Richard Altick, author of *The English Common Reader*, remarks that 'the appeal of many number-publications [during the nineteenth century] resided as much in their illustrations as in their literary content'.[55] Further evidence of the popularity and importance of illustration, even in the latter part of the century when sketches and illustrated material were more common, is reflected in the circulation of secular periodicals, including the *Illustrated London News*, which was said to have reached an average circulation in the 1860s of 70,000 copies weekly, and also the *Graphic*, which commenced publication in 1866 and which fifteen years later had achieved a circulation of 250,000 copies.[56]

The CMS was the first missionary society to publish illustrated material, the first picture in a missionary magazine (representing a scene from West Africa) appearing in the *Missionary Register* of April 1816.[57] Throughout the term of its publication until the appearance of the last number in 1855, the journal continued to include illustrations of Hindu devotees, iconography, institutions and practice. Between 1816 and 1840 (a peak period in the debate on the nature of Hinduism), it published more than forty page-size pictures illustrating different aspects of Hindu religion. All of these (most of them reproduced as woodcuts) also appeared as illustrations for the CMS *Missionary Papers* during the same period. The LMS *Missionary Sketches*, the *Missionary Magazine and Chronicle* which began publication in 1836, *Papers Relative to the Wesleyan Missions*, and other journals such as *The Free Church of Scotland Quarterly Missionary Paper*, the *Church Missionary Gleaner* and the juvenile magazines all followed suit, publishing sketches and other pictures illustrating Hindu religion and practice.

While some editors gave no information on who the artists were or details relating to provenance of the work, others, such as Pratt in the *Missionary Register*, were more inclined to provide information on both the origin and subsequent history of illustrated material. Thus it appears that a number of sketches relating to Indian religion were executed by or copied from 'native artists'. This indigenous material, reflected for example in illustrations done by Indian artists in the *Missionary Register* and the CMS *Missionary Papers*, was supplemented by drawings or engravings of brass and other images of deities used in worship by the people themselves. This input from 'native artists' was apparently encouraged by Europeans

[55] Altick 1957: 265.
[56] *Deacon's Newspaper Handbook*, London, 1881.
[57] Stock 1899, Vol. 1: 128.

commissioning local artists to draw subjects that would be of interest in missionary or other circles in Britain. Among these illustrations appearing in missionary magazines were drawings of the great temple of Jagannath in Orissa, commissioned by Lt. Col. Phipps, who lived for a long period in India and was one of the supporters of the CMS.[58] Another illustration by a 'native' artist was a drawing of a fakir (which appeared in an early volume of the *Missionary Register*), commissioned by another member of the CMS.[59] A third example of Indian artistry is a drawing of 'Purrum Soatuntre, a Hindoo Fakeer of Benares' which was originally commissioned by Jonathan Duncan (1756), Resident and Superintendent at Benares and a member of the Asiatic Society of Bengal.[60]

As well as including the work done by Indian artists, editors also incorporated drawings executed by missionaries and other European observers. In the absence of photographs, some missionaries (adopting Bishop Heber's habit of illustrating his own work)—sent in sketches, together with written reports. Among the more significant of these representations which were eventually published were illustrations in *Papers Relative to the Wesleyan Missions* by the Rev. Samuel Hardey (WMMS) of a 'Statue of Siven, "the Destroyer"' and 'A Hindoo Idol', and sketches by the Rev. Thomas Hodson, a Wesleyan who was stationed in Calcutta in the 1830s.

Factors Affecting the Construction of Hinduism in Home-based Periodical Literature

What, then, were the fundamental factors affecting the way in which Hinduism was constructed and presented in the material as outlined above?

In our discussion of the role of editors we have already referred incidentally to at least two possible influences affecting the way in which editors understood or portrayed Hinduism. One factor was the extent of the editor's knowledge and/or experience of Hinduism in India; and a second element, probably of considerable importance, was the constant need for editors to focus on propaganda rather than on depth of understanding. Bound up with these general limitations and pressures were a number of other conditions that served to further undermine any attempt at an objective assessment.

---

[58] *MR* 1824 and CMS, *MP*, No. 36, 1824.
[59] *MR*, Vol. 2, September 1816: 388; and CMS, *MP*, No. 2, 1816.
[60] *MR*, Vol. 4, June 1819: 281–82; and CMS, *MP*, No. 15, 1819. See Figure 1.1.

First, apart from the *Missionary Register*, which was broad in its coverage and included the comments and observations of missionaries of all Protestant societies based in mission stations all over India, other journals and papers (being more strictly denominational) concentrated their focus on developments in those parts of India where missionaries of their own society were either active or intended to go. Hence, while readers of almost all periodicals were encouraged to think of Hinduism as an all-embracing pan-Indian system, what they often encountered in their reading or viewing of mission material was a more localized view. And some mission society publications were more limited or regional in their focus than others. Thus journals, supporting a greater range of missions in India, such as those associated with the CMS or LMS, provided more information about conditions throughout India than others, such as the Wesleyan journals, simply because Wesleyan activity on the subcontinent was more limited. In these circumstances, it might be expected that editors and supporters of the larger missionary societies with a major stake in India were, generally speaking, better informed about the nature of India's religion as a whole than those with a minor interest in evangelism in that part of the world.

Another factor affecting the way in which Hinduism was depicted, especially in the more popular quarterly papers and juvenile material, was the need to choose a topic which could be illustrated visually. Editors were aware of the need for varied methods of presentation, and in the case of the literature produced for less well-educated readers, this meant focusing on other down-to-earth topics, such as an object, a person, a custom, or ritual practice—something which could be represented visually and discussed in the accompanying text. In other words, the very nature of popular periodical literature tended to dictate what could be said about Hinduism, the accent being on description and externalities, rather than on lengthy discussion of more theoretical, theological or abstract themes.

Third, there was also the pressure to choose particular kinds of topics because of their intrinsic interest or fascination for British readers. These included unusual, strange, bizarre or even macabre subjects which would excite the reader's attention. Bodies being crushed under the wheels of massive temple carts, the sati leaping into the flames consuming her husband's body, the relaxed figure lying on a bed of nails, devotees hanging upside down from the branch of a tree or being swung in the air with hooks embedded in the back, 'deluded votaries' paying homage to the image of a snake, or cringing before the 'weird' image of some horrific god, all these images and more (so it was thought) were bound to arrest attention, encourage a readership, and also create an even greater sense that Christians were so much better off. Indeed, in their presentation of Hinduism, missionary periodicals appealed to the same sense of 'otherness', the same sense of difference between East and West, and the same sense of superiority, that Said has described in his early work on 'Orientalism' and which was such a strong force influencing the attitude of travellers, administrators and many others who were quite unconnected with the missionary movement.

Fourth, there was the issue of language, distortion and simplification. Hindu beliefs and practices (if they were to be mentioned) needed to be described briefly and in simple English for the benefit of poorly educated working class readers, as well as for those who could cope with more sophisticated texts. These problems not only encouraged gross generalization and simplification whereby 'all' Hindus did this or believed that, but created a need to translate Hindu terminology into Christian language. The pressure was on editors, as well as on missionaries communicating with a European audience, to Christianize Hinduism. This issue has already been referred to by Peter Marshall in his book on *The British Discovery of Hinduism*, and has always been a problem in translating Hindu (usually Sanskrit) terminology into English. Then, as now, the problem was how to find the best *equivalents* in English without losing too much of the original meaning. Often, however, something was lost in translation, and when Pratt or other editors referred to Hindu ideas of God, incarnation, salvation and so on, this sometimes suggested closer parallels between Hindu and Christian thought than was actually the case.

Finally, there was the editor's more general purpose, which included an attempt to highlight the plight of the heathen overseas. The immediate and pressing need was to raise funds and recruit candidates for the mission field. Perhaps the most effective way of doing this was to dwell on the difference between Christianity and Hinduism, to arouse a sense of pity, and to make as plain as possible the urgent need to improve the Hindus' present condition and, above all, to save Hindus from the threat of eternal damnation.

In order to motivate readers editors therefore tended to focus on topics which underlined the more negative aspects of Hinduism. The editor of *Papers Relative to Wesleyan Missions* had, for example, a very clear idea of the role he should play in presenting material on 'the Hindu religion'. Writing in 1832, he declared that 'in attempting to convey to our readers a correct idea of the spiritual darkness and moral wretchedness of the heathen world, we have had frequent occasion to advert to the absurdities

of Hindooism, and the miseries inflicted by the reigning superstition on
the bodies as well as the souls of its deluded votaries'.[61] While Pratt in his
Missionary Register did appear to be genuinely curious about the nature
of Hindu deities, and while, occasionally, there were sustained and in-
depth discussions in some of the more highbrow missionary journals
published in Britain, the transparent underlying theme and motivation
was to demonstrate the superiority of Protestant Christianity.

Hinduism as Depicted in Domestic Periodical Literature, 1810–50

What, then, is the final and overall picture of Hinduism that emerges from
all this material up to about 1850? And how does this compare with the
dominant paradigm as developed by influential Protestant missionary
writers active in India during the same period?

The author's analysis, including a consideration of some of the highbrow as well as popular papers, confirms the view that the Britain-based
literature tended to echo what we have described as the dominant paradigm.[62] In the first place, the shape of imagined Hinduism in this material
was not very different from what it was according to Ward, Duff and other
missionaries in the field. There was the very occasional suggestion that the
Indian religious context was more complex and diverse than was at first
apparent. For example, the Rev. William Holwell (LMS) whose report
was published in the *Missionary Chronicle* in 1824, was (like Buchanan
in his early work) one of the few Protestants who began with the idea
of India having a diversity of religions. In Holwell's view, not only was
Indian 'heathenism' different from 'heathenism' elsewhere, but it included
more than one religion. Referring to a learned weaver who professed to
belong properly to no sect and who had been visiting him for some time,
Holwell remarked that the man disagreed in many points with 'the Hindoo
religions'.[63]

---

[61] *PRWM*, No. L, December 1832.

[62] See the *MR*, the CMS *MP*, *PRWM* and the LMS *Missionary Sketches*, as well as articles
and comment in widely read 'juvenile' literature produced by the CMS, the SPG, the LMS
and the WMMS.

[63] *Quarterly Chronicles of Transactions of the LMS*, Vol. 3: 114–15 (author's italics). At
a slightly later date, the increasing influence of the dominant paradigm was reflected in an
extract from J. W. Massie's book on *Continental India* appearing in the *Chronicle* in 1848.
While Massie felt compelled to pay homage to 'the religion of brahmanism' as the universal

However, for the most part, editors and missionary contributors, influenced by Ward and others, conveyed the generally accepted idea that Hinduism was a unitary religious system. And as was the case with missionaries in the field, this conviction involved contributors in the search for appropriate terminology. Thus commentators in the various periodicals refer to 'Indian heathenism', 'Hindu idolatry', 'the Hindoo system', 'the Hindoo Superstition', 'the Hindoo religion', 'the Brahminical system' and finally 'Hindooism'.[64] Despite the appearance of the term 'Hindooism' in Grant's *Observations* and its early use in Bengal, it did not appear in Pratt's influential *Missionary Register* until May 1818, nor in the LMS *Quarterly Chronicle* until July 1824; and in both cases the term was used not directly but when quoting missionary reports and correspondence.[65] In missionary society periodicals therefore the term was first introduced and used alongside other possible alternatives (such as the ones noted above) and only became popular in Britain, as in India, through a very gradual process until it became the dominant and most common word denoting Hindu religion.

The idea of a distinct unified system, implicit in the development of this terminology, was reinforced by those who, like Ward and Duff, argued that the Hindu system was created and held together by brahmans. Evidence of the effectiveness of brahman control was seen especially in the varna or caste system—a system which, it was argued, was invented by brahmans for their own benefit and which kept all the other classes in a state of religious as well as social subordination. According to the CMS *Missionary Papers* the scheme led to 'great pride and tyranny particularly in the Brahmins'[66]—a point taken up and developed in the LMS *Missionary*

---

religion, he suggested that, in reality, this interpretation made little sense. 'It is true the religion of Brahminism possesses sway in the principal seats of commerce and of population throughout British India, and religion is the general modeller of human character. But the unity is a name rather than a reality, and that which is prevalent is susceptible of shades as varying as the changes of colour.... The theory of Brahminism itself affords scope for schism and distraction' (*Chronicle*, Vol. XXVI, 1848: 42).

[64] 'Indian heathenism' (*PRWM*, No. XLIX, September 1832); 'Hindu idolatry' (*PRWM*, No. XXXIX, March 1830); 'the Hindoo system' (*Sketches*, CV, October 1844); 'the Hindoo Superstition' (*MP*, Nos. XXVI, 1822, and XXXIII, 1824); 'the Hindoo religion' (*Chronicle*, Vol. 1: 210); 'the Brahminical system' (*PRWM*, No. LX, March 1833); 'Hindooism' (*MP*, No. LXXI, 1833, and No. LXXXII, 1836; *PRWM*, No. L, December 1832, No. LI, March 1833; *Sketches*, CV, October 1844, CXVI, July 1847, CXXVIII, July 1850; *Chronicle*, Vol. 2, July 1824: 448). When first introduced, the word 'Hindooism' was often used in terms of its contrast with Christianity, and with the latter's 'true' nature and beneficial effects.

[65] *MR*, May 1818: 204–5; *Quarterly Chronicle*, Vol. 2, July 1824.

[66] *MP*, No. XL, 1818.

Sketches, which included a picture of a Bengali brahman with his foot on the neck of a prostrate devotee.[67] 'But now mark,' exclaimed the CMS paper, 'how artfully the whole system is contrived to keep the wretched people in bondage!'[68]

This system, which appears in the mind of missionaries to have been a form of slavery was, according to contributors to the periodical literature, further reinforced by the imposition of a common social and doctrinal belief. Hinduism was maintained through brahman teachings and the careful manipulation of a people who had no agency and few thoughts of their own. The brahmans, knowing that knowledge is power, maintained a secret knowledge, keeping control over their own Vedas and the people in a state of ignorance and delusion. In words which seem to echo Protestant views of priestcraft during the Reformation, the CMS Papers complained that the brahmans invented 'idle tales' about the gods, refusing to tell the people the truth, and teaching doctrines which continued to make the people dependent upon their ministrations.[69] Commenting on the role of brahmans in ritual bathing one paper reflected further that 'the deceived people are made to believe that they shall have much good, from this detestable idolatry, both in this life and hereafter'.[70]

According to the literature the teachings that helped bind Hindus together included a belief in transmigration. Not bothering, or perhaps not wanting to qualify its statement, and assuming all those described as Hindus believed in transmigration, the CMS *Missionary Paper* declared for example, that 'the Hindoos believe, that as soon as their souls leave their bodies, they go into other bodies: they call this transmigration'.[71] Again failing to acknowledge that Shaivites and many other Hindus did not worship Vishnu, the paper declared that 'the Hindoos suppose that the Deity has appeared at ten different periods. They call these appearances 'Avatars', which means Descent of the Deity, in some particular form.'[72] The *Papers Relative to Wesleyan Missions* were likewise inclined to over-simplified generalization. Either unaware of or ignoring the fact that Hindus had varied notions of 'Heaven' the paper claimed that Indra's heaven 'is the heaven the Hindoos wish to attain'.[73] But more extraordinary

[67] *Sketches*, CXLIV, July 1854.
[68] *MP*, No. XI, 1818.
[69] *MP*, No. XIX, 1820.
[70] *MP*, No. XXVII, 1822.
[71] *MP*, No. II, 1818.
[72] *MP*, No. 19, 1820.
[73] *PRWM*, No. 29, March 1830.

were the editor's comments in the same paper in 1836. Referring to a woodcut illustrating the worship of 'Dooga', he cried, 'how dark must be the state of that people [Hindus] who *universally* consider such an idol as this to be a proper object of worship!'[74] Moreover, more than one of the papers gave the impression that all Hindus were equally aware and determined to die within the sight of the Ganges.

In their comment on different aspects of what was essentially an imagined whole, periodical papers detailed all the practices listed in earlier travel and missionary literature. In this sense the literature recycled and reinforced much of what was already there in the popular imagination. Amongst other things, discussion during the period from about 1818 to 1850 focussed on the iconography, history and characteristics of important or popular deities. The *Missionary Register*, the CMS *Missionary Papers*, the *Papers Relative to the Wesleyan Missions*, and the LMS *Magazine and Missionary Chronicle* all included engravings and details about Hindu gods and Hindu mythology, some of the material being taken from *Asiatic Researches*, Ward's work and from Edward Moor's *The Hindoo Pantheon*. Among these deities Jagannath received very special attention. Another recurring and well-illustrated topic was his importance for Hindus, his temple at Puri, and associated activities including the pilgrimage and annual festivals honouring his name. Religious leaders, including brahmans and especially ascetics, also came in for a great deal of attention—illustrations of the latter's amazing bodily feats being the centrepiece of several missionary papers. Also depicted and discussed were various forms of self-torture such as hook-swinging and other methods employed at the *charak puja* in Bengal, the horrors of sati including the burial of widows, ceremonial bathing in rivers, human sacrifice and other epiphenomena.

Evaluation and Comparison with the Protestant Way

Periodical literature was perhaps less geared towards creating a genuine understanding of Hinduism than for example the writings of Carey and Duff. The overriding objective was to underline the point that Protestant Christianity was infinitely superior as a moral and social system and way of salvation than Hinduism, which was not only cruel and inhuman, but which also led its 'deluded votaries' straight into hell. The moral, social and

[74] *PRWM*, No. 63, March 1836.

even rational failures of the Hindu system were often illustrated through a discussion of the attitude and behaviour of Hindu deities. When discussing Hindu deities the editor of the Wesleyan *Papers* declared, for example, that 'The worship of Shiva...is equal in absurdity, cruelty, and obscenity, to that of any other of the Hindu idols.' Josiah Pratt, who produced a series of illustrated articles on Hindu iconography for the *Missionary Register*, was relatively restrained, but the CMS *Missionary Papers* remarked that 'indecent and cruel rites' were practised in connection with the worship of Shiva and his wife Parvati,[75] and that Kali was represented by the symbols of 'cruelty and blood'. These sentiments with regard to Kali were echoed by the editor of the LMS *Juvenile Magazine*[76] who argued that her worship was 'full of cruelty and abomination'. Krishna in the Vaishnava tradition was also attacked. 'Cruel and impure' stories were told of him, while the representation of him as a playful child 'shews us what low and mean ideas the Hindoos are taught to form of their gods'.[77] Referring to an illustrated tale of Hindu mythology taken from a book entitled the *Hindu Pantheon* the editor of the LMS *Missionary Magazine and Chronicle* remarked that, from these and similar sources, readers would learn of the 'wicked and degraded character of the gods worshipped by the Hindoos, and the silly legends of which their sacred history is chiefly composed'.[78]

The 'abominations' associated with Hindu deities and forms of worship were given even greater scope in periodical literature through the inclusion of illustrations and detailed reports of particular incidents. Since much of this has already been mentioned, and was hardly new, little needs to be added except to stress the frequency with which these themes were taken up and illustrated, especially in the more popular missionary society literature. A constant stream of material, representing Hinduism as something like a chamber of horrors, underlined the urgent need for social reform and evangelism that would save the poor heathen from the consequences on a truly horrific religious system.

Conclusion

It is difficult to find sustained relatively detached analysis of Hindu religion in missionary periodical literature during the early to mid-nineteenth

[75] *MP*, No. XXIII.
[76] December 1845: 279.
[77] *MP*, No. XXV, 1822; No. XXIX, 1825.
[78] *Chronicle*, Vol. XXIV, 1846: 378.

century. As we have seen, much of it was carefully selected, brief and descriptive with a strong emphasis on externalities rather than on what Hindus really thought, or on their discussion of inner life or meaning. Furthermore, the selection of illustrations and comment in popular litera-ture on the subject tended to mirror the beliefs and assumptions of ordinary British people—of the working-class as well as the middle-class readership. Indeed, this type of material tells us at least as much about British society as it does about the religion it was supposed to depict.

According to both missionaries and editors of periodical literature, Hinduism was therefore both like and unlike Christianity. The Hindus, like Christians, were seen as having a distinctive 'religion', a discrete and objec-tive system, which had its essence and boundaries, and which, in that sense, could be compared with all other 'religions' including Christianity. They might also have the same concerns as Christians about happiness in the afterlife, about sin and salvation, but here most similarities ended. And if 'religions' were to be compared and evaluated (as they must be) then Christianity came out on top and Hinduism either very low or at the bottom. In fact, for some writers, Hinduism came to represent almost everything that was the *opposite* of the Protestant faith. For the most part the Hindu religion was demonized[79] and the term Hinduism, invested with the appropriate demonic connotations, was used as a powerful weapon in the campaign to galvanize the missionary movement. This was done by contrasting the thraldom and misery of India's people, oppressed by the horrors of Hindu 'idolatry', with the progress, well-being and happiness of Christian converts secure in the knowledge and love of the one true God.

Largely because of the nature of the readership of periodical literature there was even less discussion of Hindu forms of theology than, for example, in Ward's or Duff's books. There are some references to studies of Hinduism which were appearing elsewhere during this period, but, generally speaking, the focus was on the more tangible and easily

---

[79] By the 1840s there were a few grudging concessions (almost hidden in the text) that there was something of value in contemporary Hindu tradition. Expressions of admiration for the 'devotion' of pilgrims and 'zeal' of sannyasis, was occasionally supplemented by complimentary remarks on some aspects of Hindu religious literature. Elizabeth Hoole's *Juvenile Offering* reproduced Marathi proverbs without comment, and the editor of the *Chronicle*, referring to the Mahabharata as a 'celebrated poem of great antiquity, chiefly related to the doctrines and precepts of Hindooism', remarked that it was 'not wholly destitute of the traces of true religion and pure morality' (*CMG*, No. 9, New Series, December 1850: 107. See also *Juvenile Missionary Magazine*, August 1845: 172 [Hasell]; *Juvenile Offering*, October 1850: 133; *Chronicle*, Vol. XXVI, 1848: 42).

No. L.   **Papers**
RELATIVE TO THE
WESLEYAN MISSIONS,
And to the State of Heathen Countries.
(PUBLISHED QUARTERLY.)

सन्न्यासी

SANYASI,

OR

HINDOO RELIGIOUS MENDICANT.

Figure 7.2
A Missionary Sketch of a 'Sanyasi, or Hindoo Religious Mendicant'

In 1832, when two Methodist missionaries, Peter Percival and Thomas Hodson, were walking along the banks of the river in Calcutta 'to distribute tracts and converse with the natives', they met with a religious devotee 'of whom the accompanying sketch is an excellent likeness'. Shortly afterwards, when Percival was preaching, and had attracted the crowd's and the mendicant's full attention, Hodson 'sketched the devotee on the cuff of his white jacket'; and after the missionaries returned home, he presented Percival with the drawing which, as the latter explained, 'is all the more interesting as it is an exact likeness of the man' (*PRWM*, No. L, December 1832).

understood epiphenomena. Even more than was the case in missionary comment on the subject the emphasis was on Hinduism as a way of works, on the things Hindus did, rather than on what they thought or on Hindu theology. Perhaps the nearest the journals came to discussing Hindu concepts at any length was through a discussion either of caste or of Hindu mythology. A discussion of caste naturally led to some remarks on the Hindu theory of transmigration which, it was assumed, was a universal belief among all Hindus. Furthermore, a discussion of illustrations and engravings, for example of Hindu deities, occasionally led to a slightly deeper excursion into meaning. But whether they liked it or not, editors were very much bound by the readership and, at least at the level of the most popular literature, were unlikely to include material which was too abstract or demanding for less-accomplished readers.

There was the occasional reference to devotion among Hindus but generally speaking the notions of *bhakti* or the way of devotion and ideas associated with *gyana yoga* or the way of knowledge were absent from discussion. The basic impression that one gained from most of the literature was that the vast majority of Hindus, including even sannyasis, were intent on salvation through some kind of way of works—a method of outward performance which could be seen in the enormous extent of ceremonial and ritual. As Duff argued, these rituals (imposed by brahmans on the populace as a method of control) really amounted to a complicated series of tests or hurdles which the suffering people were expected to pass if they were to have any hope of benefits in the life hereafter.

This view of Hinduism, imagined as a way of works, was not only easy to illustrate and describe, but had a special resonance for Protestants. Had not Martin Luther learned that the way of works was totally futile—and that, no matter how many steps he took up the Santa Scala in Rome, salvation was still as remote and far away as it was when he began his climb? Second, not only was salvation not possible through a way of works, but works in Hinduism, the things people were expected to do, had the most appalling social and moral consequences. Religion, in the Protestant view, was clearly linked with morality and with a moral view of the universe. There was a belief that God Himself was moral and that He made moral demands upon His people. Protestants therefore expected that other religions would have their own systems of morality and these should be judged, like everything else, by the standards of revealed religion, or, in other words, by contemporary Protestant standards. However (seeming to forget that for Hindus morality was often closely associated with caste duties), what contributors and editors of missionary society publications usually argued was that not only did the gods in Hinduism ignore morality or behave in immoral ways, but that the works in Hinduism were not 'good' works. The emphasis on the lack of moral concern in Hinduism was reiterated ad nauseam in most of the periodical publications. It was also one of the main concerns and driving forces behind the campaign in periodical literature for the suppression of sati and certain other 'dreadful practices'.

Criticism of different rituals and observances in periodical literature reflected a wide variety of British Victorian concerns. In some cases there was a cultural issue, the Hindu gods being seen as 'ugly' and Hindu music heard as 'discordant'. The Protestant and contemporary concern with the work ethic is also apparent in the complaint that Hindu sannyasis were idle, living off the earnings of others. Contemporary British standards were also reflected in the outrage at displays of Hindu sexuality and especially in the Hindu practice of linking sex with different forms of deity. And apart from obscenity there was also cruelty. As we have seen, much of the criticism of Hindu practice was linked with its apparent inhumanity and cruelty and also with social injustice. Some comments on brahmans and the caste system, and comparisons of Hinduism with slavery, implied the injustice as well as the brutality of a system which readers had heard about in the West Indies and other parts of the world. Finally, among the exponents of education and enlightenment, as well as of Protestant ideas, there was a widespread conviction that, in order to be valid, religion needed to be 'rational'. While it was supposed that Christian beliefs could be tested and declared to be 'true' through the application of rules of evidence, Hinduism was clearly 'absurd'. Indeed, its teachings conflicted with the discoveries of modern science, and were unworthy of rational human beings.

8

A Changing Context: Some General Developments Affecting Missionary Perceptions of Hinduism, 1850–1900

Changes in missionary ideas and depictions of Hinduism during the period 1850–1900 were clearly affected by developments both in India and overseas. The principal focus of this chapter is on the changes taking place outside India—mainly in Britain. While some of the relevant developments in India are also mentioned, a more detailed treatment of these and other Indian contextual issues is given in subsequent chapters.

Developments affecting missionary concepts or models of Hinduism included (*a*) an increase in sources of information, (*b*) the rise and growth of the women's missionary movement (leading to an increase in women's reporting on Hinduism) and (*c*) the growth of studies in comparative religion. Furthermore, the missionaries were not only concerned with models or interpretations of Hinduism, but also with its moral values or worth. Among developments affecting their evaluation was an increase in scholarly knowledge and understanding of Indian religion, and also, significant changes within Protestant Christianity itself. New ways of understanding God and the Christian gospel, and discussions in Britain about the relationship between Christianity and other faiths, were undoubtedly of some importance for missionaries in the mission field. But just how important these changes taking place outside of India were in creating new attitudes of sympathy for Hinduism in the mission field is a question which will be discussed in chapter 10.

Increasing Availability of Sources of Information

Published Material

An important development affecting missionary representations of Hinduism in the second half of the nineteenth century was the enormous increase in general knowledge, and in information available on Indian religions, a point already noted in the Introduction. Opportunities for study and research into Hinduism were obviously very much greater than they had been when the first British missionaries settled at Serampore. Commenting on what he described as 'the growing inter-community of thought between the East and the West', Monier-Williams in his influential book, *Indian Wisdom*, published in 1875, remarked that:

> It cannot indeed be right, nor is it even possible for educated Englishmen to remain any longer ignorant of the literary productions, laws, institutions, religious creed, and moral precepts of their Hindu fellow-creatures and fellow subjects. The East and West are everyday being drawn nearer to each other, and British India, in particular, is now brought so close to us by steam, electricity and the Suez Canal, that the condition of the Hindu community—mental, moral and physical—forces itself peremptorily to our attention. Nor is it any longer justifiable to plead the difficulty of obtaining accurate official information as an excuse for ignorance. Our Government has for a long period addressed itself most energetically to the investigation of every detail capable of throwing light on the past and present history of the Queen's Indian dominions.[1]

Information available on India had greatly increased and continued to expand at a rapid rate thanks to continuing imperial and informal connections. Added to material which had long been available in *Parliamentary Papers* was information on India's religious and social conditions contained in the India-wide census (the first census of British India being held in 1871), and in other official publications such as the district gazetteers which also began to appear in the second half of the nineteenth century. In addition to this material were unofficial accounts and sources of information provided increasingly by Indians, as well as by missionaries and other Europeans with experience in the country. In addition, missionary societies continued to expand their own outlets, including propaganda and information on religious and social conditions in the subcontinent.

Especially important was the progress being made in the translation of Sanskrit texts into English—a trend which tended to underline the brahmanical approach, but which, nevertheless, provided Europeans with more accurate knowledge of a range of influential texts. Among the most important of these translations was Frederick Max Müller's three-volume edition of the *Rig Veda* (1849–56). This was followed by the publication of John Muir's five-volume series entitled *Original Sanskrit Texts on the*

---

[1] Monier-Williams 1875: iv.

Origin and History of the People of India, Their Religion and Institutions (1871–73).

Other major developments in the translation of Sanskrit texts during this period included the publication of M. Monier-Williams' *Introduction to Indian Wisdom or Examples of the Religious, Philosophical, and Ethical Doctrines of the Hindus* (1875) and the appearance of the first volumes in the series known as the *Sacred Books of the East*. Edited initially by Max Müller, and published (with an appropriate introduction) over a period of about thirty years, they provided more ordinary readers with easier access to the translation of some of the most influential and basic sources in the brahmanical tradition. They included Max Müller's translation of the *Upanishads* in two volumes (1879, 1884); Georg Bühler's edition of the *Laws of Manu* (1886); Kashinath Trimback Telang's translation of the *Bhagavadgita* (1879); Julius Jolly's edition of the *Institutes of Vishnu* (1880); and Georg Thibaut's edition of the *Vedanta-Sutras of Badarayana* with Shankaracharya's Commentary (1890–96).

As shall become apparent, some of these translations, particularly those of Muir, Monier-Williams and Müller, were influential and proved to be of considerable use in the study and writings of some of the more prominent missionary authors.[2]

Informal Sources of Information: Personal Contact, Family and Relatives in the Mission Field

An important additional element in the growth of knowledge (however inadequate) was the increased information and detail supplied by relatives and friends already in the mission field. There were increasingly informal as well as formal methods of communicating information, ideas and views about Hindu practice and tradition. The extent to which missionaries working in India during the second half of the nineteenth century were related to current or former missionaries with Indian experience can be illustrated in different ways through missionary records. Two sets of these are the registers of the London Missionary Society (LMS) and the Church Missionary Society (CMS). Another source is the data gleaned

---

[2] A number of the leading missionary authors refer to Max Müller's work, and/or Monier-Williams' *Indian Wisdom*. Also popular were Muir's translations—these being used, for example, by John Murray Mitchell, John Robson, W. J. Wilkins and T. E. Slater. For laudatory comments on the usefulness of translations and commentaries on Sanskrit texts by Monier-Williams, Müller and Muir see the remarks of the Rev. T. Williams (SPG, Rewari) in his annual report for 1886 (*MF*, 1887, Vol. XXXII: 311–22).

from candidates' papers and other manuscript material relating to female missionaries who joined the Church of England Zenana Missionary Society (CEZMS) during the period 1883–1900.

The difference in the missionaries' experience and background during the first and the second half of the nineteenth century is clearly reflected in Sibree's entries on LMS missionaries in India.[3] Of the 335 LMS missionaries sent to India during the period 1807 to 1900, nine were sons and nine were daughters of missionaries—the combined total of eighteen representing 5 per cent of those sent out. While this represents a small proportion of missionaries, it says nothing about brothers, sisters, uncles, aunts and more distant relatives also working in India.[4] The crucial point, however, is the way in which these relationships were multiplying in India over time. All but two of these recruits with parents in the Indian mission field took up their appointment during the second half of the century—a development which illustrates the increasing importance of family relationships in India and, with this, the probability of an increasing knowledge of Hinduism through family connections during that period.[5]

The CEZMS records are also informative. The society adopted a strategy of employing women in both foreign and local connection. Those 'in local connection' were Eurasian and other women recruited in India itself, while those in the foreign connection were CEZMS workers recruited in Britain. While the women 'in local connection' could obviously be expected to have a greater local knowledge than those who joined the society from overseas, it is, nevertheless, clearly apparent that some of those in the 'foreign' category were not only born in India to missionary or non-missionary parents, but had some knowledge of Hindu ideas and practice even before joining the society in Britain.

Of the 123 CEZMS women recruited *in Britain* whose place of birth is known, and who subsequently worked in India during the period 1875 to 1900, at least fifteen (or 12 per cent) were born in India—the majority

---

[3] Sibree 1923.

[4] For further commentary on relationships between LMS missionaries in the field see Semple 2003 (pp. 95, 103–5).

[5] Of the 471 CMS missionaries sent to India during the period 1850 to 1900, thirty-three, or 7 per cent, are recorded as sons of missionaries who had worked there. For the most part they returned to the region or that part of India where they had been born, if not reared in childhood. Other missionaries had other immediate members of the family—uncles, cousins, brothers and eventually (when the CMS admitted women) sisters who were also working in India (CMS *Register of Missionaries*, etc.).

being daughters of missionaries with the CMS.[6] Among these were the sisters Maria and Louise Daeuble who, before joining the CEZMS, accompanied their father, the Rev. C. M. Daeuble (CMS) when he went on preaching tours in the Benares region. Edith Alexander, who spent the first thirty-two years of her life in India, was the daughter of the veteran CMS missionary F. W. N. Alexander, a pioneer worker in the Telugu mission established in 1842. Emily Sandys, who had much to say about Hindu religious practice, was born in Calcutta in 1860. Her father, who died when she was eleven, was a well known CMS missionary, while her mother, who continued active work with the CMS in Calcutta, eventually became Vice-President of the CEZMS in London. Gertrude Kember, Katherine Valpy, Eleanor Sell and Annie Thomas were all born into CMS missionary families in south India—Gertrude's fluency in Tamil standing her in good stead when she was appointed to Ootacamund in 1895. Other CEZMS missionaries were born of parents in secular occupations. The father of Alice and Annie Ward was a 'Barrack Master', apparently in Bombay; Catherine Newnham's father had also been in military service, while Lilian Jenning's father was a retired judge living in Mysore. Once again, and as in the case of some of the late nineteenth century CMS and LMS recruits, experience of India, most notably with parents who were working among Hindus, must have served as an introduction (however inadequate) to Hindu teachings and religious life.

Rise of the Women's Missionary Movement

Another significant change, and one reflected in the data on families and relatives in India, was the rise of the women's missionary movement in Britain and America during the second half of the nineteenth century. The British women's account of their experience and their depiction of Indian religious belief and practice became an increasingly important additional element in missionary constructions of Hinduism during this period.

The British women's enthusiasm for Christian mission (already apparent in their support of the existing male dominated societies) is also shown in the decision of male organizations to accept women as missionaries. Alongside this development, and sometimes even before, was the

[6] For these and other details mentioned in this paragraph see CEZMS archives Birmingham University, CEZ/C/AMI, Register of Missionaries with particulars of service, Vol. 1; papers of individual missionaries; Barnes 1897: esp. 233–60; and Stock 1899.

umber————

formation of independent female societies sending their own candidates to India or elsewhere.

European women were in fact involved 'informally' in British Protestant missions in India from the very beginning—often as unpaid and officially unrecognized workers in 'women's work for women'.[7] The great majority were the wives, sisters, widows or even daughters of men in the mission field.[8] Apart from carrying out what was for most of them their normal supervisory and domestic duties in the European household, it was hoped and perhaps even expected that they would do something to further the spread of Christianity among Indian women.[9] This was seen as essential partly because Hindu women were perceived as religiously conservative, as the bulwark of Hinduism in the home, and as a powerful and effective force undermining missionary attempts to influence the younger generation.[10] Wives and other female relatives of male missionaries conducted and taught in elementary girls' schools, and were active in the establishment and ongoing management of women's teacher-training institutions. They founded homes for female orphans, visited Indian women in the zenana or the humbler home, and also spent much time in the training or overseeing of Bible women and other Indian assistants. Like their husbands, brothers or fathers they were often called upon to give elementary medical assistance and even to help in the organizing of famine relief. Among pioneer British women were Hannah Marshman, Margaret Wilson (nee Cooke), Hanna Mullens and, as well as these, many other dedicated wives, widows and spinsters who followed in their footsteps and whose story is yet to be told.[11]

But while it is true that this work was officially unrecognized and was scarcely acknowledged in annual reports or at annual meetings, some understanding of the importance of women's work was beginning to

---

[7] For a brief overview see Richter 1901 (pp. 329–46) and, for the women's pioneering work in the establishment and conduct of mission schools for girls, see Ingham 1956: 86–7.

[8] For example, in a resolution of 1867, reaffirming their policy of not employing single women, the CMS claimed that the Society was already doing a good deal of work through the 'wives, sisters and daughters' of CMS missionaries (Stock 1899, Vol. 2: 398–99).

[9] On this issue see Bowie et al. 1993: 25–6.

[10] See especially Weitbrecht 1875: 47–9 and Vaughan 1876: 271. The paradox implicit in this conviction has been noted by several commentators including Rosemary Fitzgerald, who argues that while women were represented as depressed, debased and neglected, they were also represented as an 'almighty power' and 'the final guardians of the inner core of traditional culture' (Bickers and Seton 1996: 180–81).

[11] For brief biographies of these and other pioneering missionary women who worked in India, see Weitbrecht 1875: 144–222.

influence and affect the attitude of mission supporters. There was some discussion of women's work in missionary periodical literature even during the first half of the nineteenth century.[12] Missionary wives and other women occasionally contributed articles in influential missionary publications. Furthermore, the need for women's work for women, and the value of what had already been accomplished was publicized by some of the more prominent and experienced male missionaries working in the field. Indeed, it was this growing appreciation and awareness of the importance of the work undertaken by female missionary workers (usually on a voluntary basis) that was one of the factors stimulating the further growth of the women's missionary movement in subsequent decades.

In an article published in 1986, Geraldine Forbes suggests that British women's increasing involvement in missionary work was one solution to the middle-class problem of 'surplus women'.[13] This argument has recently been challenged by Jennifer Morawiecki in a doctoral thesis on the selection and preparation of women missionaries of the CEZMS, 1880–1920.[14] She argues that there were increasingly other opportunities for middle-class women outside the home, not only in nursing, but also in teaching—a point she establishes with reference to the census. She also points out that the number of women choosing mission work compared with the number of those entering other occupations was 'a tiny minority', and that the mission work option was seen to have its own problems and disadvantages.[15] But irrespective of the question as to how far women's increasing involvement in mission can be seen as one aspect of their search for 'suitable' employment, other influences encouraging women's work in the mission field are also apparent. One of these was a trend towards the increasing participation of women in religious affairs in Britain, especially in preaching and in the management and organization of religious associations,[16] and also towards a closer *link* between spiritual and humanistic views of the world. This latter trend, which has often been seen as a strengthening of the idea of the 'social Gospel', involved a growing conviction that people of all classes were not merely abstract 'souls' which required 'salvation', but men and women yearning for a more holistic

---

[12] *CMP*, No. 34, 1824, and No. 86, 1837; *Sketches*, No. 102, January 1844, and No. 123, April 1849. *Juvenile Offering*, Vol. 4, December 1847: 133–37; *Juvenile Missionary Magazine*, Vol. 1, 1844: 35–9; Vol. 2, 1845: 211, and Vol. 3, 1846: 209–10.

[13] Forbes 1986.

[14] Morawiecki 1998.

[15] Ibid.: 90–2.

[16] Ibid.: 90.

approach.[17] Christian women in Britain were, therefore, ideally placed for this type of outreach. While becoming more prominent as leaders in religious affairs, they were, at the same time, and as Frank Prochaska has noted, increasingly active in philanthropy in England in the nineteenth century.[18] Hence, women's work for women in India offered them a combination of the two roles which they were already developing in public life in Britain. While in one sense it was challenging and comparatively new, it also offered a certain degree of continuity and another arena in which middle-class women would be able to utilize their experience and expertise for the benefit of their 'benighted' and 'down-trodden' sisters in India.

Nor, in all probability, were women (any more than men) immune from a sense of romance and excitement which was sometimes connected with mission overseas. When presenting her paper at the second decennial missionary conference in Calcutta in 1883, Mrs Etherington of the Baptist Missionary Society (BMS), Benares, asked:

> [A]re all who come here to do Zenana work, as it is called, honestly desirous of working for God in this land? In not a few cases has there not been too much of mere romance and pleasant excitement, and too little of honest searching of heart, and calm counting of the cost at starting, and consequently have there not been many cases of disappointment and failure at the end? ... [I]t must be admitted that mistakes are often made, either by those who come or by those who send them; which seriously affect our work both here and at home.[19]

In addition to these factors operating in Britain were the changing situation and increasing opportunities for work in India.[20] The missionary ladies' access to zenanas (apartments reserved for secluded women) appears largely to have depended on the attitude of Indian men. These were usually the fathers or husbands who had power to decide whether they were willing to allow foreign women to visit and teach in what was regarded as their private inner sanctum. Alexander Duff had hoped that the young higher caste male students exposed to Western education and 'enlightenment' would eventually want more satisfactory relationships and education for their women,[21] and as the number of male students

[17] Oddie 1976: 26–30.

[18] Prochaska 1980.

[19] *Report of the Second Decennial Missionary Conference held at Calcutta, 1882–83*: 199.

[20] See Storrow's remarks in his introduction to Leslie 1868: xiii.

[21] Smith 1879, Vol. 1: 151.

exposed to Western influences increased, so did requests for European or other educated women to teach Hindu women in the home.

The first well-known experiment took place in 1854 when John Fordyce of the Free Church of Scotland (FCS) arranged for a Eurasian missionary, Miss Toogood, to visit Kumar Tagore's home in Calcutta.[22] Kumar Tagore's attitude and position as a cultivated and liberal-minded man is indeed significant as a reminder that the success of zenana visiting depended very largely on men such as these who had already received a Western education and were favourably disposed towards missionaries.[23] But this event might also be taken as a warning that the missionary women's depiction of the zenana was likely to be based on a somewhat unrepresentative sample of high-caste Hindu homes, since they were unable to visit homes opposed to missionaries, or those unaffected by Western education or 'enlightened' views of the need for female education.

One of the consequences of these expanding opportunities and the Protestant women's increasing involvement in other aspects of missionary activity in India during the second half of the nineteenth century was the grudging and belated admission of women as members of interdenominational missionary conferences. These included regular or somewhat intermittent gatherings of Protestant missionaries at the local, regional and all-India levels. Regular monthly meetings of urban ecumenical conferences, such as those of the Calcutta, Bombay, Madras and Bangalore Missionary Conferences, were supplemented by the holding of an increasing number of more general conferences which met during the second half of the nineteenth century. One of the first of the regional gatherings was a conference of Bengal missionaries which met in Calcutta in 1855.[24] This was followed by a conference of Protestant missionaries in Benares in 1857, the South India Missionary Conference held at Ootacamund in 1858, and the Punjab Missionary Conference held at Lahore in 1862–63.[25] India-wide conferences attracting increasing numbers of missionaries were to follow. The first of these decennial gatherings was the General Missionary Conference, attracting 136 delegates, which was held at Allahabad in

[22] Richter 1901: 338–39.

[23] For the attitude of some other leading Bengalis who were prepared to open their homes to visits from female missionaries, see Weitbrecht 1875: 66–7.

[24] *Proceedings of a General Conference of Bengal Protestant Missionaries held in Calcutta, Sept. 4–7 1855.*

[25] *Proceedings of the South India Missionary Conference held at Ootacamund 19 April– 5 May 1858,* and *Report of the Punjab Missionary Conference held at Lahore, December to January, 1862–1863.*

1872–73.[26] This was followed by the conference in Calcutta (1882–83) with 475 members, and the Bombay conference (1892–93) with 620.[27]

Women do not appear to have been admitted as members to these local, regional or general conferences at least till the 1870s. There were no women listed as members of the Calcutta Missionary Conference (the largest local conference) in a list which appeared in the minutes in April 1878. There were no women listed as members of the Bengal, Benares, south India or Punjab regional gatherings. Indeed, the usual practice was for the men to read papers on female education or to discuss among themselves any other matters that touched on work among India's women or children. Women were allowed to attend meetings of the Punjab Missionary Conference, but were asked to leave during the discussion of polygamy and divorce. However, a breakthrough appears to have come with the further influx of single as well as married women in the mission field—a development which roughly coincided with the holding of the first decennial missionary meeting at Allahabad in 1872. Murray Mitchell, Convenor of the Sub-Committee of the Allahabad meeting, asked Miss Brittan of the American Zenana Mission in Calcutta to read a paper. While, like some of the male paper givers, she and Mrs Winter of the Society for the Propagation of the Gospel (SPG) mission, Delhi, were unable to attend, they appear to have been the first women permitted to make some kind of contribution to conference deliberations. Women were physically present at subsequent decennial conferences, reading and discussing papers on work among women and children. But male generosity appears to have gone only so far as permitting women to discuss women's issues. For example, there is no indication that women were able to participate or comment on general issues relating to Hinduism. Certainly they made comments on Hindu attitudes and domestic rituals but were not involved in discussions of more, general topics and issues relating to Hindus. In that sense, and in spite of their increased importance as workers in the mission field, the woman's voice is conspicuously absent from many of the most important deliberations on Hinduism which took place during the second half of the nineteenth century.

British missionary views of the position of Indian women in Hinduism and British female missionary depictions of Hinduism are discussed further in chapter 11.

[26] *Report of the General Missionary Conference held at Allahabad, 1872–73.*
[27] *Report of the Second Decennial Missionary Conference held at Calcutta 1882–83*, and *Report of the Third Decennial Missionary Conference held at Bombay 1892–93.*

Advances in Empirical Studies, Religious Controversy and Changes in Christian Theology

As is well known, religious controversy was a marked feature of intellectual life in Victorian England. Developments in the fields of geology, natural science, biblical criticism and comparative religion all had their effect on theology and on those usually referred to as 'thinking Christians'. One of the more succinct accounts of the way in which these developments may have affected the missionary movement, including missionary depictions of Hinduism, was given by T. E. Slater (LMS). As the author of *The Philosophy of Missions: A Present-day Plea* (1882) and one who had long been interested in intellectual changes in Britain and Europe, as well as in India, he was well qualified to comment on major trends in Christian thought. Speaking at the Bangalore Missionary Conference in 1887, he remarked that:

> There can be no doubt that within the last few years there has been a marked change in the mode of preaching to the people. It used to be the fashion to attack their religion, to revile their gods, and to represent Christianity as sounding the knell of doom over all non-Christian nations. But altered views, mainly of the nature and character of God, have altered the views of most with reference to their fellow men. Not the wrath, but the love of God is now, I imagine, the chief inspiration of Christian preaching and of Christian missions. Not the thought that the heathen, as we call them, are all going to hell, because they are heathen, but that God yearns over them as His lost children, and that it is our duty and delight to recover them for Him, and to raise them, and make them happier and better *now*.[28]

The new developments such as those in scientific and historical enquiry did not affect all missionary societies or supporters of mission in the same way. While, for example, the Anglican SPG and Society for the Promotion of Christian Knowledge (SPCK) tended to reflect Broad-Church views and incorporate the results of these enquiries into their changing theology and views of the world, evangelical organizations, including the CMS, were more prone to panic and more defensive. They were, according to Brian Hatcher, more inclined to publicly ignore religious controversies, but, when unavoidable, reaffirm what they regarded as established evangelical

[28] *HF*, Vol. 7, No. 9, March 1887: 257.

truths.[29] Furthermore, as the case of Bishop Colenso demonstrates, it cannot be assumed that members of the same missionary organization were necessarily always unanimous in their views about how to react to the advances in modern knowledge.[30] Lastly, some changes were easier to accommodate and appeared less threatening to the fundamental basis of mission than others. It was perfectly possible, for example, for the advocates of mission like Eugene Stock of the CMS 'to recognize and admire the works of God throughout geologic ages', and 'to delight in the archaeological discoveries'.[31] But when it came to issues of comparative religion, such as Max Müller's 'science of religion', this was a difficult issue involving assumptions which appeared to place Christianity on the same footing and in the same category as 'heathen' religions.[32] In this view, Christianity was no longer quite so unique or quite so different from Hinduism; and, as Bishop Azariah averred many years later, doubts about Christianity's claim to be the only 'true' religion could be seen as undermining the success of missionary enterprise.[33]

Hindus, Hinduism and the Doctrine of Eternal Punishment

One of the more critical developments affecting missionary responses to Hinduism and the Hindu 'heathen' was the questioning of the doctrine of eternal punishment. Ever since its origins, the evangelical branch of the Protestant missionary movement had held as one of its basic assumptions the idea of 'the perishing heathen'.[34] This included the notion that unless they heard and responded to the Gospel, all those outside the fold of Protestant Christianity were doomed to everlasting punishment. Mission was therefore 'rescue mission' and the *primary* task of missionaries was to save individuals by plucking them like burning brands from the fires of hell. The horrific vision of millions of unregenerate heathens rushing into

[29] Hatcher 1990. According to Thompson (1951: 115) the SPG, in establishing the Archbishop's Board of Examiners in 1846 'made quite clear its determination to impose no doctrinal tests of its own upon its missionaries, but to send them out as representatives of the Church, not of a Society'.

[30] SPG, archives, *The Bishop of Natal and the SPG. Report of a meeting held at 79 Pall Mall*, London, 20/2/1863.

[31] Stock 1899, Vol. 2: 345.

[32] See especially the article by Ridgeway, Associate Secretary of the CMS, in *CMI*, September 1866.

[33] Harper 2000: 242.

[34] Piggin 1984: 139–41.

an eternity of suffering without hope of salvation was enough to disturb the sleep of many a devout Christian and a powerful incentive to mission for much of the nineteenth century. Writing as late as 1914, A. E. Garvie, author of *The Missionary Obligation in the light of the changes in modern thought*, recalled that 'When I was a boy, it was thought a heresy of the deepest dye to question or doubt the everlasting duration of future penalty for all those who did not die believing in Christ.'[35] In common with missionaries deployed elsewhere, many of those destined for India were deeply impressed with the urgency of saving souls. When applying for service with the CMS in 1838, James Long declared that 'the thought of 800 millions passing into eternity every 30 years without a ray of hope often overwhelms me as I ask myself the question am I doing my part to avert these dire consequences.'[36] In his application for work with the LMS in 1852, M. A. Sherring stressed with impeccable correctness the orthodox view that 'they who do not believe on Christ shall at the Great Day of Judgement be banished by Him then sitting as Judge into everlasting punishment'. He wanted to go out, he said, for 'the sole purpose' of preaching the Gospel to the natives 'now perishing' for lack of knowledge. Others offering their services to the LMS, and also destined for work in India, were influenced by similar considerations. They too were deeply affected by what they believed was the urgent necessity of going out and snatching the 'precious and immortal souls' of the heathen from imminent destruction in the fires of hell.[37]

These considerations—not infrequently the dominant motive for mission—declined in importance during the last quarter of the nine-teenth century. Increasing doubts that the 'heathen' who had never heard the Gospel would in fact be 'rushing into hell', were reflected in public controversy and subsequently in candidates' papers. A waning of convic-tion on this point coincided with the growth of a more liberal theology and with the development of a more tolerant attitude towards non-Christian religions. Belief in eternity of punishment, challenged by F. D. Maurice in his *Theological Essays* in 1853 but strongly defended in

[35] For these and subsequent quotations from missionary candidates' papers see Oddie 1974.

[36] Oddie 1999: 12.

[37] 'I see millions of my fellow immortals', wrote F. Baylis in 1850, 'destined to live for ever either in happiness or misery, going fast into eternity, without ever having heard of Him, who died to save them'. 'The deep necessity of the heathen who are perishing without a knowledge of the Saviour', wrote G. Shrewsbury in 1858, 'prompts me to go' (Oddie 1974: 68).

orthodox circles,[38] again became the subject of debate in 1860 as a result of the widely-publicised *Essays and Reviews*. By the 1870s and despite the determined resistance of evangelicals, it was becoming clear that the old evangelical doctrine of 'the perishing sinner' no longer represented the theological consensus.[39] In 1877 there was a controversy over the question of eternal punishment in the Congregational Union, and by 1888, even the Baptists, noted for their conservative theology, were divided over the issue.

These doubts were even acknowledged on missionary platforms and are reflected in Slater's observation in 1882 that

> the ghastly argument drawn from the appalling picture of the future misery of the heathen, which once roused missionary assemblies, has been abandoned.... The lurid verse of Montgomery's missionary hymn, 'The heathen perish' which begins with the words, 'see the short course of vain delight', and which to so many presented the great impelling motive to missionary activity is seldom sung—indeed, it has disappeared from many of the hymn books.[40]

Doubts about the doctrine of eternal punishment are also apparent in the LMS candidates' papers. Edwin Greaves, who subsequently wrote an account of the *Kumbh Mela*, complained in his application form that too much had been made of the doctrine of reward and punishment.[41] C. G. Marshall stated his belief that at the Second Coming, rewards and punishments would be bestowed upon all men according to their deeds, but that they would be 'modified by the light & opportunity given to each'.[42] Andrew Parker explicitly rejected belief in any doctrine of everlasting punishment, stating that he could not believe 'that any theory of punishment is conceived in the true spirit of Scripture wh. represents God's love as everlastingly baulked & evil eternally dividing the universe with God'.[43] In 1883, S. Long declared that the full nature and duration of punishment 'is unknown to us in detail'.[44]

---

[38] Stock 1899, Vol. 2: 341. So disturbed were evangelicals and other adherents of the Church of England that a statement signed by 11,000 clergy and 137,000 laymen was issued reiterating the signatories' belief that the 'punishment' of the 'cursed' equally with the 'life' of the righteous is 'everlasting'.

[39] Hatcher 1990: 54.

[40] Slater 1882: 26–30.

[41] CWM, *CP*, Answers to Printed Questions (n.d.).

[42] CWM, *CP*, 1888.

[43] Ibid.

[44] CWM, *CP*, April 1883.

Since the fate of the heathen was becoming less certain, this lessened the feeling of distance between European Christians (including missionaries) convinced of their own acceptance before God, and Hindus, characterized as 'unsaved', and clearly different in the sense that they were *undoubtedly* facing an afterlife of eternal misery. These developments might also be seen as affecting attitudes to Hinduism. Since it was no longer certain that 'heathen' souls were passing into hell, then Hinduism could not always be blamed for endangering the future state of its devotees. Hinduism, as some missionaries in the second half of the nineteenth century were wont to plead, was not always an instrument of the devil. On the contrary, and as we shall argue, aspects of Hinduism were seen increasingly as countering evil and as being part and parcel of God's redemptive purpose.

Values of Christianity in the Here and Now

During the latter part of the century there was, as Sharpe suggests, 'a general trend away from transcendentalism towards immanentism in theological and philosophical thought'.[45] Growing doubts about the ultimate fate of the heathen were to some extent replaced with a much greater focus on the *love* of God and on the benefits of Christianity as distinct from other systems, in the here and now. By conceiving of heaven and hell not as places but as two possible relationships with God, Maurice in particular, 'shifted the emphasis from the future to the present'.[46] For those who adopted this position there was no longer such intense concern with saving the lost, but a change in focus which encouraged greater reflection on issues of welfare, social justice and what J. J. Dennis described as 'Christian Missions and Social Progress'.[47] For some, the thought of saving 'the perishing heathen' remained as their primary motivation; but the worldly benefits of spreading the Gospel were increasingly stressed. Clear examples of this trend can again be seen in the LMS candidates' papers and in the comments of young men destined for India. In his application A. A. Dignam stressed that, as far as possible, 'I shall interest myself in the social conditions of the people, & with increasing knowledge of their wants, try to improve their mode of living & if I can do something towards

[45] Sharpe 1965: 39.
[46] Hatcher 1990: 46.
[47] Dennis 1897–99.

relieving or lessening their bodily ailments I shall not fail to do so.'[48] H. F. W. Lester, like an increasing number of Christians during this period, also placed a clear emphasis on the redeeming qualities of the Gospel in the here and now: 'I feel that Christ is just what the world wants,' he wrote, 'that he is the only possible solace in time of trouble & need, and the only possible inspiration in time of ignorance & dejection. And I feel too,' he continued, 'the deep need of the world for Christ. I have heard (but faintly I know) some of the awful cries of men & women who daily are suffering unutterable woes which the knowledge and love of Christ only can spare them.'[49]

It is obvious that quite apart from their passion for saving souls, early evangelical missionaries in India had also been concerned with moral and social questions. After campaigning for the suppression of what were seen as some of the most offensive social evils in India, there was then something of a hiatus in the mid-nineteenth century when social issues were not so prominent. However, changes in the understanding of the Christian Gospel led to a more rounded and integrated view of the purpose of Christian mission; and, as noted above, an increasingly important argument for missions in India was that Christian teaching and the Christian ethic had much more beneficial social effects than Hindu practice. Apart from continuing complaints about the way in which the lower orders were oppressed in the caste system, which was seen increasingly as being based on a Hindu religious foundation,[50] there was probably an even greater British public concern about the treatment of women as a result of the rapid growth of zenana missions. Indeed, the British women's mission to their 'Hindu sisters' was justified, at least in part, on the basis of what it was doing for women in the here and now.

Three Exponents of the New Theology

F. D. Maurice (1805–72)

One of the first to reject the doctrine of eternal punishment, Maurice was also prominent in stressing the universality of God's love and His presence in non-Christian religious systems. His writings, including books such as *The Kingdom of Christ* (1838) and *Theological Essays* (1853), as well as his

[48] CWM, *CP*, 10/1/1882.
[49] CWM, *CP*, Answers to Printed Questions, June 1885.
[50] Oddie 1976: esp. 47–50.

lectures, had a considerable influence on the Christian thought of his day.[51] It was Maurice who, like the early Christians of the Alexandrian school, advocated the policy of preserving the best in other traditions and of building Christianity on the basis of what was already there. He spelled out this idea in what became known as the fulfilment theory in his Boyle lectures on 'The Religions of the World and their Relations to Christianity'. The lectures, delivered in 1845–46, were published in book form in 1847— the popularity of the work being such that it was reprinted at least six times before 1900.[52]

Maurice argued that Christians must never cease to look for all that is good in the world's religious traditions. Among other things, he drew attention to the relevance of Paul's discourse on Mar's hill and implied that the Hindu religious aspirations and insights would find their completion or fulfilment 'in the disclosure of the Word become flesh in Jesus Christ'.

M. Monier-Williams (1819–99)

Perhaps even more influential in missionary circles during much the same period was M. Monier-Williams who became the Boden Professor of Sanskrit at Oxford in 1860. Among his best known and most influential works was *Indian Wisdom*, published in 1875. A series of lectures offering examples of 'the most remarkable religious, philosophical and ethical teachings of ancient Hindu authors', its chief purpose was to present 'the bright side of the picture' and to give prominence 'to all that is good and true in the Hindu system'.[53] Adopting a position similar to that of Maurice, Williams claimed that the ground was rapidly being cleared 'for a fair and impartial study' of the writings of Eastern nations and appealed especially to missionaries to be 'absolutely fair' in their examination and representation of other religions.[54] Like Max Müller he declared his conviction that all religions, however they are to be judged and whatever stages of development they may have reached, are expressions of a fundamental and deep-seated instinct in man. The central task, he averred in his early work, was to search for 'common ground' between Christianity and other religions and to look forward to the time when all that was good and true in other faiths would find completion in Christianity. Indeed, it was Monier-Williams who in his later book entitled *Modern India*, published

[51] Cracknell 1995: 35–60.
[52] Ibid.: 311.
[53] Monier-Williams 1875: xxxii.
[54] Ibid.: 3.

in 1878, spelled out in some further detail his idea of fulfilment or, more correctly, fulfilment in Christianity. This, he argued, was a process which could be envisioned in two ways: first, there is the idea that Christianity is that form of religion which satisfies or fulfils the religious instincts and desires in the heart of every individual, of whatever religion he or she may be; and second, the term might be used in the sense that the lower religions (each religion taken as a whole) are fulfilled or completed in the 'higher' religion through the process of evolution, Christianity being the fulfilment of Hinduism.

In a much publicized volte-face at a CMS annual meeting in 1887, Monier-Williams renounced this evolutionary view of the development of religions, arguing that far from finding their fulfilment in Christianity, non-Christian religious development was in the wrong direction. 'They [non-Christian religions] all begin with some flashes of true light and end up in utter darkness'. He not only claimed that there was 'a veritable gulf' between Christianity and these non-Christian systems, but also criticized 'the limp, flabby, jelly-fish kind of tolerance' which he now believed was unworthy of 'a manly' Christianity. However, his change in attitude was not perhaps as marked as it might have been, as he also reminded his audience that 'our Bible tells us that God has not left Himself without a witness, and that in every nation he that feareth God and worketh righteousness is accepted by Him'.[55] Furthermore, ideas expressed in his earlier work which suggested that Christianity was comparable with other religions had possibly already had some effect on conservative supporters of Christian mission. During the period in which he expressed these more liberal views, from the time of his publication of *Indian Wisdom* in 1875 up until his change of mind in 1887, he remained influential in CMS and missionary circles. It was during this period that, as the saying goes, 'he let the genie out of the bottle'. Once having sown the seeds of an idea it was difficult for at least some people to forget it altogether.

Friedrich Max Müller (1823–1900)

A third important scholarly influence on the changing missionary evaluation of Hinduism was the work and influence of Friedrich Max Müller (1823–1900). He was well known and widely respected for his work on early Sanskrit texts, especially for his translation of the *Rig Veda*. Indeed, among his papers in Oxford is a list of missionary societies that applied to the East India Company for copies of his translation. Applicants included

---

[55] Monier-Williams 1887.

the CMS, SPG, Wesleyan Methodist Missionary Society (WMMS), and the Free Church of Scotland and Irish Presbyterian missions. Max Müller was also known through his lectures and other publications, including works dealing with 'the science of religion'—a term which he coined to describe the comparative method as applied to the study of religion.[56] Challenging the view that, because of its claim to a special revelation, Christianity was unlike any other religion, he insisted that all religions must be treated as being on the same footing. They were all part of a religious evolutionary process and, though Christianity had reached a superior stage, its position was, nevertheless, relative to that of others. Thus, for John Robson, T. E. Slater and other missionaries who, as we shall see, were influenced by Max Müller's views, it was no longer possible to think of non-Christian religions as totally 'other'.

While Monier-Williams and Max Müller eventually came to differ on the relative distance between Christianity and non-Christian religions, both men, in common with Maurice, stressed the necessity of missionaries adopting a sensitive, positive and sympathetic approach in their preaching and dealings with Hindus.

According to Max Müller's vicar, who appears to have known him well, 'he had the strongest aversion for those mistaken champions of Christianity who cannot recommend the salvation and grace of our Lord Jesus Christ except by vilifying human nature'.[57] In his various writings he consistently advocated the adoption of a more generous approach. 'There is hardly one religion which does not contain some…important truth,' he said in his lecture on the Vedas delivered in Leeds in 1865.[58] Christianity, he suggested, must be

> compared not with Judaism only, but with the religious aspirations of the whole world, with all, in fact, that Christianity came either to destroy or fulfil…. Every religion, even the most imperfect and degraded, has something that ought to be sacred to us, for there is in all religions a yearning after the true, though unknown, God.

Writing in his review of a work by Charles Hardwick entitled *Christ and other Masters* some years later, he remarked that 'Surely it is not necessary, in order to prove that our own religion is the only true religion, that we should insist on the utter falseness of all other forms of belief.' 'We need

[56] Sharpe 1965: 45.
[57] Indian Institute Oxford, Max Müller Papers, MS. Eng. C. 2814.
[58] Quoted in Wolffe 1998, Vol. 5: 210.

not be frightened,' he continued, 'if we discover traces of truth, traces even
of Christian truth, among sages and lawgivers of other nations.'[59] Like
William Miller of Madras Christian College, his studies and reflection
confirmed him in his belief that God's providence was to be discerned in
the history of the world as a whole and not just in the Judaeo-Christian
revelation.[60] Hence like Monier-Williams, at least in his early phase, he
argued that the necessary task was not to dwell on points of difference,
but to welcome truths and insights in other religions and build on common ground.

The New Theology and Ideas in the Mission Field

There is evidence in LMS candidates' papers that some applicants for
service, including those sent to India, had already read works by Maurice,
Monier-Williams, or Max Müller.[61] One of these young men was Edwin
Greaves who was later to write a detailed description of the *Kumbh Mela*.[62]
Another was W. H. Campbell, who wrote accounts of Hindu belief and
practice in south India and who was also a contributor to the radical and
free ranging *Christian College Magazine*.[63] Nor, as we shall see, was the
reading of works associated with the new theology confined to missionaries associated with the LMS. Some notable examples of missionaries of
other societies influenced by the same body of literature are John Robson
(United Church of Scotland) and James Vaughan (CMS).

[59] Müller 1868, Vol. 1: 55. Those, he wrote, 'who throw themselves under the car of
Juggernath to be crushed to death by the idol they believe in—where the plaintiff who
cannot get redress starves himself to death at the door of his judge, and the philosopher,
longing for absorption into the Deity, quietly drowns himself in the Ganges, all these actions
"are not mere cruelty and brutality"'. 'They contain a religious element, and presuppose a
belief in immortality, and an indifference with regard to worldly pleasures, which if directed
in a different channel, might produce martyrs and heroes' (ibid.: 58–9).

[60] Wolffe 1997: 206.

[61] CWM, *CP*: A. P. Begg, E. Greaves, W. H. Campbell.

[62] 'Hinduism in its Strength and Weakness', *Chronicle*, Vol. 3, New series, May 1894:
115–18.

[63] Campbell, who spent many years as a missionary in Cuddapah and was writing in 1910,
remarked that, questions of higher criticism and the new theology 'have affected and do
affect' the opinions and attitudes of missionaries, but that there were few signs of these
developments affecting native Christians. Most missionaries connected with the LMS in
south India, he wrote, 'while firmly holding to the great essential truths of the Gospel accept
the results of intelligent criticism and in their teaching and preaching recognize the fact that
there has been a change in theological thought' (Henry Martyn Institute, Cambridge: Correspondence preparatory to the World Missionary Conference, Edinburgh, 1910, No. 133).

But in spite of the fact that missionaries in India were acquainted with some of this literature, it should not be inferred (as Sharpe appears to do) that the influence of British scholars was all one way, and that the missionaries had no influence on the British commentators as discussed above. As we shall see, some missionaries had a notion of Christianity being a fulfilment of Hindu ideas even before Maurice delivered his lectures on the relationship between Christianity and other religions in 1845–46. Nor should it be assumed that Monier-Williams, for example, was unaffected by the views of missionaries he met during his travels in India in 1873 prior to his publication of *Indian Wisdom* two years later.[64]

[64] Though influenced by ideas generated in Britain, missionaries also appear to have made these ideas even more popular in their place of origin. A clear illustration of this process is Vaughan's study entitled *The Trident, the Crescent and the Cross* (1876). Vaughan, who was clearly influenced by Williams's arguments, reproduced them in a modified version of his own book which appeared in serial form in the *Church Missionary Gleaner* (Vol. V, January 1878: 8–9). Using Williams's language he drew attention to the better as well as to the darker features of the Hindu tradition. 'There could be no doubt', wrote the *Gleaner*, quoting Vaughan, that in the early stages of religious life in India, the Hindus 'looked through Nature up to Nature's God', and that even in the present day, 'a Hindu, while acknowledging that India has 330 millions of gods, always speaks of the great God as *One*'. While continuing to underline parallels between Hindu and Christian beliefs, the paper also remarked that 'No other heathen religion, again, has so profound a sense of sin, and the need for atonement; and the Hindus firmly believe that sacrifices are of Divine origin.' Thus Vaughan was performing the function of popularizing for a British readership views which had originally emerged in Britain and at a more academic level.

9

Critics and Commentators on the Dominant View, 1850–1900

Context and Change

As has been noted, changes in missionary ideas and depictions of Hinduism during the period 1850–1900 were clearly influenced by developments in both India and Britain.

A decline in the need to focus so much attention on the externals of Hindu religion, and a growing familiarity with Hinduism both at home and abroad cleared the way for more careful reflection on the nature of the Hindu's inner life, including teachings, faith and beliefs.

Hinduism and Pantheism

Interest in pantheism was, in one sense, an extension of interest in brahmanism; since it was thought to be the essence of what brahmans had taught and of what was contained in the most important brahmanical texts. Indeed, pantheism (the belief that all, including the material universe, is God)[1] was seen increasingly by Protestant missionaries, as well as by the more secular European commentators, as the central message and kernel of 'the real Hinduism'.

An early indication of missionary interest in the texts and basis of pantheism, after Duff had discussed the subject in *India and India Missions*, was an advertisement appearing in the Calcutta press in September 1849. Issued on behalf of the Committee of the Calcutta Christian Tract and Book Society it was a proposal to award a prize of 300 rupees to the best essay, either in English or Bengali, on 'Vedantism, or the system included under that name'.[2] The advertisement stated that

[the essayist would] be required to give an account of the Origin and Antiquity of Vedantism, and of its true character and dogmas, illustrated by

[1] Eliade 1987, Vol. 11: 165–71.
[2] Mullens 1852.

copious quotations from Vyasa and his followers; and to discuss in like manner the question whether any such system is really to be found in the Vedas.

A growing interest in Vedantism, which in missionary thinking was usually associated with pantheism, was linked with Rammohan Roy's translations and commentaries on the Upanishads and with the subsequent development of the Brahmo Samaj. Fuelling missionary interest in the new society was the hope that Brahmoism would prove the first step in a more general movement towards Christianity. Hence the essayist, in the second part of the enquiry was asked 'to examine whether the modern system so called, as taught in the Brahma Sabha, be identical with the Vedanta of Vyasa; and if not, what its peculiar doctrines are, and on what foundation they rest'. Finally, as might be expected from a missionary organization, the essayist was required 'to point out the insuperable difficulties which lie in the way of receiving either of these systems as a revelation from God; and to contrast them with Christianity, as adopted to be the religion of man kind.' In other words, one of the preconditions of the investigation was not to search for parallels between Vedantic doctrines and the Christian faith, but to highlight differences and underline the superiority of the Christian movement.

The challenge, which was quite clearly a result of missionary concerns with Vedantism and the Brahmo Samaj, was taken up by a number of candidates, and the prize was eventually awarded to Joseph Mullens, a well-known missionary with the London Missionary Society (LMS). A graduate of University College, London, and a man who prided himself on 'his facility in acquiring languages', he had already spent eight years in Calcutta, much of it involving work in Bengali.[3] His essay, appearing under the title of *Vedantism, Brahmanism, and Christianity Examined and Compared*, was published by the Calcutta Christian Tract and Book Society in Calcutta in 1852. In it Mullens argued that, next to the writings of Vyasa (the traditional author of the *Mahabharata*) the *Sutras* and *Bhagavad Gita*, Sankara's commentaries on the Vedant and the Vedas were 'the best authorities for the Vedant system'.[4] He does not include a bibliography with his essay, but cites a range of references in the body of his work. This makes it abundantly clear that he took advantage of more recent translations, and especially of the work of Dr E. Roer 'whose duty it has recently been to

[3] CWM, CP, Box 26, F. 7, Mullens to Sec., 21/6/42. Sibree 1923: 57.
[4] Mullens 1852: 18.

read the whole of the Upanishads through, with the commentary of
Sankar Acharyya upon them'.[5] In addition to Colebrooke's translations and
essays, Mullens also referred to 'various elementary works which have been
published on the system'. One of the latest and most popular, was the
Vedanta Sar which he mentioned because it had recently been made
accessible to students in Bengal. 'Written by Sadananda, the disciple of
Adwaitananda,' he continued, 'it gives a systematic outline of the chief
doctrines of the Vedant with arguments in their favour'.[6]

While Mullens' book dealt with a number of issues, such as the developing doctrines of the Brahmo Samaj, the crucial point is that it stressed
the importance and popularity of Vedantism, and with that, the importance of pantheism as a key factor in Hinduism. Referring to a brief
definition of Vedanta as contained in the Calcutta edition of the *Vedanta
Sar*, Mullens stated that the name Vedanta applied to 'the arguments of
the Upanishads, also to the Saririk Sutras and other Shastras auxiliary
thereto'. The object of the system, he wrote, was to show 'the unity between
the sentient soul and Brahma, the soul in its pure state'. In the course of
his analysis he declared that 'undisguised Pantheism' was the very basis
upon which the vedantic system rested.[7] The early sources of Hindu
philosophy, he wrote, such as the *Sutras* and *Gita* and *Vedanta Sar* all
taught that

> there is but one real, existent Being, the supreme creator of the universe; that
> all productions and forms of matter in that universe are only emanations
> from him; that man also both in body and mind is but a product of the sole
> entity; that whatever appears to prove him an independent and separate
> being is the offspring of illusion and ignorance.[8]

Reinforcing his message, Mullens claimed that no one who read the
Upanishads could fail to notice the continual reference to 'the supreme
Brahma, as *pervading* all things',[9] or the various passages which he quoted
from the same source which 'directly assert' that 'All this universe is
Brahma: from him it springs, into him it is dissolved; in him it breathes.'[10]
Mullens' clearly focused exposition, both reflected and reinforced
a growing conviction among some of the more prominent Protestant

[5] Ibid.: 90.
[6] Ibid.: 18.
[7] Ibid.: 26; see also p. 32.
[8] Ibid.: 60–61; see also his comments on the *Upanishads* (p. 89).
[9] Ibid.: 81.
[10] Ibid.: 85.

missionary commentators on Hinduism during the second half of the nineteenth century that pantheism was the essence of the Hindu system.

Dr John Robson (1836–1908), one of the pioneers of the United Presbyterian Church of Scotland (UPS) mission in Rajputana, was well known as the author of *Hinduism and Its Relations to Christianity*. The book, hailed as bringing out the underlying philosophy of Hinduism,[11] was published in 1874 and again in two further editions, in 1893 and 1905.[12] The elder son of Dr John Robson, the popular minister of Wellington Street United Presbyterian Church, Glasgow, Robson volunteered for India in 1860, in response to a call for missionaries to staff and develop the United Presbyterian mission in Rajputana.[13] The headquarters of the mission, established by the Rev. Schoolbred in 1859, was at Beawar; but, after their arrival, and Robson's rapid progress in language studies, he and his wife settled at Ajmer, the most important town in the province, and headquarters of the Viceroy's representative. It was there that Robson opened a school and spent much of his time in work among the educated classes.

His first detailed treatment of the subject of Hinduism was in a booklet of twenty-five pages in length, published in Glasgow in 1867 and entitled *Hinduism: Its Philosophy and Popular Worship*. This was followed by the publication of the three editions of the volume already mentioned, the second volume appearing in 1893. During the whole of this twenty-six-year period the author's basic views on the nature of Hinduism scarcely changed. Indeed some of the key descriptive phrases appearing in the original pamphlet of 1867 are repeated verbatim in 1893.

In his pamphlet and again in the different editions of his book, Robson described Hinduism as 'a union of subtle Pantheistic philosophy, with a gross popular idolatry'.[14] What he meant by that was that Hinduism was comprised of two basic and interrelated components, the first of which might be described as the *Advaita* or monistic tradition. 'The fundamental principle of Hinduism,' wrote Robson, 'is, that there is only one really existent being in the universe, and that is the Supreme Lord [Parameshwar], or the Supreme Spirit [Paramatma]. He is everywhere present; therefore, our spirits must be part of Him'.[15] The way of salvation was the way of

---

[11] See 'Opinions of the press' at the back of the second edition, Edinburgh and London, 1893.

[12] The 1905 edition was cited as a further reference in an article on Hinduism in the *Cambridge Encyclopaedia*, 1910.

[13] Ashcroft 1909: 17–43.

[14] Robson 1867: 6 and 1893: 4.

[15] Robson 1867: 7. See also Robson 1893: 71–2.

knowledge—the one object of all Hindus, living in the world of *maya* (illusion) and trapped in the cycle of transmigration, was, therefore, recognition of their condition and final 'absorption,' like a drop of water, into the 'ocean of emancipation'.[16] The metaphysical difference between Christianity and Hinduism was in Robson's view that 'whereas Christianity teaches the personality of the divine and human spirits, Hinduism teaches their impersonality'.[17] Indeed, in Robson's view, 'the immortality' of Hinduism differed little from 'the annihilation' of Buddhism.[18]

The second part of the equation was popular worship and how this was related to *Advaita* or the monistic view of reality. It was here that Robson's idea of pantheism again became important.

> The worship of images was designed first of all, I believe, as an aid to meditation, and this is a plea which Hindus often put forward. We are apt, they say, to forget God, but when we see the stone, it reminds us of Him, and we invoke his name. But more generally it is thought that the god is, in some mysterious way, present in the stone, and is pleased and brought under obligation by worship done to it as by worship done to himself. It is curious, indeed, to see how the pantheism of the Hindus comes in as an aid to their image worship.... As god may be present in a stone, so he may be present in any locality, in a grove, a stream, or lake.... All I wish to do is, to show the connection between their pantheism and their polytheism—between their belief in the Supreme Spirit and the worship of the numerous popular gods of the land.[19]

Not only did Robson argue that Hindus at the popular level saw images as 'aids to meditation', but that they looked on 'absorption into the Supreme Spirit' as the great end of their existence. Furthermore, as a means to this end they sought 'to be absorbed meanwhile into one of their inferior spirits which, as it were, lead unto Him'.[20] Thus all Hindus from the most learned and sophisticated brahmans to the illiterate and low-caste villager were, as Ward and Duff had argued, integrated in the one metaphysical or religious system.

One of the first and most widely read of later missionary authors influenced by Robson's work was James Vaughan. He was, as we have seen, a Calcutta-based CMS missionary of nineteen years' experience—a man

[16] Robson 1867: 14.
[17] Ibid.: 11.
[18] Robson 1893: 84.
[19] Robson 1867: 20–1.
[20] Ibid.: 21.

who like Robson mixed a good deal among the educated classes and who had also gone on extensive preaching tours in the countryside.[21] The book he wrote which had considerable influence and was widely read especially in CMS circles, was written while he was on furlough in England in 1874, and as a solace in his grief for his wife's death a short time before. Its long title *The Trident, the Crescent and the Cross: A view of the religious history of India during the Hindu, Buddhist, Mohammedan, and Christian periods*, gives the reader some idea of the breadth of its scope.

In a section referring to the character of 'Early Hinduism' Vaughan conceded that 'erroneous as their conceptions of Him have been, still it cannot be doubted that they [the Hindus] have approached nearer the true ideal than any other people unblessed with the light of Revelation'. But like Robson and others he also thought that Hinduism had gone through a process of 'declension and deterioration'.[22] Emphasizing the point, he argued that 'Hinduism' 'utterly failed' in leading its 'votaries' to a right perception of God, and ultimately lapsed into 'a system of degraded polytheism and idolatry'.[23] But he continued, amongst the Hindus, and side by side with this tendency to polytheism 'a corresponding tendency towards Pantheism has ever been discernible'.[24] But, he contended, 'it is hardly correct to speak of these as two separate tendencies running in parallel lines; they actually intermingle and intersect with each other in a way that is most puzzling, and all but unaccountable'. Hindus may 'invoke each deity in turn as if he were supreme', but gradually 'the feeling after the Infinite led to a denial of the Finite'.

> What had been considered separate entities came to be regarded as parts of the great whole, and all other beings to be merged in the one All-pervading, All-comprising being; all other existences but the one Self-existent, came to be viewed as visionary and unreal.[25]

One commentator, reviewing Vaughan's work in the *Indian Evangelical Review* and noting that the author had acknowledged Robson's *Hinduism and Its Relations to Christianity* as one of his sources, was still somewhat surprised at the extent to which the author appeared to be using Robson's work. 'So many cases occur of similarity or even identity with statements

---

[21] See especially his annual reports to the Secretary, CMS, London, 1858–66.
[22] Vaughan 1876: 41.
[23] Ibid.
[24] Ibid.: 63.
[25] Ibid.: 64.

occurring in Robson's work, including several identical quotations from current newspapers,' he remarked, 'that one feels as if in such instances special acknowledgements are due.'[26] Indeed, there can be little doubt that Vaughan relied heavily on Robson's work. Nor can there be much doubt that Vaughan's central argument[27] that 'the Pantheistic element' pervaded every Hindu system including popular religion, was based largely on Robson's earlier account.

However, even though the above model of Hinduism was not original the fact remains that, in arguing his case, Vaughan was able to draw upon his own experience and in doing so introduced some doubts and possible qualifications.[28] This emerges clearly in his discussion of ideas of Ultimate Reality among the common people. Referring to the two poles of polytheistic and pantheistic belief, he stated that, without doubt, 'the Pundits, and learned class, gravitate more towards pantheism than do the common people; to these latter', he argued, 'polytheism must ever be more comprehensible and more popular than the abstruse conception which teaches them to ignore their own individuality.' 'Yet', he wrote, it was 'strange but true' that every now and again one heard from the lips of illiterate persons—persons steeped in polytheistic 'superstition'—a remark which showed that 'they in some rude way, do really grasp and apply the principles of pantheism'.[29]

It was not only Vaughan who during this period was inclined to echo Robson's views, or arrive more independently at the same conclusion that pantheism was the key concept in attempting to understand Hinduism. James Kennedy (1825–99) a LMS missionary stationed in Benares from 1839 to 1867, reached much the same conclusion. In a pamphlet on *Christianity and the Religions of India* published in 1874 he referred to 'the main features' or 'essential qualities' of Hinduism and identified pantheism as being at its heart. The Hindus he argued were pantheists and polytheists. 'They believe the universe to be God, sometimes making God the soul of the universe, sometimes making the universe the development

---

[26] *IER*, Vol. V, October 1877: 227–29; Vaughan's plagiarism, whether deliberate or otherwise, also got him into trouble with M. Monier-Williams who, writing in 1883, complained that 'A very energetic and useful Missionary, the late Rev. James Vaughan, in his work called "The Trident, the Crescent, and the Cross," copied from "Indian Wisdom" a large number of my translations from Sanskrit literature, and interspersed them everywhere throughout his account of Hinduism *without asking my leave*, and without any marks of quotation or references in his foot-notes' (Monier-Williams 1883: iv).

[27] Vaughan 1876: 90, 104.

[28] Ibid.: 65.

[29] Ibid.

of God, con-substantial with Him, or according to the most approved philosophic system, representing all as mere illusion.'[30] In Kennedy's view, the Vedantin philosophy, which maintained 'the doctrines of emanation and absorption', was 'so predominant in India' that it could be said 'to have swallowed up every other system'[31] while the popular and influential *Puranas* were also characterized by a 'pronounced Pantheism' which was largely derived from philosophical writings.[32] Indeed, pantheism, which was such a marked characteristic of both the philosophic and Puranic literature, had also had a profound effect on the *Bhagavad Gita*, which perhaps stood higher in Hindu estimation than any other book.[33] The *Gita*, was in Kennedy's opinion, 'intensely pantheistic', insisting 'in every chapter' on 'liberation' or absorption into the deity.

If, as we shall see, Kennedy subsequently had doubts about the all-embracing effects of pantheism and about pantheism as the essence of Hinduism, the same was not the case with some of the later missionary writers and speakers who insisted that pantheism was the clue, and heart of the Hindu faith. W. J. Wilkins (1843–1902) LMS, erstwhile teacher at the Bhowanipur College, Calcutta, was author of *Hindu Mythology, Vedic and Puranic*, published in 1882 (and still on sale in Calcutta book-stalls more than a century later), and *Modern Hinduism*, published in 1887. Wilkins, like many others, took the view that the essence of Hinduism was the idea of the unity of the godhead and, connected with this, *maya* and the belief in pantheism. '"God is everything, everything is God" is the common creed', he explained.[34] William Miller, the eminent and experienced principal of Madras Christian College, was another influential exponent of the same idea.[35] His exposition of these views before the Free Church of Scotland's General Assembly in 1888, was followed by T. E. Slater's claim to the same effect.[36] Once having suggested that there was no unity in Hinduism, Slater then implied that there was and based his claims on two main arguments. First, he revived the traditional argument, which through its insistence on the importance of brahman control and the caste system, focused on overall structure or instrumentality. The brahmans, he argued, met the threat of Buddhism half way 'by

---

[30] Kennedy 1874: 186–87.
[31] Ibid.: 174–75.
[32] Ibid.: 172.
[33] Ibid.: 177.
[34] Wilkins 1900: 136–41.
[35] *Free Church of Scotland Quarterly Paper*, No. CXVI, September 1888: 2–3.
[36] Slater 1906.

popularizing their own faith, and by providing popular deities for the
people'. Second, introducing the increasingly popular concept of 'the Indian
mind' (an idea based on the *assumption* that there was some kind of unity,
or common way of thinking), he then went on to claim that it (the Indian
mind) 'sees the Divine in everything'.[37]

Slater's ultimate view that pantheism was somehow the kernel of
Hinduism, was then clearly in line with a long list of missionary and other
European commentators. Furthermore, in his view, as in the opinion of
many others, pantheism and polytheism were in principle the same. 'They
are but a higher and lower form of one and the same view of the world.
Pantheism is the refined, polytheism the vulgar, mode of deifying
Nature.... All men, it is held, have finally to reach the same goal—union
with the Supreme.' Thus 'when a Hindu begins to think seriously upon
higher things, and to reason out his relation to the unseen and eternal, he
invariably does so on the lines laid down some 3,000 years ago by Indian
rishis, or seers, in what is called the Vedanta philosophy'.[38]

Views Critical of the Pantheistic Model

Not all those missionaries working in northern India, even in the Benares
region, and in what was sometimes regarded as the heartland of Sanskritic
culture, were convinced that the common people were influenced by what
their colleagues claimed was the Vedantic view of life. Even Kennedy,
erstwhile advocate of the idea that pantheism was the key concept in
Hinduism, appears to have modified his views, possibly as a result of
further experience and contact with ordinary Hindus. In an article on the
Gita published in the *Indian Evangelical Review* (one year after emphasizing that pantheism was the main feature of Hinduism) he again argued
that 'the pantheistic theory that God and the universe are one' not only
saturated Sanskrit literature, but dominated 'the learned and unlearned to
the present hour'.[39] However, despite having argued strongly along these
lines, he appears to have been developing some doubts about the attitude
of ordinary Hindus. Towards the end of his article he suddenly appears
ambiguous, and confessed that

> notwithstanding the Pantheism of the *Gita*, which is so accordant with the
> avowed belief of the people, and notwithstanding its manifestly injurious

[37] Ibid.: 7.
[38] Ibid.: 10.
[39] *IER*, Vol. II, April 1875: 395.

influence on their character, the Hindus often speak of God as the glorious One who is entirely distinct from themselves, whom they ought to revere, love and serve.[40]

Writing in 1887 the Rev. James Hewlett (one of Kennedy's colleagues) noted with some surprise, that

on questioning some of the Vaishnavas of the city [Benares] I have found that the highest object of their desire seems to be not an unconscious absorption into their supreme god, but what they call bhakti, faith or devotion, which they hope to enjoy after death.[41]

While there are indications that some missionaries in northern India were beginning to have doubts about an exclusive pantheistic model of Hinduism, colleagues elsewhere also challenged the dominant view. These men included K. S. Macdonald and John Morrison, both of them Scottish missionaries in higher education in Calcutta, J. Murray Mitchell, from western India, and a range of missionaries from the south. Among the latter were Robert Caldwell, subsequently Bishop of Madras, C. Egbert Kennet and G. U. Pope, all of them with the Society for the Propagation of the Gospel (SPG), and G. McKenzie Cobban of the Wesleyan Methodise Missionary Society (WMMS).

Robert Caldwell, scholar and linguist, was among the most careful of missionary observers in a period when Locke's philosophy and the importance of first-hand observation had become a widely accepted principle among British commentators on India's religious and social life. Recalling his early life, he remarked that:

My first year in Tinnevelly commenced as has been seen near the end of 1841, and before the end of 1842 I had succeeded in visiting all the Mission stations then in Tinnevelly and most of the more important places in the province. Being already acquainted with Tamil, I endeavoured to get information from the people themselves about the ideas and characteristics of each class, whether already Christian or not, and to judge for myself as to the measures that should be adopted for the spread of Christianity, for the better organization of the Mission and for the improvement of the native community in general.[42]

[40] Ibid.: 41.
[41] *IER*, Vol. XIII, 1887: 295.
[42] Quoted in Wyatt 1894: 79.

Caldwell was quite specific, like an increasing number of missionary writers, in drawing attention to differences between religious traditions often held to be part of the same system.

> Many a person who has derived his ideas of Hinduism from some particular school of Hindu metaphysics, or from the doctrines and rites considered as orthodox in a particular locality, has imagined himself acquainted with the whole subject. Whereas he has become acquainted with only one phase of Hinduism; and in other parts of India, amongst races of a different origin and speaking a different tongue, [he] would probably find the same system either quite unknown or considered heretical. For instance, who has not heard of Vedantism? And what Missionary coming out to India has not felt some misgivings as to the result of his first controversy with Vedantist brahmans? Yet in Tinnevelly, among a population of more than 800,000 souls, I think I may assert with safety that there are not to be found eight individuals who know so much about Vedantism as may be picked up by an European student in an hour from a perusal of any European tractate on the subject. And though I have no doubt but that some persons may be found in Tinnevelly who profess the system, I have not yet myself met with, or heard of a single person who is supposed to profess it as a whole, much less understand it.[43]

Other missionaries operating in south India either endorsed Caldwell's argument that the religion of the Shanars and other low-caste groups had no connection with Vedantism, or the brahmanical tradition, or pointed to evidence relating to other groups in society which challenged the view that Hinduism was, generally speaking, pantheistic.[44] Henry Rice, a Church of Scotland missionary in Madras and scion of a well-known missionary family who had a long association with south India, made the obvious point (overlooked even by the Madras-based William Miller) that, at least in the south, the brahmans themselves were divided in their views of the unity of all things and the relationship between God and the soul.

> The Brahmins of South India are largely worshippers of Shiva, but there are also Vishnuvites and Lingayets among them. They are divided into three classes, according to their religious philosophy, viz., Smartas, Madhwas, and Sri Veishnavas. The Smartas are followers of Sankaracharya and worshippers of Shiva. They are Adwaitas in philosophy, that is, they believe that

---

[43] Caldwell 1840: 7.

[44] For other commentators on Shanar religion or what was known as 'demonism' or 'the system of devil worship', see Pettitt 1851: 483–505; Edward Sargent's account in *CMI*, Vol. 1, 1850: 34–7, 60–2, 84–5 and Mateer 1871: 190–218.

the soul of man and the soul of God are identical. The Madhwas are followers of Madhwacharya, and worshippers of Vishnu. In philosophy they are Dwaitas, that is, they believe that the soul of man and the soul of God are distinct. The Sri Veishnavas follow the teachings of Ramanujacharya and worship Vishnu. They are called Visishta-Adwaitas, or 'Adwaitas with a difference,' because they hold that while the Divine and human souls are in some respects identical, yet that in life the human soul is subordinate to the Divine soul.[45]

Reasons for the Dominance of the Pantheistic Model

How then does one explain these divisions in missionary opinion, and the apparent majority view that pantheism was the dominant strand or essence of Hindu belief?

One factor which accounts for the expression of different opinions was almost certainly the existence of local and regional variations in Hindu views in different parts of India. At least to some extent, therefore, missionary estimates of the popularity or insignificance of pantheism reflect real differences in the local situation. While, for example, it is impossible to doubt Caldwell's claim (based on extensive local knowledge) that Vedantists were rare in Tinnevelly district, it is equally difficult to doubt Robson's claim (also based on local knowledge) that Vedantism/pantheism was the dominant strand of Hinduism where he was living in Rajasthan.

Whatever he had read in other people's work about contemporary Hinduism appeared to Robson to be of secondary importance, when compared with the knowledge and insights gained through years of 'practical study' and contact with Hindus in and around Ajmer. In the preface to his book published in 1874 (in which his arguments were the same as they had been in 1867) he explained that, apart from the section dealing with the early religions of India, 'the remainder of the book is mainly the result of my own observation and study of the sacred literature now most current among the Hindus'.[46] What really mattered from Robson's point of view were the texts in use and the views and opinions of the people

---

[45] Rice 1889: 25–6.
[46] Robson 1867: vi. In writing his short sketch on the earlier religions of India he made use of 'Max Muller's Early Sanskrit Literature, and Science of Religion; Professor H. H. Wilson's translations from the Rig Veda; Dr John Wilson's India Three Thousand Years Ago; Lassen's Indische Alterthumskunde; and that thesaurus of Indian Literature, Sanskrit Texts, by Dr. John Muir.'

themselves. Indeed, he stressed that what he wrote was confirmed by the pundits, individual brahmans and the peasantry.

Writing in his pamphlet, one of the first of his publications, he attacked many of the ideas about Hinduism circulating in England and pointed out that his own analysis (one which he long continued to espouse) was based entirely on what Hindus were saying about themselves. Moreover, referring to the central argument of his work (which was that Hinduism is 'a union of a subtle Pantheistic philosophy with a gross popular idolatry'), he declared that this view of the subject was the one that all his experience of conversing and reading with Hindus had convinced him was correct. He had, he stressed, 'stated no doctrines which are not held by them [the Hindus], nor referred to any practices which are not common among them. All I have done is to show the bearing which they have on one another, and the connection which I believe exists in the minds of all who hold and practice them.'[47]

Clearly then one of the most important clues to Robson's views lies in the earliest years of his mission work in Rajputana, from the time of his arrival in 1860 until he produced his pamphlet in 1867. This was a period of his life in which he was not only involved in preaching to common people, but in which he was also engaged in close discussion with pundits, holy men, and pupils from his own school as well as from the Government College. It is in fact possible to identify some of the individuals who may have helped the missionary construct and consolidate his primary thesis which was centred on monism and pantheistic views of the world. Apart from the various pundits he quotes as sources for his views, he mentions 'a Vedantist brahman',[48] who came to the rescue as a teacher at the mission school when other staff left. He also mentions his conversations with Sohan Lall, master at the Government College and the editor of what Robson claimed was the only 'native' newspaper in Rajputana. Like many others, Sohan Lall espoused *Advaita* Vedanta and became involved in discussion with Robson about the comparative merits of Christianity and 'Vedantic pantheism'. Last but not least were a series of remarkable interviews that Robson and his colleague the Rev. J. Gray had with the Hindu revivalist leader, Dayananda Sarasvati, at the beginning of 1866. One of the effects of this on Robson was to reinforce his conviction of the overriding importance of *Advaita* Vedanta in Hindu philosophical tradition. He explained in his book published in 1893 that at the time in 1866 Dayananda

---

[47] Robson 1867: 23.

[48] *United Presbyterian Missionary Record*, Vol. XVII, October 1862: 191.

'had not broken with orthodox Hinduism, nor did he seem to doubt his pantheistic creed, though theistic instincts seemed to trouble him and embarrass him in discussion.'[49] In his original and more detailed account of the meeting published in the *United Presbyterian Missionary Record* in September 1866, Robson explained that they finally came to 'the capital question as to the identity of the divine and human spirits', which Dayananda maintained, and 'we of course', denied. 'To all the arguments from our consciousness and sinfulness, he gave the stereotyped answer of the Hindoo philosophy, founded on our ignorance, and being under the influence of delusion. His argument was based chiefly on the omnipresence of the Divine Spirit.'[50]

While there can be no doubt as to the importance of Robson's experience as a factor in convincing him of the centrality of pantheism in Hinduism, like the experience of other commentators it was essentially limited, and in his case largely confined to certain parts of Rajasthan. As an educator and scholar he mixed primarily among the higher castes, and as a resident of Ajmer, he appears to have lived in an area where the proportion of brahmans in the population was exceptionally high and well above the India-wide average of 3 per cent. According to Ashcroft, author of *The Story of Our Rajputana Mission*, the brahmans around Ajmer during this period comprised about one-tenth of the population and 'are found everywhere'.[51] In this situation (compared, for example, with the situation in Tinnevelly district, where, according to Caldwell, there were very few brahmans) brahman ideas and influence, including notions of pantheism, were likely to be much more in evidence.

Although Caldwell and Robson appear to have been especially careful in their research into trends in Hindu or Indian thinking, Robson had a tendency to over-generalize, and not all missionaries were equally careful or reliable as commentators. Indeed, there seem to have been other factors, apart from their own direct knowledge and experience, which, in the case of these debates, swayed missionary views in favour of the pantheistic model.

First, pantheism seemed to flow out of brahman ideology and could easily be understood as further evidence of the brahmanical construction of Hinduism. Its importance for many missionaries was endorsed by their long-term tendency to privilege philosophy in religion, to think of the 'real' religion as opposed to the customs and beliefs of the lower classes, and to

[49] Robson 1893: 218–19.
[50] *United Presbyterian Missionary Record*, Vol. 1 (N.S.), 1 September 1866: 168–69.
[51] Ashcroft 1909: 17.

266

search for it in texts and among the higher and more educated classes in society. This elitist view clearly affected William Miller's argument about the centrality of pantheism in Hinduism. In his view, and contrary to most claims in the census, he argued that untouchable groups, such as pariahs and chamars, were not followers of Hinduism. Thus in dismissing the views of untouchables as being of no account, he could strengthen his case based on the views of a more select higher status sample, namely those more likely to reflect a pantheistic view of the world.

Second, the missionaries who, like Robson, were swayed at least partly by the attitude of pundits, were almost certainly exposed to the unrepresentative views of scholars, who, more than most Hindus, valued and expounded pantheistic ideas. As Vaughan pointed out, 'without doubt, the Pundits, the learned class, gravitate more towards pantheism than do the common people'.[52]

Third, an additional pressure in favour of pantheism as a key to Hinduism, was the increasing popularity of this interpretation among other European writers.[53] Many non-missionary scholars, some of whom the missionaries read, such as M. Monier-Williams, A. Barth, G. A. Jacob, Flint and others were also inclined to argue that pantheism was the key element in Hinduism. For example, referring to different Hindu philosophies, Monier-Williams wrote that 'the so-called pantheistic theory of the Vedanta philosophy is even more attractive to the majority of Hindu thinkers'.[54] Professor R. Flint claimed that 'Pantheism pervades all Hindu religion' and Jacob remarked that 'if the people of India can be said to have now any system of religion at all, apart from mere caste observances, it is to be found in the vedanta philosophy, the leading tenets of which are known to some extent in every village'.[55] Furthermore, the popularity of the pantheistic interpretation of Hinduism generally was reflected in an article published by Kenneth Macdonald in the *Indian Evangelical Review* in 1887 entitled 'Pantheism and Vedantism; or the Deification of the Universe'.[56] As is well known, and has been demonstrated again by recent scholars, the popularity

[52] Vaughan 1876: 65.

[53] On continental writers on this issue, see especially Inden 1990: 93–6.

[54] Referring to pantheism he described it as 'a belief in the non-duality and non-plurality of Spirit-that is to say, in one eternal Spirit, called Atman (nom. Atma) or Brahman (nom. Brahma) instead of in many,—a belief in the identification of the human spirit and of all the phenomena of nature with that one Spirit, when enveloped in illusion. In other words, the separate existence of man's soul and of all natural phenomena is only illusory' (Monier-Williams 1883: 33; see also Monier-Williams 1877: 13, 51).

[55] Murdoch 1895: 52.

[56] *IER*, Vol. XIV, No. 25, 1887–88.

of the pantheistic view of Hinduism during the nineteenth century was not confined to British scholars, but included philosophers and writers such as the German idealists Friedrich von Schlegel (1772–1829), G. W. F. Hegel (1770–1831) and Arthur Schopenhauer (1788–1860).[57]

Fourth, while in the absence of accurate India-wide surveys etc., it is impossible to establish the validity of claims about Hindu attitudes in general, there is every indication that pantheism or, more strictly speaking, *Advaita* Vedanta became increasingly influential among the Western educated classes during the course of the nineteenth century.[58] This was, at least in part, a result of the influence of religious leaders from Rammohan Roy to Vivekananda and of the attractiveness especially of Shankara's philosophy as an alternative and counterweight to missionary propaganda. The spread of Vedantism in elite circles may well have coloured the thinking of missionaries who were working among the educated classes and who, like many other observers, were inclined to generalize from their own essentially limited experience. For them it may have appeared that pantheism more generally was growing from strength to strength.

Last, the increasing popularity of pantheistic ideas among the educated classes raised the subject as a central issue in the Hindu–Christian encounter. A Christian assault on pantheism was all the more necessary; and, as Richard King has pointed out, the equation of Vedanta with the essence of Hinduism provided an easy target for Christian missionaries wishing to engage the Hindu religion in debates about theology and ethics. 'By

[57] Inden 1990: 94–7; King 1999: Ch. 6.

[58] James Long (CMS), a missionary who had taught in Calcutta for nine years, wrote in his annual report that 'I have painfully observed, those boys who have long resisted the strivings of the Spirit generally become quite hardened, and take up their quarters in that half-way house Vedantism, or else adopt a species of Socinianism, recognizing the morality of the Gospel, but divorced from its mysteries' (*CMR*, Vol. 1, July 1850: 147). K. M. Bannerjea, another trustworthy commentator on developments in the same city, remarked in one of his earlier lectures that his fellow countrymen were 'striving to find shelter in it [Vedantism]'. And there can be no doubt that there was a revival of interest in Vedantism among many Hindus in other parts of India during the course of the nineteenth century. Dr. Murray Mitchell, who spent much of his time in western India, initially among the educated classes, declared in 1894 that Vedanta was *by that time* 'by far the most widely prevalent system of Hindu philosophy'. Nehemiah Goreh, another eminent convert, and one familiar with the situation in north India, claimed in a book published in 1862 that the Vedanta was held by 'a large majority' of Hindus, and Kenneth Macdonald, who surveyed religious developments throughout India at the turn of the century, suggested that the revival movement associated with Vedantism had 'spread all over a large part of India' (Bannerjea 1851; Gore 1862: 156–60; *IA*, Vol. II, 1882: 116; Macdonald 1902; Mitchell 1894: 187).

characterizing Hinduism as a monistic religion, Christian theologians and apologists were able to criticize the mystical monism of Hinduism, thereby highlighting the moral superiority of Christianity.'[59] A clear example of this approach is the relevant section in Peter Percival's book, *Land of the Veda*, published in 1854 and based on lectures he gave to SPG missionary candidates in St Augustine's College Canterbury. Highly regarded as a Tamil scholar, Percival had spent fifteen years (1835–50) revising the Tamil Bible[60]—at least seven of these working in close association with his pundit, Arumuka Navalar. The latter, while continuing his work of translation and maintaining a close and friendly relationship with Percival, became increasingly active and well known as the leading advocate of *Shaiva Siddhanta*.[61] Notwithstanding this friendly and long-term association with Ceylon's best-known exponent of *Siddhanta*, and notwithstanding the findings of more recent scholars (who emphasize the movement's doctrine of the continued separation of God and the soul in the state of liberation)[62] Percival managed to squeeze his reference to *Shaiva Siddhanta* into his Vedantic model. Such was the power of the dominant interpretation, and such was Percival's determination to contrast Hindu teachings with Christianity.

At one point in his argument Percival appears to support the widely accepted modern view that in *Shaiva Siddhanta* the world and individual souls are real entities independent of God and that the soul retains its independent identity, even in the final state of release or liberation. 'The advocates of this system of philosophy', he wrote, 'seem to maintain the co-existence of three entities, all of which are eternal as to the past, viz., God, the soul, and maya or illusion, which is the substratum of the material universe'.[63] However, in spite of these observations which appear to suggest that in *Shaiva Siddhanta* the soul retains its independent existence, the writer went on to argue that when this subtle system of

---

[59] King 1999: 132.

[60] In recommending Percival for employment with the SPG, A. R. Symonds, Secretary of the local committee in Madras, explained in a confidential note to the General Secretary in London in 1852 that Percival was 'a man of very superior attainments. He is in the full vigour of his mind and body. He has been Chairman of the Wesleyan Mission and has proved himself a very efficient Missionary as well as an eminent Tamil Scholar, (Symonds to Hawkins, 12 February 1852, USPG, CLR/48/439–42).

[61] See especially Young and Jebanesan 1995: 108–26. A convert to Methodism in his youth, Percival rejoined the Church of England on his return from India in 1852.

[62] See, for example, Clothey's article on 'Tamil Religions' in Eliade 1987, Vol. 14; Devasenapathi 1974: 287–88 and von Stietencron 1995.

[63] Percival 1854: 204.

philosophy was finally unravelled, 'it differs but little from the Vedanta'.[64] This enabled the author to develop his grand conclusion that Hinduism taught that 'Brahma, Vishnu, Siva, the moral and material universe, however efformed... is indeed nothing but the one sole, self-existing, and essential spirit, and must merge into the ineffable ocean of being.'[65] Having established this point, and quoting from Duff, Percival then delivers the *coup de grace*—'What a contrast to all this do the statements of the Bible exhibit!' How much more attractive was the solid theism of the Christian faith, the God of the Bible 'possessed of independent personality, of freedom of will, and of absolute power'. And how much better was the Christian way of salvation, the 'moral elevation' and other benefits associated with it, and the continued sense of individuality and 'endless felicities... for those who confide in the infinite merits of his atonement'.[66]

Unlike the European scholars King mentions in his analysis of attitudes towards Indian religions,[67] the missionaries do not appear to have been in the habit of using India as a battleground to promote their views, and win points in religious conflicts and controversies *in Europe*. Unlike Voltaire, for example, their real focus was not so much on what was happening in Europe, but on the mission field and on questions about how to convert the Hindu population. Instead of being conscious of strengthening the Christian side of a debate on pantheism in Europe, they seemed to feel they had much to gain from the arguments which European Christians had already developed in controversies with their British or Continental opponents. Indeed, there was a certain residue of feeling that in arguing against Hindu pantheism they were on familiar ground, and were siding with European Christians in a historic debate which had already taken place in Europe and which had already demonstrated the fallacies of pantheistic views of God and the world. Rightly or wrongly Duff, Mullens, Kennedy, Robson and Macdonald all refer to the parallels between pantheism or *Advaita Vedanta* on the one hand and certain elements in the Western philosophical tradition on the other.[68] For example, Duff, drawing attention to 'the denigration of the existence of sensible objects' in Greek and Roman philosophies, took the opportunity of describing them as the 'whimsies and the reveries of fallible man'; and Macdonald, referring to pantheism in India, and quoting from Christlieb's *Modern Doubt*, argued

[64] Ibid.: 205.
[65] Ibid.: 240.
[66] Ibid.: 246–47.
[67] King 1999: 126.
[68] Duff 1840: 85; Kennedy 1874: 176; Mullens 1852: 62; Robson 1893: 85.

that Spinoza's 'utterances' in his *Practical Philosophy*, 'completely destroy all morality.'[69]

Missionaries and *Bhakti*

One final consideration, which is largely problematic, is that missionaries may have placed undue emphasis on pantheism partly because of their ignorance of *bhakti* (loving devotion to a personal god) or failure to see it as a distinctive tradition. There was, indeed, comparatively little discussion of *bhakti* among European scholars for the greater part of the nineteenth century and it was only in the 1880s and 1890s that Ramanuja's philosophy, 'dualism', and the ideas implicit in *bhakti* movements appear to have received much more systematic attention. Nevertheless, as we shall see in the case of Murray Mitchell, the importance of *bhakti* was acknowledged by some Protestant missionaries earlier in the nineteenth century.

As early as 1844 Elijah Hoole argued that there are 'some devotional compositions of his [Shiva's] worshippers, in which, addressing Siven as the Supreme, they have attained to the truly sublime; and, in the most appropriate language, have displayed a correctness of sentiment and ardency of devotion, which we cannot but admire.'[70] The emotional exuberance of Tukaram (1598–1650) a man whom Mitchell claimed had acquired 'immense influence' all over the Maratha country;[71] the chanting of passages from the *Gita* in the remote and humble homes of devotees in the United Provinces, a custom observed by Kennedy,[72] and the agony and ecstasy of the Tamil poets who longed for communion with their Lord,[73] these were all expressions of *bhakti* mentioned in the British Protestant missionary literature of the nineteenth century.

While there is evidence that some of the missionaries were increasingly aware of the importance of *bhakti* or loving devotion to God as one of the principal paths of Hindu religious life, the further problem is that as the Christian convert, Nehemiah Gore, and some missionaries argued, *bhakti* does not necessarily or invariably contradict the idea of pantheism.[74]

---

[69] *IER*, Vol. XIV, 1888: 430.
[70] Hoole 1844: 380.
[71] Mitchell 1899: 166.
[72] *IER*, Vol. 2, 1875: 390.
[73] Pope 1900: ix, xxxiv.
[74] See especially K. S. Macdonald, 'Pantheism and Vedantism', *IER*, Vol. XIV, 1888: 424–31.

Bhaktas were not always consistent, while some were more 'pantheistic' than others. As Carman reminds us 'Vaishnava bhakti has expressed itself in a range of positions between the "pure nondualism" (suddhadvaita) of Vallabha and the "dualism" of Madhva, and Saiva *bhakti* ranges from the monistic philosophy of Kashmir Saivism to the dualistic or pluralistic position of the Tamil Saiva Siddhanta.'[75] While therefore, some expected to preserve their sense of self, looking forward to being in the same heaven 'with a continuous vision of the Lord', others longed for an almost total absorption—a state which is 'dramatically portrayed in the stories of the merger of two of the Tamil *Vaisnava* saints (Atal and Tiruppan Alvar) into the Lord's image incarnation, Ranganatha'.[76]

Further Criticism of the Dominant Paradigm

Those missionaries who were critical of the pantheistic interpretation of Hinduism, were joined increasingly by others dissatisfied on other grounds with the received wisdom of the day. They too challenged the notion of the one uniform India-wide integrated system.

After a period of initial confusion, there appears to have been a growing conviction that tribal religions, such as those found in central and northern India, had their own distinctive characteristics, and were different from the religion as seen and practised by other inhabitants of India. However, to suggest that tribal religions needed to be distinguished from Hinduism was only a minor modification of the idea of their being an all-embracing brahmanical system. The question was how uniform and homogenized was Hindu religion outside of tribal areas, on the plains and in other parts of India? The more outspoken missionary commentators challenging this idea of a unitary brahmanical system (in areas outside of tribal regions), placed an emphasis on one of two different lines of argument critical of the dominant paradigm. One of these was to stress the importance of local or regional variations, a view which is seen most clearly in the emphasis on the distinctive nature of Tamil culture and also on *Shaiva Siddhanta* as a separate religion. A second approach was to stress the importance of horizontal divisions, especially the differences between popular and elite tradition, while at the same time contesting the strength of linkages between them.

---

[75] Eliade 1987, Vol. 2: 130–34.
[76] Ibid.: 132.

Tribal Religions

The spread of the idea among British Protestant missionaries that there was a difference between the Hindu and tribal religions was encouraged at least as much by official government reports as by their own experience of work among tribals. Carey noted what he perceived as a distinction between the Hindu and tribal religions as early as 1797.[77] However, the distinction was largely if not entirely ignored by Ward and Duff in their monumental works and was seldom raised in other missionary material during the first half of the nineteenth century. British Protestant missionaries were not especially active among so-called tribals until well after the middle of the nineteenth century when, in 1869, the Society for the Propagation of the Gospel (SPG) took over the work of the Gossner mission among thousands of tribals in Chota Nagpur.[78] In the meantime, however, British officials extended their contacts with tribals in the more remote areas and British missionaries, partly for that reason, became increasingly aware of the importance of tribal areas as a field for missionary activity.

In his book published in 1854, which in so many other ways produced arguments in favour of the dominant paradigm, Peter Percival insisted on a distinction between the 'Aborigines of India' and the 'Hindus' who were the 'Brahmanized inhabitants of the country' and 'foreign in their origin'.[79] Citing a report of Lieutenant General Briggs in support of his arguments he included a list of differences in religious and social practice. These emphasized the point that tribals or aboriginal people rejected brahman priests, offered blood sacrifice to their deities, drank alcohol, ate meat, buried their dead and in other ways differed in their customs from brahmans. The distinction between tribal and brahmanical religion reinforced by the Censuses of 1871 and 1881 was again noted in Protestant missionary comment in James Bradbury's book entitled *India: Its Condition, Religion, and Manners*, published in London in 1884. In this he also stressed the absence of caste and 'the absence of a corrupt priesthood in most tribes'.[80] By this time differences between tribals and Hindus were more or less taken for granted and the debate both among missionaries and census officials had shifted to the question of where to draw the line. While, for example, in his account of aboriginal people, Percival suggested

[77] Carey to Rylands, 6/7/1797, *PA*: Vol. I: 377.
[78] Thompson 1951: 349–52.
[79] Percival 1854: 33.
[80] Bradbury 1884: 8.

that Shanar religion was different from Hinduism, Caldwell took a different view. Although he doubted the usefulness of any idea of Hinduism
he nevertheless insisted that the Shanars (whatever their religion might
be) were quite clearly Hindus.

Growing Recognition of Regional and Local Variations

One of the primary reasons for increasing dissatisfaction with the dominant model as reflected especially in William Ward's account of Hinduism,
was not merely the feeling that tribal religions were different and failed to
fit the model, but the consolidation of missionary work more generally in
other parts of India outside of Bengal.

William Buyers (LMS) a missionary of nine years' experience of work
in Benares, declared in his *Letters on India* published in 1840, that:

> Mr Ward's Book on the Hindoos is no more applicable to a great variety
> of nations inhabiting India, than a description of the people of Yorkshire
> would apply to all the various nations of Europe. Hinduism itself is not one
> but many. What is called Hinduism in the Madras country, is very different
> from that which bears the same name at Benares.... It is true they are one
> to a certain extent—that is, as far as abstract speculations are concerned, but
> the system as it lives among the people is composed principally of local
> usages and traditions, varying in every district. Many of these local customs
> are set down in most works on India, as essential principles of Hinduism.[81]

Amos Sutton was one of the most prominent of the General Baptist
Missionary Society missionaries working in Orissa. After his arrival in
India in 1825 he wrote at least two books on missionary work in its
regional, religious and social context, and was author of the three-volume
Oriya Dictionary published at Cuttack in 1841. Writing in *Orissa and its
Evangelization* (1850), and as a missionary of twenty-five years' experience
of work in the region he, like Buyers some years earlier, emphasized the
importance of regional variations. While agreeing that the word 'Hindooism'
was adequate as a term referring to 'the essentials of the Hindoo religion
wherever seen' he attacked William Ward's account as a work based on
the assumption that the Bengali model applied elsewhere. There were, he
averred, 'local variations' which 'in many particulars, render an account
of Hindooism in one part of India inapplicable to Hindooism in another
part of India'. This consideration, he continued, 'explains many of the

---

[81] Buyers 1840: 2.

objections raised against Mr Ward's View of the Hindoos, a book which would have been more correctly entitled a View of the Bengallees. For to them alone it is, in its widest extent, fully applicable'.[82]

The importance of regional variations in Hinduism was stressed by other missionary writers from time to time. For example, Caldwell who argued that there were few Vedantists to be found in Tinnevelly, questioned the usefulness of the term Hinduism and also used, as one of his arguments, differences in ideas and practice as between different localities.

> Many a person who has derived his ideas of Hinduism from some particular school of Hindu metaphysics, or from the doctrines and rites considered as orthodox in a particular locality, has imagined himself acquainted with the whole subject. Whereas he has become acquainted with only one phase of Hinduism; and in other parts of India, amongst races of a different origin and speaking a different tongue, [he] would probably find the same system either quite unknown, or considered heretical.[83]

In his *Letters to Indian Youth* and as one writing from western India John Murray Mitchell made a similar point when he explained that 'the Hinduism of Bengal or Madras is not the same as the Hinduism of Bombay' and that the systems 'even of neighbouring provinces, such as Kannada and Maharashtra' were also different.[84]

Indeed, a consciousness of regional and local differences in Hindu religious and social life was the fundamental reason for the creation of a considerable body of missionary literature dealing with Hinduism in its local and regional context. A growing number of missionary works of this nature appeared in the press during the course of the second half of the nineteenth century. Among these books and articles, all based on experience and observation of local conditions, as well as on secondary sources, were works such as John F. Kearns's study of the marriage and funeral ceremonies of Hindus of south India (1868),[85] M. A. Sherring's, *Sacred City of the Hindus, An Account of Benares* (1868), Samuel Mateer's, *The Land of Charity: A Descriptive Account of Travancore and Its People* (1871), John Hewlett's account of 'The Hindu Sects of Benares', published in the

[82] Sutton 1850: 67.
[83] Caldwell 1840: 7.
[84] Mitchell 1861: 91.
[85] Born and educated in Ireland, J. F. Kearns joined the SPG and sailed for India in 1849. After some years of educational work in Madras he was appointed to the Puthiamputhur Mission in the northern part of Tinnevelly district where he had further experience of work among the Tamil population.

Indian Evangelical Review in 1887 (Vol. XIII), W. J. Wilkins's *Modern Hinduism: An Account of the Religion and Life of the Hindus of Northern India* (1887), Henry Rice's *Native Life in South India, being Sketches of the Social and Religious Characteristics of the Hindus* (1889) and J. E. Padfield's *The Hindu at Home, being Sketches of Hindu Daily Life* (1896)—a study of religious and social life in Andhra Pradesh. There may well be other works which could be added to this collection, but the list is sufficient to demonstrate the growing awareness of the importance of regional religious as well as social differences among Hindus.

Linguistic Developments and Tamil Religion in Missionary Thinking

An underlying assumption reinforcing the view that Hinduism was fundamentally brahmanism, or ideas flowing from brahmanic texts, was the increasingly discredited theory that, apart from tribal languages, all the rest, including those in south India, were derived from Sanskrit. According to this view Sanskrit, as the basis of all these languages, contained in its literature all that was worth knowing of ancient Indian customs and religion. As Alexander Dow declared in 1768 the Sanskrit language was 'the grand repository of the religion, philosophy, and history of the Hindoos',[86] and it followed from this that, if Europeans like Dow, Halhed, Jones, Wilkins and others had access to all the sacred Sanskrit texts, and if they could master the language, then they would know and understand the entire range of Hindu religious teaching. But this, as already implied, overlooked teachings in the non-Sanskrit texts, for example, in the Tamil *agamas* as well as teachings in more localised *oral* traditions which appear to have had no connection with the Sanskrit heritage.

The earlier conviction that the Sanskritic and therefore brahmanical literature was the only true source of Hinduism, was dealt a mortal blow by the publication of Caldwell's book on Dravidian Grammar in 1856. It had long been suspected by some Protestant missionary linguists that Jones, Carey and others were wrong in holding that Sanskrit was the parent of all Indian vernacular languages. Writing as early as 1833 Sutton announced that 'most of the languages of northern India as the Bengalee, Assamese, Hindee, etc., are radically the same, being derived from Sanskrut; those of southern India as the Tamul, Teloogoo, Kanarese, etc., appear to

---

[86] Quoted in Marshall 1970: 108.

belong to a distinct family'.[87] The Rev. W. Campbell (LMS) a missionary in Mysore in the 1830s and member of the working committee on the revision of the Kannada Bible was of a similar opinion.[88] This emerging alternative interpretation, developed and refined in Caldwell's book, ultimately convinced the European scholarly world that the southern languages belonged to a different family from those of the north. This conclusion greatly strengthened the argument that European scholars attempting to understand Indian religion or religions needed to take into account, not only the influence of tribals on the formation of Hinduism, but also the effect of a separate non-Sanskritic culture and literature on the development of religion in the south.

As is well known, south Indians as well as Europeans became increasingly aware of the importance and separateness of 'Dravidian' culture towards the end of the nineteenth century. Caldwell's work on Dravidian languages was a major factor in the growth especially of Tamil consciousness—Tamil, of all the south Indian languages, being the purest or least affected by what was imagined as 'Aryan' culture. The collection, editing and publication of ancient Tamil classics stimulated a resurgence in Tamil literature. Coincidental with this interest in Tamil literature and language was the emergence of attempts to delve into the Tamil past and discover the origin, growth and decline of Tamil civilization. Caldwell's theory that Tamil culture had a separate and independent existence before the coming of brahmans to south India was greeted with enthusiasm and soon became the basis for research into whatever was thought to have been distinctive in ancient Tamil religion and society. One of the more important of the Tamil scholars following this line of enquiry was Professor P. Sundaram Pillai (1855–97) who, in a series of articles published in the *Madras Christian College Magazine* in 1891, developed the theory that 'there was a period, lost altogether in hoary antiquity, when the native Dravidian religion was alone in vogue'.[89]

The impact of the new linguistic theories in focusing attention on the value of non-Sanskritic literature as an independent source for a better and more complete understanding of Indian religion is apparent in missionary comments in 1879. Maurice Phillips (LMS) a well-known preacher in Tamil in Madras was quick to dispute Monier-Williams's sweeping claim that Sanskrit literature 'is the only key to a correct knowledge of the

[87] Sutton 1833: 27.
[88] Campbell 1839: 108–9.
[89] Quoted in Arooran 1980: 20.

opinions and practices of the Hindu people'.[90] Writing in the *Indian Evangelical Review* Phillips observed that:

> It is true that a knowledge of Sanscrit is not absolutely necessary to one's efficiency as a missionary in the South of India where the languages are Turanian and not Indo-European. I cannot therefore agree with Professor Monier Williams, that ignorance of Sanscrit on the part of missionaries, in the south at least, is a great hindrance to the success of the work. A knowledge of Sanscrit however is very desirable, and gives a man great influence with the Brahmans, whose sacred books are locked up in that language.[91]

According to this view, brahmanical writings which encapsulated the brahmanical view of the world, were only one of a number of writings or sources for an understanding of what had come to be called Hinduism. Indian religion was based on both brahmanical and non-brahmanical ideas—the importance of the latter being insufficiently recognized in Monier-Williams' interpretation.

The notion of a distinctive Tamil religious tradition, different from those as reflected in north Indian brahmanical texts and teachings, was promoted by a number of British Protestant missionaries in the south. Indeed, they were increasingly convinced that instead of thinking in terms of one Hindu system, it would be more accurate to think of several independent religions.

Elijah Hoole, one of the first British missionaries to draw attention to the south Indian Shaiva saints, refers specifically to the work of Manikkavasagar, in the ninth century. In the narrative of his time in India, *Madras, Mysore and the South of India* (the first edition of which was published in 1844), Hoole drew attention to the saint's *Tiruvasagam*, citing passages in order to illustrate *Shaiva* 'doctrine'.[92] Peter Percival, writing ten years later, was possibly the first British missionary to refer to *Shaiva Siddhanta* as a specific school of philosophy in his book discussing Hinduism. However, as noted earlier in this chapter, he dismissed *Shaiva Siddhanta* as being much the same as Vedanta. In 1854, the same year in which Percival published his book, *The Land of the Veda*, Henry Hoisington, an American missionary who had also been working in Jaffna, published translations of three of the most important *Shaiva Siddhanta* texts. He thus made its teaching more accessible to American, British and other European readers.

[90] Monier-Williams 1875: xv.
[91] *IER*, Vol. VI, 1879: 318–19.
[92] Hoole 1844: 380–82.

Charles Egbert Kennet (1826–84) of the SPG (sometimes known as the Pusey of India) provided further details in what was perhaps a more objective account of *Shaiva Siddhanta* in an entry in the *Indian Antiquary* in 1873. After studying at Bishop's College, Calcutta, and passing his examinations in Tamil, Kennet spent thirteen years in Tinnevelly district before being transferred to a position in St John's Church, Madras in 1868 and appointed as Divinity Lecturer, Sullivan's Gardens, Madras in 1872.[93] As a theologian who according to one historian 'had probably no equal in India',[94] and as one familiar with Tamil attitudes and debates in south India, he was well placed to comment on south Indian systems. Drawing attention to the Rev. Hoisington's earlier work on *Shaiva Siddhanta* printed in America in 1854, Kennet remarked that independently of the esoteric and popular worship connected with the great temples of Madura, 'there is at that place a well-organized school of esoteric religious teaching in full vigour and operation, representing the *Shaiva Siddhanta* system, the most popular system of philosophy and religion among the Tamil people.' He stated further that it was based on 'the eight-and-twenty *Shaiva* books, or Agamas', and that its philosophy was essentially antagonistic to Vedantism.[95]

Another missionary resident in Madras city, and one whose stay there overlapped with Kennet's residence by eight years, was G. McKenzie Cobban, a Methodist missionary who arrived in India in 1877. He was a vernacular preacher and, like Kennet, a man with scholarly interests, who also drew attention to the separateness and insights of *Shaiva Siddhanta*.[96] An enthusiastic reader of Tamil religious literature and one who, again like Kennet, was probably aware of the student involvement in the Shaiva religious revival, Cobban argued that Tamils believed that Shiva is God and rejected the brahmanical notion of him as the destroyer.[97] In an article in the *Madras Christian College Magazine* in 1889 he reiterated Kennet's point that the followers of *Shaiva Siddhanta* believed that the soul when united nevertheless remained different from God, and added that God comes as Guru to instruct man.[98]

It was, however, G. U. Pope, the well-known SPG missionary scholar and exponent of Tamil tradition, who, writing at the end of the century, did the most to describe and publicize *Shaiva Siddhanta* as a distinctive

[93] *MF*, 1885: 49–52.
[94] Pascoe 1901: 918.
[95] *IA*, Vol. 2, December 1873: 343.
[96] *HF*, Vol. 3, December 1891: 227.
[97] *MCCM*, Vol. 3, July 1885: 24.
[98] *MCCM*, Vol. 7, No. 3, September 1889: 196.

tradition separate from other Hindu religions. Writing in the preface to his translation of the *Tiruvasagam*, Pope described *Shaiva Siddhanta* as 'the most elaborate, influential and undoubtedly the most intrinsically valuable of all the religions of India'.[99] The old prehistoric religion of South India, 'essentially existing from pre-Aryan times', it was something which had 'touched for generations the hearts of the great majority of the Tamil-speaking people'.[100] According to Pope, the essential teachings of *Shaiva Siddhanta* (which he, Kennet and Cobban all argued was an independent system) were reflected in the 'sacred utterances' of the Tamil saint who taught that:

> there was one supreme personal God—no mere physical abstraction, but the Lord of gods and men. He also taught that it was the gracious will of Çivan to assume humanity, to come to earth as a Guru, and to make disciples of those who sought Him with adequate preparation. He announced that this way of salvation was open to all classes of the community. He also taught very emphatically the immortality of the released soul—its conscious immortality.[101]

Horizontal Divisions: Great and Little Traditions?

British Protestant missionaries like secular orientalist and other European commentators, had always believed that Indian religion was a layered system. Whether there were two, three or even more layers, was a matter of debate. The most common assumption, explicit in the dominant model was that one could make some kind of legitimate distinction between elite and popular religion. The questions had always been: what is the nature of each layer, and what is the relationship between them? And, if in fact these layers are connected, what holds them together? These questions, which are still raised and discussed by modern anthropologists such as Redfield and Lawrence Babb, elicited a wide range of answers.

As we have noted, the dominant early and mid-nineteenth century perception was that the basic distinction was between brahmanism and popular religion including idolatry and polytheism. This concept evolved into the notion, explicit in Monier-Williams' work, of a distinction between brahmanism on the one hand and Hinduism on the other—a

[99] Pope 1900: lxxiv.
[100] Ibid.: xxxiv.
[101] Ibid.: xxxiii–xxxiv.

distinction implicit in Mitchell's book on Hinduism first published in 1883.

In the meantime, Carey had introduced the idea that one could draw a distinction between the views of 'the learned' and the uninformed or ignorant Hindus. He like many others also relied on a basic line between textual (genuine) and popular religion, a distinction very close to Rammohan Roy's 'real' and inauthentic Hinduism.[102] This idea, which usually embodied the notion of the sacred text, was especially acceptable among missionaries, Hindu reformers and some members of the East India Company searching for a way to justify the suppression of sati, hook-swinging and other practices by saying that these rituals had nothing to do with the real or textual Hinduism. But while on the one hand the missionaries, such as the Baptists Carey, Ward and Peggs, argued that the British authorities could abolish these customs without interfering with real religion, they still appear to have been complicit in the opposite idea that these customs were a product of brahmanism and not really distinct from it.

The conventional view which remained popular throughout most of the nineteenth century was that the basic unity as seen in Hinduism was created by the brahmans and enforced through their control over the castes and classes below. Furthermore, this unity emerged and was maintained not because of, but in spite of, the wishes of the common people. In short, Indian religion was a system of slavery. It was held together basically through fear and coercion—a detailed analysis of how this was done being contained in, for example, Duff's *India and India Missions*.

However, as the century progressed, there was less certainty about this model of oppression and exploitation, and about the attitudes of the common people who had so often been regarded as 'victims', or a people without agency of their own. As a result of their own investigation some missionaries like John Murray Mitchell were beginning to discover the variations and complexities in lower caste and class religion. For example, while on a preaching excursion in the Deccan, Mitchell interviewed people and took notes about their attitude and understanding of 'idol worship'. What he discovered was that the devotee's self-understanding and notion of what they were doing varied considerably. In fact, as a result of further experience (experience being especially necessary in the absence of written texts) missionaries were less confident about what they really knew.

[102] On this aspect of Rammohan Roy's thought see especially Killingley 1993: Ch. 4.

Added to this uncertainty about the nature of non-brahmanical religion or religions was a greater variety of models or types of explanation of what was happening at the popular level. There was continued uncertainty and disagreement about how many layers of religion there actually were and where certain types of religious expression, such as *bhakti* movements, might be placed in the hierarchy, if that is what it was. For example, in an open letter to the churches in 1889 the Madras Missionary Conference declared that the idolatry of south India fell naturally into two sections—'Brahmanical and non-Brahmanical'.[103] On the other hand, Samuel Mateer (LMS) a well-known missionary commentator on the religious situation in Travancore, had a somewhat more complicated view of the different levels there. In his third book, *The Gospel in South India*, published in 1886, he argued that:

> Besides the worship of the ordinary Hindu gods by the Brahmans and other high castes, which has been so fully described in most works on India, Travancore is also a principal seat of the demon worship practised by many aboriginal races in Asia and Africa.... Though not a Brahmanic form of religion, the Sudras of Malabar practise it to a great extent, along with the adoration of Hindu deities, Vishnu and Shiva, and their subordinate gods.[104]

While the notion of two basic systems producing a mixed tradition in the middle may have applied to Travancore, it was not necessarily the sort of model which missionaries always argued would apply to Hindu religion elsewhere. Indeed, it was not always clear what kind of layered model might apply to the various provinces and parts of India, let alone how far one could generalize about the religious strata in an India-wide system.

A striking example of the difficulty the more thinking and experienced missionaries had in making up their minds is reflected in the story of Murray Mitchell's varied attempts at a definition of Hinduism, including questions relating to its various layers.

One of the earliest statements of what he meant by Hinduism can be found in the 1861 edition of his well-known *Letters to Indian Youth*—a booklet first written for the benefit of one of his students and which was later used and in wide demand among missionaries throughout India. According to Mitchell, the answer to the question 'What is the system which we call Hinduism?' was far from easy because of regional variations. But the best answer was 'Genuine Hinduism is that which is contained in

---

[103] *Free Church of Scotland Quarterly Missionary Paper*, CXXII, March 1890: 1–2.
[104] Mateer 1886: 18–19.

the Shastras. The Shastras are books supposed by the Hindus to be divinely inspired; and what is not in them may be held to be but local or temporary'. In answer to the next question which was 'What are the Shastras?' he declared that the general answer would be 'the four Vedas, the six philosophical Shastras, and the eighteen Puranas'. He added that there were many Sanskrit works not included among them, but the writings enumerated were 'the peculiarly sacred and accredited books of the Hindus.'

However, this initial answer was qualified in Mitchell's later editions of the *Letters to Indian Youth* (1894 and others). During the intervening years between the two different editions he had accumulated a great deal more knowledge and experience, especially of Hindu religious life in western India. As we have seen, he joined with pilgrims and visited several of the most popular shrines and centres of worship in the region, as well as coming to sense something of the emotional appeal, as well as the widespread influence, of Tukaram's poetry.[105] In the later edition of the work, the author introduced a greater historical dimension to his definition of Hinduism by comparing its development to a river like the Ganges when it joins the sea.

> The Ganges where it joins the sea in a vast labyrinth of muddy waters is very unlike the stream which breaks out of the Himilayas at Hardwar. Equally unlike are Hinduism in it original form as presented in the Veda, and Hinduism in any of its modern manifestations.[106]

Equally significant were Mitchell's qualifications about sacred texts and his slide into taking into account more of non-brahmanical religion. Having reservations about his original list of 'peculiarly sacred' Sanskrit texts, he added a footnote explaining that although this list was the one accepted 'universally' in western India, it was somewhat different in Bengal where the *Tantras* were held in great esteem by many. Indeed, he added, 'an influential leader of the Adi Brahma Samaj in Calcutta has excluded the philosophical Shastras, and included the Tantras, among the authoritative books.[107]

Also significant was Mitchell's second footnote reflecting something of his further experience of religion in western India. 'The writings of Tukaram', he explained, 'mould the minds of the common people in Maharashtra

---

[105] For his account of his visit to Pandharpur and of Tukaram and his poetry see *IA*, March and June 1882.

[106] Mitchell 1894: 152.

[107] Ibid.

more than the acknowledged sacred books; on which, however, they profess to be founded'.[108]

It was this very notion of devotion to God, or *bhakti*, which Mitchell came to feel was central to an understanding of popular religion in western India, and which comprised the second layer of religion in an overall system. In a letter to Dr George Smith (Foreign Secretary of the Free Church of Scotland) in July 1882 he stated that:

> I have given of late a good deal of attention to the form which popular Hinduism assumes in Western India. It is not Brahmanism that most powerfully sways the mind of the Marathas; it is a very remarkable form of *bhakti*—the religion which, in Bengal, is connected mainly to the name of Chaitanya.... Some of the American Missionaries last October, in their great Conference, said it would be of no small consequence to have a full exposition of the *bhakti* system. A full exposition will not be easily supplied; but I hope to make some contribution towards it. I may refer to this later again. I would have sent you a copy of two papers I have already published, but I seem to have no copies at hand.[109]

One problem with this view was that it did not take account of everything that was significant in Mitchell's own contact with popular religion. As he subsequently realized *bhakti* was not quite the right term to explain the fear, bargaining and propitiation which he witnessed at Jejuri. Towards the end of his life, in 1899, when he wrote his recollections he offered the reader a summary of Hinduism in western India. With reference to the worship of Khandoba, the deity at Jejuri, he described it as a remnant of that 'demon-worship' which appeared to have been the religion of the earlier inhabitants of this country. 'In some parts of India and in Ceylon,' he continued, 'this still exists in a state so little affected by foreign elements as to permit its analysis and classification'. At that point in the discussion Mitchell gave his readers a summary of his last reflections, not on Hinduism as a whole, but on Hinduism in Maharashtra.

> In the Maratha country we have three systems of Hinduism—distinguishable, yet interpenetrating and modifying each other. We have first, Hinduism 'according to the Shastras'; next, the worship of Vithoba, as set forth in the popular Marathi poets; and lastly, we have the system which clusters around Khandoba and his brother deities. These are too numerous to name—

---

[108] Ibid.
[109] NLS, MS 7826, F. 114, Mitchell to Smith, 22–24/7/1882.

Khandoba, Kanhoba, Bhairoba, Mhasoba, Mhaskoba, Nauloba, Rokodoba, Jotiba, Siddhoba, and so on.[110]

Having begun with the idea of the essentials of Hinduism being embodied in brahmanical texts, Mitchell's commentaries ended with the notion of a three-tiered system in Maharashtra. And how far this model applied to other parts of India he seems to have been unwilling to say.

Increasing Doubts and Denials of Hinduism as a Unified System

While there were missionaries, such as the Rev. Sawday (WMMS, Mysore) and others who, even at the turn of the nineteenth century, continued to reiterate a model of Hinduism little different from that of William Ward or Alexander Duff, their views, and what possibly remained as the dominant paradigm, were increasingly challenged during the second half of the century. The notion of the one unified brahmanically constructed system was if anything reinforced by the idea of pantheism, since this was understood in many quarters as the key component or essence of the same system. Pantheism was, in this view, a brahman invention. Yet as a result of increasing knowledge and experience, and possibly even changing assumptions about what constituted religion, this conviction that there was the one unified Hindu system was increasingly questioned in missionary literature. As already mentioned, there was a growing acknowledgement of the importance of regional and local variations and a better and more informed understanding of the complexities of the India-wide situation. This included an increasing reluctance to generalize about the nature of popular religion. In some cases, the more the missionaries learned of the situation the more intricate and confusing it appeared to be. There was little agreement about either the relationship between the so-called 'great and little traditions', or the nature of the hierarchy which was supposed to extend across the subcontinent. As we have noted different missionaries from different parts of India gave different descriptions. Increasing experience in the mission field, much more evidence and information, and possibly other factors, were beginning to erode what had long been the dominant model. Hence, in the light of these factors, it is hardly surprising that some commentators were coming to doubt whether

[110] Mitchell 1899: 297.

there was such a phenomenon as Hinduism or the one all-embracing Hindu system.

The basic challenge and questioning of the dominant paradigm came from a handful of individual missionary scholars, and also from the Madras Missionary Conference that represented missionaries of different denominations who resided in and around Madras. The one characteristic the individual missionary dissenters tended to have in common was the high standard of their scholarly or academic achievement. Most were recognized as eminent scholars, had Masters or Ph.D. degrees, and had written books or contributed articles on various aspects of Hinduism in reputed journals. Many had had long-term experience of mission work among both the elites (often Western-educated) and lower-caste or outcaste people. As already pointed out, their exposure to Indian religion was therefore broader and more all-encompassing when compared with secular orientalists who usually confined themselves to the study of Sanskrit texts.

Murray Mitchell's research and reflection, not only helped to illuminate the mysteries of Indian religion, but also continued to raise further issues. As we noted, the conclusion at the end of his life was that in the Maratha country 'we have three systems of Hinduism'. The problem with this statement is that, in spite of his insistence that these systems were all a part of an overarching larger entity, he still does not explain what that entity was or what the three systems had in common. We can only guess that he felt there was some unity, but was unprepared to say what it was.

A clearer and more decided view was proposed by the independent-minded Caldwell who was one of the first to challenge the current orthodoxy—the view that almost any aspect of Indian religion was automatically a part of Hinduism. In 1840, after having spent some time investigating religious and social life in Tinnevelly district, he wrote as follows:

It does not throw much light upon the Shanar religion to describe it as a form of Hinduism. It is no doubt equally deserving of the name with most of the religions of India; but as those religions are not only multiform, but mutually opposed, the use of the common term 'Hinduism' is liable to mislead. It is true that certain general theosophic ideas are supposed to pervade all the Hindu systems, and that theoretical unity is said to lurk beneath practical diversity. But this representation, though in some degree correct, is strictly applicable only to the mystical or metaphysical systems. Practically, the Hindu religions have few ideas and but few practices in common; and the vast majority of their votaries would be indignant at the supposition that their own religion, and the detested heresy of their opponents, are after all one and the same.... The term 'Hinduism,' like the geographical term 'India,' is an European generalization unknown to the Hindus. The Hindus themselves call their religions by the name of the particular deity they worship, as 'Siva bhacti,' 'Vishnu bhacti,' etc.... Europeans popularly imagine that the temples and images and processions which they so frequently see belong to one and the same system. But the fact is that in many cases they belong to totally different religions.[111]

However, even Caldwell, independent-minded as he was, could not for long withstand the weight of the dominant paradigm. By the 1850s and 1860s the idea of Hinduism had become more firmly entrenched in missionary and popular circles. In fact, readers of missionary and other reports on Indian religion were beginning to expect at least a chapter on Hinduism. Although Caldwell writing in 1840 had declared that the term Hinduism could have very little meaning, yet when speaking to an assembled audience at the Church of England Brighton Congress in 1874 he called his address 'The Relation of Christianity to Hinduism'.[112] Whether he liked it or not, the term Hinduism had come to stay and was a concept around which he could try to build some kind of meaningful argument.

Another important assault on the idea of Hinduism came in 1889 in G. McKenzie Cobban's article entitled significantly 'Christianity and Hindu Faiths' published in the *Madras Christian College Magazine*. 'Men often write and speak of "the Hindu faith" as if it were a unity', he wrote. 'It is not a unity. The term "Hinduism" is misleading. Never during historic times has there been one faith for the two hundred millions of Hindus, and there is not one faith now.'[113]

Two years later the Madras Missionary Conference, in an open letter to the churches, made much the same point. 'The popular religion of India', they averred, 'though often called by one name, *viz*. Hinduism, is not a unity. Hindus have never had only one religion.'[114] Similar views are implicit in Pope's work on the *Tiruvasagam* where he argues that *Shaiva Siddhanta*, was a separate system 'among all the religions of India'.

These views from the south, critical of a paradigm based primarily on a study of north Indian texts and movements, were echoed by at least two commentators in Bengal. One of them was Rev. Kenneth Macdonald who

---

[111] Caldwell 1840: 6.

[112] Caldwell 1874.

[113] *MCCM*, Vol. VII, No. 3, September 1899: 197.

[114] *Free Church of Scotland Quarterly Paper*, CXXII, March 1890.

taught in the Free Church of Scotland's institution in Calcutta and was also editor of the *Indian Evangelical Review*—a journal which devoted a good deal of space to articles and comment on Indian religious ideas and movements. In 1890 Macdonald published a tract of eight pages entitled 'Is Hinduism a Religion?' arguing that if Hinduism was anything, it was a social system. In his view it could not possibly be considered 'a religion'. It was the Europeans, he pointed out, who had introduced and developed the idea of Hinduism and 'even the English educated people of India were in their ignorance led to believe or to pretend to believe that there was one religion called Hinduism'. If they had 'looked under the surface', he continued, 'they would soon have discovered that there was no such common religion, that the bond tying the people together was not religion but social rules known as caste rules'.[115] He not only referred to the diverse religious customs and allegiances of 'Hindus' in a typical Bengali village, but claimed that *Vaishnavism, Shaivism, Saktaism*, the *Tantric* system, *Surya* worship and other traditions were 'different religions'.[116] This sceptical view of the usefulness of the term Hinduism, was subsequently endorsed by the Rev. John Morrison, principal of Macdonald's old college in Calcutta. Writing in his book *New Ideas in India*, the latter declared that

> to the student of 'Hinduism'... the first fact that emerges is that there are no distinctive Hindu doctrines. No one doctrine is distinctive of Hinduism. There is no canonical book, nowhere any stated body of doctrine that might be called the Hindu creed.[117]

Thus at least in one sense Protestant and missionary debates on Hinduism had come full circle. The early claims of Claudius Buchanan that even the brahmans were divided in faith and belief and that 'in Hindostan alone there is a great variety of religions',[118] re-emerge in the discussions of the late nineteenth century. This was clearly because of increased missionary knowledge and understanding, because of the long-term experience of missionaries working in different localities and interacting with diverse groups of people, and possibly also because of the influence of the government's census reports—documents which missionaries and missionary societies consulted with considerable interest.[119]

---

[115] Macdonald 1890. See also the reference to the tract in the *Harvest Field*, December 1891.

[116] Macdonald 1890: 3–8.

[117] Morrison 1906: 151.

[118] Pearson 1819, Vol. 1: 394.

[119] See for example *CMI*, Vol. XI, 1875: 235–36, 261–63.

First introduced in British India in 1871 and taken at an all-India level at ten-yearly intervals thereafter, these reports contained an overview, as well as details, of the different religions including Hinduism. Once having introduced the term Hinduism which the census commissioner in 1891 confessed was a 'clumsy' name, 'only justifiable by convention',[120] enumerators and others were faced with the impossible task of agreeing on a definition. As a way of solving the problem, commissioners settled on the idea that Hinduism could be defined only in negative terms (by what it was not) and Hindus, or the followers of Hinduism, by what was termed a policy of 'successive exclusion'.[121] Once it was decided who was a Sikh, a Jain, a Buddhist and so on, then these adherents were enumerated and placed in their separate categories; those who were left were described as Hindus or the followers of Hinduism. This policy of last resort, reflecting the failure to agree that there was any central doctrine, creed or structure which could be identified as the essence of Hinduism, could not but encourage the idea that the term had little meaning.[122] Once again, if nothing could be forced into a meaningful overall structure, the only realistic alternative was to think in terms of smaller categories and a plurality of religions.

10

Empathy or Otherness? Changing Evaluations of Hinduism in the Nineteenth Century

Natural Religion and Hinduism

Any assessment of the extent to which attitudes towards Indian religions, including Hinduism, were changing in the nineteenth century must necessarily involve some discussion of missionary views of natural religion. No matter how far apart missionaries may have felt from 'the natives' of India, no matter how critical of the evils of Hinduism, or of other aspects of Hindu culture, they never believed that Hindus were totally 'other'. In their view, all people were descended from Adam and hence were the children of the one Creator. All races shared in the same common humanity and were sinful and in need of salvation which came through an acceptance of the Christian Gospel.

The source of this conviction was biblical teaching reinforced by the underlying assumption, shared in by leaders of the European Enlightenment, that there was such a thing as a common or universal human nature.[1] Even Charles Grant who, as we have seen, was one of the most vituperative and outspoken critics of Hindus and Hinduism assumed that underneath it all Hindus were little different from Europeans. Of course Hinduism was an abomination and Hindus no better than their lying and immoral deities; but in spite of the awfulness of their religion, they, like everyone else, had been endowed with reason and conscience; and conscience 'though smothered' was 'not extinct'.[2] As mentioned in chapter 5, Baptist missionaries, including Peggs, Ward and Sutton, en route for India in 1821, held regular meetings on the long voyage out. At one of these they discussed passages in Paul's epistle to the Romans, including his assumption that the Gentiles had originally been endowed by 'the light of nature', while at a subsequent meeting, the missionaries considered 'the degree of

---

[1] For comment on this issue and reference to recent scholarship on religion and the Enlightenment, see especially Porter 1990.
[2] Grant 1792: 62.

the knowledge of the natural and moral perfections' which existed 'in modern and heathen nations'.[3]

Furthermore, it was the well-known Serampore-based Baptist *Friend of India*, which clashed with Alexander Duff on precisely the issue of how far one should take into account the fact that Hindus already shared with Christians common feelings and attitudes towards God. Referring to a speech which Duff made in Scotland in 1835, the paper argued that the missionary methods which he developed and somewhat arrogantly promoted as a model for others to follow, failed to take advantage of the full range of the Hindus' natural and God-given gifts which included not only their rationality, but a conscience and sense of sin.[4] Duff, who according to the editor, had confined his work to addressing a 'few young men who had...drunk in the poison of European infidelity', was focusing too exclusively on the historical and other 'external' evidences of the Christian faith, overlooking the persuasive power of 'internal' evidence 'in every human heart'. The Gospel, repeated the editor, was such as to commend itself to men's conscience as well as reason, 'notwithstanding all their accidental differences'.

> Now the fact is, that there is amongst the people an almost universal acknowledgement of the Divine existence, and the various attributes of the deity both natural and moral—of the sinfulness of men, and of future suffering as its natural and necessary consequence—and of the principle of propitiation and atonement as the great means of its accomplishment. Other minor points also are generally held, which, in conjunction with these, afford the Christian preacher wide ground of argument with Hindus of all classes. These truths...furnish abundant materials with which to assail Hindooism itself, and also to shew the intrinsic value of the Gospel and consequently the internal evidence of its having proceeded from God.[5]

The view that Hindus already had the ability to reason, a conscience, and some knowledge of God's work and activity in the world, was a presupposition that both sustained the missionary movement and was linked with the widely accepted notion of 'natural religion'. In his *Dictionary of the English Language* (the first edition of which was published in 1773) Samuel Johnson cited Charles Wilkins to the effect that 'I call that *natural* religion, which men might know, and should be obliged unto, by

[3] Sutton 1833: 17–18.
[4] *Friend of India*, 26/11/1835: 378–80.
[5] Ibid.

the meer principles of reason, improved by consideration and experience, without the help of revelation.[6] About a hundred years later, John Murray Mitchell gave a slightly more elaborate definition. He argued that, in addition to revelation, 'there is what we call the Light of Nature':

> It denotes all that knowledge of God which we might derive from the works of Nature around us, the providence of God, and the constitution of our own minds. When we unite into a system all the instruction which these things communicate respecting God, we term that system—Natural Religion.[7]

Protestant missionaries generally throughout most of the nineteenth century continued to draw a distinction between natural religion (including certain universal God-given characteristics) on the one hand and all religious systems including Christianity on the other. There was no argument that God's light had shone and was working in nature and human nature; but, as we have seen, one question was how far was this, God's activity, still apparent among Hindus? A second question related to the way in which different religious systems responded or reacted to natural religion. They could build upon it, leave the natural condition unchanged, or even undermine or stifle what God had already given. While, for example, Charles Grant and Heber appear to have differed in their estimate of the original God-given qualities which were still apparent among Hindus, both believed 'the Hindu system' tended to undermine these original gifts. The commonly accepted Christian belief, clearly spelt out by Murray Mitchell, was that 'there is not a single truth recognized by Natural Religion nor a single duty inculcated by it which Christianity does not equally recognize and inculcate'.[8] On the other hand, and according to the same source, the 'unanswerable argument against the Hindu religion is this, that it is often entirely opposed to Natural Religion'.[9]

The extent to which missionaries could go in separating natural religion from Hinduism is apparent in Elijah Hoole's book on missions and Hinduism in south India published in 1844. Like Ward and Duff whom he referred to as the best authorities on the 'pretended mysteries' of 'Hindoo Mythology', he proceeded to condemn Hinduism in a style typical of his generation, as a system that abounded in 'the grossest absurdities' and

---

[6] Johnson 1834: 785.

[7] Mitchell 1894: 93. For recent comment on the history of the idea of natural religion, see J. Z. Smith 1998: 271–73.

[8] Mitchell 1894: 95.

[9] Ibid.: 165.

contradictions and which gratified the most corrupt tendencies of the human heart.[10] And yet substantial passages quoted in his book comprise translations from Tamil devotional and moral works which seem to suggest the opposite, and which, as the author explains, illustrate just how far the Tamils still retained ideas and insights given to them through the light of nature, and in spite of the imposition of 'the Hindoo system'. For example, he declared that the Hindus generally 'acknowledge the existence of one Supreme and Eternal Being, from whom all things have proceeded, and for whose pleasure they exist'. Furthermore, he introduced a substantial passage from the *Tiruvasagam* with the explanation that there are 'some' devotional compositions of Shiva's worshippers, in which, addressing Shiva as the Supreme, 'they have attained to the truly sublime; and in the most appropriate language, have displayed a correctness of sentiment and ardency of devotion, which we cannot but admire'.[11]

According to Hoole, these and other sentiments, 'many of which are so opposite the prevailing superstition', were not only popular, but proved that amongst the heathen 'there is a degree of knowledge and truth contending with ignorance and error'.[12]

Finally, in his summing up, he declared that:

It may not be denied morality, kindness, natural affection, and hospitality, in some measure, exist amongst the Hindoos; but it may be safely averred that none of these are owing to their religion—a system which would influence the mind to close its vision against that 'light which lighteth every man that cometh into the world'.[13]

The idea of natural religion remained as a strand in missionary thinking throughout the nineteenth century. Kennedy, Mateer, Macdonald (editor of the *Indian Evangelical Review*), Caldwell, Mitchell, Robson, Slater and others all refer to God's activity in the conscience, heart or mind of the Hindu people. Vaughan went as far, if not further than most, when he declared that it could not be doubted that, of all people, the Hindus had 'approached nearer the true ideal than any other people unblessed with the light of Revelation'.[14] And even when they lapsed into a system of 'degraded polytheism and idolatry' they still retained much that was

---

[10] Hoole 1844: 377, 408–10.
[11] Ibid.: 380
[12] Ibid.: 392.
[13] Ibid.: 410.
[14] Vaughan 1876: 41.

admirable: 'the lamp of devotion still burnt bright in many a soul, and sublime sentiments breathed in many a fervid page'.[15]

While the distinction between natural and revealed religion may or may not have been used as a deliberate strategy, it enabled missionaries to quarantine those aspects of Indian religion which they respected (and which had parallels with Christianity) from other elements which they disliked and demonized as attributes of 'the Hindu system'. In other words, the best things in Indian religion were reflections of natural religion and the worst features were represented as components of Hinduism. However, it became increasingly clear that the distinction between natural and Hindu religion was not always sustainable. How, for example, could it be maintained that some aspects of the *Tiruvasagam* were reflections of natural religion, while other aspects were part of 'the Hindu system'? Was it not all part of a coherent *Shaiva Siddhanta* tradition—the so-called 'good' and 'bad' elements being all part of the whole? It was problems such as these that led Max Müller to declare in a lecture in 1873 that the idea of a 'universal primeval revelation' (only another name for natural religion), 'rested on no authority but the speculation of philosophers'. He suggested that instead of trying to maintain a distinction between what were in effect three classes of religion, 'the primitive or natural, the debased or idolatrous, and the revealed' it was better to recognize that all religions were based on natural religion involving conscience and the use of reason.[16] Indeed, as missionaries developed a more sympathetic attitude towards Hinduism, a process increasingly in evidence during the last quarter of the nineteenth century, there was greater recognition that aspects of religious life and thought previously associated with natural religion were part and parcel of Hinduism.[17]

One noteworthy example of what became an increasing tendency to blur the distinction between natural religion and Hinduism can be seen in John Robson's depictions of Hinduism during the period from 1867 to

---

[15] Ibid.: 104. Vaughan's admiration for the fortitude and spirit of devotion among Hindu pilgrims he met while on a preaching tour in 1846 is clearly apparent in his annual letter to the CMS. 'It is truly saddening to behold the degrading scenes of idolatry wh. go on around', he wrote, 'Yet there is an air of earnestness & sincerity over all. Persons who take a journey of 1500 miles to a shrine are undoubtedly in earnest. They have an object before them; they labour, suffer, pray & pray for a blessing. One cannot help feeling the deepest commiseration for those who are thus groping in the dark after an unknown good' (CMS, CIi/0 299/40, Annual Report, 6/1/1865).

[16] Müller 1873: 124–39.

[17] Significant also is the ambiguity in Robson's (1874) book on Hinduism.

294 IMAGINED HINDUISM

1874. A reading of his early lecture on Hinduism, delivered in Scotland in 1867, shows that his early evaluation of it was essentially negative and not very different from that of many other missionaries active earlier in the nineteenth century.[18] Like many of his predecessors he pointed to 'the law of God' which, he averred, was written on the hearts of Hindus as well as on those of other men. And like earlier commentators he went on to argue that natural religion was in conflict with Hinduism. 'Thus while many of the Hindus feel and strive to act according to the dictates of their con-science, it is obvious', he remarked, 'that the whole tendency of religion must be to make them indifferent to its promptings'. However, seven years later, and probably after he had read Max Müller's lectures on 'the Science of Religion', he appears to have changed his idea about the sources of goodness and truth in Indian religious life and tradition. In the text of his work entitled *Hinduism and Its Relations to Christianity*, published in 1874, he again drew attention to the positive role of natural religion, but in a seemingly contradictory fashion appears to blur the distinction between natural religion and Hinduism in the preface. According to the preface not only did Hinduism, with all its faults, 'contain a subtle philosophy, express high moral truths and enjoin many social virtues; it even in one guise or another embodies many of the leading truths which Christianity teaches'.[19] A greater willingness to make concessions to Hinduism, and to attribute the insights of natural religion to 'truths' in Hinduism itself, was clearly a symptom of more basic changes in the overall process of evaluation. This process reflecting the growth of more positive attitudes towards Hinduism was beginning to influence a larger number of missionaries, and was a development which we shall now examine in greater detail.

Factors in the Growth of More Sympathetic Views

Kenneth Ballhatchet, referring to Christian missionary writings mainly on Hinduism in the nineteenth and twentieth centuries, has argued that two attitudes towards non-Christian religions can be distinguished—one of hostility and one of sympathy. 'The former,' he contends, 'was predomin-ant during the greater part of the nineteenth century, the latter there-after.'[20] While this general conclusion remains undisputed, there is continued

[18] Robson 1867.

[19] Robson 1874: v–vi. See also his positive evaluation of Hinduism in the text itself (for example, pp. 3, 8, 13, 31, 119, 158).

[20] Ballhatchet 1961: 344.

uncertainty about the extent to which changes in attitude occurred towards the end of the nineteenth century, as well as disagreement about why this shift in opinion was taking place. In his explanation of what he believed was an increasingly sympathetic approach Ballhatchet placed his emphasis on developments in both India *and* overseas. By way of contrast, Sharpe and Cracknell concentrate much more on changing theologies and movements of thought in Britain and Europe—developments which they suggest were fundamental to an understanding of the more respectful and sympathetic approach.[21] While they convey the impression that the growth of a more measured response was almost entirely due to developments in the West, Hugald Grafe, writing about Christianity in south India, argues that the changes in outlook among missionaries there were a result, not of influences coming from outside of India, but of changing circumstances in the local south Indian context.[22]

One of the arguments of this chapter is that while developments in Britain and Europe were important as a factor in changing attitudes towards Hinduism, missionary experience was a fundamental element in the growth of these more sympathetic views. Notions of fulfilment and other ideas important in developing the new approach were already there *in India* before the pronouncements of British scholars such as Maurice, Max Müller and Monier-Williams. As we have noted, missionaries like Hoole had long grappled with the issue of parallels between the Christian faith and traditions within Hinduism. Increased knowledge led Carey into a deeper dislike of the Hindu system. But for others, like Cobban, the discovery of Hindu devotional literature, *Shaiva Siddhanta* and teachings which seemed to echo Christian sentiment, was a revelation and an important part of their Indian experience. Feelings of frustration and failure, linked with the counterproductive nature of the hard-line approach, and a real life exposure to Hindus and Hindu teachings was, in a sense, a *prepario evangelica* in reverse. It was an experience and exposure which prepared the missionaries themselves for a change of heart. It raised afresh questions about the relationship between Christianity and Hinduism and encouraged evangelists to recognize and acknowledge more fully the values inherent in Hindu traditions.

In addition to the changes in the theological and intellectual climate in Europe already discussed, the following developments in India appear to have been especially important in encouraging a more generous and

---

[21] Cracknell 1995; Sharpe 1965: Chs 1–3.
[22] Grafe 1990: 140–45.

sympathetic approach. First, there were changes within Hinduism itself. These included the virtual disappearance of sati—a potent symbol and reminder of much of what Protestants felt was objectionable in Hindu tradition. Indeed, the Company's measures in banning sati, the regulations against drowning of infants at Sagar, and the decline in the number of deaths through accident or ritual suicide at the Jagannath festival at Puri (another potent symbol of imagined Hinduism) were all developments which helped mollify the British public and open the way for a less emotive and more considered and sympathetic approach to the subject. It is true that caste with all its supposed 'evils' was seen increasingly as an essential part of Hinduism and that the sufferings of Hindu women, frequently attributed to the teachings and ethos of the same religion, were matters of considerable or increasing concern during the second half of the nineteenth century. But while these issues were the topics of frequent discussion they seldom evoked the same intense horror or sense of outrage as the sati's cry or the sickening remains of bodies crushed beneath the wheels of a ponderous cart.

Second, there were not the same political pressures on Christians to highlight the remaining humanitarian abuses within Hinduism during the second half of the nineteenth century. Because of the growth of Hindu socio-religious reform movements and the continued expansion of an 'enlightened' public opinion in India, it was increasingly recognized that Hindus themselves were the most appropriate group to deal with these matters. As a result of these considerations, the issues of hook-swinging and child marriage, only seldom appeared on the missionary agenda. Missionaries in India appealed to the government on both of these issues;[23] but, generally speaking, missionary supporters were more relaxed and there were no long sustained political campaigns in Britain as there had been in the first half of the century with an almost unwavering focus on the bloody and constantly running sores of imagined Hinduism. Candidates for the mission field, and the younger men and women who arrived in India in the latter period no longer carried with them quite the same imagery or ideas of the 'evils' of Hinduism as Duff and others had in the 1820s and 1830s.

Third, quite apart from the greater knowledge of Hinduism, as reflected in the translation of texts and in commentaries in Europe, the missionaries gradually acquired, more directly and through their experience of work in different parts of India, a greater knowledge and understanding of contemporary Hinduism at the local and regional levels. Prominent among those

---

[23] Oddie 1976: 96–102; and 1995: 102–4.

involved in a re-evaluation of Hinduism were missionaries with impressive linguistic accomplishments who had spent long periods at work among the people as well as in study. Indeed, some of them, like Hoole, Mitchell and Pope, brought to light texts and devotional traditions which were little known or understood in Europe. Encounters with Hindu devotees, the hearing of Hindu songs and the reading for the first time certain types of devotional literature like Tukaram's poetry, or the insights and feelings after God as reflected in the *Turuvasagam* or Vaishnavite texts were for these evangelists something like 'a revelation'. Thus, unlike many of the Europe-based scholars of Hinduism, their conclusions were often based on fieldwork as well as on reading, and were, as noted in chapter 3, the outcome of a process of research more comparable with the approach of the modern anthropologist than with the methods of the armchair philosopher. It was this new knowledge which encouraged a greater tolerance and a greater sympathy and feeling for various aspects of Hindu tradition.

Also important in the process of re-evaluation of Hinduism was what appears to have been a greater degree of intellectual freedom in the mission field than in most missionary circles in Britain. Missionaries in India learnt a great deal from each other at local, regional and India-wide conferences which were ecumenical in nature and largely free from the constraints imposed on missionaries by their societies at home. Furthermore, in India, they had their own in-house publications (evangelical or otherwise) that display a remarkable degree of diversity and openness in debates about the character of Hindu religion. The *Indian Evangelical Review*, established in 1875, was for 'the free discussion' of all topics relating to religion and the welfare of the people of India,[24] and displayed through its columns considerable diversity of opinion. The *Harvest Field*, nominally under the control of Methodists, was also a vehicle for very different views on the relative merits of Hinduism and Christianity. Last, but not least, was the *Madras Christian College Magazine*, which bore the imprint of its founder William Miller, certainly a radical and pioneer. The magazine continued to nurture and disseminate liberal views of the relationship between faiths that would be unacceptable (if not unthinkable) in certain missionary society journals in Britain.[25] In these circumstances in India, missionaries with conservative views were perhaps more likely to be challenged by alternative and more radical points of view than they were in the more sheltered missionary society environments in Britain.

---

[24] *IER*, Vol. I: 96.
[25] For example, in the *Church Missionary Gleaner*.

Another reason for the missionaries' change of approach to Hinduism, evident in the second half of the nineteenth century, was a practical problem and the growing realization that attacks on Hinduism were counterproductive. Hence, there was a deliberate attempt to adopt a less confrontational approach, and also note the merits as well as defects in Hindu religion.

There are clear indications that from about the middle of the nineteenth century missionaries were becoming increasingly doubtful about the wisdom of frequently attacking Hinduism and related ideas. The gradual and long-term accumulation of missionary experience had made it more obvious that the outright denunciations of Hindu behaviour and belief, including the denigration of Hindu gods, was often unhelpful and counterproductive. It was therefore necessary, as a matter of tactics, to experiment with a more positive and conciliatory approach. The issue emerged as a major consideration at a general conference of Bengal missionaries meeting in Calcutta in 1855.[26] The Rev. John Wenger (Baptist Missionary Society, BMS) claimed that there had sometimes been 'too great an eagerness to assail the vulnerable and sore points of Hinduism and Mahommadanism, and to make the hearers ashamed of their religious systems'.[27] In the discussion which followed there was considerable agreement that this aggressive method was already changing and that missionaries should, as far as possible, adopt a more conciliatory approach. For example, the Rev. Boaz (London Missionary Society, LMS) said that he understood that satirical allusions to the gods and goddesses had 'long ago' been discontinued,[28] while the Rev. W. Smith (CMS, Benares) stated his belief that all missionaries were agreed that 'we ought to preach the Gospel first, as far as we are permitted , and to do it in a way that shall give the least possible offence to the prejudices of the people'.[29]

These sentiments were echoed at conferences and by British missionaries elsewhere. A resolution passed at the South India Missionary Conference meeting at Ootacamund in 1858 noted that the missionaries' primary duty was to 'testify the Gospel of the grace of God' and avoid unnecessary disputes and confrontation.[30] Five out of the six British

---

[26] *Proceedings of a General Conference of Bengal Protestant Missionaries held at Calcutta, Sept. 4–7, 1855.*

[27] Ibid.: 47–8.

[28] Ibid.: 63.

[29] Ibid.: 170.

[30] *Proceedings of the South India Missionary Conference held at Ootacamund, 19 April–5 May 1858*: 230–31.

missionaries who spoke on the subject at the general missionary conferences held at Allahabad (1872–73) and Calcutta (1882–83) namely J.
Kennedy, J. Murray Mitchell, J. Smith, M. Phillips and J. P. Hughes (CMS,
Peshwar) counselled a sympathetic and tactful approach.[31] Lastly, there is
evidence of British missionary attitudes supplied by the Rev. P. J. Jones of
the American Madurai mission in 1889.[32] Jones, whose chief activity was
preaching to Hindus, sent sixty letters of enquiry to twenty-two missions
asking missionaries a range of questions on the topic. After having received
thirty-eight replies from eighteen missions and analysed responses he
remarked that the method of conciliation and simple presentation of the
Gospel prevailed 'almost universally among missionaries'.[33] Among those
who adopted this approach were the Revs. H. Rice (LMS), H. Haig (Wesleyan
Methodist Missionary Society, WMMS), who 'formerly sought to be
argumentative', and G. McKenzie Cobban. The latter declared it was
better to know truth than error in Hindu tradition and that, if he could
stir truth 'which is in the Hindu mind', then 'Christ and Christianity must
soon find a welcome there'.[34]

The need to adopt a conciliatory approach, even if only as a continuing
point of contact and effective method of communication, was made
clearly apparent in a variety of comments elsewhere. Kennedy, for example, argued that missionaries must win the people if they would do
them good, and that, unless Hindus believed them to be their friends and
were treated with courtesy, they would not hear the message. But instead
of treating Hindus in a courteous manner, he said, they were sometimes
'rudely assailed'.[35] The Rev. Hewett was likewise aware of the need for a
sympathetic approach if the preacher was really going to communicate.
'Will God hold us guiltless,' he wondered, 'if we fail to carry the Gospel
home to their hearts through our own inability to sympathise with their
honest spiritual experiences?'[36]

[31] *Report of the General Missionary Conference held at Allahabad, 1872–73*: 48, 50; *Report
of the Second Decennial Missionary Conference held at Calcutta, 1882–83*: 18, 26–8.
[32] *IER*, Vol. XVI, 1889: 129–47.
[33] Ibid.: 138.
[34] Ibid.: 138, 141.
[35] His attempt to reinforce his message by citing as rude and unacceptable the comments
of two Indian catechists, prompted a retort by Kailas Chandra Bose (catechist) that it was
'the besetting sin of catechists to attack Hinduism and Muhammedanism', but that they had
picked this habit up from tracts and books written by Europeans. *Report of the General
Missionary Conference held at Allahabad, 1872–73*: 48, 84–5.
[36] *IER*, Vol. XIII, 1887: 299.

If anything the need for tact and a conciliatory approach increased towards the end of the century as a result of the growth of Hindu revival movements, the rise of nationalism and an increase in anti-European and anti-Christian feeling. Kenneth Cracknell, has given (in 1995) as part of the title of his book the words 'Justice, Courtesy and Love', the three principles which Slater recommended should govern Christians in their dealings with Hindus and Hinduism. However, what is important to note is that, in this particular instance, Slater's recommendation has to be understood in the context of his attempt to adopt suitable strategies for conversion. The complete sentence from which the quotation is drawn is *'We shall never gain the non-Christian world* until we treat its religions with justice, courtesy and love.'[37] Indeed, what the full sentence reflects is Slater's experience of attempting to cope with one of the most hostile groups of Hindus missionaries had ever had to face. These were the Western-educated young men heavily influenced by European rationalism, the Hindu revival and anti-Christian movements reflected in the activities of the Hindu Tract and Preaching Societies.[38] Of course when addressing audiences in this atmosphere the only possible approach was to treat Hindus and Hinduism with 'justice, courtesy and love'. As Slater (whose time was set aside for work among the educated classes) reminded his society at home 'to be tolerant and yet faithful; and thoroughly to secure their confidence and affection, is not an easy task'.[39]

However, what appears to have begun as a matter of tactics and a recognition that outright attacks on Hinduism were in many cases ineffectual or counterproductive, gradually merged with the growth of more sympathetic and positive views of Indian religion and Hinduism itself. Evidence of these changes, reflecting a growing recognition of the value and degree of truth and enlightenment in Hindu religious tradition, is apparent in a range of different kinds of sources. Reports of discussion at missionary conferences, articles written in the *Indian Evangelical Review*, largely for the benefit of the missionaries themselves, and comments in publications intended for a more general readership all point in the same

[37] Slater 1906: 2 (author's italics).

[38] On the activities of the Hindu Tract and Preaching Societies see especially Oddie 1982: 217–43.

[39] Hartle 1978: 121. Indeed, it was easier for Duff and his contemporaries to be critical of Hinduism in the absence of strong revival movements and also in view of the fact that Duff in particular often spoke to an audience which was already in many ways alienated from Hinduism, and perhaps less influenced by the strong political feelings of the later nineteenth century.

direction and towards a gradual shift in the missionary evaluation. Of course there are indications that among some missionaries the older more condemnatory attitudes, worthy of Duff or William Ward, persisted.[40] Furthermore, there were complaints that the new and more sympathetic approach had gone too far. 'There was a time when persons who wrote about Hinduism too generally fell into the error of indiscriminate depreciation,' said Caldwell in 1874. 'That period has passed away, and the error into which people at present, as it appears to me, are too apt to fall, is that of indiscriminate laudation.'[41] Another commentator, reviewing a book by W. J. Wilkins (LMS) on *Hindu Mythology* (1882), also felt that the balance was going too much the other way—in favour of Hinduism. Wilkins, he complained, was 'more ready to tell all that is good of a Hindu god than what is bad'.[42] What is significant about these protests is that they highlight a general change and one that Caldwell felt as early as 1874.

If then there is clear evidence of a growing trend in favour of more positive approaches towards Hinduism what were the basic and emerging views about the relationship between Christianity and Hinduism?

Three Types of Approach

As the century developed, three schools of thought on the relationship between Christianity and Hinduism gradually emerged. Two of them came to represent significant sections of missionary opinion. The third, which was reflected in William Miller's philosophy and voice of dissent, gained further followers and greater strength in the twentieth century.

The first of these approaches was what Cracknell has described as the policy of 'radical displacement'. This was the idea which dominated missionary thinking about Hinduism during the first half of the nineteenth century—the belief that the purpose of mission was to wage war and destroy Hinduism (the citadel of Satan) replacing it with what amounted to a European version of Christianity. Among the best known and most influential exponents of this approach were William Ward and Alexander Duff. Religious encounter was warfare and the object was the

---

[40] See, for example, Dr John Wilson's reference to Hinduism as still being 'the grandest embodiment of Gentile error' (*Report of the General Missionary Conference held at Allahabad, 1872–73*: 14); and his article, published posthumously, on 'Hindu gods and their incarnations' in *IER*, Vol. VIII, 1882 (pp. 323–40).

[41] Caldwell 1874: 5.

[42] *IER*, Vol. IX, 1882: 239.

total obliteration of the enemy. There was nothing ultimately good in Hinduism, 'a system' which led its 'deluded votaries' astray. And just as light replaces darkness, so Christianity would, in the fullness of time, triumph and shine forth as the only true and meaningful faith for the people of India.

The attraction of this view, which lay partly in its simplicity (not to mention the Europeans' sense of superiority), was seen in the way it continued to linger on into the twentieth century. In spite of the growth of a more sympathetic, understanding and discriminating view of Hinduism reflected in comments at conferences and elsewhere, there is plenty of evidence of the continuation of the traditional hardline approach. It is apparent among a few of the older missionaries, and also in the attitude of some of those involved in work among Hindus at the grassroots level. The older, conservative approach was reflected, for example, in the views of the much respected and elderly Dr John Wilson, a man of whom it was said that he had 'ceased to learn',[43] and whose denunciations of Hindu deities were reprinted in the *Indian Evangelical Review* in 1882. The same views were also echoed in the protests of one Methodist missionary, J. R. Broadhead who, in the same year, in response to pleas for a more sympathetic approach, described popular Hinduism as 'a system of idolatry, a refuge of lies, [and] a sink of iniquity', which 'belonged to those works of the devil which Jesus Christ came to destroy'.[44]

Among other voices of dissatisfaction with the tendency to overlook the evils of the Hindu system were commentators not only at conferences, but also contributors to missionary journals. One of these was the Rev. George Sawday (WMMS, Mysore), who penned a series of articles on Hinduism for the *Harvest Field* in 1885 and 1886 in which he made few concessions to the more positive aspects of Hindu religion. There was also a symposium in the same periodical in 1887 on 'How shall we preach to the Hindus?'— the Revs. J. A. Vanes (WMMS) and William Robinson (LMS, Madras) reiterating a conservative approach. According to Vanes the central question was whether Hinduism was adequate as a means of salvation. Denying that this was so, he argued that missionaries should make the foundation of their preaching not any excellencies of the Hindu religion but 'defects in that religion'. Robinson went further, denying that there was any truth in Hinduism as 'found in every village [in south India] and practised by all the people'. To consolidate his argument he quoted at length from

[43] *IA*, Vol. 6, 1877: 233.
[44] *Report of the Second Decennial Missionary Conference held at Calcutta, 1882–83*: 31.

Macaulay's Gates of Somnath speech of 1843 and reiterated the point that in his (Robinson's) view Hinduism in its popular form was 'nothing but a collection of degrading superstitions'.[45]

Christianity as Fulfilment of Hinduism

A second way of viewing the relationship between the two religions, an approach which was becoming increasingly influential, was to think of Christianity as the *fulfilment* of all that was best in Hinduism. Hindu religious aspirations, insights and truly devotional authentic practice would all find their completion in the Christian Gospel. Hence, in certain circumstances the missionaries in practice were like Paul, who while preaching to the Athenians on Mars' Hill, declared that he had found an altar to the unknown god. 'Whom therefore you ignorantly worship,' he said, 'him declare I unto you'.[46] Protestants therefore might follow de Nobili and other Jesuits in building the faith on much of what was already there. Indeed, up to a certain point, this was probably the only way missionaries could function and communicate the Gospel in different cultures.

Whether they liked it or not, evangelists in India, as in other parts of the world, were compelled to use the language of the people. This included terms for God and associated ideas which already had an indigenous meaning and which from the missionary point of view, also had certain undesirable connotations associated with heathenism. However, if anything was to be understood it involved some form of translation, a process of understanding one idea or belief in terms of another and a gradual incorporation of new concepts by building on pre-existing ideas and parallels which were seldom if ever an exact equivalent. As one Protestant missionary confessed with reference to Hindi in 1875, 'nearly all our theological terms are of heathen origin, and are used in Hindu writing in senses far different from those in which we employ them'.[47] The extent of missionary dependence on key Hindu theological concepts becomes clearly apparent in John Murdoch's *Renderings of Important Scripture Terms in the Principal Languages of India*, a booklet published in Madras in 1876.[48] Based on extensive enquiries into missionary practice all over India, it sets

---

[45] *HF*, Vol. VII, March 1887: 257–65; April 1887: 297–300; May 1887: 333–39; June 1887: 357–61.

[46] Bible, Acts 17: 23.

[47] *IER*, Vol. II, 1875: 497–98.

[48] A copy of this work is available in the UTC archives, Bangalore.

out equivalents in fifteen different languages ranging from English, Hebrew and Greek on the one hand to the major indigenous languages on the other. Thus we learn that when the missionaries referred to 'the true God' in Hindi and Bengali they used the term *Ishwar*, and when they referred to God in Tamil they use the word *Devan*. There may have been debates among linguists about which of these and other words were the most suitable, but none of them was free from the context in which it developed; and the only alternative (apart from developing a completely new word which locals would not recognize) was to build on terms already in use.

The tradition of building Christianity on the basis of what was already there was well known in Protestant circles, and was, for example, one of the themes in the theology and writing of F. D. Maurice (1805–72). It was Maurice who according to Paul Hedges, author of a recent study of fulfilment theology, spelled out ideas of fulfilment in his well-known Boyle lectures on 'The Religions of the World and their Relations to Christianity'.[49] The lectures, delivered in 1845–46, and published in book form in 1847, were reprinted at least six times before 1900. As noted in Chapter 8, Maurice urged Christians to seek out whatever was good and true in other faiths and, like St Paul on Mars' Hill, build Christian teaching on the basis of what was already there. In this way the religious aspirations, insights and perceptions of Hindus, among others, would find their completion and fulfilment in the Christian revelation.

Hedges argues that themes and ideas in these lectures provided a basis for ideas of fulfilment which were subsequently discussed in the works of Max Müller and Monier-Williams during the latter part of the nineteenth century. However, it should be noted, that the world of Britain-based academic scholarship was not the only source of these ideas, and that Protestant missionary comments relating to Hinduism and the idea of fulfilment *pre-date* the works of all of these English scholars. The notion of fulfilment was there in the mission field in India before it was seriously discussed in lectures, books and writing in Britain. The names of two missionaries, Robert Caldwell (SPG) and Robert Noble (CMS), both of them working in south India, are important in this respect, as examples of earlier exponents and also *practitioners* of the idea of fulfilment.

Robert Caldwell, who was a great admirer of the Jesuit priest, Father Beschi (a well-known advocate of the policy of adaptation) referred to the idea of developing Christian teaching on the basis of some Shanar (Nadar)

[49] Hedges 2001: 51.

beliefs in his book on the Shanars published in 1840.[50] Having devoted considerable space to a discussion of Shanar belief and practice he declared that:

> From the particulars now mentioned it is sufficiently obvious that, if in some things the Shanars are further than other Hindus from Christianity, they are in a better position for understanding the grand Christian doctrine of redemption by sacrifice.... The fact of the prevalence of bloody sacrifices for the removal of the anger of superior powers is one of the most striking in the religious condition of the Shanars, and is appealed to by the Christian Missionary with the best effect.[51]

It might be noted that Caldwell's comments were published seven years before Maurice delivered his Boyle lectures, and before he suggested that even the worst of non-Christian practices (such as human sacrifice) had grown up in response to the needs of the soul.[52] It was Caldwell who, in a lecture in 1874, also discussed the idea of fulfilment, *before* Monier-Williams drew attention to much the same idea in his *Indian Wisdom* or explored it at greater length in his *Modern India* which appeared in 1878. Referring to Hinduism, Caldwell declared that 'Christianity would be the best realization of the visions of its seers, and the best fulfilment of the longings of its sages.'[53] Furthermore, he pointed out that missionaries had long used Indian books of authority not only to show their contradictions, but also to demonstrate that Christianity 'is not, as Hindus are apt to fancy, an outlandish novelty', but is in reality 'in accordance with the best sentiments of India's best minds'.[54]

The second early pioneer and advocate of the policy of fulfilment was Robert Noble. The youngest son of a country vicar and a graduate of Sidney Sussex College, Cambridge, he volunteered for the new CMS mission to the Telugu people in 1839.[55] The work, which was commenced two years later, included the establishment of a senior boys' school in Masulipatam. From an initial intake of two students it gradually developed to become

[50] On his attitude to Beschi, see Caldwell 1982: 238–43.

[51] Caldwell 1840: 22. The Rev. John Hay, LMS, Vizagapatam, writing in the *Indian Evangelical Review* on the use of sacrificial terms in Indian languages, drew attention to what he believed was common between Christianity and other faiths when he remarked that 'The idea of sacrifice seems to lie at the foundation of all religion' (*IER*, Vol. I, 1874: 280).

[52] Hedges 2001: 56.

[53] Caldwell 1874: 4.

[54] Ibid.: 9.

[55] Noble 1867: 70–78.

one of the most popular and highly-regarded educational institutions in south India. In a letter to the Rev. John Tucker, Secretary of the CMS Corresponding Committee in Madras, in December 1843, Noble described his early work in the school:

> We commence daily—the Lord's Day excepted—at seven o'clock, and con-
> tinue our instructions till nine o'clock. We begin with a Gospel; by it
> teaching Grammar, and gently, every now and then, urging the truth
> upon them, or rather setting it before them.... After a portion of the
> first chapter of St Luke we passed on to Exercises on the English Verbs, and
> after that to a portion of the Bhagavat gita, which I propose reading through
> with the first class. Our Lord's words seem very applicable: Think not that
> I am come to destroy Law, or the Prophets: I am not come to destroy, but
> to fulfil! So I wish them to think that we have not come to set aside the light
> of nature, and the truths which it has set down, but to enforce, to correct,
> to fulfil, with the additional light of Revelation.[56]

Like Caldwell's suggestions about using the Shanar idea of sacrifice as a basis for Christian teachings, Noble's practice of introducing readings on Indian religious texts as the basis for Christian teaching may have appeared unpalatable to mission supporters in England.[57] But, as Caldwell pointed out, the use of Indian books to show that Christianity was not 'an out-landish novelty', had long been practised in India. Nevertheless, Noble's remarks are especially significant as they show that (a) he was highly conscious of the idea and theology of fulfilment prior to Maurice's lectures in England and that (b) he was putting the idea of fulfilment into practice. Furthermore, these references to the idea of fulfilment also show that the idea was not merely one dreamed up by armchair academics in Britain, but emerged as a response to the real-life needs and situation in India.

Ideas of Fulfilment in the Later Nineteenth Century

Further interest in the philosophy and policies of fulfilment is clearly apparent during the period from about 1870 to 1900. Missionary

---

[56] *MR*, December 1844: 526.

[57] Even if news of this approach, which was printed in the CMS edited *Missionary Register*, caused concern at the head office in London, there was little if anything the London or the Madras committees of the CMS could do. Noble agreed to his appointment to Masulipatam only on condition he was allowed freedom of action in his educational measures (see Noble 1867: 78–89).

commentators advocating this approach included men drawn from most of the Protestant societies. Among the more conspicuous were John Robson (United Presbyterian Church of Scotland, UPCS), J. Murray Mitchell (Free Church of Scotland, FCS), James Vaughan (CMS), G. McKenzie Cobban (WMMS), John Hewlett and T. E. Slater (LMS) and, in addition to Caldwell, Charles Egbert Kennet and G. U. Pope, all connected to the Society for the Propagation of the Gospel, SPG.

In 1873 some years after his return to Madras Kennet published his notes on *Shaiva Siddhanta*.[58] Referring to the basic teachings of the movement, which was then some years away from what has been described as its 'revival',[59] he declared that 'the coincidence of thought and language' of *Shaiva Siddhanta* with Christian teaching was 'remarkable'. These parallels, he wrote, suggested 'the possibility of these speculations of an extraordinary school of Hindu religious philosophy being made meeting-places for higher truths, which can alone supply what is lacking in them, and satisfy the deep natural yearnings which gave them birth'.

Kennet who, according to the writer of his obituary, was 'exceedingly well read in the writings of the early Christian Fathers',[60] was also interested in how their ideas might apply to the relationship between Hinduism and Christianity. In a pamphlet entitled *The Catechetical School of Alexandria; Its Lessons to the Missionary Clergy of India*, published in about 1881,[61] he reiterated his belief in Christianity as the fulfilment of all that was best and true in India's religious tradition. According to Kennet, St Clement (*c.* A.D. 150–215), implied that

> one need not fear to seek even in heathen literature whatever traces of truth he may find in it, and appropriate what is useful in it, for all comes from God, and as such is pure. For he saw in it a gift of God, imperfect indeed and corrupted by human devices, but designed by God for the training of the Gentile world, and education preparing the Gentiles for the coming of Christ, as the Law prepared the Jews.... The Christian Fathers... certainly thought and believed that whatever was good or true in heathen philosophy and literature came from the Light of God's Spirit.

In the very first edition of his *Hinduism and its Relations to Christianity*, a book published in 1874, Robson also argued that Hindu literature, probably more than the literature of any other nation, gave utterance to

---

[58] *IA*, Vol. 2, 1873: 343–44.

[59] Arooran 1980: 20–26.

[60] *MF*, 1885: 50.

[61] Calcutta and London. The date (1881) is a British Library entry.

those feelings of reverence, trust and truth, which showed that the image of God within the individual, 'though defaced is not destroyed'. Rather than speaking of Christianity as fulfilling specific Hindu doctrines, he preferred to emphasize its capacity to satisfy the Hindus' religious needs.[62] Referring to 'multitudes' of stray verses, and 'even whole hymns' 'in which a Christian might express many of his feelings of devotion', he remarked that these were 'cries of the human conscience, expressions of the religious wants which all men feel'. The practical value of any religion, he declared, could be seen in 'the response which it gives to these cries, in the satisfaction which it offers to these wants, in the help which it gives man to lead a godly life'.[63] Much the same views, which were expressed in Robson's subsequent *Science of Religion*, are also echoed in Vaughan's work which appeared in 1876. Adverting to all that was good and true in the religious life and teachings of the Hindu people, he too declared that 'Christianity alone satisfies those soul-cravings, for it points to the one true revelation of God's will, it reveals the only efficient sacrifice for sin, and presents to the believing gaze the one true incarnation.'[64]

Discussions about preaching and missionary methods not infrequently brought to the fore similar deep-seated convictions that missionaries should build on the 'truths and half-truths' available in Hindu tradition. For example, John Hewlett (LMS, Benares) commented that it was important to know enough of Hindu belief and practice 'to enable the missionary wisely and sympathetically to show the worshipper how all their loftiest aspirations can be gloriously realized by that conscious union with God in Christ'.[65] Speaking in London some years later he remarked that 'we must admit that there are some grains of truth and some grains of goodness in their system, and we should make these the basis of our reasoning with them about Christianity'. Referring to his own practice he added that

> I have in conversation with many of the Pundits in the Schools of Philosophy in Benares, and with the Monks in the Monasteries, found men who seemed to be most sincere, and I tried to lay hold of their beliefs, and make them the basis of my talking to them about Christianity.[66]

[62] Hedges 2001: 189.
[63] Robson 1874: 184–85.
[64] Vaughan 1876: 222.
[65] *IER*, Vol. XIII, 1887: 298. See also comments by Phillips, *IER*, Vol. VI, 1879: 317; Cobban, *IER*, Vol. XVI, 1889: 141 and Timory, *Report of the Third Decennial Missionary Conference, Bombay*, 1892–93 (p. 307).
[66] *Report of the Centenary Conference on the Protestant Missions of the World*, London, 1888: 93.

The growing recognition of the need to construct Christianity on the basis of what was already there is reflected in discussions elsewhere. For example, speaking at a conference in Bombay in 1882 Murray Mitchell, not only argued that missionaries should acknowledge all that was 'good and pure' in Hinduism, but also suggested that they should deal with Hindus 'as the great apostle did at Athens' with 'the remarkable quotation which he made from "certain of their poets"'.[67] Hence, instead of quoting Old Testament passages about the destruction of idols and idolatry, it was becoming almost fashionable to refer to New Testament comments and especially to Paul's proceedings at Mars' Hill when he used the people's worship of 'the unknown God' as a basis for his comments about what could be known of God through Jesus.

G. McKenzie Cobban, berated in England for views sympathetic to Hinduism, was also an advocate of the policy of constructing Indian Christianity, as far as possible, on the truths and insights reflected in Hindu religion. Like Kennet, he was aware of the approach adopted by the Alexandrian Fathers—a policy which he felt was the only way forward. Speaking at the conference in London in 1888 he stressed that 'with regard to the truths known in India, these would be used by the wise Missionary as allies. And since there was in embryo among the Hindus a doctrine of Christ, this especially should be used'.[68] In the following year he published a major article in the *Madras Christian College Magazine* which set out in greater detail his views on the relationship between Christianity and Hindu faiths.[69] In this he drew attention to what he regarded as the truths in both Vedanta and Siddhanta and argued that missionaries could make effective use of some of their basic teachings. Taking as an example one of the central ideas in Indian religion, the Hindu doctrine of the Sat-Guru, he explained:

> It is a doctrine of God manifest, and is, altogether apart from the ten incarnations, familiar to English readers. As held among the Siddhantists at its best it is as follows: God is manifest as Guru or Divine teacher. The Guru is not one of the souls, that is, not a man. He is God with a human form. His manifestations may be said to correspond to the theophanies of the Hebrews. He is the giver of truth and grace. He enlightens man; He saves him; He destroys the spell of the senses; He is the Shepherd of man, and his Lord. He preserves all living creatures, and conducts man to heaven. These

[67] *Report of the Second Decennial Missionary Conference held at Calcutta, 1882–83*: 29.
[68] *Report of the Centenary Conference on Protestant Missions of the World*, London, 1888: 89.
[69] *MCCM*, Vol. VII, 1889: 197–211.

FREE CHURCH OF SCOTLAND
Quarterly Missionary Paper.

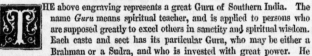

A CELEBRATED BRAHMAN GURU.

T HE above engraving represents a great Guru of Southern India. The name *Guru* means spiritual teacher, and is applied to persons who are supposed greatly to excel others in sanctity and spiritual wisdom. Each caste and sect has its particular Guru, who may be either a Brahman or a Sudra, and who is invested with great power. He superintends the people belonging to his sect in his jurisdiction, and enforces the due observance of the rules and customs, by punishing the refractory. He has also the power of expelling from the caste, and of restoring those who had been

No. XLI.   DECEMBER 1869.

Figure 10.1
'A Celebrated Brahman Guru'

An etching from the *Free Church of Scotland Missionary Paper* (December 1869) of the spiritual head of the Shankaracharya Mutt or monastery at Sringeri in Mysore state. It not only reflects the missionaries' increasing specialized knowledge of different Hindu traditions, but also some attempt to be fairer and more objective in depicting Hindu belief and practice.

are Hindu expressions in which the doctrine is set forth. For the Christian missionary, this doctrine forms an easy and direct way to approach the Hindu. Jesus Christ is the Sat-Guru, the Divine teacher; greater and more wonderful than these Hindu glimpses.[70]

Thus for Cobban, like others cited here, the central task in India was not to sweep away the whole of Hindu tradition, but, as far as possible, to build Christianity on the basis of what was already there. Christianity could and would satisfy the religious yearnings of the Hindu heart, and fulfil the greatest of its truths as reflected in the teachings of sage and saint. In the writings of these commentators, however, the idea of fulfilment was only part of what Monier-Williams and Max Müller had implied when they addressed the issue. For them, and subsequently for T. E. Slater, fulfilment also meant something which was more corporate and evolutionary in the sense that lower religions would gradually be transformed and evolve towards the higher—the highest of all being Christianity itself.

T. E. Slater

It is not clear from some missionary comments, such as the passage from Vaughan's work quoted here, whether they were thinking of 'fulfilment' merely as satisfying certain longings or crowning certain beliefs in the life of the individual, or whether they were thinking of it as a broader process involving the building of one entire system or religion on the basis of another. There can be no doubt, however, that T. E. Slater, like Monier-Williams in his *Modern India*, had all of these models in mind. In fact, Slater's exposition of the idea of fulfilment was perhaps the most detailed and elaborate missionary analysis of the concept and process prior to the end of the nineteenth century. As we have seen, his ideas were hardly original, and what he was doing (admittedly as early as the 1880s) was to bring together insights and reflections in contemporary thought.

A well developed version of his ideas of fulfilment appeared in his book on *The Philosophy of Missions*, published in 1882. There the author went beyond references to the religious needs of individuals in other religions finding satisfaction in Christianity, to a comparison of religious systems in general. In the history of religions, declared Slater, it was simply a question of 'the survival of the fittest'.[71] All other religions (which do not

---

[70] Ibid.: 205.
[71] Slater 1882: 111.

contain the same amount of truth) were waiting 'for their fulfilment in Christianity'.[72] Summarizing his views in an article in the *Harvest Field* he wrote that the main burden of his argument was as follows:

> The old religions of India are a serious indication of man's deepest wants, and also a serious attempt to supply them; all the truth, however, which Hinduism offers or even suggests, is to be found in Christ, who has also revealed certain essential complementary truths, thereby fitting Christianity to become the religion of every race and of all time.[73]

In some of his later comments, and especially in his book *The Higher Hinduism in Relation to Christianity* (the manuscript of which appears to have been finished in 1901) Slater spelled out in greater detail how some of the more specific Hindu ideas or practices would find their satisfaction and, in a sense, correction in Christianity. Thus for example, there are parallels between the Christian doctrine of the incarnation and Hindu doctrines of *avataras* or descents. The latter prefigures 'the historical Deliverer to come'. And yet there are also major differences between the Christian and Hindu teachings. Vishnu's incarnations were 'diverse and numerous' and therefore 'portions only' of 'the Divine essence united in created things'. Furthermore, when Vishnu returns to his heaven he lays aside his human nature. Divine manhood is therefore 'apparent only, not real'. On the other hand, 'Christ not only fulfils the unconscious prophecy', but corrects Hindu misconceptions of the true relationship between God and men. It was in the life of Christ, 'the Word made flesh', that God revealed 'both the Divinity of man and the humanity of God'.[74]

Slater's work was important not only because he clarified and developed many of the underlying ideas associated with fulfilment theology, but also because of his influence upon his contemporaries including colleagues in the mission field. A regular contributor to missionary journals, he was an effective publicist and tireless advocate of the new ideas. He seldom seems to have passed up an opportunity to challenge his conservative colleagues to think again, gave papers at some of the most important missionary conferences, and wrote a great deal.

---

[72] Ibid.: 112.

[73] *IER*, Vol. XI, 1884: 286.

[74] Slater 1906: 30–2. For further discussion of Slater's comments on parallels and differences between Hindu and Christian teachings, see Hedges 2001: 169–77.

William Miller: One Christ and Many Religions

A third and somewhat different way of looking at the relationship between Christianity and Hinduism is reflected in the thinking of William Miller (1838–1923). A long-term principal of Madras Christian College, he was well known as a pioneer in missionary higher education and a controversial commentator on the role of Christianity in India. As Sharpe rightly says he 'provided Christian colleges with a new and controversial *raison d'etre*— not to convert, but to spread Christian thought and Christian influence throughout non-Christian India'.[75]

Many of the newer more liberal ideas about the relationship between Christianity and other religions which were beginning to emerge in the last quarter of the nineteenth century were integrated in Miller's philosophy of mission and also in his understanding of God's overriding providence. However, his arguments and insights were not only the result of his building on earlier developments, but reflect challenging original thinking, and anticipate the views of some of the most prominent Christian commentators on inter-faith relations in recent times.

Little is known about his specific views on fulfilment. Soon after his arrival in India in 1863 he gave a lecture on 'Christ the Fulfiller' and, according to his biographer, claimed that 'Christ's religion was the one which sought to fulfil the aspirations in other religions and which itself sought its own fulfilment or completion by being furnished with the peculiar contributions of other religions'.[76] A significant aspect of this version of fulfilment is that it implies that all religions, including Christianity, are imperfect and incomplete and need to borrow something from each other.

Miller's concern was, however, less with these specific notions of fulfilment and more with the nature of God's activity in the whole of creation. In his writing and speeches he referred to what were for him key biblical passages illustrating the nature of God's care and concern for all people and all nations throughout the world.[77] One such passage was Psalm 24:1. 'The earth is the Lord's and the fullness thereof; the world and they that dwell therein. For he has founded it upon the seas, and established it upon the floods'. Like an increasing number of missionaries during this period, Miller also drew attention to Paul's preaching to the Athenians on Mars' Hill. Especially relevant was the latter's declaration

[75] Sharpe 1965: 82.
[76] Ibid.: 87.
[77] Reuben 2002: 124–25.

that 'God made of one every nation of men to dwell on all the face of the earth, having determined their appointed seasons, and the bounds of their habitation, that they should seek God, haply they might feel after Him and find Him.'[78] Hence for Miller, people outside the Church were as much under God's care as those within, and in no nation or situation was it impossible to find God.

The key to an understanding of Miller's position is, however, the clear distinction he drew between Christianity and Christ, between the historic churches, denominations, creeds, and Christian organizations on the one hand and God's spirit as revealed in Jesus Christ on the other.[79] Once again this distinction was hardly new. As the nineteenth century progressed missionaries became increasingly aware of the importance of their role in preaching Christ as distinct from their task of enrolling converts in the churches. As early as 1855 the Rev. John Wenger, speaking at a missionary conference in Calcutta, declared that all missionaries 'should preach Christ rather than Christianity' and, in response, the Rev. W. Smith (CMS) stated his conviction that 'all missionaries' were agreed that 'we ought to preach the Gospel first'.[80] Indeed, the idea of preaching Christ rather than spending time in endorsing the values of particular Christian churches or structures seems to have been taken for granted, the discussion at the Bangalore conference of 1888 having, for example, moved on to the distinction between Christ and philosophies about Christ. In the Rev. J. Hudson's view missionaries 'gencrally' fully agreed with Slater's remarks on 'the necessity of preaching Christ rather than a philosophy about Christ'.[81] In all of this the notion of enrolling converts into European type denominational churches appears to have been far removed from the ideas involved in missionary preaching, even though this may have been the actual result.

Miller's idea of separating Christ from Christianity was not therefore quite as innovative or radical as it may seem. Indeed, it is quite possible that the missionaries more generally were less wedded to particular versions of

[78] Bible, Acts 17: 26.

[79] Reuben 2002: 125–26.

[80] *Proceedings of a General Conference of Bengal Protestant Missionaries held in Calcutta, 4–7 Sept. 1855*: 48, 170. One of the issues was, of course, what is meant by 'preaching Christ', or preaching 'the simple gospel'? The highly esteemed 'vernacular' preacher the Rev. A. F. Lacroix (LMS) believed that preaching the simple gospel was 'to preach Christ, the story of his life, his death, his resurrection and ascension, his presence with us now and the certainty of his future judgement' (p. 63).

[81] *HF*, Vol. VII, May 1887: 334–35.

Christianity than they had been earlier in the century. But, whatever the case, what Miller did was to press the idea of the difference between Christ and Christianity as far as possible. And having drawn a clear distinction between the two he then freely admitted all the evils and shortcomings of the historic church. According to Gabriel, he 'never undermined the importance of the Church as God's divinely ordained agency to reveal Christ to the world',[82] but he was severe in his comments on the evils of its arrogance, complacency and state of decay. Furthermore, in his view, there was real danger in the church's conquering mentality and in the belief that God could be found only within her walls.

Christ's care for the whole of the world was for Miller reflected in His operation in all religious systems. All religions including Christianity were imperfect and incomplete. They all needed each other as they struggled to grow in the truth and reflect the light of Christ. If individuals felt they should be baptized into the Christian church then baptism should occur, but, generally speaking, there was no need for baptism as people drawn from all nations and communities could continue to develop Christian ideas and ideals while continuing to operate within their existing communities, and without 'a shifting of camps'. It was, therefore, the task of the church and of Christian colleges to diffuse Christ's teachings and ideals throughout the country so as to enable Hindus to follow Christ within their own particular tradition. It was this last point that was especially challenging for most missionaries. Many if not all, had been conditioned to the notion that baptism was a necessary further step in commitment to Christ, and the debate raged, for example, in the pages of the *Harvest Field*. It remained, however, as a central issue which continued to alienate Miller from many of his colleagues.

While it might be argued that Miller's voice was like one crying in the wilderness, some thinking in the mission field (though not thinking on baptism) was already moving in his direction. Even in the early days of British Protestant missions, the missionaries believed that God was active through natural religion, and that He was present in India even before they set foot in the country to begin working among the Hindu people. They were not therefore going to a strange place, but to pray and work for their Lord who had already gone there before them even though, in many cases, He was hidden from view by the evils of the Hindu system. Miller's Christ, active in Hinduism, was a further extension of these embryonic ideas. Nor in one sense was it so far removed from ideas of fulfilment. While the

---

[82] Reuben 2002: 123.

different religions could enrich each other, it was Christ alone who would bring them all to completion, who was the climax and apotheosis of all striving for truth and goodness. It is ideas such as these that have influenced both Western and Indian Christian theologians of the twentieth century.

Extent of Sympathetic Views

In his study of J. N. Farquhar, Sharpe concluded that

> before the turn of the century, those missionaries who were prepared to turn their backs on the accepted Evangelical attitude to non-Christian religions and strike out in the direction indicated by Max Muller and Monier Williams were few and far between, and often isolated in their opinions.[83]

However, subsequent research suggests that those who endorsed a more sympathetic approach to Hinduism were not quite so 'few' or 'far between' and that, Sharpe's comments are, quite possibly, an underestimation of the extent of changes that took place in missionary attitudes during the period from1875 to 1900.

The number of missionaries who were prepared to state their conviction that God was operating in Hinduism gradually increased; and some of these, as we have argued, began to place less emphasis on God's activity through natural religion and more on the evidence of His presence in the Hindu religious system itself. The names of Kennedy, Smith, Phillips, Hughes, Rice, Haig, Timory, Murray Mitchell, Noble, Kennet, Robson, Wilkins, Cobban, Caldwell, Slater, Miller and Pope have all been mentioned as missionaries who were prepared, at the very least, to adopt a more sympathetic approach. Most also thought in terms of building Christianity on one or more of the elements in Hinduism—an outstanding exception to this view being Miller who was less concerned with the formation of Christian churches and more with the diffusion of a Christ-like spirit within Hinduism. But these are not the only missionaries who might have been mentioned as favouring the 'new' approach. Others were J. Hudson (WMMS) who, while not going as far as some, stressed that 'it is...of great importance to exhibit the truth of Hinduism as well as its falsehood',[84] D. Mackichan (CS) who also emphasized the need for a sympathetic response,[85] and F. W. Kellett (WMMS) whose views on the subject had

[83] Sharpe 1965: 55.
[84] *HF*, Vol. VII: 338.
[85] *Report of the Third Decennial Missionary Conference held at Bombay, 1892–93*: 298.

much in common with those of Slater. In 1896, when Kellett was teaching at Madras Christian College, he published a pamphlet entitled 'Christ the Fulfilment of Hinduism'.[86] Written for a Christian Literature Society (CLS) series of *Papers for Thoughtful Hindus*, it was based on the idea of God's progressive revelation of Himself, and suggested that this progressive disclosure, as evidenced in particular ways in Hindu religion would find its ultimate completion in the person and work of Christ.

But apart from taking note of individual comments and papers on approaches to Hinduism it is also important to examine what contemporaries themselves were saying about trends in opinion. In his paper read at a meeting of the Bangalore Missionary Conference in February 1887 Slater stated that:

> I think there can be no doubt that within the last few years there has been a marked change in the mode of preaching to the people. It used to be the fashion to attack their religion, to revile their gods, and to represent Christianity as sounding the knell of doom over all non-Christian nations. But altered views, mainly of the nature and character of god, have altered the views of most with reference to their fellow men. Not the wrath, but the love of god is now, I imagine, the chief inspiration of Christian preaching and of Christian missions.[87]

The trend towards a more generous and sympathetic view of Hinduism was noted, though not with entire approval, by one of the speakers at the Conference in Bombay in 1892. The experienced and much respected Indian Christian minister, Samuel Satthianadhan, agreed that in dealing with non-Christian religions, missionaries should be capable of 'recognizing and fully appreciating the glimpses of truth' that reveal themselves in those systems. 'At the same time', he added, 'there should be no attempt at compromise. *This is often done now-a-days*, I regret to say, with the most disasterous results.'[88]

---

[86] Sharpe 1965: 105–6.

[87] *HF*, Vol. VII, March 1887: 257. The trend towards a more sympathetic view of Hinduism was also noted by Bishop Caldwell at an Anglican confernce in Brighton in 1874, though, in his case, it is not clear whether he was including missionaries in his generalization. 'Very different estimates of Hinduism have been formed at different times, and by different persons at the same time', he said. 'There was a time when persons who wrote about Hinduism too generally fell into the error of indiscriminate depreciation. That period has passed away, and the error into which people at present, as it appears to me, are too apt to fall, is that of indiscriminate laudation' (Caldwell 1874: 5).

[88] Author's italics. *Report of the Third Decennial Missionary Conference held at Bombay, 1892–93*: 271.

Finally, while missionaries were not in the habit of passing resolutions at their gatherings which would indicate their position on this issue, an examination of conference reports does occasionally leave the reader with a general impression. An analysis of the relevant sections of the reports of the second and third decennial missionary conferences in Calcutta and Bombay (1882–83 and 1892–93) is in this respect especially illuminating. These reports do indeed provide plenty of evidence of positive comment and suggest that, if there was a hidden silent majority swayed by more traditional views, advocates of a more sympathetic approach still had considerable vocal support.[89] It was the more liberal-minded speakers and writers advocating sympathy for Hinduism who tended to dominate, who set the agenda and who suggested how Christian–Hindu relations should be conducted in the future.

One of the more unusual corporate statements made by missionaries was a resolution of the Calcutta Missionary Conference on the subject of the Barrows lectureship in 1895. This was a statement which at least implies a tentative movement on the part of evangelical missionaries towards the idea of embracing comparative religion. In a resolution, adopted unanimously, and giving their qualified approval for the project, they declared:

> That the conference recognising, as they do, the importance of the study of Comparative Religion, have heard with much interest that, through the generosity of a Christian lady, courses of lectures on that subject are to be delivered in Calcutta, under the auspices of the University of Chicago. They observe with satisfaction, that it is proposed that the Lecturers shall be able and prominent Christian men, who have the confidence of Evangelical Christendom and who, it may be presumed, will not only make the comparison in a reverend and impartial spirit, but will also carry it out in reference to definite topics as the Divine Attributes, the Incarnation, the Resurrection and the nature of Sin and Atonement.[90]

While there is a certain degree of caution reflected in the wording, a resolution of this nature implying that Christianity was not totally different from other religions was unthinkable thirty years before. Moreover, the conference resolution was an expression of *evangelical* opinion, the views of broad Church Anglicans, such as those connected with the SPG, not being included in the statement.

---

[89] *Report of the Second Decennial Missionary Conference held at Calcutta, 1882–83*: 26–31; and *Report of the Third Decennial Missionary Conference held at Bombay, 1892–93*: 298–310.

[90] *IER*, Vol. XXI, 1895: 501.

The story of these changes in the British Protestant missionary evaluation of Hinduism must however remain somewhat incomplete, at least until more is known about the attitudes of missionary women who were active in India in increasing numbers during the second half of the nineteenth century. One of the reasons for this is the enforced absence of females at the relevant discussions of Hinduism at regional and general conferences. It is to the question of the women's depiction of Hinduism that we now must turn.

11

Gender Issues in the Construction of Hinduism with Special Reference to the Church of England Zenana Missionary Society, 1880–1900

We have already noted the rise of the women's missionary movement in Protestant circles during the second half of the nineteenth century. The purpose of this chapter is to focus more specifically on developments in India, and to explore the women's experience and representation of Hinduism with special reference to the Church of England Zenana Missionary Society (CEZMS) missionaries who served in India during the last quarter of the nineteenth century.

The central question is how far, if at all, did the women's views, models and assessments of Hinduism differ from those of men? What did these women really know of Hinduism? To what extent did they acquire special new information and develop new insights through their contact with Indian women and their entry into Hindu homes? Furthermore, is it possible to detect in their more general response, a distinctive female voice and interpretation? Before exploring these issues something more needs to be said about the Indian context, including the way in which women's work was linked with the idea of Hinduism.

Hinduism in Propaganda on behalf of Hindu Women

To some men in the mission field, as well as wives or daughters, it was very clear that there was a need for some kind of intervention on behalf of the Hindu woman. Among the most effective male advocates of the Hindu woman's protection and 'emancipation' were James Peggs and William Ward (both Baptists) Alexander Duff, and Edward Storrow (London Missionary Society, LMS) in his introduction to Mary Leslie's book *A Dawn of Light*, published in 1868. Among the most outstanding women publicists, who followed the male lead in the same direction, and who continued to press for women's work for women, were Mary Weitbrecht in *The Women of India and Christian Work in the Zenana* (1875) and Emma Raymond Pitman author of *Indian Zenana Missions* which was one of the contributions to the *Outline of Missionary Series* published in 1881.

Not all of these speakers and writers had precisely the same goals in mind. As we have seen, the early publicists on women's issues such as Peggs and Ward were especially disturbed by the prevalence of 'certain dreadful practices' such as sati and were intent on bringing public pressure to bear on British Indian authorities to outlaw these and other practices affecting Hindu women. They and later writers were also concerned with the extent of women's ignorance and the importance of developing female education. Linked with this latter objective, including the conversion of females, was the growing realization that the best and perhaps only way forward was through an expansion of 'women's work for women' and the recruitment of female missionaries in what was becoming known as the women's missionary movement. The work of publicists such as those mentioned above must therefore be taken into account in any attempt to explain the growth of women's work for Indian women. The advocacy and pleas of individuals as well as a growing volume of general and graphic literature gradually began to have its effect. Thus, while Miss Cooke (Mrs Wilson), one of the best known and most successful European pioneers of women's educational work in India, was encouraged to go there partly in response to Ward's special pleas on behalf of India's womanhood, Duff's passionate and dramatic accounts of the Hindu woman's plight and suffering aroused further concern and prompted the formation of women's committees in Scotland.[1]

The most prominent writers on women's condition in India from William Ward in the 1820s to Emma Pittman in the 1880s wrote as if the Hindu woman's life was seldom if ever cheered by hope, goodness or the light of learning. As Morawiecki has pointed out, they seem to have assumed that it was almost impossible for Hindu women to feel any joy, contentment or happiness in the life they led. The basic assumption appears to have been that unless they and their homes could in some way measure up to the standards established by middle-class Christians in Britain then their life must be truly miserable indeed.

The two points that weighed most heavily in propaganda in favour of women's missions in India were (*a*) the magnitude of the Hindu woman's misery and suffering and (*b*) the root cause of these problems which, it was argued, lay in Hinduism. Two examples of this type of approach can

[1] Weitbrecht 1875: 60; Smith 1879, Vol. 1: 373–74 and Duff 1839.

be seen in Duff's speech on 'Female Education in India', delivered in Edinburgh in 1839, and in Mary Weitbrecht's book *The Women of India and Christian Work in the Zenana,* published in 1875.

The source of much of Duff's information and also of his basic arguments appears to have been in Bengali accounts, especially the statements and views of the radicals known as 'Young Bengal'. Among students who attended Duff's lectures, were young men strongly influenced by European ideas of the Enlightenment, and like Duff, fiercely critical of Hindu religious tradition. While in Calcutta in about 1831 Duff sought and was granted permission to attend the young men's debating clubs some of which allowed discussion of women's rights and emancipation. According to George Smith, Duff's biographer, it was there while attending these somewhat revolutionary sessions that Duff first formulated his policy on female education.[2] Duff returned to Scotland in 1835, but not to forget the issue of female education, and it was while there that he delivered his well-known lectures on Hinduism and the plight of India's women. In what appears to have been a remarkable coincidence, he and a young man called Mahesh Chundra Deb (though far apart and in different countries) delivered parallel lectures on female oppression and education in 1839. Deb speaking in the Calcutta Sanskrit College Hall in January 1839,[3] and Duff speaking in Edinburgh a little later both made many similar points about women's subjection.

Both began by describing the depth of the Bengali woman's suffering and degradation and attributed her condition to the influence of religion and superstition. And once having compared the oppressed condition of women in nations 'unblessed with the light of revelation', with the freedom and 'equality' of women in Christian countries, Duff turned to Hindu teachings on women. These he found in Halhed's translation of the laws of Manu, a text also referred to by Deb in his address. Making the usual assumption that these laws were universally applicable and accepted among Hindus throughout the subcontinent, Duff drew attention to what he declared was 'the conclusion of the whole matter.' This was that

> from her birth to her death, woman must never in anything have a will of her own—must never dare to aspire to independence. Instead of being a help meet for man, she must for ever and ever be satisfied with being his humble slave—his crouching and submissive drudge.[4]

[2] Smith 1879: 149.
[3] See the full text of this address in Chattopadhyay 1965, Vol. 1: 105–30.
[4] Duff 1839: 7.

He noted the influence of the doctrine of the transmigration of souls and the way in which it was used to justify women's oppression through its teaching that severities and suffering in the present life is a direct result of sins or crimes committed in a former existence. Furthermore, like Deb, he consolidated his argument about the close relationship between Hinduism and the treatment of women by drawing attention to other specific religious injunctions designed to curb the freedom and independence of females. Among these requirements were practices already embedded in the imagination of at least some members of the Christian public. These included the requirement of infant marriage, the lifestyle of poverty and renunciation expected of Hindu widows and the ban on widow remarriage. But unlike Deb, Duff had something also to say about the way in which some women treated their own kind. Referring to the excess in the number of males over females in areas like Rajputana he wasted no time in building up his picture of the slaughter of innocent females. And this he argued was done by 'the unhappy mothers' who 'in the name of false honour, and false religion', had no compassion on the fruit of their own womb.[5] And in case his audience were still not fully aware of the role of Hindu religion in these atrocities he reiterated that the driving engine behind them was, not only the power of 'demon pride', but of 'hellish superstition'.

The other example of an influential publicist who pointed to Hinduism, or rather Brahmanism, as the root cause of the Hindu woman's misery and degradation is Mrs Weitbrecht—widow of the venerated Church Missionary Society (CMS) missionary who died in Bengal in 1852.[6] While she had read Duff's work on women's issues and echoed many of his sentiments,[7] her depiction of the condition and circumstances of India's women was somewhat more sophisticated. This was partly because she had had much more direct and extensive contact with Indian women, and had gained her information and insights over a very long period, having spent forty years in women's work in Bengal.[8] By comparison with Duff, Weitbrecht also appears to have been more aware of the limitations of her knowledge and experience, freely acknowledging that what she had to say applied principally to Bengal and northern India and only to a lesser extent to southern and western regions.

[5] Ibid.: 17.
[6] Stock 1899, Vol. 2: 164.
[7] Weitbrecht 1875: 38.
[8] For references to her marriage and early work among females in Burdwan, see Christopher 1854: esp. 105–9.

In the early section of her book she discussed the position of women and ideals of Indian womanhood as reflected especially in epic literature such as the *Ramayana* and *Mahabharata*. Although she found something there which she could admire, for example the Hindu women's virtuous character, and evidence of the right of choice in marriage, she argued that, ultimately, notions of faithfulness, duty and obedience led to the Indian woman's downfall. 'The principle of unquestioning obedience, embodied in these poems,' she wrote, 'has continued most rigorously to be applied to the conjugal relations in India, and has brought about the enslavement of women'.[9] While Duff referred to the oppressive role of Hinduism, her chief assault was more specific, on the role of brahmans and on the way in which they eventually consolidated all that was most oppressive in relation to women over previous centuries. She held that their influence had gradually increased 'till at length they had enclosed the nation in a network of religious observances, extending to the inward impulses no less than to the outward movements'.[10] The brahmanical *Laws of Manu*, she claimed, represented 'the actual institutions of Indian life' after the expulsion of Buddhism. She referred to the total loss of women's independence, the part played by the doctrine of transmigration in justifying and reinforcing women's oppression, the ranking of women with inferior castes and other disabilities, such as those mentioned in Duff's papers. But she also introduced the idea that the germs of the zenana system 'the principle that it is needful to seclude woman by confinement from the outer world', were to be found in the code.[11] The consequence of this system, she declared, was that 'the poor little girl' was torn away at a tender age from the home of her infancy 'to reside among strangers...to wake in her prison home, and to begin a life of seclusion and inanition'.[12]

The argument of these leading publicists was, if anything, reinforced by the somewhat misleading impression that various commentators left, and that was that the zenana was basically a Hindu institution. This was an issue which Monier-Williams felt compelled to address in 1898 when he remarked that 'it must be clear that the seclusion of women, with their consequent degradation, is not properly a Hindu custom'.[13] But so long as individuals or the public viewed the zenana as a Hindu establishment then Hinduism received the blame: and ideas of deprivation and imprisonment

[9] Weitbrecht 1875: 28.

[10] Ibid.: 30.

[11] Ibid.

[12] Ibid.: 43.

[13] *IW*, Vol. 18, April 1898.

associated with the zenana endured, working within the imagination as yet another potent symbol of Hindu oppression and disregard for the values of human life. Indeed, much has been written about the zenana, its symbolism and meaning, and all that requires to be mentioned here is that for some supporters of the missionary movement it came to represent all that was dark, dismal, isolated and dreary—a dungeon, a 'prison home', a place where women, cut off from all outside contact, including the delights of nature, spent their life in ignorance, drudgery and superstition. If towards the end of the century the symbolism, especially of Jagannath, was beginning to fade, it was replaced, at least to some extent, by the imagery of the zenana—the place of darkness and misery. And no matter how much some of the missionaries themselves protested that women's life and living conditions varied throughout the subcontinent,[14] it must have been difficult to efface the power of the stereotype and fixed idea.

Discussion of the Hindu woman's condition in India became then an occasion for underlining the way in which Hinduism was responsible for her plight and suffering. And just as the missionaries had come to feel that caste was, in the last analysis, a religious institution, so now there was widespread agreement that the root cause and underlying reason for the maltreatment of women on the subcontinent was, once again, the religious system. Certainly it is true that Mary Weitbrecht was able to point to the freedom of choice that women in Hinduism had once enjoyed, as well as to the virtues of loyalty, obedience and devotion as exemplified in the lives of Hindu heroines of the heroic age. But these features were understood as developments in a period long before the age of decline; and the overall picture of women in Hinduism, as presented in the more general promotional literature for much of the nineteenth century, was of females suffering from a loss of freedom and rights most usually understood as a consequence of the rise and establishment of brahmanical control.

Women's Organizations Working for Hindu Women

The more general developments which prompted the rise of the women's missionary movement, together with the establishment of women's organizations for missionary activity overseas have already been discussed in Chapter 8. One of the first of these organizations was the Society for Promoting Female Education in the East which was founded in London

---

[14] See for example Small 1890: 46–50.

in 1834.[15] An all-female inter-denominational association, its object was to carry on missionary labour among the women of India. In 1838 women in Scotland, swayed by Duff's appeals and depiction of the plight of Hindu females, established the 'Scottish Ladies' Association for the Advancement of Female Education in India'. It split into two groups as a result of the Disruption of the Church of Scotland in 1843—the work of the ladies of the Free Church of Scotland (which had control of almost all the missions in India) being conducted through the 'Female Society of the Free Church of Scotland for Promoting the Christian Education of Females of India'. In 1849 it had forty-eight auxiliary societies in various parts of Scotland.[16]

In the meantime, female schools and related organizations were developing in Calcutta—an important development which meant that, at least initially, much of the British focus was on Bengal and northern India and most of the knowledge of women's conditions 'in India' derived from the same source. As a result of Miss Cooke's determined efforts twenty-two girls' schools were in operation in Calcutta and its vicinity by the year 1823 and, in the following year, a Ladies Society for Native Female Education in Calcutta was formed to control their affairs.[17] A central girls' school was opened in 1826 and the Calcutta Normal School for training female teachers (the cradle of the CEZMS) was established in 1852.

The pioneering work of the churches in Scotland in establishing their own ladies committees for work among women in India and elsewhere, was followed by the establishment of similar denominational auxiliaries in England. A 'Ladies Committee for Ameliorating the condition of Women in Heathen Countries' was set up by the Wesleyan Methodist Missionary Society (WMMS) in 1858[18] and similar ladies committees were established in connection with the Society for the Propagation of the Gospel, SPG (1866), the Baptist Missionary Society, BMS (1868) and the LMS (1875). The society which is conspicuously absent from this list is the CMS. It had already been funding committees active in women's work in Calcutta and elsewhere but seems to have had even greater problems accepting the idea of sending out single ladies than the other organizations mentioned earlier.

As is apparent from discussion in Chapter 8, established male missionary organizations in India, including conference committees, were at least

---

[15] Richter 1901: 335–36; Weitbrecht 1875: 135–36; Stock 1899, Vol. 1: 377.

[16] Sixth Annual Report 1849: 26–27.

[17] Barnes 1897: 3.

[18] Findlay and Holdsworth 1922, Vol. 4: 13–24.

as slow in adjusting themselves to the influx and increased professionalism of female missionaries as most societies at home. While, as Semple has shown, there were problems over the admission of women to at least some denominational district committees, it is also obvious that women had to deal with discrimination at the level of regional or all-India inter-church conferences.[19]

Origin of the CEZMS

In 1851 a meeting of ladies in London formed themselves into a committee to select staff and obtain funds for the Calcutta Normal School. Ten years later this association, which became known as the Indian Female Normal School and Instruction Society (IFNSIS) (and was in effect the parent body of the CEZMS) decided to embrace the whole of India as its sphere of activity, sending out its first missionary to south India in 1862.[20] According to its own brochure published in 1875 it had, by that time, 131 'agents' in different parts of India. These comprised twenty-eight 'English ladies', sixty 'Native and Eurasian Christian teachers', eight 'Native Christian ladies' employed in zenanas, and thirty-five 'Native Bible women'.[21] The brochure claimed that 622 zenanas were being visited in which there were 1,043 pupils, and that in addition to this, there were 1,437 female scholars in schools under the society's management. The society published its own quarterly, *The Indian Female Evangelist* established in 1872 and edited by Mrs Watson, daughter of Alexander Duff.[22]

While the IFNSIS, or IFNS for short, was intended as an inter-denominational association, Henry Venn, General Secretary of the CMS, had been active in the framing of its constitution and, in actual practice, it was, both in its origin and continuing membership, closely connected with the Church of England.[23] According to Eugene Stock, historian of the CMS, in 1880 Lady Kinnaird and some other members of the Committee wanted to give more emphasis to the society's non-denominational basis (primarily in order to secure more support in Scotland), by appointing an additional secretary—a well-known Presbyterian missionary.[24] These proposals led to a split within the society, many on the committee, including

[19] Semple 2003: 97–98.
[20] Weitbrecht 1875: 139.
[21] CEZMS archives (University of Birmingham) CEZ/G AP2 1875–1880.
[22] *IER*, Vol. VII, 1879: 167.
[23] Stock 1899, Vol. 3: 258.
[24] Ibid.; and CEZMS brochure, 21/6/1880.

Mrs Sandys and Mrs Weitbrecht (both of them widows of CMS Bengal missionaries), leaving to form their own separate organization. From this point onwards there were two societies, continuing supporters of the older society regrouping as the Zenana Bible and Medical Mission while those who left formed the CEZMS.

In 1880 when it was formed, the CEZMS had for its nucleus the entire charge of the Normal School, Calcutta, and also responsibility for seventeen other stations, with a staff of thirty-one 'ladies' (three-quarters of the former IFNS European staff) as well as assistant missionaries and Bible women.[25] According to its first annual report it had six centres in Bengal, seven in north and north-west India, and four in the south where the society was fairly heavily reliant on its 'native' assistants. The stated objects of the society were 'to make known the Gospel of Christ to the Women of India, in accordance with the Protestant and Evangelical teaching of the articles and formularies of the Church of England'.[26] However, this statement of objectives was clearly open to different interpretations. What was meant by the Gospel of Christ? How far did this mean showing forth the love of Christ and improving conditions for women in the here and now? Furthermore, in 1880 the term 'evangelical' was becoming increasingly vague and was appropriated by missionaries in particular with a wide range of different views. The stated objects of the CEZMS therefore left the way open for a certain degree of flexibility for women who wanted to test and explore varied roles in the mission field.

Hinduism in CEZMS Missionary Training

As noted in earlier comments, applicants for service with British missionary societies, including the CEZMS, had greater opportunities for obtaining information about the mission field and Indian religious traditions than the men and women who went to India in the early nineteenth century. There was more information on India and its religious life available in Britain in the last quarter of the nineteenth century—though the bulk of this information was still collected or compiled by men. Almost all the systematic or major studies of Hinduism, and many of the lesser ones, were undertaken by men and reflected a male perspective. However, many of the candidates who worked in India in the last quarter of the century, including some recruited by the CEZMS, had the additional

[25] Barnes 1897: 9.
[26] CEZMS brochure, 21/6/1880.

advantage of being more familiar with India and even Hinduism through earlier life and experience in India. In the case of the women under consideration, this included personal contact with females in India during childhood or continuing contact with female friends or relatives in the mission field.

While much of the CEZMS archival material was destroyed in bombing during the Second World War, some of what remains is especially significant for our purpose.[27] Among the documents are candidates' papers that include answers to questions about what they knew of non-Christian religions. These papers are especially valuable as, unlike many earlier missionary archival collections, they provide specific and organized information on what some of the candidates knew or understood of Hinduism while they were still in Britain and before their college training for work overseas.

When applying for service with the CEZMS applicants (like those who applied to some other societies such as the LMS) were asked a series of questions about their background, education and knowledge, as well as about the chief motives which led them 'to desire to be a missionary'. But as mentioned earlier and in the case of those applying for service with the CEZMS questions also included one on the nature of India's non-Christian religions.[28] Applicants were asked to state 'shortly' what they knew of 'the different idolatrous systems of India'. The question was changed in the 1890s to read 'State shortly what you know of the chief non-Christian religious systems in heathen and Mohammedan lands' and then again to 'State shortly what you know of the different religious systems in India and China'. Thus the all-important reference to religions as 'systems' remained as part of the question throughout. However, reference to them being 'idolatrous' was dropped—presumably in order to incorporate Islam in the question, but possibly also because the idea of describing Hinduism or Buddhism and so on as idolatrous was less fashionable, or even seen as more problematic than it appeared to be in the earlier part of the century.

In some of their replies candidates confessed they were unable to answer the question. Edith Potter, for example, writing in 1893 explained that she was unable to answer the question without reading some book on the idolatrous systems of India. A few years later, Emily Barton, also apologizing for being unable to answer the question, stated that she hoped

[27] These papers, included under the general reference CEZ/C AM5, are filed in individual folders under the initial for the missionary's surname.
[28] CEZMS archives, CEZ/C AM5 (Candidates Papers) and Annual Reports, 1883–1900.

'to learn enough' during her period of training. However, a number of applicants did attempt the question, some giving longer and more detailed answers than others. Among these were summaries of what the applicant knew of Hinduism.

Encouraged by the question itself, the basic assumption was that Hinduism was a unified system, and, reflecting this view, were the answers which emphasized the supremacy of one god and the inter-relationship between all the deities mentioned. Thus, for Mary Cooper, Hinduism involved 'the worship of one supreme being Brahm, & of numerous other gods [springing?] from him'. According to Amy Townsend, who answered the question under the heading of 'Brahmanism', pantheism appeared to be at the core of its teaching. 'Brahma is worshipped as the personification of goodness & man's chief aim is to become absorbed in his being. Everything has emanated from Brahma'. Kathleen Loader declared that 'the Hindus are followers of the teachings of Brahma, they have many gods, but principally the Triad—Brahma, Vishnu & Kali'. In her answer, Evelyn Karney (daughter of Edward Karney Secretary of the CEZMS) and Blanche Carey (recruited for Karachi) underlined the complementary functions of the different deities, declaring that Hindus worshipped Brahma the Creator, Vishnu the Preserver and Shiva the Destroyer. However, neither candidate explained whether Hindus worshipped all three as somehow connected or whether they understood them as independent deities. Phoebe Grover who was subsequently sent as one of the society's missionaries to Ootacamund had a somewhat different view. 'Hinduism', she wrote, 'is a form of religion in which several gods are worshipped, some superior, some inferior deities, but no one universal.' And lastly, Charlotte Harding (sent out to Calcutta in 1885), had yet another different and evolutionary view—one which was more in line with the orientalists and Rammohan Roy's understanding of the decline of India's religion.

> After ages of effort to see the Unseen to know the Unknowable to grasp the infinite, the Hindus betook themselves to deify mortals and to worship objects by which they were surrounded. Hinduism utterly failed to lead its votaries to a high perception of God & ultimately passed into a system of degraded polytheism & idolatry—From regarding objects as symbols of the true God they have come to honour these as actual deities.

Allied with these comments about deities and the relationship or lack of relationship between them were occasional references to brahmans as the mentors and guardians of Hindu tradition. 'The Brahmanists', wrote Clara Elwin, 'teach that Brahma was the Supreme God & that the priests were formed from the head etc.'[29] One of the other candidates, Kathleen Loader, was, however, more absorbed with the much loved image of the fakir. 'There is one class called Fakirs, or religious beggars', she wrote, 'who mutilate & exhibit themselves & live on the alms of their devotees.' Lastly, a not uncommon theme throughout, was the idea that Hinduism was closely linked with the social system. Several candidates spelled out the idea and implication of transmigration.[30] Margaret Church argued that the rules of caste 'form a great part of their religion'. Florence Cooper averred that 'their widows are not allowed to marry', while Loader referred to Hinduism as 'a cruel and superstitious religion involving the close seclusion of women, early marriages [and] strict caste regulations'.

In describing what they knew, some candidates attempted an admirable objectivity. Others, such as Margaret Loader, found it difficult to resist moral judgements. The two deities, apart from Brahma, Vishnu and Shiva, most frequently mentioned were Krishna and the goddess Kali. But while in Karney's view 'Krishnu indulged in every form of vice', Carey drew attention to the fact that Vishnu 'is represented as having come down to offer a sacrifice for the good of the human race'. Furthermore, while there was a conventional concentration on the character of Hindu deities and the usual absorption with the unhappy social consequences of 'the Hindu system', Harding's short statement was somewhat different in that she was able to empathize with the Hindu's initial search for meaning. It is apparent therefore that, even at this stage, some women were prepared to adopt something of the more modern sympathetic approach.

Views and Representations of Hinduism in the Mission Field

These were the views of applicants before they entered college and attended lectures on Hinduism. While there is an absence of information as to how far, if at all, their ideas of Hinduism changed as a result of exposure to lectures or further study, it is possible to capture something of women's views and constructions of Hinduism in the mission field. It is important to note that, at least up until the time they entered college, much of what they read or heard of Hinduism was from the perspective of men. It was mostly the men who had written books or commented on Indian religions: there was not so much material composed by women available.

[29] See also comments by Hilare Brown and Florence Cooper.
[30] See comments by Carey, Loader, Townsend and Margaret Church.

Figure 11.1
'Teaching in a Zenana at Umritsur'
From the CM *Gleaner*, Vol. VI, No. 61, January 1879.

As already noted, once in India, one of the most important sources of information about Hindu religion and practice was the munshi or pundit. As in the case of other missionaries he was one of the first of the more learned Indians whom the women encountered and met at frequent intervals, usually over a period of two or more years. In addition to this was the women's association with workers in local connection and assistant missionaries who were often Indian Christians. Soon after its formation (with a nucleus of Church of England missionaries who had been working for the IFNS) the CEZMS recruited an increasing number of Indian and Anglo-Indian workers who together with European women resident in India were categorized as being those 'in local connection' to distinguish them from the European missionaries recruited and trained in Britain. According to the CEZMS annual reports the combined total of locally recruited workers, the majority of whom appear to have been Indian Christians, outnumbered European missionaries by over five to one in 1887; the situation remaining much the same in subsequent years up until the end of the century.[31] Apart from the school teachers there were the bible women who became increasingly important as assistants in the task of visiting the zenanas or even Hindu festivals in the company of the European women, or in pursuing their own independent activities in the villages or elsewhere. Like converts more generally, they too were an important source of information and guidance.[32]

But perhaps the most important indigenous source of information, and the greatest teacher of all, was the women's direct experience of work among Hindu women. Some of this work involving teaching in girls' schools or in training colleges was not especially new, but even this was gender specific, and something that was outside the experience and direct responsibility of male missionaries. More innovative as projects which drew European women into the Hindu women's world of activity and meaning were their journeys into the countryside, village preaching, work among Hindu women on pilgrimage or attending Hindu festivals, medical work and visits to the Hindu home. It was the latter type of endeavour (visits to the zenana) which excited the greatest interest and which had a considerable impact on the missionaries themselves. This may have been partly because female missionaries could feel greater rapport with people who appeared to be closer to their own 'class' than ordinary village women;[33]

[31] AR, 1880, 1887, 1897.

[32] Christina Hall, IW, 1899, Vol. XIX: 6.

[33] On the middle-class background of CEZMS missionaries during this period, see Morawiecki 1998.

but, as will be argued in a later part of this chapter, it was also because many of them were able to develop and consolidate meaningful long-term relationships through this form of activity.

CEZMS missionary reports referring to zenana visits often reflect the sense of discovery or even excitement on the part of female missionaries at being let into some kind of secret world hitherto protected and hidden very securely from the European gaze. These sources are in fact a repository of new types of European knowledge and information about the details especially of higher caste Indian women's life and affairs. In this sense they complement indigenous biographical material such as Pundita Ramabhai's *The High Caste Hindu Woman*. The missionaries not only had the opportunity of witnessing Hindu women's participation in rituals, and of exploring their views on matters of religious belief, but also gained further knowledge and insights into gender relations within the family, such as marriage and widowhood—social practices which some European commentators continued to associate with Hinduism.

What then did the CEZMS missionaries discover or learn in these encounters? What did they make of their experience? How far, if at all, did their increasing knowledge and experience lead to an identifiable female view or construction of Hinduism? There were perhaps three ways in which the women's representation of Hinduism was different from that of men.

First, women tended to notice and report on what Hindu women thought and did to a greater extent than the male missionaries, even when giving an account of the same event. Especially interesting in this respect is an account of the Jagannath car festival at Serampore which was published in the *Indian Female Evangelist* in 1874. The author, J. C. S. (Mrs Sutton?) appears to have gone with other European women to observe Hindu female devotees and certainly wrote them into her account. 'The idol was bathed', she wrote, 'amidst the shouts of men and cries of the women'. At the beginning of the procession the 'idol' was exposed 'and the peculiar shrill crying of the women is heard all around'. Expressing her pity for 'the many poor women' who, 'from a fear of calamity, or in hope of good' had come to honour or propitiate the idol, the writer explained that women of all ages and types were among them.[34] Here then was an account different in focus from the usual male accounts of similar festivals where the women's activity received little if any attention.

---

[34] *IFE*, Vol. 2: 9–13.

A second difference in the way in which European missionary women portrayed Hinduism when compared with men (especially in the details) arose partly as a result of their different type of work and experience. In 1894 the veteran CMS missionary J. E. Padfield published a series of articles in the *Madras Christian College Magazine* on different aspects of Hindu daily life. These articles, which proved popular, were published in book form and under the title of *The Hindu at Home* in 1896. Much, though not all, of the author's discussion was about male brahman rituals. When he came to the section on 'The Hindu Woman's Religion' he drew attention to the difficulty he had with lack of sources.

> There is great difficulty in arriving at anything like a clear knowledge of the Hindu woman's religion. Little help can be gained from books and the Hindus themselves have very confused and conflicting ideas on the subject. I have consulted with learned Hindus and others likely to have the best information, and I give it in as clear a way as it seems to me possible in anything so conflicting and confusing as Hinduism.[35]

One of Padfield's problems was, of course, the difficulties he had in attempting generalizations valid for the whole of India. But other problems appears to have been that (*a*) he was male and therefore largely debarred from familiar interaction with Hindu women and (*b*) he appears to have been either ignorant, or somewhat dismissive of what European missionary women had already written on the Hindu women's religion. Even if male missionaries seldom read female missionary reports, it is surprising that Padfield failed to include, or give prominence to material derived from the female missionaries' observations.

The female missionaries' zenana visits in particular gave them a unique opportunity to observe and investigate the more private and enclosed world of the Hindu home. Indeed, much of the fascination and impact of CEZMS reports lay in the fact that missionary women were able to expose for Europeans generally many things Western observers had not known before. In giving an account of life and developments in the zenana missionary commentators not only elaborate on the Hindu females' life and place in the home and on her relationship with the husband, but also include detailed descriptions of domestic rituals and a range of different female attitudes and beliefs. What these accounts tend to have in common with Padfield's account is an accent on upper-caste culture.

[35] Padfield 1908: 50.

Some reports make it clear that in some places the European women's visit to zenanas was still something of an issue, especially for the more conservative Hindus who were still afraid of pollution. For example Miss Todd, writing from Ellore in the mid-1880s, explained that she had hoped to visit brahman homes, but was told by neighbours that these visits would result in them being obliged 'to cleanse thoroughly the place we occupied while visiting them'.[36] Miss D'Albedyll, who was also working in south India and who visited the Rajah of Cochin's wife, gave her little girl of five a doll. In this case, the missionary obtained feedback from the bible women who told her the doll was washed and hung up to dry—the little girl explaining that 'The English lady is not high caste like me, and I could not touch the doll unless I washed it, as she had had it in her hands'.[37] However, when missionaries visited the same place on a number of occasions fear of pollution sometimes seemed to disappear. In one of her reports from Madras, Miss Oxley explained that formerly the children used to drop books into her hand 'for fear of pollution', but that, in recent times, 'the pupils *now usually* sit too close'.[38]

In some cases, especially in north India, the question of pollution was not such an issue and European zenana visitors had greater freedom of movement and opportunities for observation. They were able to describe, first hand and in detail, domestic rituals involving women and girls. For example, Miss Highton of Calcutta explained that one of her pupils (a girl of twelve), showed her into a room which was full of brass platters containing sweet meats, rice cakes, flowers, and so on. A brahman sitting among them was 'muttering' prayers and ringing a bell; and, while the grandfather was looking on and 'doing anything he was told', the grandmother was called to blow a conch-shell, 'which she did with a will, and then fell down upon her face before the Brahmin'.[39] The Hindu women's devotion and enthusiasm for ritual practice was also noted. Mrs Lewis of Palamcotta remarked that a favourite pupil, accompanied by other widows, 'visited one of those so-called holy shrines, and were all persuaded to cut off their hair and present it to the gods'.[40] Sophia Oxley, who reported that her pupil came 'gorgeously dressed' on her way to the temple dance', noted that this practice was common among brahman girls.[41]

[36] *IW*, Vol. 5, 1885: 261.
[37] *IW*, Vol. 19, 1899: 75.
[38] *IW*, Vol. 8, 1888: 238. See also Vol. 1, 1880: 31.
[39] *IW*, Vol. 1, 1881: 70.
[40] Ibid.: 14.
[41] *IW*, Vol. 8, 1888: 242.

The Hindu woman's role in family, marriage and death rituals was also noted in missionary correspondence. Of considerable importance in the timing of marriages, and an influence on the life of Hindu women, was the horoscope. 'Since January, there has been a number of marriages', wrote Miss Brandon from Masulipatam, 'A lucky star is in the ascendancy, and the Shastres have ordered all the ceremonies to take place this spring; afterwards for two years it will be very unlucky to marry. Accordingly even little girls of three have been married, and our schools have been almost deserted'.[42] The high-caste woman's role in funeral ceremonies was also noted. One revelation, no doubt new to many readers of *India's Women*, was Miss Highton's reference to a girl whose mother died and who, according to Hindu custom, was expected to provide for the funeral ceremonies.[43] In another instance it was reported that the 'new-made' widow had a special rite to perform. As she was childless, and hence had no son to perform the usual duties, she was given the task of putting fire to the dead man's mouth.[44]

Also significant are references to the strategies Hindu women employed in attempting to deal with poverty, illness and disease. Writing from Karachi, Alice Dawson, remarked that it was the custom amongst 'heathen' girls in the month of June 'to sow corn in small earthen pots, and when the blade is well grown, to keep a fast, sing round it, worship it, and finally throw it into the tank'. This was done, she explained, 'to ensure themselves against want when they go to their husband's house'.[45] Miss Sandys, referring to illness, commented on a woman who believed she could be healed from a swollen leg (the result of a dog bite) by taking grains of rice 'brought all the way from Juggernath'.[46] Miss Basoe, referring to an outbreak of cholera near Masulipatam described in some detail the villagers' attempts to propitiate the deity through animal sacrifice and other methods.[47]

These comments are merely samples of the kind of knowledge and information female missionaries gleaned from regular contact and activities with Hindu women. *India's Women,* and a range of other female missionary periodicals, gradually increased the British women's awareness (and possibly the British males' awareness) of domestic life and women's concerns and rituals—especially in the high-caste Hindu home. This was

[42] *IW*, Vol. 5, 1885: 256.
[43] *IW*, Vol. 4, 1884: 18.
[44] *IW*, Vol. 19, 1899: 3.
[45] Ibid.: 82.
[46] *IW*, Vol. 7, 1887: 32.
[47] *IW*, Vol. 19, 1899: 55.

at the very time in which male missionaries were becoming more involved in administration and less involved in Hindu affairs. The women's reports not only focus on women, but unlike Padfield's account of the Hindu woman's religion, are less concerned with textual statements and idealized versions of what the woman was supposed to do. As noted earlier, the women's depictions are usually first-hand accounts and much more grounded in empirical observation.

A third way in which the women's descriptions of Hindu religious life and thought differed from dominant male depictions relates to the women's focus on detail. Despite their earlier education in the big picture and in male theories of Hinduism, female missionaries, or at least those associated with the CEZMS, tended to ignore general theories and concepts. There appear to be few references to Hinduism in CEZMS reports,[48] and so little interest in the wider picture that the Rev. W. Ball felt constrained to remind women attending the Society's twentieth anniversary of broader and more encompassing views.[49] Despite there being many books on Hinduism written by male missionaries, there are no important general studies of the subject written by British women—at least up until 1900. Furthermore, when the women wrote about the religious life and beliefs they tended to write about individuals and detailed circumstances rather than explore the macro dimension.

The reasons for this approach may relate to levels of education and the nature of training. Semple in her recent study of British missionary women who worked with the LMS, the Church of Scotland and the China Inland Mission in the Victorian era has argued that there were major differences in the way in which men and women were selected and trained for the mission field. Because men came from more specific educational institutions where standards could be more easily assessed than was the case with women, it was easier to select men on the basis of educational achievement. 'This meant that criteria other than academic excellence had to be used to assess female candidates'.[50] Moreover, while a woman's educational background might be considered, 'middle class respectability' and other factors in the woman's background, counted more than education.

---

[48] For example, in all the reports and correspondence about work in India in the society's journal (*IW*, Vol. 18, 1898) there are no more than four (mostly brief) missionary references to Hinduism.

[49] In this he resorted to Duff's favourite imagery of warfare between the two great religious systems (*IW*, Vol. 20, 1900: 129.)

[50] Semple 2003: 17.

Much the same general considerations appear to have affected the selection and training of women at 'The Willows' where, up until 1896, almost all CEZMS women were trained. There, as in other training institutions, female candidates were not encouraged to be as academic as men.[51] They were not expected to operate in an especially abstract, philosophical or intellectual manner. While, for example, Miss Schroder, principal of The Willows, recognized that students trained in the college should have 'an intellectual grasp of Christian doctrine', this was not necessarily the same grasp which male missionaries, and, in particular, ordained clergymen, were required to have.[52] Indeed, as Morawiecki has argued, 'the effort made to give only limited theological training to women missionaries was deliberate, as it was feared that too deep an understanding might tempt women to undertake work in the field which was restricted to ordained clergymen'. Hence academic training at the Willows, like academic training in other Protestant missionary colleges for women, was much less extensive than that for men. The training that was given was felt to be more useful and better suited to women candidates, with an emphasis on such subjects as educational method, domestic knowledge and basic medical skills. Certainly it was expected that female missionaries would be well versed in their knowledge of the Bible, and even have some understanding of non-Christian religions: but much of the emphasis was on training for the practical and caring side of the women's work, including the development of their 'natural' skills as healers and comforters.

It can also be argued that by the time women were in a position to write general accounts of Hinduism, there was no longer the same need for them as there had been earlier in the century. General studies of Hinduism by men such as Mitchell, Robson and Vaughan dominated the field.

But perhaps, in the last analysis, the lack of women wanting or being able to comment on Hinduism as a general system has more to do with the women's world of meaning, and with what was perceived to be the most satisfying and effective approach.

The women's correspondence suggests that, as time progressed, it was not so much abstract ideas, or theories about Hinduism in general that seemed to require the greatest attention, but rather the Hindu women's immediate needs. Linked with this was the perceived importance of developing meaningful relationships between mission workers on the one

[51] Morawiecki 1998: 192–93.
[52] Ibid.: 192.

hand and the Hindu women and families on the other.[53] Certainly it
mattered that the Indian women were 'heathen', but the focus was on the
individual, the individual's story, and the immediate context in which
relationships within the Hindu family and with the missionary developed.
Hence what brought zenana visitors and others the greatest pleasure was
'the particular', the Hindu women and children they met and came to
value, perhaps even as friends.

The depth of feeling and emotional nature of these relationships is
apparent in widespread comment.[54] Moreover, they were all the more
important for single European women somewhat isolated and deprived
of the friendships and comforts of home. Women such as these were
perhaps more likely to take up these more personal and practical matters
than they were to focus on broader questions and produce an intellectual
or theoretical analysis of 'the Hindu system'. One illustration of this point
is the work of Amy Carmichael—the most successful and influential
publicist among CEZMS missionaries in the very first years of the twentieth century. Recruited for the CEZMS in 1895[55] she became well known
for her stories about the suffering and enlightenment of individuals and
families in southern India.[56] The Hindu religious and social context and
other influences and forces at work are referred to in her book. But rather
than being the point of focus, or being put there for systematic intellectual
analysis, they are more like shadows in the background, and, as the author
remarks, remain as something 'undescribed'.[57]

[53] This point comes through constantly in their correspondence. See for example
extracts from Miss Brandon in Masulipatam (IW, Vol. 5, 1885: 253); Mrs Lewis in Palamcotta
(IW, Vol. 1, 1881: 13); Miss Mulvaney in Calcutta (IW, Vol. 8, 1888: 76); and Miss Gore in
Burdwan (IW, Vol. 8, 1888: 78).

[54] According to Mrs Lewis of Palamcotta, 'Dear Kemala Bai, when I visited her to-day,
threw her arms round me and embraced me warmly' (IW, Vol. 1, 1881: 13). Miss Mulvaney
who visited a high-class zenana in the company of two other European ladies noted that
one of the zenana women 'who used to make my heart sad and my eyes tearful by the
blasphemous way in which she opposed the Divinity of our Lord, came up to me after Miss
Clymer's faithful, loving words, and threw her arms around my neck before all, saying she
loved me, and I was like one of her own, and I must tell the lady she would never forget
the words she had spoken'(IW, Vol. 8, 1888: 76). Mary Gore, describing her feelings and
experience of visiting zenanas in Burdwan, wrote that 'I may truly say that I have spent some
of the happiest moments of my life while sitting among them. In Burdwan they say to Miss
Mulvaney, "You are our own," and in Royan they say the same to me' (IW, Vol. 8, 1888: 78).

[55] CEZ/C/AMI, Vol. 2; Houghton 1953.

[56] For example, most of the chapters in her first book published in 1903, and based on
her work in Tinnevelly district, addressed the difficulties 'heathen' men, women and children faced in their ordinary every-day life (Carmichael 1903).

[57] Ibid.: 3.

Conclusion

This book has been about assumptions and imagination. It has also been about how further learning, and especially experience, informed and refined the imagination, changing ideas and models of Hinduism into something different. While there were some missionaries who saw no point in investigating the niceties or even the broad outlines of Hindu religion, there were others who, like William Carey, an admirer of Captain Cook, had a passion for discovery. Some like Carey and Bishop Heber were led into the depths of disappointment, and to an even greater sense that Hinduism was one of the worst inventions the devil had ever concocted. Others, over many years, seemed to be led into different waters and developed different feelings—a sense of respect, even admiration, for things they discovered partially hidden or invisible beneath the surface.

The initial assumptions included a deeply-held conviction that the basic religious structures of the world were exemplified in the Christian model. It was taken for granted that the Christian model and experience of religion provided one with the framework and insights with which to judge other religious systems. Christianity was therefore not only the best and true religion, but also the best guide as to what religion itself was all about. If it had some kind of unity, basic creeds, underlying philosophy, priests and hierarchies, followers and outward forms then so too did the other religions of the world. The questions one asked were the same sort of questions one could ask of the Christian faith. What did Hindus 'believe'? Where were the priests and interpreters of the faith? What was its equivalent to the Bible? What was the 'real Hinduism' as opposed to the beliefs and practice of the ignorant multitude? Where were the boundaries of the faith, what kept it together and what explained its essence?

It was questions such as these arising out of the British and European context and history that produced the dominant missionary brahmanical model of Hinduism. It was an idea of Indian religion which probably tells us as much about the thought processes of British people as it does about the essentials of Hindu belief and practice. A construct gradually built up over time, it mirrored British and European ideas, moulding Hinduism into something like the opposite of Christianity.

Especially important in the process of disseminating this were missionary society periodicals and graphic literature. Editors and others who produced this material were clearly constrained by the limitations in the education and literacy of potential readers. How could one convey ideas about an alien or unknown religion in ways which would be entertaining and understood even at the level of the humble cottager? And how could editors and others do this in such a way as to inspire support for a movement designed to save Hindus from themselves? The most effective method of approach was to discuss Hinduism in terms of what readers already knew, using familiar Christian language and concepts and simplifying the message even further at the popular level. There, most clearly, was the pressure to re-mould Hindu practice and views of the world into the parameters of Christian thinking, to ignore distinctions, qualifications and refinements, and to shock readers with images of customs and behaviour which contradicted values as expressed in Protestant tradition. Like Christianity, Hinduism was also 'a religion'. That much they had in common. But at this level of presentation, this is where similarities ended. In all other things the contrast was as stark as day and night.

While, as we noted in chapter 2, evangelicals and missionaries were among the first, if not the first, to employ and popularize the term 'Hinduism', their depiction of its nature and characteristics during the first half of the nineteenth century was hardly original. The notion of Indian religion as brahmanism, as an India-wide all embracing construct and system invented and controlled by brahmans essentially for their own benefit was a view of Indian religion already apparent in earlier literature. Susan Bayly is surely correct when she suggests that Ward's vision of immoral brahman despotism 'clearly drew on popular English Protestant mythology of a priest-ridden, tyrannised papist Europe awaiting liberation by the triumph of the Reformation spirit'.[1] But, ironically, the view of Indian religion as something like brahmanical despotism was shared by some Catholics as well. Early travel, Jesuit and other non-missionary accounts available in Britain emphasized the importance of brahmans as all-powerful leaders who invented, justified and continued to control the Hindu system. These ideas, worked out in great detail by Ward, Duff and others, were reinforced by non-missionary writers such as secular orientalists, James Mill and others. Indeed so convinced were Westerners that brahmans had a fundamental vested interest in Hinduism and were the props and key to the entire system that writers like J. W. Kaye suggested that brahmans (whose religion, the British had threatened to undermine) were the chief instigators of the Indian mutiny and civil

[1] Bayly 1999: 110.

rebellion. Furthermore, this view of the absolute centrality of brahmans was shared by many missionary and non-missionary commentators during the second half of the nineteenth century when the idea of pantheism (a brahmanical teaching) was proposed as 'the essence' of the Hindu system.

But if initially the missionaries and evangelicals tended to echo, support and develop a long-term and popular theory about the leadership and unified character of the Hindu religious system, some of them began to express different ideas mostly in the second half of the nineteenth century. In the end it was the missionaries' Indian experience, even more than theological changes in the West, which chipped away at the dominant paradigm and began to reshape missionary ideas and interpretations of Indian religion. As noted in chapter 5, the impact of Carey's experience on his knowledge and understanding of Hindu rituals is clearly apparent in his letters and diaries. Indeed, it was his own observation of hook-swinging and sati, his presence on the spot, that seems to have provided him with greater insights than pre-reading and earlier discussions with other people.

While Carey's experience was a powerful factor in his changing evaluation of Hinduism, Duff's limited experience of life in Calcutta seems to have made very little difference to his overall views. Having rejected opportunities to work in the vernacular and concentrating on developing Western education through English he had little contact with Indians and Indian culture outside a small select group of largely alienated Bengali youth. What experience he had in India seemed to convince him even further that Enlightenment ideas and what he learned of Christianity in Scotland were entirely sufficient for the progress and salvation of India's people. The students he taught and counselled appeared, for the most part, to have already rejected much in their Hindu background and, because of their familiarity with Western skeptical and other literature, they could readily appreciate Western and Christian arguments designed to counteract the influence of the Western 'infidelity' they had absorbed so well.

If Duff's ideas about the nature of Hinduism and its relationship with Christianity remained unchanged partly because of his essentially limited and confined experience of India, some other missionaries who did have a broader experience seem to have been unable to make anything of it. As we noted in chapter 5, William Ward, who had extensive and frequent contact with Kartabhajas appears to have had problems about what emphasis to place on them in his imagined system. Peter Percival, another exponent of the conventional view, also had difficulty in accommodating the evidence and material he acquired through a long-term and close association with a leading advocate of *Shaiva Siddhanta*. It almost appears as if, in these cases, the conventional and dominant paradigm had made such a deep impression that some commentators were reluctant to accept the clear results of their own experience. Instead of coming to terms with what they found and offering a new interpretation, they continued to defer to the more comfortable and conventional view of the one brahman-controlled unitary system.

There were, however, increasing numbers of vocal missionary critics of the dominant paradigm. Unlike the secular orientalist scholars who focused on brahmanical texts as a key to an understanding of India's ancient history, law and religious life, the missionaries as a body had always had broader interests, including a determination to understand the views and attitudes of Hindus at the grassroots level. As mission workers fanned out in greater numbers outside Bengal (and away from the hub and influence of secular oriental studies), settling and working in the more remote parts of India, they gained more extensive knowledge and experience of the extraordinary variety of Hindu religious ideas, traditions and practices. In this ever-extending and, for them, little-known environment they became increasingly dissatisfied with dominant and conventional views.

First, there was increasing contact with lower- and outcaste Hindus and an increasing recognition that these people, even in their religious life, were not merely puppets manipulated by those above, but people who had their own independent agenda. Especially important, for example, in Murray Mitchell's intellectual development was his visit to pilgrim centres in Maharastra, his amazement at the outpouring of devotional feeling and his increasing sense that *bhakti* rather than *Advaita* Vedanta or pantheism was, in these instances, the Hindus' vital and operative faith. Caldwell, Mateer, Campbell, Whitehead, to name a few, were all beginning to insist that there was little in common between brahmanism and lower-caste expressions of religious faith. These views were reinforced by the missionaries' increasing experience of work among the mass movement enquirers and converts drawn to Christianity from the lowest castes and classes in Hindu society.[2]

Second, alongside this trend, but in some ways bound up with it, was a growing recognition of the influence and importance of regional ideas

[2] Webster 1992.

and of the inadequacy of William Ward's model for the whole of India. Especially noteworthy was an increasing acknowledgement of the importance and comparative independence of south Indian traditions including the south Indian version of *Shaiva Siddhanta* which even then, in the late nineteenth century, was undergoing revival. Alongside the frank admission of socio-religious and regional religious diversity (views expounded by Sutton, Buyers, Mitchell, Long, Caldwell and many others) was dissatisfaction with the idea that pantheism represented the essence of Hinduism throughout the subcontinent. There was in fact increasing disagreement over what constituted the essential core of Hinduism, if it had a core; and also an inclination among some missionaries to dispute the idea that Hindu religion could be described as a unitary system. These developments, highlighting the essential diversity and complexity of Indian religious phenomena, were boosted by the growth of knowledge and insights into women's religious views and activity gained as a result of female missionary contact and visits to the Hindu home. Again the impression of diversity, reflected in the growth of specialized or local missionary studies, tended to coincide with the findings of the Indian census first introduced in 1871. Finding it impossible to define Hinduism, census commissioners resorted increasingly to the technique of describing it as the residue, after all other religions had been accounted for.

By the end of the century therefore there were a number of missionaries, Macdonald, Cobban and Pope among them, who argued that instead of the notion of the one Hinduism, there should be a concept of the many Hindu religions. In one sense the debate had come full circle—the idea of diversity, clearly apparent in Buchanan's early writing, finding confirmation at the end of the nineteenth century. And, as is clearly apparent from more recent publications this debate among what is now a wide range of secular scholars continues into the twenty-first century.

Among the factors which have been discussed and which might be said to constitute missionary 'experience' in India was the missionaries' encounter with pundits, as well as with the more ordinary people they met while on preaching tours throughout the countryside. The debate about the extent to which Western knowledge of India was entirely Western in its origin has been widely discussed in recent years. While it is now more generally accepted that Western knowledge included indigenous knowledge, the precise nature of this 'native' information and learning, as well as methods of transmission, is still a matter of some discussion. It has often been noted that brahmans were active in providing Company officials with information, for example brahmanical texts, arguments and views of the world. Indeed, it was almost certainly the brahmans' influence that was one of the key factors in convincing Europeans that brahmanism was Hinduism and that the brahmans were the key to the entire religious and social system. However, as noted in chapter 4, not all of the missionaries' pundits were drawn from the same brahman schools of learning. Nor were they always brahmans. Indeed, it is very likely that the growing disillusionment with the dominant brahmanical model was encouraged by the fact that missionaries did not always have brahman mentors and were exposed to a diversity of different views and interpretations.

Experience was not only a crucial factor in the growing recognition of diversity. At least as much as changing theologies and ideas in Europe, it was a powerful catalyst in the emergence of more sympathetic views of Hinduism. It is not true that greater knowledge or more extensive experience necessarily encouraged a greater sympathy for Hindu religion. The more Carey and Heber knew of Hinduism, for example, the more they disliked it. It may be argued that they still did not know enough, and that if they had known even more, then their desire to condemn the system may again have changed and their views again become more sympathetic. But while increasing knowledge was important in changing evaluation it was not the only factor which determined missionary views. Also important were missionary values and priorities in what they admired or disliked. Both Carey and Heber came to dislike Hinduism even more because they thought they discovered more about the extent of its cruelty and inhumanity. On the other hand Cobban, like Pope, was amazed as a result of his deeper knowledge of *Shaiva Siddhanta* to find that it tended to reflect many of those values he most admired.

But working in and through these later changes in missionary evaluation was a changing climate of opinion—a more positive general attitude to other religions apparent outside of India as well as at missionary conferences in India itself. These changes arising partly out of missionary experience and frustration in the field itself encouraged missionaries to discuss and explore the best as well as the worst in other traditions. The notion of natural religion, incorporating the idea of God's universal activity in human reason and conscience, long kept separate from the idea of Hinduism, and used to explain all that was good and true in Indian religious thought and activity, was, at least in some cases, gradually supplanted by a more generous attitude towards Hinduism itself. As in the case of Robson, Murray Mitchell and others whatever was seen as good and true in Hindu belief and practice was acknowledged, increasingly, as a part of Hinduism.

Finally, what was the overall effect of missionary and missionary society representations of Hinduism in the nineteenth century? First, there was the impact of Protestant missionary views and models of Hinduism on the Hindus themselves. This issue has already been explored in some detail in the author's recent contribution to a collection of papers edited by R. E. Frykenberg.[3] Briefly stated, the argument is that Hindu religion in the form of the one all-embracing unified brahman controlled system is not clearly apparent in the pre-modern period. Nevertheless, some Hindus were beginning to compare themselves with Islamic intruders in the sixteenth and seventeenth centuries and in some parts of India (especialy among the Marathas) a sense of being Hindu in a religious sense was beginning to modify some of the divisions apparent among the followers of different sects, cults and religious traditions. A growing consciousness of being Hindu in a religious sense was further encouraged by the activity of the Protestant missionaries—especially those who were active and preaching in India during the first half of the nineteenth century. As we have seen, they tended to assume that Hindus were incorporated into the one overarching religious system. A tendency to lump all Hindus of different persuasions together and to assume that they all belonged to the one system was, not infrequently, accompanied by generalized attacks on the views of Hindu people as a whole. This approach, including the use of abusive language, tended to unite different Hindus in common op-position to what they perceived as missionary insults. But even more important in creating a sense of unity especially among the higher and more educated classes was the threat of conversion. This was a process which was thought to be working especially through the mission schools and government collaboration with the missionary movement—a semi-secret partnership seen in the assault on sati and in the undermining of Hindu laws of inheritance. While many Hindus were feeling threatened at both the grassroots and higher levels their cause was taken up and championed by Hindu leaders who began to think of themselves as de-fending a broadly-based 'system' in opposition to Christianity. The term 'Hinduism', adopted by Rammohan Roy to describe 'the real religion' of India, was introduced increasingly into the discourse of Western-educated reformers and others who came to think of themselves as belonging to the one unified all-pervasive system. Ironically, however, this transition in Indian thinking was continuing to take place at the very time during the second half of the nineteenth century when, as we have shown, the

[3] Oddie 2003.

Protestant missionaries were developing increasing doubts about the validity of the unified model.

Second, there is the question of the impact of missionary depictions of Hinduism, together with the effect of missionary society periodical comment, on Europeans, especially in the West. Of considerable importance, for example, was the influence of mission society propaganda on the public in Britain, many of whom were church-goers. Enough has been said in chapter 7 to indicate the ever-increasing extent to which popular missionary periodicals were sold and/or distributed on a regular basis from the time of the first appearance of the *Missionary Register* through to the end of the nineteenth century. Apart from the sheer and increasing volume of this material, it is noteworthy (for the most part) for its repetitiveness, the closeness with which it adhered to the dominant model, and its demonizing of Hindu religion—a general negativity which, in contrast to what was happening on the mission field, appears to have been only slightly dented towards the end of the nineteenth century. Produced by editors, many of whom had not been exposed to the same influences or faced with the same challenges as missionaries in India, and who by the nature of their task spent more time in attempting to enlist the British publics' support of missions, it is not surprising that it maintained for even longer the sharp contrasts between the blessings of Christianity on the one hand and the piteous plight of Hindus in Hinduism on the other. It was also a literature which played perhaps the crucial role in creating popular impressions—stereotypical views of Hinduism which captured and remained lodged in the British imagination. Moreover, it was used and amplified in the well-known evangelical and missionary society campaigns against sati and the East India Company's continued connection with Hindu religious institutions. Campaigns in the periodical press detailing the horrors of Hinduism were supplemented by what was said at rallies and annual meetings, and even in parliamentary reports.

These popular campaigns and forms of representation might be taken as examples of 'orientalism' in what (according to David Smith) has now become its simple meaning—namely 'Western misunderstanding and mistreatment of the East'.[4] However, in this case, it was the editors as well as missionaries who were responsible for popular literature designed to arouse middle- and working-class people. Furthermore, these accounts, accessible to and read by ordinary people in Britain, need to be set alongside the more serious and scholarly missionary contributions to European

---

[4] Smith 2003: 89.

understandings of Hinduism. These accounts include books on the subject written by missionaries such as Robson, Murray Mitchell and Wilkins, all of whose writings were recommended in the article on Hinduism appearing in the *Cambridge Encyclopaedia* published in 1910. As noted in chapter 3, missionary publications in the nineteenth century also included scholarly articles on different aspects of Hinduism published in non-missionary journals such as the *Journal of the Bombay Asiatic Society*, the *Indian Antiquary* and the *Contemporary Review*, as well as highly original contributions in the *Indian Evangelical Review*. Indeed, what secular British and European scholars were attempting to do by way of spreading knowledge of brahmanical religion, was paralleled by what the British missionaries were attempting to do by disseminating further knowledge of popular Hindu beliefs and practice. In that particular respect their work was closer to that of modern anthropologists than it was to that of secular orientalists like Max Müller, Monier-Williams or John Muir, all of whom were working on ancient texts.

Select Bibliography

Archives and Manuscript Collections

Birmingham University Library
CMS Committee Minutes; Correspondence and Annual Reports of individual missionaries (B. Bailey, J. Vaughan, J. Long, etc.).
CEZMS CEZ/C/ AM5 (Candidates' Papers and Annual Reports, 1883–1900).
CEZ/C/ AMI (Register of Missionaries with particulars of service, Vol 1: Papers of individual missionaries and other papers).

British Library, London
India Office and Oriental Collection.
MSS. EUR. E. 93 (early text of Grant's *Observations*).

Cambridge University Library
SPCK archives. *Annual Reports (AR)* and incoming correspondence of missionaries connected with the India Mission, c.1740–1800.

Henry Martyn Institute, Cambridge
Correspondence preparatory to the World Missionary Conference, Edinburgh, 1910.

Indian Institute, Oxford
Max Müller papers (MS, Eng.C.2814).

NLS (National Library of Scotland), Edinburgh
FCS archives. Alexander Duff papers (MS7530) and J. Murray Mitchell papers and correspondence.

Regents Park College, Oxford
BMS archives. Carey's papers, diary and correspondence.

Rhodes House, Oxford
USPG archives. Proceedings, letters and reports of missionaries including R.Caldwell, P. Percival, J. F. Kearns, G. U. Pope, C. E. Kennet and H. Symonds.

Serampore College archives, West Bengal
William Ward's diary.

SOAS (School of Oriental and African Studies), London
Council for World Mission (CWM) archives. Home Personal, Candidates' Papers, Incoming correspondence and reports (J. Crisp, T. Hodson, P. Percival, W. H. Campbell, J. Kennedy, W. Drew, T. E. Slater, M. A. Sherring, W. J. Wilkins, M. Phillips, E. Greaves, J. Hewlett, etc.).

WMMS archives. Papers and correspondence of individual missionaries (E. Hoole, G. M. Cobban, P. Percival, T. Hodson, E. Crisp).

UTC (United Theological College) archives, Bangalore
CEZMS Madras Committee books.

Official Records

UK Parliamentary Papers, 1812–13, Vol. X, Paper No. 282; 1821, Vol. XVIII (Commons) and
    1851, Vol. XLI, Session Paper No. 176.
Census of India, Reports, 1871–1901.

Conference Reports

Proceedings of a General Conference of Bengal Protestant Missionaries held in Calcutta, Sept.
    4–7 1855. 1855. Calcutta: Baptist Mission Press.
Proceedings of the South India Missionary Conference Held at Ootacamund, 19 April–5 May
    1858. 1858. Vepery: SPCK.
Report of the Punjab Missionary Conference held at Lahore, December to January, 1862–1863.
    1863. Lodiana: American Presbyterian Mission Press.
Report of the General Missionary Conference held at Allahabad, 1872–73. 1873. London:
    Seeley, Jackson and Halliday.
Report of the Second Decennial Missionary Conference held at Calcutta, 1882–83. 1883.
    Calcutta: Baptist Mission Press.
Report of the Centenary Conference on the Protestant Missions of the World. 1888. London:
    James Nisbet and Co.
Report of the Third Decennial Missionary Conference held at Bombay, 1892–93. 2 vols. 1893.
    Byculla: Education Society.
Report of the Fourth Decennial Indian Missionary Conference, held in Madras, 1–18 December
    1902. n.d. London and Madras: Christian Literature Society.

Other Printed Sources

An Account of the Origins and Designs of the Society for Promoting Christian Knowledge. 1734.
    London: SPCK.
Bliss, E. M., ed. 1891. The Encyclopaedia of Missions. New York, London and Toronto: Funk
    and Wagnalls.
Church Missionary Society. n.d. Register of Missionaries (Clerical, Lay and Female), and
    Native Clergy from 1804 to 1904. Printed for private circulation.
Deacon's Newspaper Handbook and Advertisers Guide. 1881. London.
Foreign Missions of the Free Church of Scotland, No. 1, 'India: A Field for Missionary Effort'.
    n.d. Edinburgh: n.p.
Johnson, S. 1834. A Dictionary of the English Language. London: Westley and Davis.
Newcomb, Harvey. 1854. Cyclopaedia of Missions; Containing a Comprehensive View of
    Missionary Operations throughout the World. New York: Scribner.

Periodicals and Newspapers

Baptist Annual Register
Baptist Magazine
Calcutta Christian Advocate
Calcutta Christian Observer
Church Missionary Gleaner
Church Missionary Intelligencer
Church Missionary Record
Church Missionary Society Juvenile Instructor
Church Missionary Society Missionary Papers
Church Missionary Society Quarterly Papers
Contemporary Review
Edinburgh Review
Free Church of Scotland Quarterly Missionary Papers
Friend of India
Harvest Field
Home and Foreign Record of the Free Church of Scotland
Indian Antiquary
Indian Church History Review
Indian Evangelical Review
Indian Female Evangelist
India's Women and China's Daughters
Juvenile Missionary Magazine
Juvenile Offering
Madras Christian College Magazine
Madras Journal of Literature and Science
Mission Field
Missionary Magazine and Chronicle
Missionary Notices
Missionary Papers
Missionary Register
Missionary Sketches
Occasional Papers from St Augustine's College
Papers Relating to Wesleyan Missions
Periodical Accounts relative to the Baptist Missionary Society
Quarterly Chronicle of the LMS
United Presbyterian Missionary Record
Wesleyan Missionary Society Missionary Notices

Books, Articles and Theses

Abbs, John. 1870. *Twenty-two Years' Missionary Experience in Travancore*. London: J. Snow and Co.

Adam, Robert. 1818. *The Religious World Displayed; or a View of the Four Grand Systems of Religion, Judaism, Paganism, Christianity and Mohammedanism*. Philadelphia: Moses Thomas.

Ali, Muhammad Mohar. 1965. *The Bengali Reaction to Christian Missionary Activities, 1833–1857*. Chittagong: Mehrub Publications.

Allnutt, M. R. 1911. *A Record of Sixty-nine Years' Ministry: Memoirs of Richard Lea Allnutt*. London: SPCK.

Altick, Richard. 1957. *The English Common Reader: A Social History of the Mass Reading Public, 1800–1900*. Chicago: University of Chicago Press.

Arooran, K. Nambi. 1980. *Tamil Renaissance and Dravidian Nationalism, 1905–1944*. Madurai: Koodal Publishers.

Arthur, William. 1902. *A Mission to the Mysore with Scenes and Facts Illustrative of India, its People, and its Religion*. London: Charles H. Kelly.

Ashcroft, Frank. 1909. *Story of Our Rajputana Mission*. Edinburgh: Oliphant, Anderson and Ferrier.

Ballhatchet, K. A. 1961. 'Some Aspects of Historical Writing on India by Protestant Christian Missionaries during the Nineteenth and Twentieth Centuries', in C. H. Philips, ed., *Historians of India, Pakistan and Ceylon*. London: Oxford University Press.

Bannerjea, K. M. 1851. *Lectures to Educated Young Men*.

Barnes, Irene H. 1897. *Behind the Pardah*. London: Marshall Brothers.

———. 1906. *In Salisbury Square*. London: CMS.

Barrow, Ian J. 2003. 'From Hindustan to India: Naming Change in Changing Names', *South Asia* n.s. XXVI (1).

Bayly, C. A. 1996. *Empire and Information. Intelligence Gathering and Social Communication in India, 1780–1870*. Cambridge: Cambridge University Press.

Bayly, Susan. 1999. *Caste, Society and Politics in India from the Eighteenth Century to the Modern Age*. The New Cambridge History of India, Vol. IV (3). Cambridge: Cambridge University Press.

Bearce, George D. 1961. *British Attitudes Towards India, 1784–1858*. London: Oxford University Press.

Bebbington, D. W. 1989. *Evangelicalism in Modern Britain. A History from the 1730s to the 1980s*. London and New York: Routledge.

Bernier, Francois. 1916. *Travels in the Mughal Empire, AD 1656–1688*. Translated on the basis of Irving Block's version and annotated by Archibald Constable. 2nd ed. London and Edinburgh: Oxford University Press.

Bickers, Robert A., and Rosemary Seton, eds. 1996. *Missionary Sources and Issues*. London: Curzon.

Biller, P. 1985. 'Words and the Medieval Notion of "Religion"', *Journal of Ecclesiastical History* 36.

Bose, N. S. 1960. *The Indian Awakening and Bengal*. Calcutta: Firma K. L. Mukhopadhyay.

Bowie, Fiona, Deborah Kirkwood and Shirley Ardener, eds. 1993. *Women and Missions: Past and Present. Anthropological and Historical Perceptions*. Providence and Oxford: Berg.

Boyce, W. B. 1872. *The Missionary World*. New York: A. D. F. Randolph.

Bradbury, James. 1884. *India, Its Condition, Religion and Missions*. London: John Snow.

Brekke, Torkel. 1999. 'The Conceptual Foundation of Missionary Hinduism', *Journal of Religious History* 23 (2).

Brewster, David, ed. 1830 [1810]. *The Edinburgh Encyclopaedia*. 3rd ed. Edinburgh: Balfour, Kirkwood and Co.

Brown, Raymond. 1986. *The English Baptists of the Eighteenth Century*. London: Baptist Historical Society.

Brunner, Daniel L. 1988. *Halle Pietists in England: Anthony William Boehm and the Society for Promoting Christian Knowledge*. Gottingen: Vandenhoeck and Ruprecht.

Buchanan, Claudius. 1805. *Memoir of the Expediency of an Ecclesiastical Establishment for British India*. Repr. in Allan K. Davidson (1990), *Evangelicals and Attitudes to India, 1786–1813*. Abingdon: Sutton Courtenay Press.

———. 1811. *Christian Researches in Asia with Notices of the Translation of the Scriptures into the Oriental Languages*. 2nd ed. London: Cadell and Davies.

———. 1814. *An Apology for Promoting Christianity in India*. London: Cadell and Davies.

Buckland, C. E. 1971 [1906]. *Dictionary of Indian Biography*. Varanasi and Delhi: Indological Book House.

Buyers, William. 1840. *Letters on India with Special Reference to the Spread of Christianity*. London: John Snow.

———. 1842. *Travels in India*. London: Blackwood.

Caldwell, Robert. 1840. *The Tinnevelly Shanars: A Sketch*. Madras: SPCK.

———. 1856. *A Comparative Grammar of the Dravidian or South Indian Family of Languages*. London: Harrison.

———. 1874. *The Relation of Christianity to Hinduism*. Repr. of a paper given at the Church Congress, Brighton, October 1874. London: R. Clay, Sons and Taylor.

———. 1879. *Christianity and Hinduism. A Lecture Addressed to Educated Hindus in Four Parts*. London: SPCK.

———. 1982 [1881]. *A History of Tinnevelly*. New Delhi: Asian Educational Services. First published in 1881 as *A Political and General History of the District of Tinnevelly, in the Presidency of Madras, from the Earliest Period to its Cession to the English Government in AD 1801*. Madras: Printed by E. Keys.

Campbell, William. 1839. *British India in Its Relation to the Decline of Hindooism*. London: John Snow.

Cannon, Garland, ed. 1970. *The Letters of Sir William Jones*. 2 vols. Oxford: Clarendon Press.

Carey, Eustace. 1836. *Memoir of William Carey, D.D.* London: Jackson and Walford.

Carey, S. P. 1926. *William Carey, D.D., Fellow of Linnaean Society*. London: Hodder and Stoughton.

Carey, W. 1934 [1792]. *An Enquiry into the Obligations of Christians to use Means for the Conversion of the Heathens*. Leicester: BMS.

Carmichael, Amy. 1903. *Things as They Are: Mission Work in Southern India*. London: Morgan and Scott.

Carson, P. 1988. 'Soldiers of Christ: Evangelicals and India, 1784–1833'. Ph.D. diss., University of London.

Chadwick, Owen. 1970. *The Victorian Church*. London: Adam and Charles Black.

Chakrabarty, Ramakanta. 1985. *Vaisnavism in Bengal, 1486–1900*. Calcutta: Shyamapada.

Chattopadhyay, Goutam, ed. 1965. *Awakening in Bengal in Early Nineteenth Century*, Vol. 1. Calcutta: Progressive Publishers.

Cheriyan, P. 1935. *The Malabar Syrians and the Church Missionary Society 1816–1840.* Kottayam: CMS.

Christopher, A. M. W., ed. 1854. *Memoir of the Rev. John James Weitbrecht by his Widow.* 2nd ed. London: James Nisbet.

Clarke, W. K. Lowther. 1959. *A History of the SPCK.* London: SPCK.

Clothey, Fred. W., ed. 1982. *Images of Man: Religion and Historical Process in South Asia.* Madras: New Era Publications.

Cohn, Bernard S. 1971. *India: The Social Anthropology of a Civilization.* New Jersey: Prentice-Hall.

————. 1990. *An Anthropologist among the Historians and Other Essays.* Delhi: Oxford University Press.

Conlon, Frank F. 1992. 'The Polemic Process in Nineteenth Century Maharashtra: Vishnubawa Brahmachari and Hindu Revival', in Kenneth W. Jones, ed., *Religious Controversies in British India: Dialogues in South Asian Languages.* New York: State University of New York Press.

Cope, Captain. 1754. *A New History of the East Indies with Brief Observations on the Religion, Customs, Manners and Trade of the Inhabitants.* London: M. Cooper, W. Reeve and C. Sympson.

Copley, Anthony. 1997. *Religions in Conflict: Ideology, Cultural Contact and Conversion in Late Colonial India.* Delhi: Oxford University Press.

Cowell, E. B., ed. 1873. *Miscellaneous Essays by H. T. Colebrooke.* 3 vols. London: Trubner and Co.

Cox, Jeffrey. 2000. *Imperial Fault Lines: Christianity and Colonial Power in India, 1818–1914.* Stanford: Stanford University Press.

Cracknell, Kenneth. 1995. *Justice, Courtesy and Love: Theologians and Missionaries Encountering World Religions, 1846–1914.* London: Epworth Press.

Craufurd, Quintin. 1792. *Sketches Chiefly Relating to the History, Religion, Learning, and Manners of the Hindoos.* 2 vols. London: Cadell.

Crooke, William. 1894. *An Introduction to the Popular Religion and Folk-lore of Northern India.* Allahabad: Government Press.

————. ed. 1968 [1903]. *Hobson-Jobson.* Delhi: Munshiram Manoharlal.

Daniel, J. T. K., and R. E. Hedlund, eds. 1993. *Carey's Obligation and India's Renaissance.* West Bengal: Serampore College.

Das, S. K. 1978. *Sahibs and Munshis: An Account of the College of Fort William.* Calcutta: Orion.

Davidson, Allan K. 1990. *Evangelicals and Attitudes to India, 1786–1813.* Abingdon: Sutton Courtenay Press.

Della Valle, Pietro. 1892. *The Travels of Pietro Della Valle in India.* London: Hakluyt Society.

Dennis, J. J. 1897–99. *Christian Missions and Social Progress: A Sociological Study of Foreign Missions.* 3 vols. Edinburgh and London: Oliphant, Anderson and Ferrier.

Devasenapathi, V. A. 1974. *Saiva Siddhantha.* Madras: University of Madras.

Dodwell, H. H., ed. 1958. *Cambridge History of India,* Vol. VI. Delhi: S. Chand and Co.

Dubois, J. A. 1897 [1806]. *Hindu Manners, Customs and Ceremonies.* 3rd ed. Edited and annotated by Henry K Beauchamp. Oxford: Clarendon Press.

————. 1977 [1823]. *Letters on the State of Christianity in India.* Edited by Sharda Paul. New Delhi: Associated Publishing House.

Duff, Alexander. 1839. *Female Education in India, being the Substance of an Address Delivered at the First Annual Meeting of the Scottish Ladies' Association, in Connection with the*

Church of Scotland, for the Promotion of Female Education in India. Edinburgh: John Johnstone.

Duff, Alexander. 1840. *India, and India Missions*. Edinburgh: John Johnstone.

Eliade, Mircea, ed. 1987. *The Encyclopaedia of Religion*. New York: Macmillan; London: Collier Macmillan.

Embree, Ainslie Thomas. 1962. *Charles Grant and British Rule in India*. London: Allen and Unwin.

Farquhar, J. N. 1967. *Modern Religious Movements in India*. Delhi: Munshiram Manoharlal.

Findlay, G. G., and W. W. Holdsworth. 1922. *The History of the Wesleyan Methodist Missionary Society*. London: J. A. Sharp.

Forbes, Geraldine H. 1986. 'In Search of the "Pure Heathen": Missionary Women in Nineteenth Century India', *Economic and Political Weekly* XXI (17); *Review of Women's Studies* 26 April.

Foster, William, ed. 1968. *Early Travels in India, 1583–1619*. Delhi: S. Chand and Co.

Fryer, John. 1909. *A New Account of East India and Persia, being Nine Year's Travels, 1672–1681*. London: Hakluyt Society.

Frykenberg, R. E. 1981. 'On Roads and Riots in Tinnevelly: Radical Change and Ideology in Madras Presidency During the 19th Century', *South Asia* n.s. 4 (2).

──────. 1993. 'Constructions of Hinduism in the Nexus of History and Religion', *Journal of Interdisciplinary History* 23 (3).

Gardella, Peter. 1985. *Innocent Ecstasy: How Christianity Gave America an Ethic of Sexual Pleasure*. New York: Oxford University Press.

Gladstone, J. W. 1984. *Protestant Christianity and People's Movements in Kerala, 1850–1936*. Trivandrum: Seminary Publications.

Gore, Nehemiah. 1862. *A Rational Refutation of the Hindu Philosophical Systems*. Calcutta: Bishops College Press.

Grafe, Hugald. 1972. 'Hindu Apologetics at the Beginning of the Protestant Mission Era in India', *Indian Church History Review* VI (1).

──────. 1990. *Tamilnadu in the Nineteenth and Twentieth Centuries. History of Christianity in India*, Vol. IV (2). Bangalore: Church History Association of India.

Grant, Charles. 1792. *Observations on the State of Society among the Asiatic Subjects of Great Britain*. Released as Paper 282 in *Parliamentary Papers*, Commons, Vol. 10, 1812–13.

Grose, J. H. 1772 [1757]. *A Voyage to the East Indies*. 3rd ed. London: S. Hooper.

Halbfass, Wilhelm. 1988. *India and Europe: An Essay in Understanding*. Albany: State University of New York Press.

Hamilton, Alexander. 1727. 'A New Account of the East Indies', in J. A. Pinkerton, ed. (1808), *A General Collection of the Best and Most Interesting Voyages and Travels, etc.*, Vol. 8. Edinburgh: n.p.

Hardgrave, Robert L. 1998. 'The Representation of Sati: Four Eighteenth-century Etchings by Baltazard Solvyns', *Bengal Past and Present* 117 (1).

Harper, Susan Billington. 2000. *In the Shadow of the Mahatma: Bishop V. S. Azariah and the Travails of Christianity in British India*. Grand Rapids and Cambridge: W. B. Erdmans; Richmond: Curzon.

Harrison, P. 1999. *'Religion' and the Religions in the English Enlightenment*. Cambridge: Cambridge University Press.

Hartle, Susan E. 1978. 'Work among the Educated Classes of Nineteenth Century India— The Thought and Work of Thomas Ebenezer Slater'. M.Litt. thesis, Lancaster University.

Hatcher, Brian A. 1990. 'Eternal Punishment and Christian Missions: The Response of the Church Missionary Society to Broad Church Theology', *Anglican Theological Review* LXXII.

————. 1996. *Idioms of Improvement. Vidyasagar and Cultural Encounter in Bengal.* Calcutta: Exford University Press.

Hawley, John Stratton. 1991. 'Naming Hinduism', *The Wilson Quarterly* 15.

Heber, Amelia. 1830. *The Life of Reginald Heber, D.D.* 2 vols. London: John Murray.

Heber, Reginald. 1828. *Narrative of a Journey through the Upper Provinces of India.* 3 vols. London: John Murray.

————. 1829. *Sermons Preached in England.* London: John Murray.

Hedges, Paul. 2001. *Preparation and Fulfilment. A History and Study of Fulfilment Theology in Modern British Thought in the Indian Context.* Berlin: P. Lang.

Hodges, William. 1793. *Travels in India during the Years 1780, 1781, 1782 & 1783.* London: n.p.

Hole, Charles. 1896. *The Early History of the Church Missionary Society for Africa and the East.* London: CMS.

Hoole, Elijah. 1844. *Madras, Mysore and the South of India.* 2nd ed. London: Longman, Brown and Green.

Hough, J. 1839. *The History of Christianity in India.* London: Seeley and Burnside.

Houghton, Frank. 1953. *Amy Carmichael of Dohnavur.* London: SPCK.

Hudson, D. Dennis. 2000. *Protestant Origins in India: Tamil Evangelical Christians, 1706–1835.* Grand Rapids and Cambridge: William B. Erdmans; Richmond: Curzon.

Inden, Ronald. 1990. *Imagining India.* Cambridge, MA, and Oxford: Blackwell.

Ingham, K. 1956. *Reformers in India:1793–1833.* Cambridge: Cambridge University Press.

Ives, Edward. 1773. *A Voyage from England to India in the Year 1754.* London: Printed by J. Edewards.

Jagadeesan, N. 1977. *History of Sri Vaishnavism in the Tamil Country (Post-Ramanuja).* Madurai: Koodal Publishers.

James, Louis, ed. 1976. *Print and People, 1819–1851.* London: Allen Lane.

James, W. R. 1888. 'Idolatry: What is It and Why is It Condemned', *Indian Evangelical Review* XV (58).

Jones, Kenneth W. 1989. *Socio-religious Reform Movements in British India.* Cambridge: Cambridge University Press.

Kaye, J. W. 1859. *Christianity in India.* London: Smith, Elder.

Kearns, J. F. 1868. *Kalyan'A Shat'Anku, or the Marriage Ceremonies of the Hindus of South India together with a Description of Karumantharum or Funeral Ceremonies.* Madras: Higginbotham.

Kejariwal, O. P. 1988. *The Asiatic Society of Bengal and the Discovery of India's Past, 1784–1838.* Delhi: Oxford University Press.

Kennedy, James. 1874. *Christianity and the Religions of India.* Mirzapore: Orphan School Press.

————. 1884. *Life and Work in Benares and Kumaon, 1839–1877.* London: T. Fisher Unwin.

Killingley, Dermot. 1993. *Rammohan Roy in Hindu and Christian Tradition.* Newcastle-upon-Tyne: Brill.

King, R. 1999. *Orientalism and Religion: Postcolonial Theory, India and the Mystic East.* London and New York: Routledge.

Kopf, David. 1969. *British Orientalism and the Bengal Renaissance: The Dynamics of Indian Modernization, 1773–1835.* Berkeley and Los Angeles: University of California Press.

Lach, Donald F. 1968. *India in the Eyes of Europe: The Sixteenth Century.* Chicago and London: University of Chicago Press.

Laird, M. A., ed. 1971. *Bishop Heber in Northern India: Selections from His Journal.* Cambridge: Cambridge University Press.

————. 1972. *Missionaries and Education in Bengal, 1793–1837.* Oxford: Clarendon Press.

Latham, S. F. n.d. *Memoirs of Zenana Mission Life.* London: CEZMS.

Leslie, Mary E. 1868. *The Dawn of Light: A Story of the Zenana Mission.* London: John Snow and Co.

Lewis, James. 1923. *William Goudie.* London: WMMS.

van Linschoten, John Huyghen [Jan Huygen van Linschoten]. 1884–85 [1598]. *The Voyage of John Huyghen van Linschoten to the East Indies. From the Old English Translation of 1598. The First Book, Containing his Description of the East.* 2 vols. Edited by Arthur Coke Burnell (First Vol.) and P. A. Tiele (Second Vol.). London: Hakluyt Society.

Lockman, J. 1743. *Travels of the Jesuits, into Various Parts of the World.* 2 vols. London: J. Noon.

Long, J. 1848. *Handbook of Bengal Missions in Connection with the Church of England.* London: J. F. Shaw.

Lovett, Richard. 1899. *The History of the London Missionary Society, 1795–1895.* 2 vols. London: Henry Frowde.

Lunt, James, ed. 1970. *From Sepoy to Subedar.* London: Routledge and Kegan Paul.

Macdonald, Kenneth S. 1890. *Is Hinduism a Religion?* Calcutta: Santal Mission Press.

————. 1902. 'Religious Movements amongst Hindus in Bengal during the Decade 1891–1901', in *Report of the Fourth Decennial Missionary Conference,* Madras, 1–18 December 1902.

Macphail, James. 1905. *M. Kenneth S.Macdonald, M.A., D.D., Missionary of the Free Church of Scotland, Calcutta.* Edinburgh and London: Oliphant and Co.

Majeed, Javed. 1992. *Ungoverned Imaginings: James Mill's* The History of British India *and Orientalism.* Oxford and New York: Clarendon Press and Oxford University Press.

Major, Andrea. 2004. '"Pious flames": European Encounters with Sati before 1805', *South Asia* n.s. XXVII (2).

Mani, Lati. 1998. *Contentious Traditions: The Debate on Sati in Colonial India.* Berkeley, Los Angeles and London: University of California Press.

Marshall, P. J., ed. 1970. *The British Discovery of Hinduism in the Eighteenth Century.* Cambridge: Cambridge University Press.

Marshman, John Clark. 1859. *The Life and Times of Carey, Marshman and Ward.* London: Longman and Co.

Mateer, Samuel. 1871. *The Land of Charity: A Descriptive Account of Travancore and Its People.* London: John Snow.

————. 1883. *Native Life in Travancore.* London: W. H. Allen and Co.

————. 1886. *The Gospel in South India.* London: The Religious Tract Society.

Maurice, Thomas. 1820. *The History of Hindostan.* 2 vols. London: W. Bulmer and W. Nicol.

Maxwell, Ian Douglas. 1995. 'Alexander Duff and the Theological and Philosophical Background to the General Assembly's Mission to Calcutta to 1840'. Ph.D. diss., University of Edinburgh.

Mill, James. 1826. *The History of British India.* 3rd ed. 6 vols. London: Baldwin, Cradock and Joy.

Mitchell, J. Murray. 1861. *Letters to Indian Youth on the Evidences of the Christian Religion*. Madras: CVES.

———. 1882a. 'Tukaram', *Indian Antiquary*, March 1882: 57–66.

———. 1882b. 'Pandharpur', *Indian Antiquary*, June 1882: 149–56.

———. 1885. *Hinduism Past and Present*. London: The Religious Tract Society. Repr. 1989 (New Delhi: Asian Educational Services).

———. 1894. *Letters to Indian Youth*. 11th ed. Madras: SPCK.

———. 1897. *Hinduism Past and Present*. Rev. ed. London: The Religious Tract Society.

———. 1899. *In Western India: Recollections of My Early Missionary Life*. Edinburgh: David Douglas.

Mitter, Partha. 1977. *Much Maligned Monsters: A History of European Reactions to Indian Art*. Chicago and London: University of Chicago Press.

Monier-Williams, M. 1874. *Religious Thought and Life in India*. London: John Murray.

———. 1875. *Indian Wisdom, or Examples of the Religious, Philosophical, and Ethical Doctrines of the Hindus*. London: W. H. Allen and Unwin.

———. 1877. *Hinduism*. London: SPCK.

———. 1878. *Modern India and the Indians*. 2nd ed. London: Trubner and Co.

———. 1883. *Religious Thought and Life in India*. London: John Murray.

———. 1887. *Address at the Anniversary Meeting of the CMS, Exeter Hall, 3 May 1887*.

Moor, Edward. 1810. *The Hindoo Pantheon*. London: Johnson.

Morawiecki, Jennifer. 1998. 'The Peculiar Mission of Christian Womanhood': The Selection and Preparation of Women Missionaries of the Church of England Zenana Missionary Society, 1880–1920'. D.Phil. diss., University of Sussex.

Morris, Henry. 1904. *The Life of Charles Grant, Sometime Member of Parliament for Inverness-Shire and Director of the East India Company*. London: John Murray.

Morrison, John. 1906. *New Ideas in India during the Nineteenth Century*. Edinburgh: George A. Morton.

Mukherjee, S. N. 1987. *Sir William Jones: A Study in Eighteenth-century British Attitudes to India*. 2nd ed. Bombay: Orient Longman.

Mullens, J. 1852. *Vedantism, Brahmanism, and Christianity Examined and Compared*. Calcutta: Calcutta Christian Tract and Book Society.

———. 1862. *The Religious Aspects of Hindu Philosophy Stated and Discussed*. London: Smith Elder and Co.

———. 1869. *London and Calcutta, Compared in their Heathenism, their Privileges and their Prospects*. London: James Nisbet and Co.

Müller, F. Max. 1868. *Essays in the Science of Religion*. 2nd. ed. London: n.p.

———. 1873. *Introduction to the Science of Religion*. London: Longmans, Green and Co.

Mundy, George. 1834. *Christianity and Hindooism Contrasted; or, a Comparative View of the Evidence by which the Respective Claims to Divine Authority of the Bible and the Hindoo Shastrus are Supported*. 2nd. ed. 2 vols. Serampore: Mission Press.

Murdoch, John. 1895. *Sacred Books of the East Described and Examined*. Madras: Christian Literature Society.

Nemer, Lawrence. 1981. *Anglican and Roman Catholic Attitudes on Missions: An Historical Study of Two English Missionary Societies in the Late Nineteenth Century (1865–1885)*. St Augustin: Steyler.

Noble, John. 1867. *A Memoir of the Rev. Robert Thurlington Noble, B.A.* London: Seeley, Jackson and Halliday.

Oberoi, Harjot. 1994. *The Construction of Religious Boundaries: Culture, Identity and Diversity in the Sikh Tradition*. Delhi: Oxford University Press.

O'Connell, Joseph T. 1993. 'The Word "Hindu" in Gaudiya Vaishnava Texts', *Journal of the American Oriental Society* 93 (3).

O'Connor, Daniel and Others. 2000. *Three Centuries of Mission: The United Society for the Propagation of the Gospel, 1701–2000*. London and New York: Continuum.

Oddie, Geoffrey A. 1974. 'India and Missionary Motives, c.1850–1900', *Journal of Ecclesiastical History* XXV (1).

————. 1976. *Social Protest in India. British Protestant Missionaries and Social Reforms, 1850–1900*. Delhi: Manohar.

————. 1982. 'Anti-missionary Feeling and Hindu Revivalism in Madras: The Hindu Preaching and Tract Societies, c.1886–1891', in Fred W. Clothey, ed., *Images of Man: Religion and Historical Process in South Asia*. Madras: New Era Publications.

————. 1991. *Hindu and Christian in South-East India. Aspects of Religious Continuity and Change, 1800–1900*. London: Curzon Press.

————. 1994. '"Orientalism" and British Protestant Missionary Constructions of India in the Nineteenth Century', *South Asia* n.s. XVII (2).

————. 1995. *Popular Religion, Elites and Reform: Hook-swinging and its Prohibition in Colonial India, 1800–1894*. Delhi: Manohar.

————. 1997. 'Old Wine in New Bottles? Kartabhaja (Vaishnava) Converts to Evangelical Christianity in Bengal, 1800–1845', in idem., ed., *Religious Conversion Movements in South Asia. Continuities and Change, 1800–1900*. London: Curzon Press.

————. 1999. *Missionaries, Rebellion and Proto-Nationalism: James Long in Bengal 1814–87*. Richmond: Curzon Press.

————. 2003. 'Constructing "Hinduism": the Impact of the Protestant Missionary Movement on Hindu Self-Understanding', in R. E. Frykenberg, ed., *Christians and Missionaries in India: Cross Cultural Communication since 1500*. Cambridge: Erdmans; London: RoutledgeCurzon.

Ovington, John. 1929. *A Voyage to Surat in the Year 1689*. Edited by H. G. Rawlinson. London: Oxford University Press.

Padfield, J. E. 1908 [1896]. *The Hindu at Home, being Sketches of Hindu Daily Life*. Madras: SPCK.

Pascoe, C. F. 1901. *Two Hundred Years of the SPG*. London: SPG.

Pearson, Hugh. 1819. *Memoirs of the Life and Writings of the Rev. Claudius Buchanan, D.D.* 2 vols. London: Cadell and Davies.

Percival, Peter. 1854. *The Land of the Veda: India Briefly Described*. London: George Bell.

Pettitt, George. 1851. *The Tinnevelly Mission of the Church Missionary Society*. London: Selleys.

Philipps, J. Thomas. 1717. *An Account of the Religion, Manners, and Learning of the People of Malabar in the East Indies*. London: W. Mears and J. Brown.

————, trans. 1719. *Thirty Four Conferences between the Danish Missionaries and the Malabarian Brahmans...together with some Letters Written by the Heathens to the said Missionaries*. London: H. Clements.

Philips, C. H. 1961. 'James Mill, Mountstuart Elphinstone, and the History of India', in C. H. Philips, ed., *Historians of India, Pakistan and Ceylon*. London: Oxford University Press.

Piggin, Stuart. 1984. *Making Evangelical Missionaries, 1789–1858*. Abingdon: Sutton Courtenay Press.

Piggin, Stuart and John Roxborogh. 1985. *The St. Andrews Seven: The Finest Flowering of Missionary Zeal in Scottish History*. Edinburgh and Carlisle, PA: Banner of Truth Trust.

Pitman, Emma Raymond. 1881. *Indian Zenana Missions*. n.p.: Outline Missionary Series.

Pope, G. U. 1900. *The Tiruvacagam or 'Sacred Utterances' of the Tamil Poet, Saint and Sage Manikka-Vacagar*. Oxford: Clarendon Press.

Porter, Andrew. 2004. *Religion versus Empire? British Protestant Missionaries and Overseas Expansion, 1700–1914*. Manchester and New York: Manchester University Press.

Porter, R. 1982. 'Mixed Feelings: The Enlightenment and Sexuality in Eighteenth-century Britain', in Paul-Gabriel Bouce, ed., *Sexuality in Eighteenth-century Britain*. Manchester: Manchester University Press.

————. 1990. *The Enlightenment*. London: Macmillan.

Potts, E. Daniel. 1967. *British Baptist Missionaries in India, 1793–1837: The History of Serampore and Its Missions*. Cambridge: Cambridge University Press.

————. 1993. 'William Ward: The Making of a Missionary in the 18th Century', in *Bicentenary Volume: William Carey's Arrival in India, 1793–1993. Serampore College, 1818–1993*. West Bengal: Serampore College.

Prasad, Ram Chandra. 1965. *Early English Travellers in India*. Delhi: Motilal Banarsi Dass.

Prochaska, Frank. 1980. *Women and Philanthropy in Nineteenth-Century England*. Oxford: Clarendon Press.

Quinlan, M. J. 1941. *Victorian Prelude*. New York: Columbia University Press.

Reuben, L. Gabriel. 2002. 'Dr William Miller—A Historical Study of His Thought and Work', *Indian Church History Review* XXXVI (2).

Rice, Henry. 1889. *Native Life in South India, being Sketches of the Social and Religious Characteristics of the Hindus*. London: The Religious Tract Society.

Richardson, A. 1950. *A Theological Word Book of the Bible*. London: SCM Press.

Richter, J. 1901. *A History of Missions in India*. Trans. Sydney H. Moore. Edinburgh and London: Oliphant, Anderson and Ferrier.

Robson, John. 1867. *Hinduism: Its Philosophy and Popular Worship*. Glasgow: David Robertson.

————. 1885. *Outlines of Protestant Missions*. Bible Class Primers, ed. D.D. Salmond. Edinburgh: n.p.

————. 1893 [1874]. *Hinduism and Its Relations to Christianity*. Edinburgh and London: Oliphant, Anderson and Ferrier.

Rocher, Rosane. 1994. 'British Orientalism in the Eighteenth Century: The Dialectics of Knowledge and Government', in Carol A. Breckenridge and Peter van der Veer, eds, *Orientalism and the Postcolonial Predicament: Perspectives on South Asia*. Delhi: Oxford University Press.

Schwab, Raymond. 1984. *The Oriental Renaissance: Europe's Rediscovery of India and the East, 1680–1880*. Trans. Gene Patterson-Black and Victor Reinking. New York: Columbia University Press.

Scott, David. 1951. *The Correspondence of David Scott, Director and Chairman of the East India Company, Relating to Indian Affairs, 1787–1805*. Edited by C. H. Philips. London: Officers of the Royal Historical Society.

Semple, Rhonda Anne. 2003. *Missionary Women: Gender, Professionalism and the Victorian Idea of Christian Mission*. Woodbridge and New York: Boydell Press.

Sencourt, Robert. 1923. *India in English Literature*. London: Simpkin, Marshall, Hamilton, Kent and Co. Ltd.

Sharpe, E. J. 1965. *Not to Destroy but to Fulfil: The Contribution of J. N. Farquhar to Protestant Missionary Thought in India before 1914*. Uppsala: Gleerup.

Sherring, M. A. 1868. *The Sacred City of the Hindus: An Account of Benaras*. London: Trubner and Co.

————. 1878. *The Hindoo Pilgrims*. London: Trubner and Co.

————. 1879. *The Missionary Life and Labours of the Rev. William Smith*. Benares: Medical Hall Press.

Sibree, James. 1923. *Register of Missionaries, Deputations etc, from 1796 to 1923*. 4th ed. London: LMS.

Singh, Brijraj. 1999. *The First Protestant Missionary to India: Bartholomaeus Ziegenbalg, 1683–1719*. Delhi and Oxford: Oxford University Press.

Slater, T. E. 1882. *Philosophy of Missions: A Present-day Plea*. London: J. Clarke and Co.

————. 1906. *The Higher Hinduism in Relation to Christianity. Certain Aspects of Hindu Thought from the Christian Standpoint*. London: Elliott Stock.

Small, Annie. 1890. *Light and Shade in Zenana Missionary Life*. London: J. and R. Parlane.

Smith, D. E. 1963. *India as a Secular State*. Princeton: Princeton University Press.

Smith, David. 2003. *Hinduism and Modernity*. Malden and Oxford: Blackwell.

Smith, George. 1879. *The Life of Alexander Duff, D.D., LL.D.* 2 vols. London: Hodder and Stoughton.

————. 1885. *The Life of William Carey: Shoe-Maker & Missionary*. London: Everyman's Library.

Smith, Jonathan Z. 1998. 'Religion, Religions, Religious', in M. C. Taylor, ed., *Critical Terms for Religious Studies*. Chicago: University of Chicago Press.

Smith, Wilfred Cantwell. 1981. 'The Crystalization of Religious Communities in Mughal India', in idem, ed., *On Understanding Islam. Selected Studies*. The Hague and New York: Moulton.

Sonthamier, D. Gunther, and Hermann Kulke, eds. 1997. *Hinduism Reconsidered*. Delhi: Manohar.

Stanley, Brian. 1990. *The Bible and the Flag: Protestant Missions and British Imperialism in the Nineteenth and Twentieth Centuries*. Leicester: Inter-varsity Fellowship.

————. 1993. *The History of the Baptist Missionary Society, 1792–1992*. 2 vols. Edinburgh: Clark.

————. ed. 2001. *Christian Missions and the Enlightenment*. Grand Rapids and Cambridge: Erdmans; London: Curzon.

Stennett. S. 1825. *Memoirs of the Life of the Rev. William Ward*. London: J. Haddon.

von Stietencron, Heinrich. 1995. 'Religious Configurations in Pre-Muslim India', in Vasudha Dalmia and Heinrich von Stietencron, eds, *Representing Hinduism: The Construction of Religious Traditions and National Identity*. New Delhi: Sage Publications.

Stock, Eugere. 1899. *A History of the Church Missionary Society*. 3 vols. London: CMS.

————. 1902. *The Centenary Volume of the Church Missionary Society*. London: CMS.

Stokes, Eric. 1992. *The English Utilitarians and India*. Delhi: Oxford University Press.

Sugirtharajah, Sharada. 2003. *Imagining Hinduism: A Postcolonial Perspective*. London and New York: Routledge.

Suntharalingam, R. 1974. *Politics and Nationalist Awakening in South India, 1852–1891*. Tucson: University of Arizona Press.

Sutton, Amos. 1833. *A Narrative of the Mission to Orissa*. Boston: Samuel N. Dickinson.

————. 1850. *Orissa and Its Evangelization; Interspersed with Suggestions Respecting the More Efficient Conducting of Indian Missions*. Derby: Wilkins and Sons.

Sweetman, Will. 2003. *Mapping Hinduism: 'Hinduism' and the Study of Indian Religions, 1600–1776*. Halle: Verlag der Franckeschen Stiftungen zu Halle.

Taggart, Norman W. 1993. *William Arthur: First among Methodists*. London: Epworth Press.

Talbot, Cynthia. 1995. 'Inscribing the Self: Hindu–Muslim Identities in Pre-colonial India', *Comparative Studies in Society and History* 37 (4).

Tavernier, J. B. 1977. *Travels in India*. Edited by William Crooke. 2 vols. Delhi: Oriental Books Reprint.

Teltscher, Kate. 1995. *India Inscribed: European and British Writing on India. 1600–1800*. Delhi: Oxford University Press.

Thapar, Romilla. 1989. 'Imagined Religious Communities? Ancient History and the Search for a Hindu Identity', *Modern Asian Studies* 23 (2).

Thompson, H. P. 1951. *Into All Lands: The History of the Society for the Propagation of the Gospel in Foreign Parts. 1701–1950*. London: SPCK.

Thurston, Edgar. 1909. *Castes and Tribes of Southern India*, Vol. 1. Madras: Government Press.

Tiliander, B. F. 1974. *Christian and Hindu Terminology: A Study in their Mutual Relations with Special Reference to the Tamil Area*. Uppsala: Almqvist and Wiksell.

Trautmann, Thomas R. 1997. *Aryans and British India*. Berkeley, Los Angeles and London: University of California Press.

Trudgill, E. 1976. *Madonnas and Magdalenes: The Origins and Development of Victorian Sexual Attitudes*. London: Heinemann.

di Varthema, Ludovico. 1863. *The Travels of Ludovico di Varthema*. Trans. George Percy Badger. London: Hakluyt Society.

Vaudeville, C. 1974. *Kabir*. Oxford: Oxford University Press.

Vaughan, James. 1876. *The Trident, the Crescent and the Cross: A View of the Religious History of India during the Hindu, Buddhist, Mohammedan, and Christian Periods*. London: Longmans, Green and Co.

Walker, Frank Deaville. 1926. *William Carey, Missionary Pioneer and Statesman*. London: Student Christian Movement.

Walls, Andrew F. 1996. *The Missionary Movement in Christian History. Studies in the Transmission of Faith*. New York: Orbis; Edinburgh: T & T Clark.

Ward, William. 1811. *Account of the Writings, Religion, and Manners, of the Hindoos: Including Translations from their Principal Works, in Four Volumes*. Serampore: Mission Press.

———. 1817–20. *History, Literature and Mythology of the Hindoos*. 3rd ed. 4 vols. Delhi: Low Price Publications.

———. 1864. *History, Literature and Religion of the Hindoos*. 5th ed. Includes Introduction by W.O. Simpson. Madras: Higginbotham.

Wardlaw. J. S. 1856. *Memoir of the late Rev. W. H. Drew*. Vizagapatam: Mission Press.

Wardlaw, Ralph. 1845. *Memoir of the Late Rev. John Reid, M.A. of Bellary, East Indies*. Glasgow: James Maclehose.

Watts, Michael R. 1978. *The Dissenters, from the Reformation to the French Revolution*. 2 vols. Oxford: Clarendon Press.

Webb, R. K. 1955. *The British Working Class Reader, 1790–1848*. London: Allen and Unwin.

Webster, J. C. B. 1992. *The Dalit Christians: A History*. Delhi: ISPCK.

Weir, Robert W. 1900. *A History of the Foreign Missions of the Church of Scotland*. Edinburgh: R & R Clark.

Weitbrecht, Mary. 1875. *The Women of India and Christian Work in the Zenana*. London: James Nisbet.

Wilberforce, W. 1958 [1797]. *A Practical View of the Prevailing Religious System of Professed Christians in the Higher and Middle Classes in this Country Contrasted with Real Christianity.* A facsimile produced by the Student Christian Movement.

Wilkins, W. J. 1882. *A Hand book of Hindu Mythology, Vedic and Puranic.* London: Thacker, Spink and Co.

————. 1888. *Daily Life and Work in India.* London: T. Unwin Fisher.

————. 1900 [1887]. *Modern Hinduism.* 2nd ed. Calcutta and London: Thacker.

Wilkinson, M. 1844. *Sketches of Christianity in North India.* London: n.p.

Wink, Andre. 1990. *Al-Hind. The Making of the Indo-Islamic World: Early Medieval India and the Expansion of Islam, 7th–11th Centuries.* Delhi: Oxford University Press.

Wolffe, John, ed. 1997. *Religion in Victorian Britain,* Vol. 5, 'Culture and Empire'. Manchester and New York: Manchester University Press.

Woodberry, Robert D. 2004. 'The Shadow of Empire: Christian Missions, Colonial Policy, and Democracy in Postcolonial Societies'. Ph.D. diss., University of North Carolina.

Wyatt, J. L., ed. 1894. *Reminiscences of Bishop Caldwell.* Madras: Addison and Co.

Young, Richard Fox. 1981. *Resistant Hinduism: Sanskrit Sources on Anti-Christian Apologetics in Early Nineteenth-century India.* Vienna: De Nobili Research Library.

————. 1987. 'Was Rammohun Roy the "True Successor" of Ramram Basu? A Critique of Certain Statements by David Kopf', in R. Lariviere and R. Solomon, eds, *Festschrift for Professor Ludo Rocher.* Madras: Adyar Library.

Young, Richard Fox, and S. Jebanesan. 1995. *The Bible Trembled: The Hindu–Christian Controversies of Nineteenth Century Ceylon.* Vienna: De Nobili Research Library.

Zupanov, Ines G. 1999. *Disputed Mission: Jesuit Experiments and Brahmanical Knowledge in Seventeenth-century India.* Delhi: Oxford University Press.

Index

Vedanta, 173
Sharpe, Eric J., 16
Sherring, M. A., 243
Shillay, J., 112
Shiva, 33, 330
Shore, John, 85
Simon, Charles, 76
Singh, Brijraj, 57
Slater, Thomas Ebenezer, 35, 122, 241,
    307, 310
slave trade and slavery, 31, 73, 158, 163, 172
Smith, Cantwell, 71
Smith, George, 283, 322
Smith, J., 299
Smith, Rev. W., 298, 314
Society for Political Information, 31
Society for Promoting Female Education
    in the East, 325
Society for the Promotion of Christian
    Knowledge (SPCK), 16, 57, 58, 59,
    61, 63, 64, 84, 204, 240, 241, 261, 272
Society for the Propagation of the
    Gospel (SPG): 17, 58, 84, 117, 307
    326; missionaries, 18, 64
Society of Jesus, 52
Solvyns, Baltazard, 212
South India Missionaries Conference
    meeting at Ootacamund, 298
Sri Rangam, idol-priests of, 26
Stanley, Brain, 25
von Stietencron, Heinrich, 71
Stock, Eugene, 242, 327
Storrow, Edward, 320
sun worship, 145, 150
superstition, Brahmanical system of, 195
Sutcliff, John, 143
Sutton, Amos, 273
Sweetman, Will, 52–4

Tagore, Kumar, 239
Tamil: 278; ancient, religion and society,
    276; civilization, growth and decline
    of, 276; devotional and moral works,
    292; religious leaders, 14; religious
    literature, 278; Shaiva Siddhanta, 271;
    Shaivism, 271
Tantras, 282

Tavernier, Jean-Baptiste, 40, 42
Telang, Kashinath Trimback, 233
Telugu mission: 235; publications of, 124
Teltscher, Kate, 49
temple: carts, 49; dancing, 92; Siva and
    Kali, 146; management, 212;
    prostitution, 25; Terry, Edward, 41,
    42, 44
Toland, John, 196
Thomas, Annie, 235
Thomas, John, 71, 136, 140
Thompson, H. P., 64
Thornton, Henry, 70
Townsend, Amy, 330
Tractarian Movement, 18, 20
Tranquebar Mission: 14, 57–9, 57, 59, 60,
    61, 103; depictions of Malabar
    religion, 65; reports and letters
    available in Britain, 62
translation: of Hindu classics, 155;
    of missionaries' letters, 58; of the
    Old Testament into Bengali, 145;
    of Sanskrit texts, 232–3; of Shaiva
    Siddhanta, 111
transmigration, doctrine of, 105, 324
travelers: European, 49, 171; British, in
    India, 41
tribal religions, 272
Tucker, Rev. John, 306
Tukaram, 111, 270

United Presbyterian Church of
    Scotland (UPS) mission, 255
Universal Soul, 172
untouchables, 107

Vaishnavas, 109
Vanes, Rev. J. A., 302
varna. See caste
di Varthema, Ludovico, 40–1
Vaughan, James, 130, 215, 250, 256, 307
Vedanta: 174, 196, 196, 253, 263, 309;
    pantheistic theory of, 266
Vedantism: and the Brahmo Samaj, 253;
    in elite circles, spread of, 267
Vedas, 101–2
Veen, Henry, 17, 18, 327

About the Author

Geoffrey A. Oddie is an Honorary Research Associate in the Department of History at the University of Sydney, Australia. He has lectured in history in the same department since 1964, and has also been a Visiting Professor at the United Theological College, Bangalore (2003).

Dr Oddie was first published in 1957. Since then he has authored, edited or contributed to a score of books on various aspects of religion in South Asia, with a focus on Hinduism and missionary Christianity in colonial and pre-colonial times. His books include *Missionaries, Rebellion and Proto-Nationalism. James Long of Bengal: 1814–87* (1998); *Religious Conversion Movements in South Asia: Continuities and Change* (edited, 1997); *Popular Religion, Elites and Reform: Hook-swinging and Its Prohibition in Colonial India, 1800–1894* (1995); and *Social Protest in India: British Protestant Missionaries and Social Reforms, 1850–1900* (1979).